Fifteen Years
In Exile

Fifteen Years In Exile

VOLUME ONE

Edited By
BARRY CALLAGHAN

Toronto
Exile Editions
1992

© Exile Editions Ltd. 1992

Cover montage of photographs by John Reeves

This Edition is published by Exile Editions Ltd.,
20 Dale Avenue, Toronto, Ontario, Canada M4W 1K4

All effort has been extended to secure copyright clearance for each
individual work. Where this has not been possible, the publisher would
welcome all correspondence

Sales distribution: General Publishing Co. Ltd., 30 Lesmill Road, Don
Mills, Ontario M3B 2T6

Typeset in *Palatino*

Printed in Canada by the *University of Toronto Press*

ISBN 1-55096-0237

FIFTEEN YEARS IN EXILE

Barry Callaghan

We are celebrating fifteen years in *Exile*. I say fifteen for a fact, except nothing is ever as it seems.

We began *Exile* in June of 1972, on a whim, not knowing where we were going or how long it would take. It took twenty years. Time fell between the cracks along the way. A month got lost here, two months there, and before we knew it, five years had leaked away. So twenty became fifteen over twenty, a way to read our blood pressure. Still, an awful lot got done in *Exile*.

We tried only once to explain why we chose the name *Exile*. Opening Volume 1, Number 1, we wrote that in many excellent reviews the writer of imaginative prose and poetry had become mere fodder for scholarly dancing horses. The writer of the critique had become "more important than the writer of the poem, especially if the writer offers a new fund of useful information. But useful for what? It is the day of the information deluge. Who sorts it all out? The imaginative writer, who can rely only on his own eyes, his own heart and sensibility for his information, is, in a sense, in exile now. There ought to be a small haven somewhere for such exiles. In these pages the imaginative writer will not be led in by a scholarly praetorian guard. He will be on his own."

That was it. That is still it. The writing's on the wall. Poems, drama, fiction. Almost no non-fiction appeared in *Exile*: Jerzy Kosinski wrote about his own novel, *Steps*; Bruce Powe wrote about Glenn Gould; Jacques Ferron wrote of his friendship for Claude Gauvreau; and Mary Meigs wrote of her friendship for Marie-Claire Blais. No essays. No book reviews at the back. The writer, the painter, the poet, the composer, the photographer, was on his own, and so, curiously enough, was the reader.

We were open to anything. We took old Alexander Pope seriously: "A perfect judge will read each work of wit/With the same spirit that its author writ." And Matthew Arnold, too: trying always to see the work, "the object as in itself it really is." So we've done a dance, it seems, with all the *isms*, the fox trot, the tango, modernism and post-modernism, the concrete cakewalk and comic book tales and gothic ghost stories and summonings in circles of sacred stones from all over the world, and especially from Ireland and Israel, home countries to our two founding contributing editors, John Montague and Yehuda Amichai.

We were happy to be a haven if a writer in Riga or Beograd or Cape Town or Qualicum Beach wanted to find his Paris in Toronto in *Exile*. Why not? And if that sounds arrogant, then you miss the laughter, because any fool knows that Toronto is no Paris while Paris aint what it used to be. *Exile*, in a world where nothing is ever as it seems, was in a hover space of its own, levitating above the tree line. Julio Cortazar, who died as an expatriate at home in Paris, got it just right: "The only true exile is the writer who lives in his own country."

As exiles, we were at home in our uncertain country. We side-stepped politics and published poems, novels, plays. We didn't scorn politics. It's just that politics is the world of false success, which is why we took Paul-Emile Borduas – painter, subversive, exile, founding father – to heart: "Together we will undertake the extravagance of living under a sharpened conscience, in open honesty, and we will see what happens. The worst can only be catastrophe, which is better by far than a false success."

Extravagance. Catastrophe. Open honesty.

As we gather the work of fifteen years over twenty, what is *Exile*? Is it of the place? Is it in the local grain?

We like to think that no one can say what *Exile* is. The world's full of people who say they know exactly who they are. Americans insist they know who they are, what they are. Who else but a dyed-in-the-flag-know-it-all could convene a House Committee of Un-American activities.

If anyone tried to call a House Committee of Un-Canadian activities, folks would fall on the floor laughing. No one in this country knows the words to the national anthem, let alone what a Canadian is. So no one can say what a Canadian must be. That's a great freedom. It means that you can go way out on a limb on your own and you can be anything you want to be. You, too, can be in exile.

Perhaps we've been more Canadian than we ever dreamed.

Though nothing is ever as it seems.

We can only say: "There is more enterprise in walking naked."

Haw.

CONTENTS

George Eliot

FUNERAL RITES

Seamus Heaney

I
I shouldered a kind of manhood
stepping in to lift the coffins
of dead relations.
They had been laid out

in tainted rooms,
their eyelids glistening,
their dough-white hands
shackled in rosary beads.

Their puffed knuckles
had unwrinkled, the nails
were darkened, the wrists
obediently sloped.

The dulse-brown shroud,
the quilted satin cribs:
I knelt courteously
admiring it all

as wax melted down
and veined the candles,
the flames hovering
to the women hovering

behind me.
And always, in a corner,
the coffin lid,
its nail-heads dressed

with little gleaming crosses.
Dear soapstone masks,
kissing their igloo brows
had to suffice

before the nails were sunk
and the black glacier
of each funeral
pushed away.

II

Now as news comes in
of each neighborly murder
we pine for ceremony,
customary rhythms:

the temperate footsteps
of a cortege, winding past
each blinded home.
I would restore
the great chambers of Boyne,
prepare a sepulchre
under the cupmarked stones.
Out of side-streets and bye-roads

purring family cars
nose into line,
the whole country tunes
to the muffled drumming

of ten thousand engines.
Somnambulant women,
left behind, move
through emptied kitchens

imagining our slow triumph
towards the mounds.
Quiet as a serpent
in its grassy boulevard

the procession drags its tail
out of the Gap of the North
as its head already enters
the megalithic doorway.

III

Before they put the stone back
in its mouth,
let us pray
that the necropolis will prove

sufficient to our appetite
for memory, that cuds behindbacks
and incubates spilled blood;
and place these remnants

in the care of Gunnar.
He lay beautiful
inside his mound,
though dead by violence

and unavenged:
it seemed that he was chanting
verses about honor,
and four lights burned

in corners of the chamber.
Which opened then, as he turned
with a joyful face
and looked at the moon.

THE SALAMANDER

Mercè Rodoreda

I walked under the willow tree, came to the patch of watercress, and knelt beside the pond. As usual, there were frogs all around. As soon as I got there they'd come out and bounce up to me. And when I began to comb my hair, the naughtiest ones would start touching my red skirt with the five little plaits on it, or pulling the scalloped border on my petticoats, all full of frills and tucks. And the water'd grow sadder and sadder, and the trees on the hillside would slowly darken. But that day the frogs leapt into the water in one jump, and the water's mirror shattered into little pieces. And when the water was all smooth again I saw his face beside mine, like two shadows watching me from the other side. And so he wouldn't think I was frightened, I got up without a word, I began walking through the grass very calmly, and as soon as I heard him following, I looked around and stopped. Everything was quiet, and one edge of the sky was already sprinkled with stars. He'd halted a little ways off, and I didn't know what to do, but suddenly I got scared and started to run. And when I realized he was catching up with me, I stopped underneath the willow with my back against the trunk. He planted himself in front of me, with his arms stretched out on both sides so I couldn't escape. And then, looking into my eyes, he pressed me against the willow and with my hair all dishevelled, between him and the willow tree, I bit my lips so I wouldn't cry out from the pain in my chest and all my bones feeling like they were about to break. He put his mouth on my neck, and it burned where he put it.

The next day the trees on the hill were already black when he came, but the grass was still warm from the sun. He held me again against the willow-trunk, and put his hand flat over my eyes. And all at once I felt like I was falling asleep, and the leaves were telling me things which made sense but which I didn't understand, saying them softer and softer and slower and slower. And when I couldn't hear them anymore and my tongue was frozen with terror, I asked him, "And your wife?" And he told me, "You're my wife. Only you." My back was crushing the grass I'd hardly dared walk on when I was going to comb my hair. Just a little, to catch the smell of it breaking. Only you. Afterwards, when I opened my eyes, I saw the blond hair falling and she was bent over, looking at us blankly. And when she realized I'd seen her, she grabbed my hair and said, "Witch." Very softly. But she let go of me immediately and grabbed him by his shirt-collar. "Go on, go on," she said. And she led him away, pushing him as they went.

We never went back to the pond. We'd meet in stables, under haystacks, in the woods with the roots. But after that day when his wife led him away, the people in the village started looking at me like they didn't see me, and some of them would cross themselves quickly as I went by. After a while,

4

when they saw me coming they'd go into their houses and lock the doors. I started hearing a word which followed me everywhere I went, as if the air whistled it or it came from the light and the darkness. Witch, witch, witch. The doors shut. I walked through the streets of a ghost town, and the eyes I saw between the slits in the curtains were always icy. One morning I had a lot of trouble opening my front door, which was old and cracked by the sun. They'd hung an ox's head in the middle of it, with two little green branches stuck in the eyes. I took it down. It was very heavy, and I left it on the ground since I didn't know what to do with it. The branches began to dry, and while they were drying the head began to stink and there was a swarm of milk-colored worms all around the neck on the side where they'd cut it.

Another day I found a headless pigeon, its breast red with blood, and another a sheep born dead before its time and two rat's-ears. And when they stopped hanging dead animals on my door, they started to throw stones. They banged against the windows and roof-tiles at night, as big as fists … Then they had a procession. It was the beginning of winter. A windy day with scurrying clouds, and the procession went very slowly, with white and purple paper flowers. I lay on the floor, watching it through the special door I'd made for the cat. And when it was almost in front of the door, with the wind, the saint, and the banners, the cat got frightened by the torches and chants and wanted to come in. And when he saw me he let out a great shriek, with his back arched like a bridge. And the procession came to a halt, and the priest gave blessing after blessing, and the altar boys sang and the wind whipped the flames on the torches, and the sexton walked up and down, and everything was a flutter of white and purple petals from the paper flowers. Finally the procession went away. And before the holy water had dried on the walls, I went out looking for him and I couldn't find him anywhere. I searched in the stables, under haystacks, in the woods with the roots – I knew it by heart. I always sat on the oldest root, which was all white and dusty like a bone. And that night, when I sat down, I suddenly realized I had no hope left. I lived facing backwards, with him inside me like a root in the earth. The next day they wrote "witch" on my door with a piece of charcoal. And that night, good and loud so I could hear them, two men said they should have burned me when I was little, along with my mother who used to fly around on eagles' wings when everyone was asleep. That they should have had me burned before they started needing me to pick garlic or tie the grain and alfalfa in sheaves or gather grapes from the poor vines.

One evening I thought I saw him at the entrance to the woods with the roots, but when I got closer he ran away and I couldn't tell if it was him or my desire for him or his shadow searching for me, lost like I was among the trees, pacing to and fro. "Witch" they said, and left me with my pain, which wasn't at all the kind they'd meant to give me. And I thought of the pond and the watercress and the willow's slender branches … The winter was dark and flat and leafless. Just ice and frost and the frozen moon. I couldn't move, because to walk around in winter is to walk in front of everybody and I didn't want them to see me. And when Spring came, with

5

its joyous little leaves, they built a fire in the middle of the square, using dry wood, carefully cut.

Four men from the village came looking for me: the elders. From inside I told them I wouldn't go with them, and then the young ones came with their big red hands, and broke down the door with an axe. And I screamed, because they were dragging me from my own house, and I bit one and he hit the middle of my head with his fist, and they grabbed my arms and legs and threw me on top of the pile like one more branch, and they bound my arms and feet and left me with my skirt pulled up. I turned my head. The square was full of people, the young in front of the old, and the children off to one side with little olive branches and new Sunday aprons. And while I was looking at the children I caught sight of him. He was standing beside his wife, who was dressed in black with her blond hair, and he had his arm around her shoulder. I turned away and closed my eyes. When I opened them again, two old men came forward with burning torches, and the boys started singing the song of the burning witch. It was a very long song, and when they'd finished it the old men said they couldn't start the fire, that I wouldn't let them light it. And then the priest came up to the boys with his bowl full of holy water, and made them wet the olive branches and throw them on top of me, and soon I was covered with little olive branches, all with tiny shoots. And a little old lady, crooked and toothless, started laughing and went away and after a while she came back with two baskets full of dry heather and told the old men to spread them on the four sides of the bonfire, and she helped them, and then the fire caught. Four columns of smoke rose, and the flames twisted upwards and it seemed like a great sigh of peace went out of the hearts of all those people. The flames rose, chasing after the smoke, and I watched everything through a red downpour. And behind that water every man, woman, and child was like a happy shadow because I was burning.

The bottom of my skirt had turned black. I felt the fire in my kidneys, and from time to time, a flame chewed at my knee. It seemed like the ropes that tied me were already burnt. And then something happened which made me grit my teeth. My arms and legs started getting shorter like the horns on a snail I once touched with my finger, and under my head where my neck and shoulders met, I felt something stretching and piercing me. And the fire howled and the resin boiled … I saw some of the people looking at me raise their arms, and others were running and bumping into the ones who hadn't moved. And one whole side of the fire collapsed in a great shower of sparks, and when the scattered wood began burning again it seemed like someone was saying "She's a salamander." And I started walking over the burning coals, very slowly, because my tail was heavy.

I walked on all fours with my face against the ground. I was going towards the willow tree, rubbing against the wall, but when I got to the corner I turned my head slightly and off in the distance I saw my house which looked like a flaming torch. There was no one in the street. I went past the stone bench, and then quickly through the house full of flames and glowing coals, towards the willow, towards the watercress, and when I was outside again I turned around because I wanted to see how the roof was burning. While I was staring at it the first drop fell, one of those hot, fat drops that give birth to toads, and then others fell, slowly at first and then faster, and soon all the water in the sky had poured down and the fire went out in a great cloud of smoke. I kept quiet. I couldn't see a thing, because night had fallen and the night was black and dense. I set out, wading through mud and puddles. My hands enjoyed sinking in the soft mush, but my feet grew weary behind me from getting stuck so often. I would have liked to run, but I couldn't. A clap of thunder threw me into the middle of the path. Then came a bolt of lightning, and through the rocks I saw the willow. I was out of breath when I reached the pond. And when after the mud, which is dirt from the ground, I found the slime, which is dirt from the bottom of the water, I crept into a corner, half-buried between two roots. And then three little eels came along.

At dawn, I don't know if it was the next day or some other, I climbed out slowly and saw the high mountains beneath a sky smudged with clouds. I ran through the watercress and stopped at the trunk of the willow tree. The first leaves were still inside the buds, but the buds were turning green. I didn't know which way to turn. If I didn't watch where I was going, the blades of grass would prick my eyes – and I fell asleep among those blades until the sun was high in the sky. When I woke up I caught a tiny mosquito, and then looked for worms in the grass. Finally I went back to the slime and pretended to be asleep, because the three eels immediately came up, acting very playful.

The night I decided to go to the village there was lots of moonlight. The air was full of smells and the leaves were already fluttering on all the branches. I followed the path with the rocks, very carefully because the smallest things frightened me. When I got to my house, I rested. There was nothing but ruin and nettle bushes, with spiders spinning and spinning. I went around back and stopped in front of his garden. Beside the holly-hocks, the sunflowers hung their round flowers. I followed the bramble hedge without thinking why I was doing it, as if someone were telling me "Do this, do that," and slipped under his door. The ashes in the hearth were still warm. I lay down for a while, and after running around a bit all over I settled down under the bed. So tired that I fell asleep and didn't see the sunrise.

When I woke up there were shadows on the ground, because night was already falling again, and his wife was walking back and forth with a burning candle. I saw her feet and part of her legs, thin at the bottom, swollen higher up, with white stockings. Then I saw his feet, big, with blue socks falling over his ankles. And I saw their clothing fall, and heard them sitting on the bed. Their feet were dangling, his next to hers, and one of his feet went up and a sock fell, and she took off her stockings, pulling them off with both hands, and then I heard the sheets rustling as they pulled them up. They were talking very softly, and after a while, when I'd gotten used to the darkness, the moonlight came in through the window, a window with four panes and two strips of wood that made a cross. And I crawled over to the light and placed myself right under the cross because inside myself, even though I wasn't dead, there was nothing inside me that was totally alive, and I prayed hard because I didn't know if I still was a person or only a little animal, or if I was half person and half animal. And

7

also I prayed to know where I was, because at times I felt like I was under water, and when I was under water I felt like I was on the ground, and I never knew where I really was. When the moon went down they woke up, and I went back to my hiding place under the bed, and started to make myself a little nest with bits of fluff. And I spent many nights between the fluff and the cross. Sometimes I'd go outside and go up to the willow tree. When I was under the bed, I'd listen. It was just like before. "Only you," he'd say. And one night when the sheet was hanging on the floor I climbed up the sheet, holding onto the folds, and got into bed beside one of his legs. And he was as quiet as a corpse. He turned a little and his leg pressed down on top of me. I couldn't move. I breathed hard because he was crushing me, and I wiped my cheek against his leg, very carefully so as not to wake him.

But one day she did a housecleaning. I saw the white stockings and the raggedy broom, and just when I least expected it blond hair was dragging on the floor and she shoved the broom under the bed. I had to run because it seemed like the broom was searching for me, and suddenly I heard a scream and saw her feet running towards the door. She came back with a burning torch and jammed half her body under the bed and wanted to burn my eyes. And I, awkward, didn't know which way to run and was dazzled and bumped into everything: the legs on the bed, the walls, the feet on the chairs. I don't know how, I found myself outside and made for the puddle of water under the horses' drinking trough, and the water covered me up, but two boys saw me and went to look for reeds and started poking me. I turned and faced them. They threw down the reeds and ran away, but immediately they came back with six or seven bigger boys, and they all threw stones and handfuls of dirt at me. A stone hit one of my little hands and broke it, but in the midst of badly-aimed stones and in utter terror I was able to get away and run into the stable. And she came looking for me there with the broom, with the children constantly shouting, watching at the door, and she poked me and wanted to make me come out of my corner full of straw and I was dazzled again and bumped into the pails, the baskets, the sacks of carob beans, the horses' hoofs, and a horse reared because I'd bumped into one of his hoofs, and I went up with him. A whack from the broom touched my broken hand and almost pulled it off, and a trickle of black spit oozed from one side of my mouth. But I still was able to get away through a crack, and as I escaped I heard the broom poking and poking.

In the dead of night I went to the woods with the roots. I came out from under some bushes in the light of the rising moon. Everything seemed hopeless. The broken hand didn't hurt, but it was dangling by a nerve, and I had to lift my arm so it wouldn't drag too much. I walked a little crookedly, now over a root, now over a stone, till I got to the root where I used to sit sometimes before they dragged me off to the bonfire in the square, and I couldn't get to the other side because I kept slipping. And on and on and on, towards the willow tree, and towards the watercress and towards my slimy home under the water. The grass rustled in the wind, which whipped up bits of dry leaves, and carried off short, bright strands from the flowers beside the path. I rubbed one side of my head against a tree trunk, and slowly went towards the pond, and entered it holding my weary arm up, with the broken hand on it.

Under the water streaked with moonlight, I saw the three eels coming. They seemed a little blurred, and intertwined with each other, winding in and out, making slippery knots till the littlest one came up to me and bit my broken hand. A little juice came out of the wrist, looking like a wisp of smoke beneath the water. The eel held onto the hand and slowly pulled on it, and while he was pulling, he kept looking at me. And when he thought I wasn't watching he gave one or two hard, stubborn jerks. And the others played at entwining as if they were making a rope, and the one who was biting my hand gave a furious yank and the nerve must have snapped because he carried off the hand and when he had it he looked at me as if to say, "Now I've got it." I closed my eyes for a while, and when I opened them the eel was still there, between the shadow and the shimmering bits of light, with the little hand in his mouth – a sheaf of bones stuck together, covered by a bit of black skin. And I don't know why, but all of a sudden I saw the path with the stones, the spiders inside my house, the legs hanging over the side of the bed. They were dangling, white and blue, like they were sitting on top of the water, but empty, like spread-out washing, and the rocking water made them sway from side to side. And I saw myself under that cross made of shadows, above that fire full of colors that rose shrieking and didn't burn me ... And while I was seeing all these things the eels were playing with that piece of me, letting it go and then grabbing it again, and the hand went from one eel to the next, whirling around like a little leaf, with all the fingers separated. And I was in both worlds: in the slime with the eels, and a little in that world of I don't know where ... till the eels got tired and slime sucked the hand under ... a dead shadow, slowly smoothing the dirt in the water, for days and days and days, in that slimy corner, among thirsty grass roots and willow roots that had drunk there since the beginning of time.

Translated by David H. Rosenthal

DEATH OF A LADY'S MAN

Leonard Cohen

The Promise

A wound in the shoulder keeps me still. The lizards sing, the sea pours in, the night upholds my promise.

I am guarded against your scorn by a spider on the ceiling and a lizard on the wall.

Adam and Eve hang from a thorn, back to back. I want them to face each other.

I will call her out of the used-up sea. I will speak her down from the pitch of terror. She will form her body around the words of longing. She will establish her beauty on the Promise of Faithfulness.

I make this promise now. The other men say: Can you?

Do you wish to see her radiant? 'She will establish her beauty on the Promise of Faithfulness.' Do you wish to see her radiant? 'No, I want to see her cunt.' This ambiguity is honored so you can bear the company.

In one form only does she recognize me, the form of wife. In every other form she is searching for her mate; she blunders past me like something going blind, a salmon or a sea-turtle, and I am landscape and water, going the other way.

Crickets and lizards make lace out of the edges of my thought. They're taking me away from the Guerero. For crimes I did against the heart.

I never thought I'd see a moth and a lizard fighting. The moth is now some darkness in the green translucent belly. No it isn't worth it. It isn't worth it at all. They've launched two red ants against the throne.

I eat too much when I'm with her. I become obscure.

Thank you for killing the moth. I never liked them.

What was the Mexican girl singing to my daughter? My wife was speaking. We were in another room. The wishbone of the song came through. The baby no more crying. The pelican with pierced breast. I was your bride all afternoon and you with the other woman. The other woman carried her here but I am your baby's mother. Cling to her or cling to me, it never makes a difference. You'll open a door in your promise and leave us both alone.

from the Notebooks 1973

The Unclean Start

I went down to the port with my wife. On the way down I accused her of continuing her relentless automatic assault on the centre of my being. I knew this was not wise. I only meant to rap her on the knuckles and direct

10

her attention to her habitual drift toward bitchiness but I lost control. There is no control in these realms. I became a thug. I attacked her spirit. Her spirit armed itself and retaliated massively. I think we were talking about valises or which of us travelled the lightest. A truce was investigated briefly by shabby deputies neither of which had the authority to begin the initiative. You always carry something extra, a shopping bag, something of string and paper that can't be checked. I'm glad you didn't pack for me. You always slow me down. I can't be an acrobat when you're around. You're sandpaper. I can't be a dancer. I'm dead when you're around. You kill. It is your nature. Observe your nature. The shoemaker looked up at us as we passed his open doorway. This humiliation made me furious. I shoved a razorblade into her nerves. Her eyes changed color. This was done by saying Jesus Christ, quickening my step slightly, minutely moving my jaw, rejecting the essence of her totally and forever. If she went down quickly I would nurse her back to love in time to get her blessings before the boat came in. But why should I, she didn't rub my back when I threw my shoulder out, even when I asked her three times. And why should she since I had defeated her smile over and over. And why should I since she was the enemy of my freedom and the smiling moon over my gradual death. And why should she since I hated her because her beauty died. Why should I because there must be a woman in Jerusalem or beside me on the airplane. Half-asleep Old John saw us but it was no humiliation since he didn't recognize me anymore and I no longer greeted him. Captain Mad Body saw us but it didn't matter because he was mute and crazy and lived on the port and knew the shames of everyone. We were on the port, in plain sunlight between the masts and the shops. The shit piled up in the One Heart which is the engine of our energy. We are married: there is only one heart. On common ground the armored spirits tried to embrace but they both fell down paralysed. Pain removed the world. They felt for the organs of sex but they were gone. There was no war, no peace, no world, the punishment of marriage spoiled. There is no Armageddon here. And fuck you. And fuck you. The horn, the boat was coming. I would have to travel without her blessing in the collapsed world. I won't accuse you of ruining my trip. I won't accuse you of ruining your absence. The Kamelia came in, its white decks above us, or was it the Portokalios Ilios. I know the name of a boat or two. I always hide her beauty from myself until it is too late to praise her for it. Ropes were flying, uniforms flashing, everywhere haste advised and the threat of lost time. I stared at her as she became beautiful and calm. I would not get the blessing. The journey had an unclean start. And she must carry still-born blessings up the hill.

In the Final Revision of My Life in Art this passage expands as follows:

What a burden for the woman being born to carry still-born blessings up the hill. When she got home she pinned a blue ribbon to the inside of my windbreaker, next to where the heart would be. She showed me this much later. Certainly a factor in my coming back alive. I must study the hatred I have for her, how it is transmuted into desire by solitude and distance

11

(and where is the hatred now, years later, as he types this out, his love for her aching through the slow-motion snow storm of her absence)

Without her blessing I didn't have the courage or joy to greet the sea or the milky shores of islands or the mountain villages of faded silver. I had these in mind for happier siteings but I couldn't call them out. I felt unworthy of the landscape, present and past. I'm ashamed to be in the rays of your reading eyes. I can't

(secret words deleted years later, as he types this out)

I sat down next to a man who had done some work. There are always such people around to illumine one's sloth. The modesty of this one was especially reproachful. His hands told me how lazy I am. His quietness told me how loud. His wrinkles told me how weak I am. His shoulders told me how proud.

I won't. I won't take another woman casually. Only when her beauty is manifest. Only when she strikes me with her juicy grace. Only when she comes forward and there is no doubt. She will not come forward now. There she is. That is part of her skin. I think it is the shadowy arc between her buttocks. I think it is her 'green intelligence.' I won't fuck in the Holy Land unless she is my True Wife. Surely this hateful one I leave behind is not my True Wife. And other such thoughts as I rode the sea

(and other such thoughts that led him to this lousy kitchen table in the middle of the night with FM jazz and consolations of the diary, and her in the arms of youth, years later, as he types this out)

Yorgo T. boarded the ship at Aegina, a cunt-struck landowner from this very island, home of the pistachio nut and superior pistachio ice-cream. I asked him if he had any news of Henrietta, an English inn-keeper of mutual acquaintance who had a sad reputation of biting into cocks, disinterested information of her existence being the mainstay of our accidental annual conversations. Yes, he had news, but not very pleasant news. She had come to Athens. She had contacted him. They had arranged a rendezvous but both turned up at different times due to a misunderstanding of clocks. Some time later when he called her hotel he was informed that she was not physically capable of using the telephone. He summoned the hotel manager to the line and he was advised not to come to see her, it was not a pretty sight. Some weeks later he received a letter from Henrietta, postmarked London, with a depressing explanation. Apparently she had been badly tortured by three Japanese tourists behind a restaurant. This was the first conversation with Yorgo T. that I had enjoyed in a long time.

— Do you believe this preposterous story? I asked him. It was amazing how clear-brained I had become. Just a little sea between me and the creature of unbeauty and the world had begun to surface. He stuffed a cigarette into an ivory tube and pretended not to hear me. We sipped our ouzos, perfectly content, giving nothing, two civilized men.

— Why aren't you in Israel? he said, thinking he had me there.

— As a matter of fact that's exactly where I'm going.

— Really? Really? He stood up delighted.

— I'll go directly to the airport as soon as we dock. That's what I'm doing here.

— Bravo, he said. Really. Bravo. Bravo. Bravo. He seized both my hands in his and squeezed them with true enthusiasm and something like gratitude. Oh I'm so pleased, he said. Bravo. Bravo. Evidently I now represented certain old virtues which he cherished deeply. More than love of cunt did we share together. We were

the Shield, we were the Men Who Defended. My house, his house. My land, his land. Because of this we were granted cigarette holders, loneliness and the right to speak of women casually.

– You must. You must, he said.

– I know. I know. I felt humble and doomed. His eyes seemed to be shining at an honored corpse. The degree of his admiration had now attracted more than several of our fellow passengers. These he commenced to address in Greek:

– This man is travelling to Israel to defend his country against his country's enemy. He leaves a well-appointed house, a woman and a child, all the comforts of his achievement. I wonder how many of you, if you lived let us say in Holland or Sweden in similar circumstances, would sacrifice your security and come back here, if the threat arose, to fight against the Turk. Bravo, Leonard. Bravo. Bravo. Bravo. With a contemptuous wave of the hand he sent the worms back to their private holes to reconsider their cowardice, and we embraced. I must be doing something really stupid, I said to myself, to make another man so happy.

The Plan

The plan to marry her in Jerusalem with Yemenite ornaments. The plan to be the man in this wild garden. The plan to undo famine with the notion of the Total Fast. The plan to lead through influence. The plan to document these daisies. The plan to fish every morning with Donald. The plan to sit an hour each day with Anthony. The plan to go on the road again. The plan of money and fast bodies. The plan to return to dignity through the use of old clothes. The plan of crossing to the other shore, landing safely on the other shore. The plan of being street father to the young writers in Montreal, using the harsh style. The miserable plan of the invisible temple, a ceremony with Asher. The plan to visit Egypt in homage to the great woman's voice. The plan to study power in Ottawa. The plan to overthrow my life with fresh love. The plan to live with Roshi and serve him in the clean drunk life. The plan to fall in love with her, to see her beauty plain in the sweat of lawful lust. The plan to teach my son that there is no light in this world. The plan to follow my true song no matter where. The plan to honor Henry M. and Mark P., the great mad spirits who tempt me with their gratitude. The plan to prevent the man from beating the horse. The plan to heed the counsel of that man on the street in San Francisco who put his finger to his lips as he passed me. The plan to be strong ordinary muscular and simple. The plan to say the daisies are shoulder high on the very day that the description obtains, or to adjust this description to other high demands. The plan to make my face noble and attractive through hard work and brave decisions. The plan for my body. The plan to greet Steve S. in the highest ritual. A plan to be the seed. A plan to give up. A plan to assume the friendship of the lizards and the nettles. A plan to sing to the Mexican gardeners if I ever go back. The plan to be thin and fast and kind. My plan for you. My throne for you. My cunning towards God. There is a cat to my left, just hidden at the edge of the daisies, moving clumsily. Is this cat injured or is this cat about to give birth. The plan to escape. The plan not to witness.

13

Every one of these plans was studied, materialized and followed. I married her in Jerusalem but I should not have allowed her to be circumcised by the old Nubian nurse. In the expanding desert of western Ethiopia I taught a simple Scientology exercise to the starving tribesmen. Soon they were gazing into each others' eyes, their hunger forgotten. I made myself immensely attractive by sucking in my cheeks, and many followed me. I wrote the Final Revision of My Life in Art. So now you know the truth, and when you are broken down enough, you will appreciate it. You will not feel so superior to those who kill in the name of Jesus Christ. You will not study so carefully the conflict between State and Society in Eastern Europe. Your sideburns will grow long and curl at length but the Jews will still despise you. You will not depend on the floor to receive your boots and you will not depend on your beard to be victimized. You will crawl without bending your knees. You will sing without parting your false grey lips. You will be thrown back. You will fall against me. And I, who could not heal myself, I will heal you. I am the Canadian and I am the French-Canadian. I am the Acadian. I am the smoke of Quebec and the kilt of Mt. Royal. I am the subtlest germ of the Quebecois and I am the mould for the pores of snow. I have defeated all your plans with the weightless carcass of a summer fly. The one who comes after me has a clear field.

O₃ Spots!

O, Spots   *Joe Rosenblatt*

MAU TO LEW: THE MAURICE RAVEL – LEWIS CARROLL FRIENDSHIP

Mavis Gallant

Villa "Les Violettes"
Saint-Jean-de-Luz
Wednesday, 8th June

Sir,

Your letter has astonished and troubled me. My mother did not comprehend it, either. First, it is based on a great misunderstanding. I am not "a frequent and lavishly-remunerated guest of well-heeled universities," nor do I know "all the smart fiddles and gimmicks" for easing my way into them. My position in life is that of any Basque poet and translator, quite modest. Surely the experience of an obscure Maurice Ravel can be of little help to a C.L. Dodgson of Christ Church, Oxford, one of the leading avant-garde composers and musicologists of our time – a little *too* avant-garde for me, I am afraid; permit me to say that after hearing your *Sacre du Printemps* I had to ask my mother to play some Edouard Lalo on her Bechstein for a full hour before the blood of my poetic vein, congealed, could begin to circulate again. Please do not take this to be criticism.

Receive, Sir, my distinguished respects.
Maurice Ravel
Member of the Saint-Jean-de-Luz Folklore Club

Villa "Les Violettes"
Friday, 1st July

Dear Dr. Dodgson,

Thank you for the score of *Ballade de la Reine Morte d'Aimer*. I'm afraid I am not much of a singer, but my mother and I are both touched by your thoughtfulness. An unexpected invitation from the University of the Thursday Revolution at Monsoon is about to take me far from "Les Violettes." (Apparently Gabriel d'Annunzio let them down at the last minute.) My mother and I are looking forward eagerly to the cultural opportunity offered. I can well understand your feeling restless at Oxford, of which I hear poor reports, particularly concerning the breakfasts. For your information, I shall be sailing third-class on a comfortable tanker flying the Liberian flag, while my mother follows with her Bechstein on a Norwegian trawler. (Monsoon has been kind enough to see to arrange-

15

ments.) Forgive my mistake about *Sacre du Printemps:* to the profane, Dodgson and Debussy sound somewhat alike. (My mother had believed it to be an act from a little known Seventeenth Century masque.) She joins me in sending distinguished thanks.

Maurice Ravel

University of the Thursday Revolution
P. O. Box 88, Monsoon
Sunday, 20th July

Good Dr. Dodgson,

A nightmarish Gordian knot brings me before you, kneeling, hands clasped: it was not a Basque poet Monsoon required, but a composer, musicologist, conductor and piano virtuoso. (The new regime is closing down the hemp plantations and recycling the workers into symphony orchestras.) Could you send, by return of post, such rudiments of musical knowledge as may permit me to glide through my stay with an appearance of serenity? In the meantime, I shall plead bursitis and tone-deafness brought about by tanker-lag and change of climate.

I pass on a nugget obtained from a friendly (not actively hostile) colleague: the University of Labrador is looking for a combination drummer and glass-blower. Might this not be good for you?

My mother is stranded in Tasmania with her Bechstein. My despair knows no frontiers.

Maurice R.

Monsoon, Saturday, 2nd August

Noble C. L. Dodgson!

My mother, her Bechstein and your *L'Enfant et ses Sortileges* arrived by airlift via Panama. Maman performed beautifully at a gala in the new President's palace, while I delivered the text in Basque – the original seemed to us to be confusing and arbitrary. It went over quite well. We are distributing copies to the wives. I thought it simpler to place the copyright in my name.

I have mastered Solfege, Harmony and Composition, thanks to the little books you sent. I made out your handwriting quite easily.

I am sorry you did not find the Labrador idea "reliable." May I put forth another? Monsoon is starting a Multiple Writing Crafts Department – too late, alas, for me: I have accepted a sympathetic invitation from the Conservatory of Music at Arkhangel'sk. However, I have taken the liberty of recommending you for a Multiple post. Submit a sample of your prose, preferably under another name: "Dodgson" may strike a familiar musical note to some. I am sure you can do it easily; you write a fair letter.

From Maurice, who never forgets a good turn.

Arkhangel'sk Conservatory of Music
Monday, 9th September

Dear Dodge,

There is no such thing as "I can't." Enclosed is a copy of an old Basque folk song my mother taught me. Work it over into English and send it to Monsoon along with your application. (*Brillig* means "feather boa," *morogoves* stands for "public prosecutor," and *mome raths* is a hung jury.) My mother is working her passage north on a freighter. "Lewis Carroll" sounds all right. It could be anything.

Lots of luck,
Mau

Arkhangel'sk, 30th September

Dear Lew,

I liked *Chansons Madécasses* and Maman did too. We are looking for someone to hum the flute part. I am sorry Monsoon has not lived up to your expectations. I realize, now, I had failed to explain they were planning to turn the campus into a hemp plantation. Why not try Rangoon? A playwright who knows something about family quarrels in Oslo would stand a good chance. I doubt if you will get any satisfaction from Harvard. They grant tenure only to candidates' *mothers*. (Have you a mother, by the way? You've never said.) My musical prowess waxes.

Keep in touch,
Mau

Aboard "Star of Lenin"
8th October

Dear Lew,

My mother sends her thanks for the piano reduction of the Ring cycle. It must have been a lot of work, but then, as you say, Sunday is a long day in Monsoon.

Thrilling developments. Maman has been named musical officer on a luxury icebreaker making a leisurely tour of Arctic ports. Could you send along a simple piece, something she can tinkle during the kvass-and-pickle hour, when passengers' spirits are apt to flag? Mail it to General Delivery, Murmansk.

Maman embraces you heartily. She speaks of fate. My own feeling is just that we have been programmed by a machine I am prepared to trust.

Maurice

17

Hôtel de Paris, Monte Carlo
Monday, 4th November

Dear Lewis Carroll,

Adélaide ou le Langage de Fleurs, which we didn't think much of at the time, has been turned into rather a delightful ballet. I insisted they mention you on the second page of the program: "Based on an Idea by Lewis Carroll." Is that all right?

"Stranded, penniless and without consular protection in bloody awful Monsoon" seems an over-reaction on your part. Counter-revolutions never have been and never will be good for money, but once the first rough bustle is over you may learn to appreciate the advantages. Some counter-revolutionary societies fix everyone's teeth, for instance.

Heidelberg has a backlog of tenure until 2090, so not much hope for you there.

It was not a handbook on reforestation I sent; it was a critical study of the Marquis de Sade. Try it on Berkeley.

I'm engaged for my first solo concert, a charity affair up at the Palace. Don't you happen to have anything in some simple key? Maman adds, as a joke, "for one hand."

How strange our fates have been and how capricious our destinies.

Maurice R.

En route to Venice
15th November

Dear Dodgson,

I am writing on my knee, my letter paper firmly in place on the back of the Modigliani I am taking to Venice as a present from Countess Rasponi to her sister, who was, as you know, a good friend of Henry James. We had a nice little run into Switzerland to see Noel Coward, who lent us the Rolls. Maman was pleased with the Alps.

Here's news: Lubyanka gives tenure on demand. In Ethiopia, you have to promise not to marry anyone in direct line to the throne. In San Marino, they make you sign a pledge not to overthrow the soccer team. You may use my name, if you wish.

We find you depressive. Just keep telling yourself that all you need in your present Monsoon predicament is a large-scale map and a smart accountant.

Cordially,
Ravel

18

Dear Friend,

My son is rehearsing his speech for the Legion of Honor ceremony, during which massed choirs numbering three thousand will render *Daphnis et Chloé*; he has asked me to answer your questions in his stead. I can see that your feelings have ceased to be rational, but was it such a good idea to implant yourself in a country on the brink of upheaval? All revolutions eat their young: the trouble with counter-revolutions is that they also eat their old. To think they are blaming you for last year's hemp harvest! My poor friend, you are like someone paying interest who has never applied for credit! As my son puts it, the creative life is just one big uncut emerald. It's a matter of knowing where to slice. Such a pity you are not here to advise us; Maurice has become keen on England. How much longer do you think they will keep you for questioning? Not too long, I hope.

With fond sympathy,
"Maman Ravel"

Christ Church, Oxford
St. Swithin's Day

My dear Dr. Dodgson,

How agreeable to hear from you.

Yes, there is a shelter for distressed authors somewhere in England, but no one can tell me where. I cannot help wondering if you would not be better off seeking healthy employment while you are still able-bodied. I have been told of a vacancy for a cleaner in the Irish Guards barracks. If you like, I could provide you with a personal introduction to Her Majesty the Queen, making no reference, of course, to your recent incarceration in Monsoon: the Guards are sticky about clean records. Should you prefer to touch on the outskirts of the world of music, as one wistful phrase of your letter suggests, you might study the possibilities offered by a new comprehensive complex, the Asia Minor Musical and Performing Arts Facility, where the post of night watchman is still up for competitive bidding. You will be given the option of tenure without salary, or room and board with agonizing insecurity: the choice is up to you. I am informed that the place is a hotbed of creative dislocation, which should suit someone starting at rock bottom. My mother suggests sending you to Saint-Jean-de-Luz, where a caretaker is desperately needed to keep the Bechstein dusted and tuned. How fluent are you in Basque?

Yours etc,
Maurice Ravel

Apparently you have been writing a lot of nonsense. Why so?

LOVERS

Ludwig Zeller

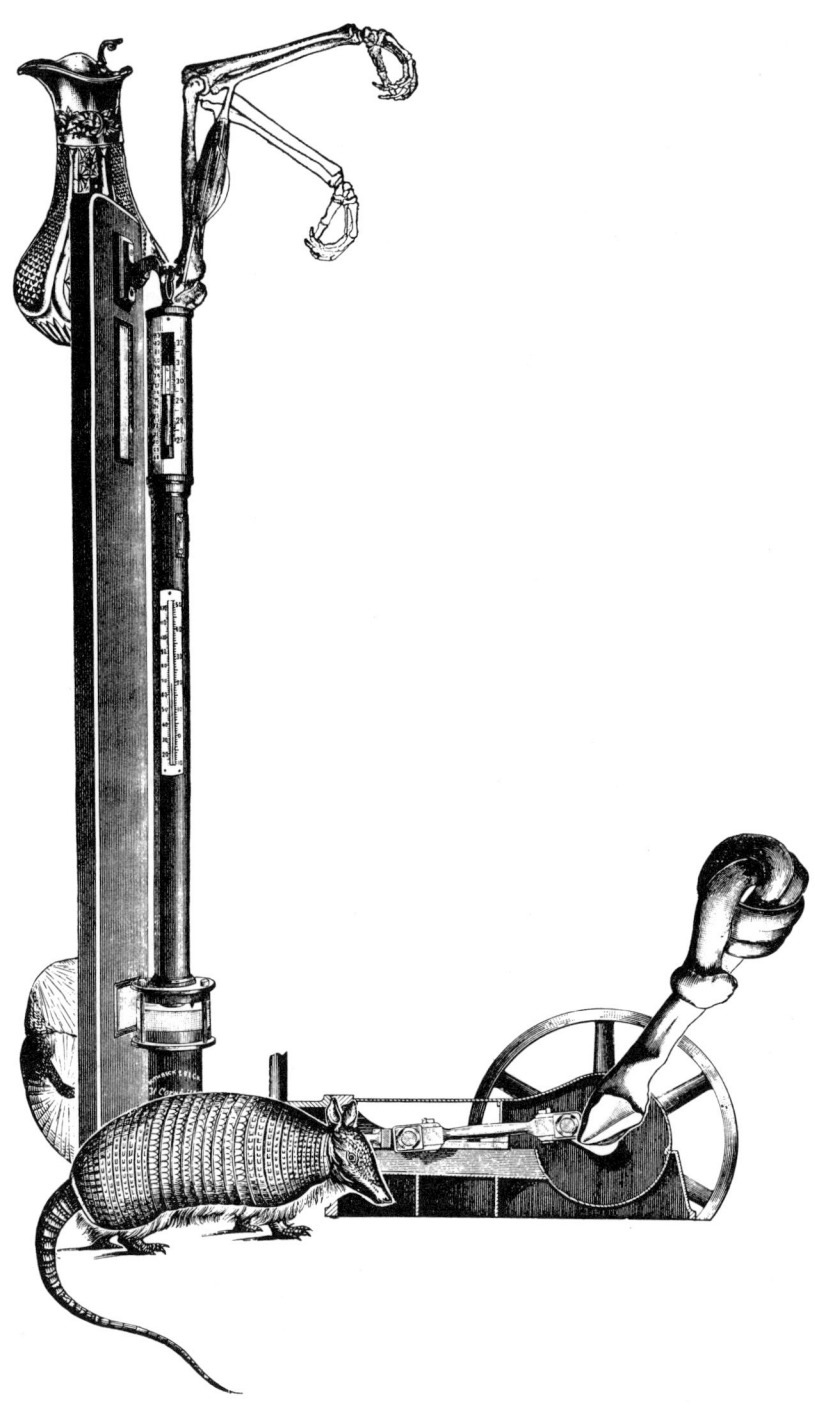

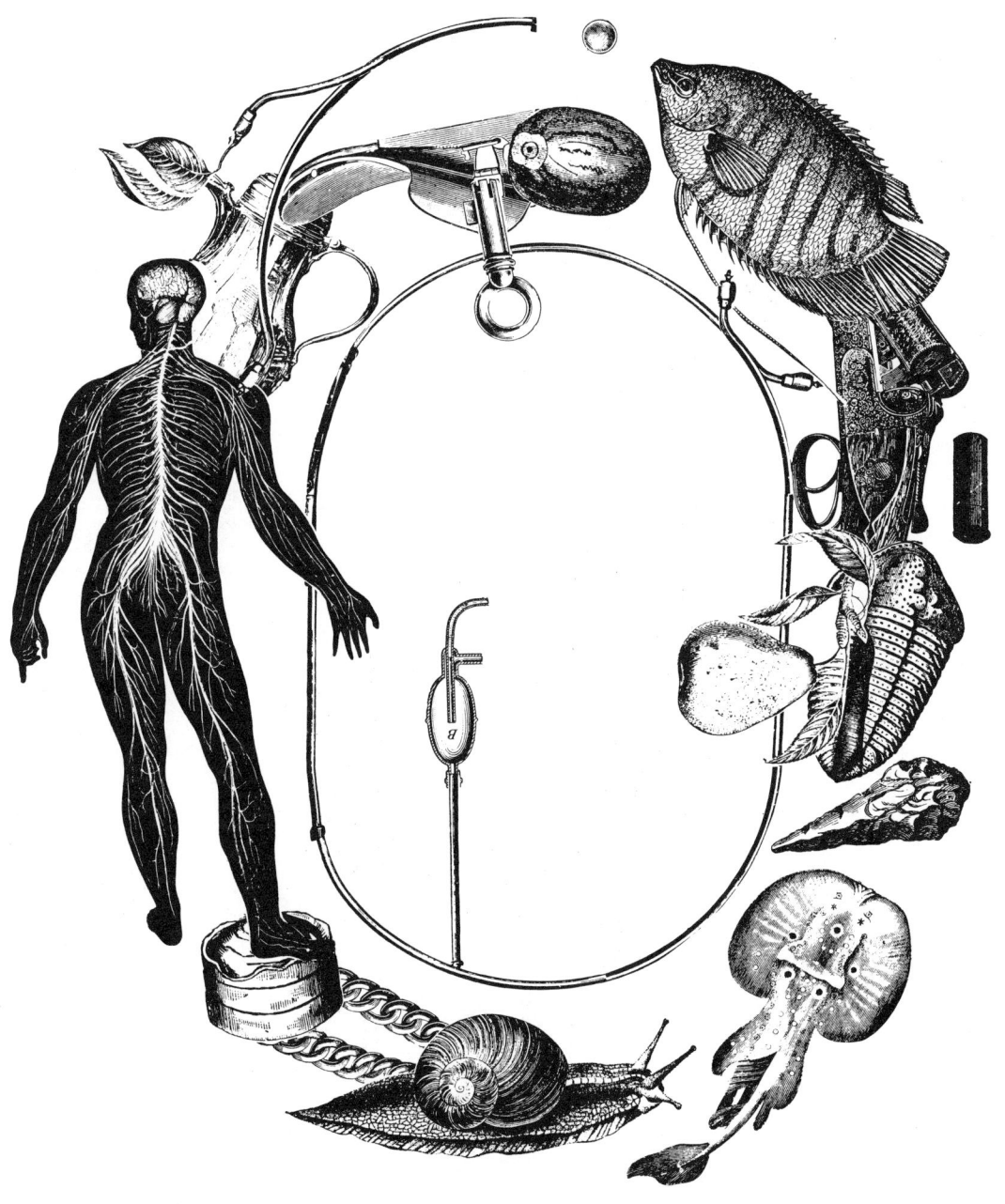

21

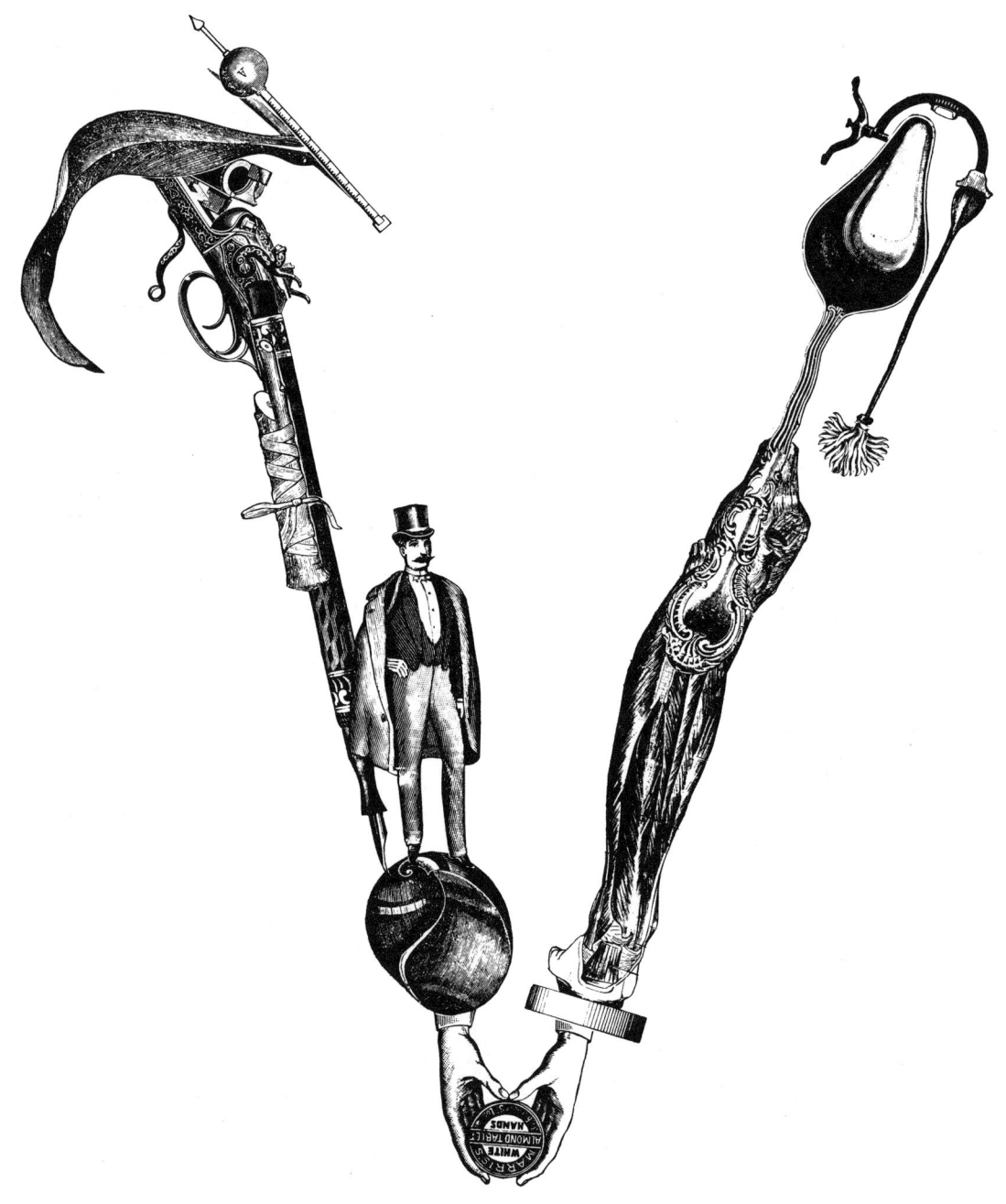

22

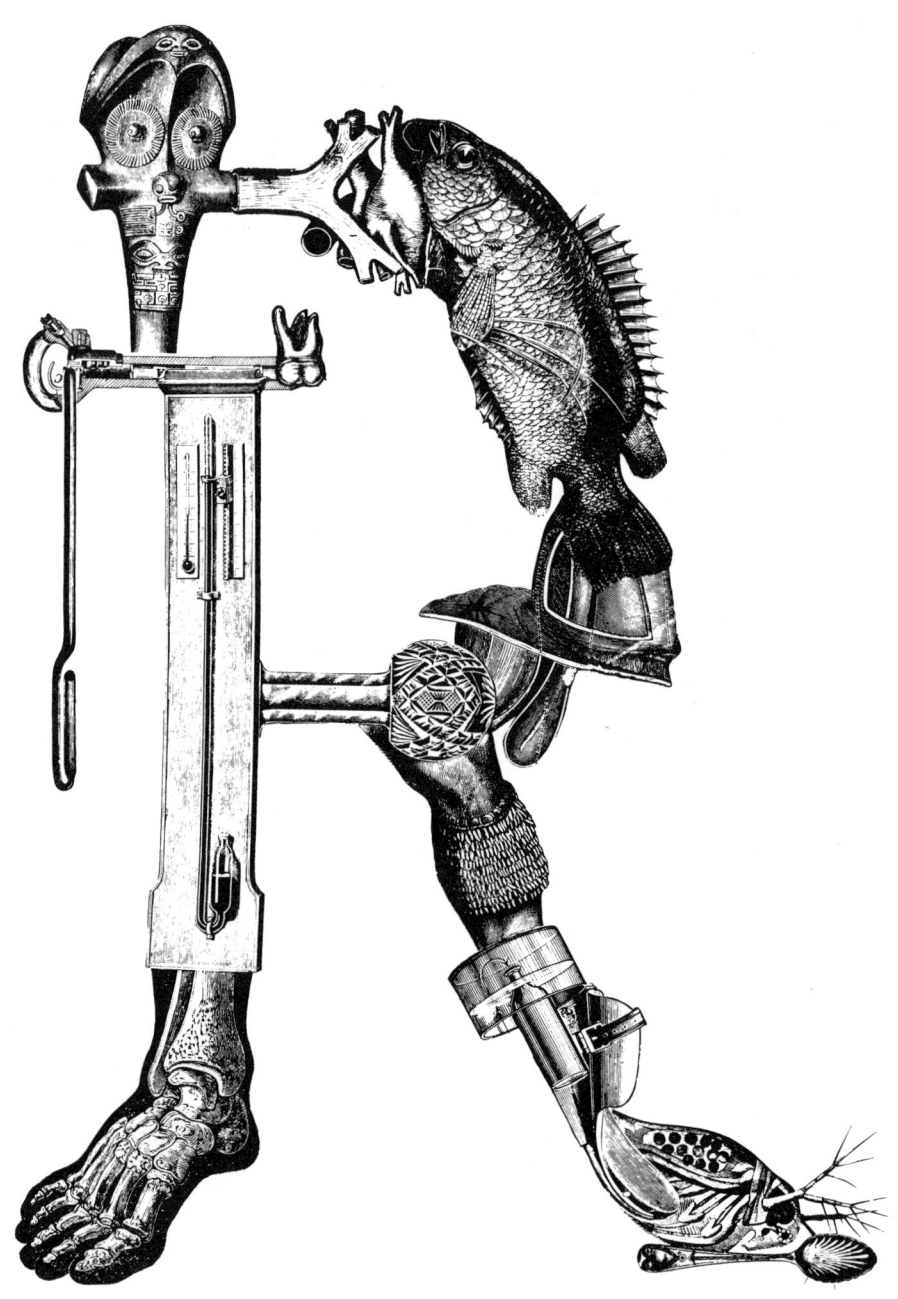

25

A QUÉBÉCOIS DREAM

Victor-Lévy Beaulieu

Cut One

((It happened when he stepped onto des Récollets Street: he could tell
something was different all of a sudden. A cloud hovering over him like a
dusky wing and right away this feeling of oppression. His legs were
hurting. Goddamn creaky knees! He lifted a foot and set it down slowly.
He took off his cap. His curly, matted hair. Damn sweat! He wiped his
forehead. If at least I had a car. He saw himself at the wheel of an old
convertible tearing through the streets of the Morial Mort. He'd put on seat
covers to hide the rips and the cigarette burns in the worn leather. The tires
squealed on the asphalt; he'd slam on the brakes at red lights, and the
Hollywood mufflers made a hell of a racket when he took off again. The
fox tail fixed on the antenna was an occult trophy, some strange symbol of
virility. He had the radio turned up all the way: it was blaring, really
blasting out of the back speaker. Think I don't know how to handle cunt,
mother-fucker! And there sure are some out on the prowl this mornin'!
Truth was, there were lots of them – girls on the street in summer outfits –
You know, the kind of clothes that show everything without showing
anything, those scanty things that show off the navel and the place where
mongoloids are made. Hey, get a load of those big, high-class asses in
those shorts! He must have been walking for an hour now, long strides
beneath a leaden sun. The arm holding the overnight bag'd gone to sleep
a long time ago. Even his bad leg was growing numb. Good thing there
were plenty of taverns along the way for old Joseph-David-Barthélémy
Dupuis! He yawned the time to let the novelist see his nicotine-stained
teeth and that tongue he could wag as fast as a nervous foot – and wasn't
it wearing a sock right now! It was the beer, it had knocked him out: KO,
CHA-O ... s. But Joseph-David-Barthélémy Dupuis didn't give a damn! The
house wasn't far, and soon, sucking his Jeanne D'Arc's tits, his barome-
ter'd show fair weather again. Yeah, sure, he was out of work – so what?
There're more than enough people workin' already! He hawked up
phlegm and spit it out on the sidewalk, then cleared his throat. Somethin'
stunk. Too many women on the rag, most likely. He figured Jeanne D'Arc
was parked naked in front of the television set watching some crummy
film, holding her heavy, brown tits in her hands. His hand tightened into
a fist; he couldn't help it: I don't trust her, an' I got good reasons not to.
Hers ain't the most Catholic cunt in the world, the lousy bitch! He might
have added that he didn't do much to help her there, and that he wasn't
exactly a model husband. But what would be the point? Everybody in
Morial Mort knew that, starting with his Jeanne D'Arc. (You're a no-good
bum, understand? That's what bugs me!) He would pinch one of her tits,
laughing a manly laugh. Usually it worked: all he had to do was tickle a tit

and she'd calm down. But this mornin' it didn't do any good: she slapped shit outta me and me too stupid to slap her back. I took my cap off the nail an' – ahhh! What he had done was simple enough: he had slammed the door, slammed it so hard a pane of glass tumbled out onto the floor and broke all to pieces. And Jeanne D'Arc screaming when he jumped over the fence – Bastard! You're nothing but a coward, a drunken bum! He'd shrugged his shoulders. Women always scream the same thing. First of all, I'm not a drunk. I have a small Labatt's every now and then but you gotta wet your whistle when it's hot like this, eh? He laughed. He liked being a holy terror with his Jeanne D'Arc. Get fed up? Her? Come on! Was anybody gonna hump her any better than him in his old parent's big bed? Yeah, well, that's what worries me: Jeanne D'Arc's got fuckin' on the brain an' maybe she says, another prick that'll keep the juices flowin'. He saw her stretched out in the middle of the old parents' big bed, her legs spread for Christie to feed her one mean sandwich. He chased the thought away in a hurry – Till I'm shown different my Jeanne D'Arc eats the same kind of sandwiches as everybody else. Joseph-David-Barthélémy Dupuis was thinking too much and had hardly noticed things as he passed them, so he was astonished to discover he was almost home. The house's gable was a white maw in the green surroundings. He had just trimmed the trees, whose branches were beating against the upstairs window and keeping Jeanne D'Arc from sleeping. I worked a lot this summer. Yes, he had. He had butchered the hedge of spirea in front of the porch trying to fashion green figures and a cross. Yeah, well, I was bound to mess it up, I got no experience with that sort of thing – I ruined the fuckin' hedge, if you wanna know! He had even hoed up the pumpkins his Jeanne D'Arc was growing by the fence in the backyard. She must really like those big, green balls warmin' their bellies in the sun! Damn if the little woman ain't vulgar! It comes from watchin' TV with all those programs full of nothin' but sex! He laughed again. He laughed a lot lately. Laughter would simply bubble up in his body like witches' brew in a cauldron. He was beginning to enjoy it. He was perfecting his laugh, thickening it and rounding it out. Because soon he was going to undertake something noble; he didn't know what yet, but he was sure he would go down in history. I'm gonna have my fine car an' then my Jeanne D'Arc's gonna be in trouble, then she's gonna get it, but good. Now des Récollets Street had changed while he was gone. What was it all about? You're too tired, probably from walkin' and drinkin' too much. Is it because you just got outta Dorémi, old Joseph-David-Barthélémy Dupuis? An' you're gonna go home and hug and squeeze your Jeanne D'Arc? He didn't really believe it, there was too much noise on des Récollets, too many helicopters circling around and landing somewhere behind the houses in huge clouds of dust with their long, sweeping propellers, too many police sirens and red bubblegum machines on top of the patrol cars, too many soldiers with long carbines on their shoulders. And des Réclollets Street closed off by a wall of cops. Joseph-David-Barthélémy Dupuis stopped. His heart. Out of breath. Hey, what's goin' on? For a second he thought it was him they were after, they were going to haul him in because his Jeanne D'Arc had reported him. He punched his cap. It was that hypocrite Jeanne D'Arc's face he was pound-

27

ing. She sold me out, crossed me. Now what's gonna become of you? He moved forward a bit; he had to go past the police if he wanted to get home. The street was full of people. Big, greasy faces, wide mouth-faces belching out left and right: Can't get through! Can't get through! Turn around! People were crowded together on the hill in the direction of Monselet. They were afraid of the rifles and of the motorcycles coming from every direction. Barthélémy thought of big, buzzing flies, black and wingless. A chill ran up and down him – Those bastards crammed me full of dope. A hand landed on his shoulder. He turned around. You were told to move back. Don't you see you can't get through? He jumped out of the way of a motorcycle. The white cop helmets were golf balls with red eyes and ears. Barthélémy started to run. What is this? The end of the world, or a war, or what? He jostled men and women alike because he wanted to get away as fast as possible from that swelling, threatening sea. On the bare shoulders of sun-blackened men, children were crying. (Could he really know there was no time left to recreate the world, to ring the past around with a heavy palisade of pious folk, a fort of sorts, to protect it against sly, slinking procedure and savage words flying at the skull with tomahawk fury? There was to be no future for him, perhaps; not even a present; for he was already condemned to what had never been, to what would never be, living out his life in dank obscurity, in a rubber snake world coiling and uncoiling around him, motion almost mechanical, banal, the randomness of mere process, the dumbness of a thing overflowing, emptiness' pure lack which sucked at his spine, leaving him only his purposeless wanderings through Morial Mort – to make sense if he could out of the phoney world of Steinberg supermarkets, Laura Secord shops, Smoker's Corners, snack bars, alleyways, cars parked in no-parking zones, houses jammed up against one another to find warmth, making sure nothing and no one holed up in those decorated wombs should ever be lonely or sick or without a telephone to call the doctor when he was ready to die. Did God alone know that the future was to be found cowering in the narrow folds of the steadily shrinking present?) Oh, push open the tavern door so that darkness might take him and bind his hands behind his back and lead him below and leave him for dead. (God almighty. Oh, God almighty!) Barthélémy's ears were still ringing with the sounds of life outside. His eyes were watering. He was an old hound who was going to die far from his bitch, she with life still beating in her. He was the same as he always was when he got out of Dorémi. Which meant he was scared. So he slapped himself hard on the forehead several times, trying to get hold of himself. But he was far gone already, water was cascading now somewhere behind his eyes and only the traditional invocations could do anything for him – Jesus fuckin' Christ! You becomin' afraid of your own shadow? Damn ugly bitch! Jeanne D'Arc's not gonna eat you. Just because you slugged her doesn't mean you oughta have the shakes. Take it easy, old buddy, take it easy! But he couldn't help himself, his teeth were chattering and hot tears fell from his eyes. He had these attacks more and more often and he was powerless against them. He was definitely going to die. He was definitely through. He kicked a table leg. His wrists came free at once. He downed his beer, stood up, then took off running between the tables and through the opening the door suddenly offered. Outside it seemed to him he was a big, unruly horse hightailing it down the street. (Whoa, whoaaa boy!) He pulled on the reins and the taps on his boot soles sent up sparks off the asphalt. You wanna break your leg and get sent to the glue factory? He laughed once again. He never thought he could be so crazy. To celebrate, he took an old harmonica out of his pocket and began to play, to the delight of the passers-by Jeanne d'Arc's favorite reel, the one she asked for when she was happy and in love with him. She'd rub up against me and take hold of my prick. Or keep time with her foot. With the very first notes he shivered violently. And those bastards at Dorémi, they hid my harp – he blew hard into his mouth organ and danced on the sidewalk, happy, so incredibly happy. But Jeanne D'Arc's waitin' for me, I gotta hurry. (Maybe she'd put perfume between her legs and in her ears. Am I ever gonna go at that with my tongue!) But he wasn't getting anywhere, his house was like a target seen through field glasses: if he went another five hundred feet he wouldn't be able to turn back, he'd have to open fire. (All this was taking place at the hour when the wild animals go down to drink in the Rivière des Prairies. All this was taking place at the hour when the mighty males stand watch, backside to backside, while the females contemplate their antlers in the still water.) Barthélémy's lungs were spitting flames. The old harmonica had turned red in his hands. His fingers were twisted with pain, his charred nails were bloody spots. Barthélémy threw the harmonica on the ground and stomped it furiously. His lips were bleeding, the eyes in his face, he knew, were burning embers. (I hate your guts. God, do I hate your guts!) Once the instrument was demolished he fell to his knees and saw the poor, squashed thing crawling along the sidewalk. He was full of remorse them, and of fierce anger against Jeanne D'Arc, who must have been waiting for him, secure behind the living room curtains. (It was no longer at watering time that this was taking place now, but at the silent hour, the hour of inner lamentation and of the sun closing its red eye behind the houses along Monselet Street. Barthélémy carefully picked up what had been his harmonica, looked at it tenderly, kissing it before putting it in his pocket next to his heart – I'm losin' my grip. I gotta get to the house before I can't find my way at all! He started walking fast, straight ahead. It was like being in a train: the coach window was distorting the lines of the houses. At least doors were opening to let him through. They know I'm in a hurry an' Jeanne D'Arc's pining for me. He'd never liked houses as much as now. He stammered out his thanks, raising his hand high, two fingers forming the ritualistic v. He was beside himself with joy. For the moment, he had to forget Dorémi, his internment, the judge's threats, Jeanne D'Arc's false witness, the night in the cell, the cops' brutality, the drugs injected into his thigh, and a lot of other shit that would come back one of these days and occupy his heart. Finally, here I am! When he reached the gate his legs were shaking. He was exhausted, as though all his energy had seeped out of the wound in his foot. He waited a while so he could catch his breath. He held on to the fence. Didn't somebody have him by the legs trying to drag him away? Weren't the devils gripping his ankles, warning him how important it was not to move an inch? He punched at thin air, then lifted the gate latch. He began to mutter to himself. A sort of song came out of his mouth, one that he must have heard on the radio, though he didn't remember the real words. He was walking now; the sound of his voice had calmed him. He was approaching the house, his paradise regained after all too much suffering. He pictured to himself Jeanne D'Arc's beautiful face as she let him caress her at the head of the stairs, her eyes glassy, her body not moving, her thoughts elsewhere, in a beery coolness, or perhaps nowhere at all, floating peacefully in darkness, an evil demon pacified by his patient aloofness. The stairs creaked under his feet. The sweat. His large check-ered handkerchief was soaking wet. He had dropped his bag to stop the muscles in his arm from twitching. He breathed deeply and walked to the other end of the porch looking at the stars, his nostrils open wide to the familiar odors they'd deprived him of for too long. Then, coming back to the door he stumbled over something and fell. He lay silent. He hoped Jeanne D'Arc hadn't heard him fall – I open the door, she doesn't know I'm there an' lookin' at her, she's got a finger in her mouth, is she ever nervous, that Jeanne D'Arc, it must be because of TV, she must think she's in the movies but she's pretty, I can't wait to put my hand on her head. (He was standing up now.) Wanna tell me what it was I tripped over, For God's sake? He reached for whatever it was that had toppled him and ran his hands over it, astonished to discover it was his old overnight bag. It's not hard to recognize it, it's missin' a handle. Jeanne D'Arc must've filled it full of bricks it's so heavy. He unzipped it and plunged both hands inside. At Dorémi I hid under the bed so I could fool around in the bag without bein' bothered. Sonsabitches, they'd want to stick me while I was asleep an' the next day there I was with my mouth hangin' open. I'd keep noddin' out all day an' I couldn't even talk 'cause my jaws wouldn't move. An' they thought I'd take it without sayin' a word. OK, I ate damn good, I'd've been fat as a pig in no time, but those pills, oh no, well, they weren't gonna get me with that. Hee-hee-hee. I fixed 'em when I began to take' em with coke. Like walkin' into a stone wall; I'd go off my damn nut, I might've killed everyone of 'em; I was highflyin'. Hee-hee-hee-hee. Joseph-David Barthélémy Dupuis began to empty his bag. Ah, Jeanne D'Arc put every-thing I own in there. He might have added: including my memory, but he didn't know the word, that is, what he was in the process of doing, laying out his personal effects, the various pieces of his past that he was anx-iously, frantically, dragging to the surface – it left him feeling so unreal that he forgot Jeanne D'Arc. The bag. A catch-all. That is, a trap. And he could never reach the end, there were too many things he considered irretrievably lost, sunk, crushed, undone under barrels and barrels of small Labatt's. Suddenly coming face to face with all this terrified him and made him almost delirious. Breath – Hey, have I ever been around! Damn, have I ever been through it or not! He looked at the westclox hands, the phosphorescent numbers. He put it to his ear and shook it because he didn't hear the tick-tock. Not surprisin' it aint runnin' it's been so long since it was wound. He had completely forgotten he was supposed to go inside and take Jeanne D'Arc in his arms. He wound the clock and listened to the noise the springs made. I'd have really liked to work in a clock factory! Of everything from his past it was the old westclox he liked most, the old dented and rusted body which was just like him, you couldn't wear it out, its stubbornness kept you from ever really getting at it. It was the world he was holding against his ear, his whole existence he held on to so tightly. The metal's hardness. The cracked glass he had never replaced because dust couldn't hurt those rock-solid works. He set the clock down on the chair beside him and stayed a long time watching the progression of its hands. It was to remember, that was why he was doing it. As a form of homage too, no doubt. Because the clock had saved his life lots of times. Too often when he was completely drunk he just couldn't stand it any more: he would see hordes of demons, monsters would leap at his face trying to disfigure him. He didn't know how to talk about those things, there were no words for what he saw, he'd have had to draw a picture. (But the big hippopotamus had reached the foot of the bed: it was breathing ferociously and soon was going to jump on him and crush him beneath its weight.) Hey, Jeanne D'Arc! Hey, damn it! He leapt to his feet. The evil spell had turned into a whirlwind, lifting dust, dead leaves and scraps of paper in the yard. It's time for me to go in an' take Jeanne D'Arc in my arms an' talk to her once and for all. I got so much to tell her, it's been three months now that I been keepin' it all inside me. A blown up balloon full of words, a long series of sentences which would flow from him the minute he opened his mouth lying at Jeanne D'Arc's side in his old parents' big bed after they'd had a good fuck. He'd be delivered from all that was afflicting him, he'd be soft and humble like in those easy, early days. Oh, the little house. The scratching of a clothes line. High banks of snow. An ass like an offering for the eye. Where and when, all of that? In what dream? Before which decisive swig of beer that had destroyed everything? He coughed softly so as not to alert Jeanne D'Arc, then he tried the door. (Locked, damn it.) He fumbled in his pockets but found nothing he could use to force the lock. He thought of the bag; he knelt down and unzipped it. There's gotta be an old piece of wire in here somewhere. His hands burrowed into his life's debris. (Casting aside the dice, the thin chains, the worn-out shoe, the medallions, the handkerchiefs, the false nose and fake eye-glasses, the doll's head, its eyes hanging out of its sockets, finally coming up with this narrow metal rod with small plastic wheels at both ends which still turned.) Barthélémy unscrewed the wheels and tossed them in the bag. The kodak. The muffled noise (Jeanne D'Arc peeking out from behind the window?) He slid the metal pin into the lock. Easy, easy, don't scare away the birds that've built their nest in there. The sound of breathing through the nose. (And that big draught-horse stepping sleepily through the potato plants. Whoa boy, don't bolt on me now, damn you!) Joseph-David-Barthélémy Dupuis was nervous, you see. And I got no patience, my nerves ain't so hot these days. he kept at it, slowly working the little truck axle into the lock. The springs (he knew there were no springs but he liked to say that word that sounded so nice, that made him think of motion, something like the wild flight of two terrified beasts down des Récollets) – so the springs, then, gave; there was a sort of click, and when he turned the door knob there it was, the long hallway of paradise regained running straight up to him. He was overjoyed, his head full of scenes of the time before Dorémi, only the nice ones, and leaning with his hand against the white plaster wall he understood how close he'd come to dying and losing his Jeanne D'Arc. (No. A mole no more. No more to roam dark holes. No more to be surrounded by stray dogs, their paws bloodied from scrabbling in ice-encrusted snow. No more. No. He was full of fine resolutions, full of tender words he was finally going to say – to himself as much as to his Jeanne D'Arc.) To keep from speaking yet he closed his mouth and sealed his lips with adhesive tape. It was thus that he wandered through paradise regained, invisible in the shadows, and silent, and terribly troubled by what was welling up inside him, all of it somehow constituting his affection for Jeanne D'Arc. I should have taken a bath before I left. And if I had my suit. And my good polished boots. And my tie with the shiny stickpin. Or if I was naked. You can't tell I'm ugly when it's dark. The scars disappear, an' the sores on my foot, too. I'm presentable then. He was sweating profusely and talking to himself in his head because inside things were churning. One wrong move an' I'm caught. Jeanne D'Arc'll be at me tooth and nail. (The truth was he didn't dare admit he was worried, that a knot of anguish had come to his throat the minute he stepped onto des Récollets Street. At a certain point I'm gonna open a door and then – Jeanne D'Arc.) He saw her naked on the sofa, her neck broken, her head, its long blond hair like a torchlight, hanging over the side, soaked in warm blood, her belly open, the smell of piss and shit. That obsession again! He was trying to calm down; he leaned against the wall and closed his eyes – Sickly, pale infant in a stroller with rusty wheels. Then battles with baseball bats somewhere along the Rivière des Prairies. And big caved-in bellies with pieces of intestine sticking out like mushrooms. And quick kisses through the bars to make of love something poor and difficult, to make it nothing but two obscene tongues trying to meet. And happiness right at hand when once alone in the huge, white room at Dorémi. (You're a little boy. Everything's big. Steinberg's parking lot is a black sea. You go one mile and you think you're at the other end of the earth. But you're not afraid; you know that what's gonna save you is the fact you're so little and everything around you's gonna get lost in its own bigness. When you get older and grown up then it's not the same at all. You walk down the streets an' think you're taller than the houses an' think the cars are goin' between your legs and think with a flick of your prick your could knock down every single one of the Steinberg's, and think everybody else is a dwarf an' if you wanted to you could scoop' em up by the handfuls. But you don't use your powers; you wait for your moment an' you're too dumb to realize it's come an' gone an' you're gettin' worn down an' becomin' as little as everybody else which means one fine mornin' you wake up and find your legs limp as dish rags an' the bones broken an' stickin' out everywhere. What're you gonna do then? You go from pillar to post, try like hell to make ends meet and don't, or start yellin' or laughin' till you're out of breath, or else you just sit back an' watch yourself sink under. Don't worry! You're gonna wind up with a little pinhead and tiny arms and no feet an' no body an' no heart especially. No heart; the heart's important. No heart, you got no diamond or club or spade either. You're nothin' but a fuckin' lump of ground beef with raggedy legs that don't run that fast any more.) He'd opened all the doors now. He saw the blind television set in the living room under the plastic palm tree, he saw the monkey hanging from a branch, he saw the hollow coconut shell, he saw the frayed burlap trunk. Jeanne D'Arc had to really be angry for him to buy her a gift like that! (At Dupuis'.) And him drunk. Jeanne D'Arc was going to leave him because of the poke in the eye he gave her, because of the insults, because of the drinking, and him, he'd gone to Dupuis'. The taxi and the tree cost him his whole pay cheque, he must have explained all that to the salesman, who pretended not to hear, turning a deaf ear to those words oozing fear. Hey, listen you, you loaded or what? You don't understand nothin', eh? Then what you doin' here? He was acting that way out of impatience and out of brutal desire for Jeanne D'Arc lying on the sofa with a tiny bag of ice on her eye. Whew! It was a hard job gettin' all that into the trunk of the car, alright. The memory made him terrible happy. He thought of the old taxi, the harsh lights, the screeching of the tires, the swarm of colors, buildings falling away behind the cars, the people, the nice-looking people walking up and down the streets, while the Pontiac was a half-tame animal let loose on Jeanne D'Arc's trail. (Ah, damn, damn!) And now there were just rooms which were too bare because Jeanne D'Arc wasn't in them. The dirt, the smell of burnt potatoes in the kitchen, of milk curdled in the container. And the living room. Jeanne D'Arc must have always watched television in the same spot, snuggled in a blanket in the rocking chair. The chair's rockers had left too many marks on the rug. And the potato chip crumbs, wasn't that proof enough? And the four coke bottles with the lipstick-stained straws. And the cigarette butts drowned in the bottles. Barthélémy remained perfectly still in the doorway. (Like on TV when they freeze the picture.) He felt nothing. His eyes were fixed in a stare and were filing up with water. A cordon of cops made an impenetrable curtain between him and the rest of the world. He was threatened and safe at the same time. If I was two people there'd be no problem. Each of us would have his place. Me, I could be mean an' him good. His ears tingled. The house was filling up with sounds, defending itself after its fashion against his intrusion; it was like a womb about to deliver, gas was escaping from it and it gave off cracking noises. How could Barthélémy not believe that he was once again a prisoner inside the white hospital where the only sounds were of needles piercing skin. He tried to move out of the doorway. Then suddenly everything went black. His knees buckled, his forehead struck the door frame, he fell on his leg (the dressing grew large and heavy with blood and pus and pain). He dragged himself down the hallway, grabbing at furniture. But running away was pointless because the guards were already at the door, the white guards were already blocking the windows – QUEBEC OCCUPIED. It was written in huge letters across the front page of the newspaper the guards brought him following his afternoon nap. (Why?) The nurses wore masks, they were naked but their faces were hidden behind squares of white gauze. The red rubber gloves. The frizzy, black hair below the belly. If it'd been any longer they'd have had real corkscrew curls. That's what he was thinking as the four nurses came towards him, he with a hard-on under the covers. They had tied him down to the bed, straps around his shoulders and knees; the nurses were really kangaroos or bloodsucking vampires. (Nothing escaped from that silent mouth.) Inside he was screaming and sirens were sounding. They took the sheet off the bed and tossed it aside, and the only vertical thing in that horizontal hospital world was his prick. The vampires were definitely going to grab him and plant passionate kisses all over him. Those teeth going into the skin. Those long draughts of blood, that prolonged sucking. Barthélémy doubled his efforts to move his trapped muscles. Warmth, and a heart bursting with love in his breast, and red tattoos on those impotent arms. Satiated, the vampires were perched on the big heating pipes which ran the length of the room. Other metamorphoses were going to take place, the vampires-kangaroos-nurses and the hypodermic needles would penetrate the flesh once again. Once again there would be inaudible cries and intense heat beneath the skin. During all this time Jeanne d'Arc's image pressing upon his eye, so small, so lovely, so pure. (Object of troubled affection rooted in the iris; a spear gouging the socket; blurred, failing sight.) Sphincters relaxing with rotten noises. Shitting and pissing. The white whale had strong breath. All around it a sheet of white, foul water in which the whaling ship was going to sink. The gold piece on the mainmast blinded Barthélémy. Unable to scream, he was crying. So, you like that book? Whales scare me. And cannibals more. The nurse was seated close by on the white chair taking his pulse. Those fingers with their long nails, and those protruding veins at his wrist, reassured him. I'm finished, eh? Why'd you have to kill me? The odor of excrement underneath him and this delicious feeling of buttocks wet with hot piss. He spit out the thermometer. You're acting like a child, monsieur Dupuis. Help us make you well. He kept his teeth clenched. His breath taken away because of the strap, his head like thunder ready to blow up the world. He would have liked to put his hand between the nurse's legs, violate her intimacy, get revenge for the indignities he was suffering. But she wasn't paying any attention to him now; the vampires had come back. They turned him over on his stomach and were holding his legs wide part. His sex hurt him, his too-stiff prick was pure pain beneath him. Could the hippopotamus have put on the rubber glove the better to get inside him and brutally explore his anus? Don't you know it was time? You'd think there was cement in there. Oh, die of shame hearing the dry turds land in the bed pan. (Let go of me! Fuck, let go of me!) A car's headlights flashed yellow into the shadows, suddenly lighting up the long hallway. Barthélémy rubbed his eyes. He was covered with sweat, his leg was bloody and his heart beat rapidly in his chest. What the hell's happenin' to me ? Heyheyhey! He lifted himself up and crawled on his knees to the door and collapsed on the porch beside his overnight bag. He was gasping for breath, tongue hanging out of his mouth, face on fire, blind and deaf and wild with excitement. Everything was turning, he couldn't tell where he was, there was too much wind and the flames were shooting out all around him now. He put his hand over his heart. Stop it, for God's sake! Stop it! He needed all his energy, something really serious must have happened while he was gone and if he didn't grab hold of himself he would be broken and destroyed before knowing what was what. He took a package of Forest out of his pocket, licked a Vogue paper, and came up with a pinch of tobacco. He was shaking so hard he lost the tobacco. His lungs were stopped up; there was no more air in the house, everything was crisp and dry. He made a sudden, violent movement with his body to break the spell and fell down the steps. Crying out – Jeanne d'Arc! Where are you, my Jeanne? He tried to get up. The back of his head struck something and all Barthélémy's strength left him. Later, he would understand that his head was stuck between two steps, that the wild grass growing beneath the porch was tickling his chin, and that he needed to laugh – It would rise on its own from somewhere deep within him, or maybe from somewhere outside him, so tired did he feel. Then the machines mounted him, caterpillar tractors flattening his back, jackhammers drilling his head; and, filling half the yard, there sat the grotesque hippopotamus, all smiles, its green teeth bared. Barthélémy couldn't keep from laughing, it made a protective wall between him and the rest of the world. I'll finally go to sleep. He wasn't aware right away of the importance of what he had just thought. He must have vomited before and wiped his lips on his shirtsleeve. Then he understood – that was the important word: sleep. He laid his head on the step and yawned. (Old lion lost in the jungle, mortally wounded, no Tarzan to bring him hunks of beef. Old fat-gut, toothless lion who's lost his roar. Go to sleep, damn it. Go to sleep. He knew Jeanne D'Arc would come back at the right moment, that first he had to wait for her deep in the heart of the night before he could take her in his arms. He let the tears flow down his cheeks and closed his eyes. He was floating down the Rivière des Prairies, gasping for breath, drowning in the blood running out of his leg) –))

Translated by Ray Chamberlain

THE DEAD SKY LETTERS

Diane Keating

Love is a planet
made from the pulp
of what we dream.
I was never more alive

but the sky was against us,
a shining casket,
meteors burrowed
like maggots into our skin.

***

For a monument we cut
our initials into a tree trunk.
Whatever is carved from a living thing
fills in … still
a sign, dear starthrower,

your scars in my skull.

***

Today I remember
how we pulled the blinds
and persuaded the universe
to come into our room,

planets rotating
around walls,
the Milky Way rising from the floor.

We were gods with mirror eyes
looking into each other's blindness.

***

Now this street into the night,
telephone poles
pointing to the Southern Cross.

Look up, dear blacksmith,
the nails are cold and sharp.

Remember the light, how it opened.
How we burst through.

***

Living in our moonshell,
the world seemed a small black stone.

What matters, you cried
is the space inside, the no-man's-land
between heart and mind.

What matters, I said, is what
comes up from the dead
and down from the boned air.

***

Sunday with its snares
and sparrows
hopping across the sill
on splintered legs.

Sunday, brighter than flowers
the new winter's blood
on the holly bush. The furnace hums:
sunlight under rock.
Keep pushing, dear snowheart,
each rebirth
we are more filled.

***

I'll love you till
your heart's so fat,
cracks its shell
and scuttles
into the boiling vat.

I'll love you till
a peacock flies up your nose.

I'll love you till
your eyepit roots a blue rose
and your skin when we touch
secretes purple rainbows.

37

So keep the sun behind bars.
God's shadow, time, is a friend.
Our story's told in the stars.
Who cares when it ends.

***

Wherever we went
white shadows of the drowned
floated across the sky.

We let go our bones
slipped into each other.
It was natural to be unbound

but love breaks
a wave leaving no message
except to swell and break again ...

my heart watching itself
I wait on the edge with my suitcase
of masks. No dream near
I shun the sun's revelations.

IF ON A WINTER'S NIGHT
A TRAVELER

Italo Calvino

The novel begins in a railway station, a locomotive huffs, steam from a piston covers the opening of the chapter, a cloud of smoke hides part of the first paragraph. In the odor of the station there is a passing whiff of station café odor. There is someone looking through the befogged glass, he opens the glass door of the bar, everything is misty, inside, too, as if seen by nearsighted eyes, or eyes irritated by coal dust. The pages of the book are clouded like the windows of an old train, the cloud of smoke rests on the sentences. It is a rainy evening; the man enters the bar; he unbuttons his damp overcoat; a cloud of steam enfolds him; a whistle dies away along tracks that are glistening with rain, as far as the eye can see.

A whistling sound, like a locomotive's, and a cloud of steam rises from the coffee machine that the old counterman puts under pressure, as if he were sending up a signal, or at least so it seems from the series of sentences in the second paragraph, in which the players at the table close the fans of cards against their chests and turn toward the newcomer with a triple twist of their necks, shoulders, and chairs, while the customers at the counter raise their little cups and blow on the surface of the coffee, lips and eyes half shut, or suck the head of their mugs of beer, taking exaggerated care not to spill. The cat arches its back, the cashier closes her cash register and it goes pling. All these signs converge to inform us that this is a little provincial station, where anyone is immediately noticed.

Stations are all alike; it doesn't matter if the lights cannot illuminate beyond their blurred halo, all of this is a setting you know by heart, with the odor of train that lingers even after all the trains have left, the special odor of stations after the last train has left. The lights of the station and the sentences you are reading seem to have the job of dissolving more than of indicating the things that surface from a veil of darkness and fog. I have landed in this station tonight for the first time in my life, entering and leaving this bar, moving from the odor of the platform to the odor of wet sawdust in the toilets, all mixed in a single odor which is that of waiting, the odor of telephone booths when all you can do is reclaim your tokens because the number called has shown no signs of life.

I am the man who comes and goes between the bar and the telephone booth. Or, rather: that man is called "I" and you know nothing else about him, just as this station is called only "station" and beyond it there exists nothing except the unanswered signal of a telephone ringing in a dark room of a distant city. I hang up the receiver. I await the rattling flush, down through the metallic throat, I push the glass door again, head toward the cups piled up to dry in a cloud of steam.

The espresso machines in station cafés boast their kinship with the locomotives, the espresso machines of yesterday and today with the locomotives and steam engines of today and yesterday. It's all very well for me to come and go, shift and turn: I am caught in a trap, in that nontemporal trap which all stations unfailingly set. A cloud of coal dust still hovers in the air of stations all these years after the lines have been totally electrified, and a novel that talks about trains and stations cannot help conveying this odor of smoke. For a couple of pages now you have been reading on, and this would be the time to tell you clearly whether this station where I have got off is a station of the past or a station of today; instead the sentences continue to move in vagueness, grayness, in a kind of no man's land of experience reduced to the lowest common denominator. Watch out: it is surely a method of involving you gradually, capturing you in the story before you realize it – a trap. Or perhaps the author still has not made up his mind, just as you, reader, for that matter, are not sure what you would most like to read: whether it is the arrival at an old station, which would give you a sense of going back, a renewed concern with lost times and places, or else a flashing of lights and sounds, which would give you the sense of being alive today, in the world where people today believe it is a pleasure to be alive. This bar (or "station buffet," as it is also called) could seem dim and misty only to my eyes, nearsighted or irritated, whereas it could also be steeped in light diffused by tubes the color of lightning and reflected by mirrors in such a way as to fill completely every passage and interstice, and the shadowless space might be overflowing with music exploding at top volume from a vibrant silence-killing machine, and the pinballs and the other electric games simulating horse races and manhunts are all in action, and colored shadows swim in the transparency of a TV and in that of an aquarium of tropical fish enlivened by a vertical stream of air bubbles. And my arm might not hold a briefcase, swollen and a bit worn, but might be pushing a square suitcase of plastic material supplied with little wheels, guided by a chrome stick that can be folded up.

You, reader, believed that there, on the platform, my gaze was glued to the hands of the round clock of an old station, hands pierced like halberds, in the vain attempt to turn them back, to move backward over the cemetery of spent hours, lying lifeless in their circular pantheon. But who can say that the clock's numbers aren't peeping from rectangular windows, where I see every minute fall on me with a click like the blade of a guillotine? However, the result would not change much: even advancing in a polished, sliding world, my hand contracted on the light rudder of the wheeled suitcase would still express an inner refusal, as if that carefree luggage represented for me an unwelcome and exhausting burden.

Something must have gone wrong for me: some misinformation, a delay, a missed connection; perhaps on arriving I should have found a contact, probably linked with this suitcase that seems to worry me so much, though whether because I am afraid of losing it or because I can't wait to be rid of it is not clear. What seems certain is that it isn't just ordinary baggage, something I can check or pretend to forget in the waiting room. There's no use my looking at my watch; if anyone had come and waited for me he would have gone away again long ago, there's no point in my furiously racking my brain to turn back clocks and calendars in the hope of reaching again the moment before something that should not have happened did happen. If I was to meet someone in this station, someone who perhaps had nothing to do with this station but was simply to get off one train and leave on another train, as I was to have done, and one of the two was to pass something to the other – for example, if I was supposed to give the other this wheeled suitcase which instead has been left on my hands and is scorching them – then the only thing to do is to try to re-establish the lost contact.

I have already crossed the café a couple of times and have looked out of the front door onto the invisible square, and each time the wall of darkness has driven back inside this sort of illuminated limbo suspended between the two darknesses, the bundle of tracks and the foggy city. Where would I go out to? The city outside there has no name yet, we don't know if it will remain outside the novel or whether the whole story will be contained within its inky blackness. I know only this first chapter is taking a while to break free of the station and the bar: it is not wise for me to move away from here where they might still come looking for me, or for me to be seen by other people with this burdensome suitcase. And so I continue to cram tokens into the public telephone, which spits them back at me every time. Many tokens, as if for a long-distance call: God knows where they are now, the people from whom I am to receive instruction or, rather – let's come right out and say it – take orders. It is obvious that I am a subordinate, I do not seem the sort of man who is travelling for personal reasons or who is in business for himself; you would say, on the contrary, that I am doing a job, a pawn in a very complicated game, a little cog in a huge gear, so little that it should not even be seen: in fact, it was established that I would go through here without leaving any traces; and instead, every minute I spend here I am leaving more traces. I leave traces if I do not speak with anyone, since I stick out as a man who won't open his mouth; I leave traces if I speak with someone because every word spoken is a word that remains and can crop up again later, with quotation marks or without. Perhaps this is why the author piles supposition on supposition in long paragraphs without dialogue, a thick, opaque layer of lead where I may pass unnoticed, disappear.

I am not at all the sort of person who attracts attention, I am an anonymous presence against an even more anonymous background. If you, reader, couldn't help picking me out among the people getting off the train and continued following me in my to-and-fro-ing between bar and telephone, this is simply because I am called "I" and this is the only thing you know about me, but this alone is reason enough for you to invest a part of yourself in the stranger "I". Just as the author, since he has no intention of telling about himself, decided to call the character "I" as if to conceal him, not having to name him or describe him, because any other name or attribute would define him more than this stark pronoun: still, by the very fact of writing "I" the author feels driven to put into this "I" a bit of himself, of what he feels or imagines he feels. Nothing could be easier for him than to identify himself with me; for the moment my external behavior is that of a traveler who has missed a connection, a situation that is part

41

of everyone's experience. But a situation that takes place at the opening of a novel always refers you to something else that has happened or is about to happen, and it is this something else that makes it risky to identify with me, risky for you the reader and for him the author; and the more gray and ordinary and undistinguished and commonplace the beginning of this novel is, the more you and the author feel a hint of danger looming over that fraction of "I" that you have heedlessly invested in the "I" of a character whose inner history you know nothing about, as you know nothing about the contents of that suitcase he is so anxious to be rid of.

Getting rid of the suitcase was to be the first condition for re-establishing the previous situation: previous to everything that happened afterward. This is what I mean when I say I would like to swim against the stream of time: I would like to erase the consequences of certain events and restore an initial condition. But every moment of my life brings with it an accumulation of new facts, and each of these new facts brings with it its consequences; so the more I seek to return to the zero moment from which I set out, the further I move away from it: though all my actions are bent on erasing the consequences of previous actions and though I manage to achieve appreciable results in this erasure, enough to open my heart to hopes of immediate relief, I must, however, bear in mind that my every move to erase previous events provokes a rain of new events, which complicate the situation worse than before and which I will then, in their turn, have to try to erase. Therefore I must calculate carefully every move so as to achieve the maximum of erasure with the minimum of recomplication.

A man whom I do not know was to meet me as soon as I got off the train, if everything hadn't gone wrong. A man with a suitcase on wheels, exactly like mine, empty. The two suitcases would bump into each other as if accidentally in the bustle of travelers on the platform, between one train and another. An event that can happen by chance, but there would have been a password that that man would have said to me, a comment on the headline of the newspaper sticking out of my pocket, on the results of the horse races. "Ah, Zeno of Elea came in first!" And at the same time we would disentangle our suitcases, shifting the metal poles, perhaps also exchanging some remarks about horses, forecasts, odds; and we would then go off toward different trains, each pushing his suitcase in his own direction. No one would have noticed, but I would have been left with the other man's suitcase and he would have taken away mine.

A perfect plan, so perfect that a trivial complication sufficed to spoil it. Now I am here not knowing what to do next, the last traveler waiting in this station where no more trains arrive or leave before tomorrow morning. It is the hour when the little provincial city crawls into its shell again. At the station bar the only people left are locals who all know one another, people who have no connection with the station but come this far through the dark square perhaps because there is no other place open in the neighborhood, or perhaps because of the attraction that stations still exercise in provincial cities, that bit of novelty that can be expected from stations, or perhaps only in recollection of the time when a station was the single point of contact with the rest of the world.

42

It's all very well for me to tell myself there are no provincial cities any more and perhaps there never were any: all places communicate instantly with all other places, a sense of isolation is felt only during the trip between one place and the other, that is, when you are in no place. I, in fact, find myself here without a here or an elsewhere, recognized as an outsider by the nonoutsiders at least as clearly as I recognize the nonoutsiders and envy them. Yes, envy. I am looking from the outside at the life of an ordinary evening in an ordinary little city, and I realize I am cut off from ordinary evenings for God knows how long, and I think of thousands of cities like this, of hundreds of thousands of lighted places where at this hour people allow the evening's darkness to descend and have none of the thoughts in their heads that I have in mine; maybe they have other thoughts that aren't at all enviable, but at this moment I would be willing to trade with any one of them. For example, with one of these young men who are making the rounds of local shopkeepers collecting signatures on a petition to City Hall, concerning the tax on neon signs, and who are now reading it to the barman.

The novel here repeats fragments of conversation that seem to have no function beyond that of depicting the daily life of a provincial city. "What about you, Armida? Have you signed yet?" they ask a woman I can see only from behind, a belt hanging from a long overcoat rimmed with fur, the collar turned up, a thread of smoke rising from the fingers gripping the stem of a glass. "Who says I want to put a neon sign over my shop?" she answers. "If the City is planning to save money on street lights, they certainly aren't going to light the streets with my money! Anyway, everybody knows where Armida's Leather Goods is. And when I've pulled down the metal blind, the street will just stay dark, and that's that."

"That's a good reason for you to sign," they say to her. They address her familiarly, as *tu*; they all call one another *tu*; their speech is half in dialect; these are people used to seeing one another daily year after year; everything they say is the continuation of things already said. They tease one another, even crudely: "Admit it, you like the street dark so nobody can see who comes to your place! Who visits you in the back of the shop after you've locked up?"

These remarks form a murmuring of indistinct voices from which a word or a phrase might emerge, decisive for what comes afterward. To read properly you must take in both the murmuring effect and the effect of the hidden intention, which you (and I, too) are as yet in no position to perceive. In reading, therefore, you must remain both oblivious and highly alert, as I am abstracted but prick up my ears, with my elbow on the counter of the bar and my cheek on my fist. And if now the novel begins to abandon its misty vagueness and give some details about the appearance of the people, the sensation it wants to transmit to you is that of faces seen for the first time but also faces that seem to have been seen thousands of times. We are in a city in whose streets the same people often run into one another; the faces bear a weight of habit which is communicated even to someone like me, who, though I have never been here before, realizes these are habitual faces, whose features the bar mirror has watched thicken or sag, whose expressions evening after evening have become

43

wrinkled or puffy. This woman was perhaps the beauty of the city; even now I feel, seeing her for the first time, she could be called an attractive woman; but if I imagine looking at her with the eyes of the other customers at the bar, then a kind of weariness settles on her, perhaps only the shadow of their weariness (or my weariness, or yours). They have known her since she was a girl, they know everything there is to know about her, some of them may have been involved with her, now water under the bridge, over and done with; in other words, there is a veil of other images that settles on her image and blurs it, a weight of memories that keep me from seeing her as a person seen for the first time, other people's memories suspended like the smoke under the lamps.

The great pastime of these customers at the bar seems to be betting: betting on trivial events of daily life. For example, one says, "Let's bet on who comes first to the bar here tonight, Dr. Marne or Chief Gorin." And another says, "And when Dr. Marne does get here, what will he do to avoid meeting his ex-wife? Will he play billiards or fill in the football-pool form?"

In an existence like mine forecasts could not be made: I never know what could happen to me in the next half hour, I can't imagine a life all made up of minimal alternatives, carefully circumscribed, on which bets can be made: either this or that.

"I don't know," I say in a low voice.

"Don't know what?" she asks.

It's a thought I feel I can also say now and not keep for myself as I do with all my thoughts, say it to the woman who is here beside me at the bar, the owner of the leather goods shop, with whom I have a slight hankering to strike up a conversation. "Is that how it is, here in your town?"

"No, it's not true," she answers me, and I knew this was how she would answer me. She insists that nothing can be foreseen, here or anywhere else: of course, every evening at this hour Dr. Marne closes his office and Chief Gorin comes off duty at the police station; and they always drop by here, first one or first the other; but what does that signify?

"In any case, nobody seems to doubt the fact that the doctor will try to avoid the former Madame Marne," I say to her.

"I am the former Madam Marne," she answers. "Don't listen to them."

Your attention, as reader, is now completely concentrated on the woman, already for several pages you have been circling around her, I have – no, the author has – been circling around the feminine presence, for several pages you have been expecting this female shadow to take shape the way female shadows take shape on the written page, and it is your expectation, reader, that drives the author toward her; and I, too, though I have other things to think about, there I let myself go, I speak to her, I strike up a conversation that I should break off as quickly as I can, in order to go away, disappear. You surely would want to know more about what she's like, but instead only a few elements surface on the written page, her face remains hidden by the smoke and her hair, you would need to understand beyond the bitter twist of her mouth what there is that isn't bitter and twisted.

44

"What stories do they tell?" I ask. "I don't know a thing. I know that you have a shop, without a neon sign. But I don't even know where it is."

She explains to me. It is a leather goods shop, selling suitcases and travel articles. It isn't in the station square but on a side street, near the grade crossing of the freight station.

"But why are you interested?"

"I wish I had arrived here earlier. I would walk along the dark street, I would see your shop all lighted up, I would go inside, I would say to you: If you like, I'll help you pull down the shutter."

She tells me she has already pulled down the shutter, but she has to go back to the shop to take inventory, and she will be staying there till late.

The men in the bar are exchanging wisecracks and slaps on the back. One bet has already been decided: the doctor is coming into the place.

"The chief's late tonight. I wonder why."

The doctor comes in and waves a general greeting; his gaze does not stop on his wife, but he has certainly noticed that a man is talking with her. He goes on to the end of the room, turning his back on the bar; he thrusts a coin into the pinball machine. Now I, who should have remained unnoticed, have been scrutinized, photographed by eyes that I cannot deceive myself I have eluded, eyes that forget nothing and no one connected with the object of jealousy and pain. Those slightly heavy, slightly watery eyes are enough to make me realize that the drama between the two has not yet ended: he continues coming to this café every evening to see her, to open the old wound again, perhaps also to know who is walking her home this evening; and she comes to this café every evening perhaps deliberately to make him suffer, or perhaps hoping that the habit of suffering will become for him a habit like any other, that it will take on the flavor of the nothingness that has coated her mouth and her life for years.

"The thing I'd like most in the world," I say to her, since at this point I might as well go on talking with her, "is to make clocks run backward."

The woman gives some ordinary answer, such as, "You only have to move the hands." "No, with thought, by concentrating until I force time to move back," I say; or, rather, it isn't clear whether I really say it or would like to say it or whether the author interprets in this way the half sentence I am muttering. "When I got here my first thought was: Maybe I achieved such an effort with my thoughts that time has made a complete revolution; here I am at the station from which I left on my first journey, it has remained as it was then, without any change. All the lives that I could have led begin here; there is the girl who could have been my girl and wasn't, with the same eyes, the same hair ..."

She looks around, as if making fun of me; I point my chin at her; she raises the corners of her mouth as if to smile, then stops: because she has changed her mind, or because this is the only way she smiles. "I don't know if that's a compliment, but I'll take it as one. And then what?"

"Then I am here, I am the I of the present, with this suitcase."

This is the first time I mention the suitcase, even though I never stop thinking about it.

And she says, "This is the evening of square suitcases on wheels."

45

I remain calm, impassive. I ask, "What do you mean?"

"I sold one today, a suitcase like that."

"Who bought it?"

"A stranger. Like you. He was on his way to the station, he was leaving. With an empty suitcase, just bought. Exactly like yours."

"What's odd about that? Don't you sell suitcases?"

"I have a lot of this model in stock at the shop, but nobody here buys them. People don't like them, or they're no use. Or people don't know them. But they must be convenient."

"Not for me. For example, just when I'm thinking that this evening could be a beautiful evening for me, I remember I have to drag this suitcase after me, and I can't think about anything else."

"Then why don't you leave it somewhere?"

"Like a suitcase shop," I say.

"Why not? Another suitcase, more or less."

She stands up from the stool, adjusts the collar of her overcoat in the mirror, the belt.

"If I come by later on and rap on the shutter, will you hear me?"

"Try."

She doesn't say good-bye to anyone. She is already outside in the square.

Dr. Marne leaves the pinball machine and approaches the bar. He wants to look me in the face, perhaps overhear some remarks from the others, or only a snicker. But they are talking of bets, the bets on him, not caring if he listens. There is a stirring of gaiety and intimacy, of slaps on the back, which surrounds Dr. Marne, a business of old jokes and teasing; but at the center of this merriment there is zone of respect that is never breached, not only because Marne is a physician, public health officer or something of the sort, but also because he is a friend, or perhaps because he's a poor bastard who bears his misfortunes while remaining a friend.

"Chief Gorin is arriving later than all the predictions tonight," someone says, because at that moment the chief enters the bar.

He enters. "Good evening, one and all!" He comes over to me, lowers his eyes to the suitcase, the newspaper, mutters through clenched teeth, "Zeno of Elea," then goes to the cigarette machine.

Have they thrown me to the police? Is he a policeman who is working for our organization? I go over to the machine as if I were also buying cigarettes.

He says, "They've killed Jan. Clear out."

"The suitcase?" I ask.

"Take it away again. We want nothing to do with it now. Catch the eleven o'clock express."

"But it doesn't stop here ..."

"It will. Go to track six. Opposite the freight station. You have three minutes."

"But ..."

"Move, or I'll have to arrest you."

The organization is powerful. It can command the police, the railroad. I trail my suitcase along the passages between the tracks until I reach track

46

six. I walk along the platform. The freight section is at the end, with the grade crossing that opens into the fog and the darkness. The chief is at the door of the station bar, keeping an eye on me. The express arrives at top speed. It slows down, erases me from the chief's sight, pulls out again.

Translated by William Weaver

Horse   *S.W. Hayter*

Three Poems

Michel Deguy

When the wind sacks the village
     Twisting cries
          The bird
Plunges into the sun

     All is ruin
          And ruin
     A spiritual outline

Reflect on the great in palaces
Where the first form was measured
From a tiger's pad on the flagstone
Grass for lucid peacocks
Urns for the swan   Marble for dogs
They grew silent near the horse
They hunted the griffon to drive it to stone
And be able to live there in turn

Every time he curdles his life's unity into rules
Every time jealous motions exactly ape his faith
he is buckled like an island with water, dim birds

Every time he fixes time
Sap encircles him   Evil thickens in his barns
His son soon deserts him   Summer makes him desperate
A new principle dishonors his daughters

A wise man would let time wind like a kestrel
Over the yard he feeds with his dead
But the unexpected expands
Then a mocking prophet is needed

Translated by John Montague

BLAZING FIGURES

Robert Markle

Elvis, in another lonesome mood, leaves us. Groucho, befuddled, follows.

On stage Sexy Sadie is on a red plush settee doing astonishing things with her legs and one of her shoes. She moves to the floor, finding an imaginary lover, but only for a moment. Like all good strippers, she has learned to live her performance in a constant state of daring. She brings to her surface all that she's got to flash. She articulates her body with the special emphasis of wired bras, sequins and tassels. Sexy Sadie is very much involved in the art of self-fascination. Strippers – the good ones – reach out through the eyes of their audience to get a better look at themselves. Beside me, and it seems inevitable, an Oriental man is silently watching, *reading* her. Why are the Orientals so curious about sex shows? Maybe it's because they're often Buddhists and Buddhism is all about conquering desire. Maybe watching is a way of conquering. I watch with the hope that desire will grow into romance.

Sexy Sadie is waving her G-string and brushing the air with the curls of her pubic hair. Blurring, trembling, naked flesh. Solid, dark nipples reminiscent of those I've painted. She's now a fire in a black space that surrounds me. At this moment, like the rarest seduction, she's capable of fulfilling any promise. The Oriental gentleman beside me is inside himself, watching his own version of her. She finishes in a flurry; a glistening patch of sweat on the small of her back becomes a mirror that catches the fading spotlight. For 20 years, obsessed with this kind of woman, with this kind of figure, I find it impossible not to keep these wonderwomen *up there*, high on pedestal shoes, safe from life's little realities.

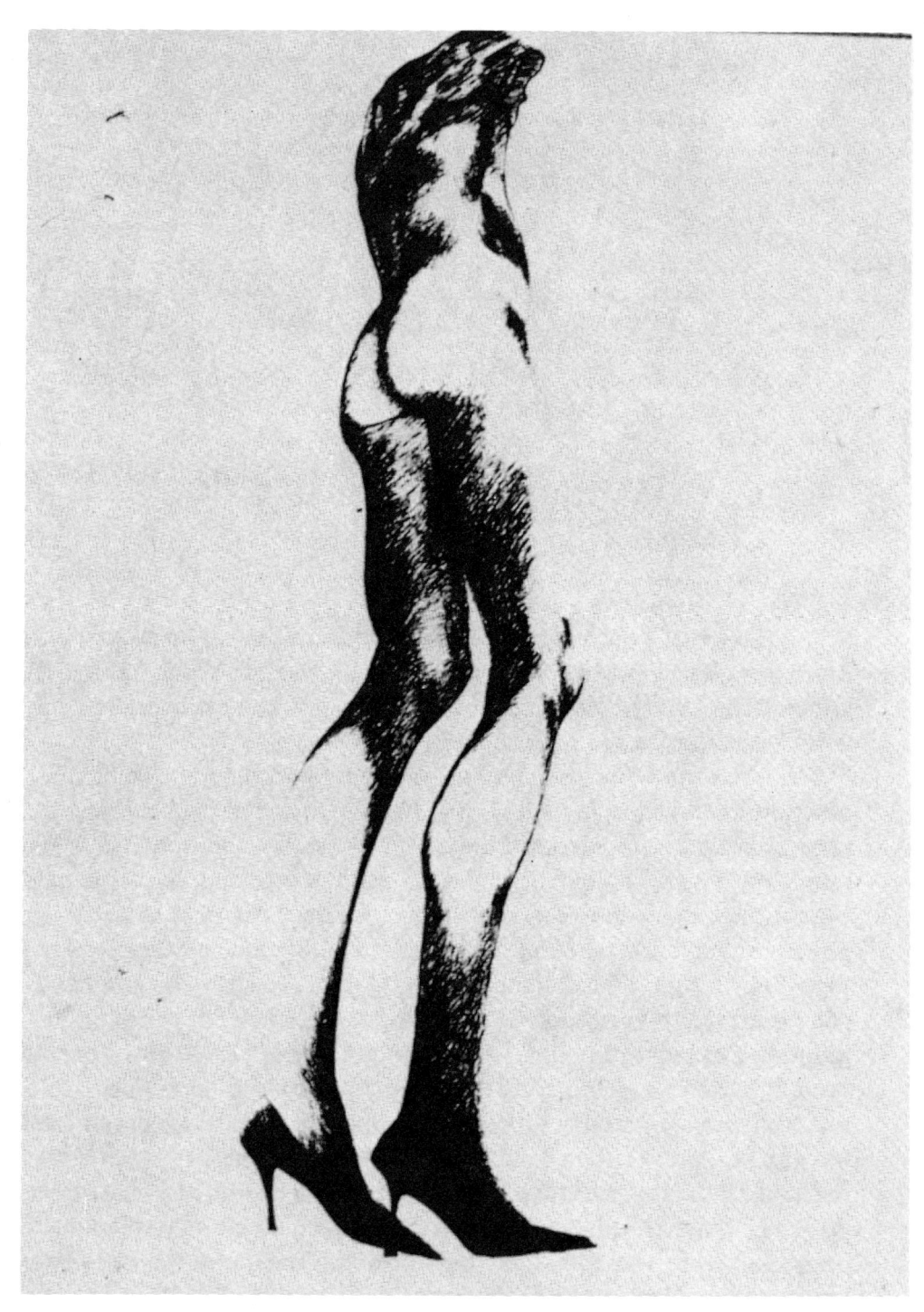

She hung the G-string from one very erect nipple and strutted, stiletto clack across the stage. Feathers in the far corner catching faint draughts, her wake. This was a beauty, she was good, she loved being good, we applauded.

She started out as a model: "I remember as a very young girl being aware of my legs. I would compare their shape with those of the grown up girls in magazines. I wanted them to be like those girls, their legs. It was too early for the rest of my body, only my legs seemed to have any real shape. I have been told that my legs were never those of a child, they were shapely, long, I was always moving, they were strong. I always thought of them as *dramatic*, so soon I was in black hose, the line of the back seam drawing the true shape of my legs. I was a little girl. I lived in an artistic community and soon I was posing for drawings and photographs. I remember catching glimpses of myself in shop windows, mirrors, and thinking that I was someone else, not me, someone to admire. The drawings helped me see myself better, I soon knew that what I wanted was to be continually on display. Of course by this time the rest of my body caught up with my legs, though not as well as I would have liked, but people wanted to see what I looked like, and I wanted them to see. I learned to use their light around me, I would roll through space … "

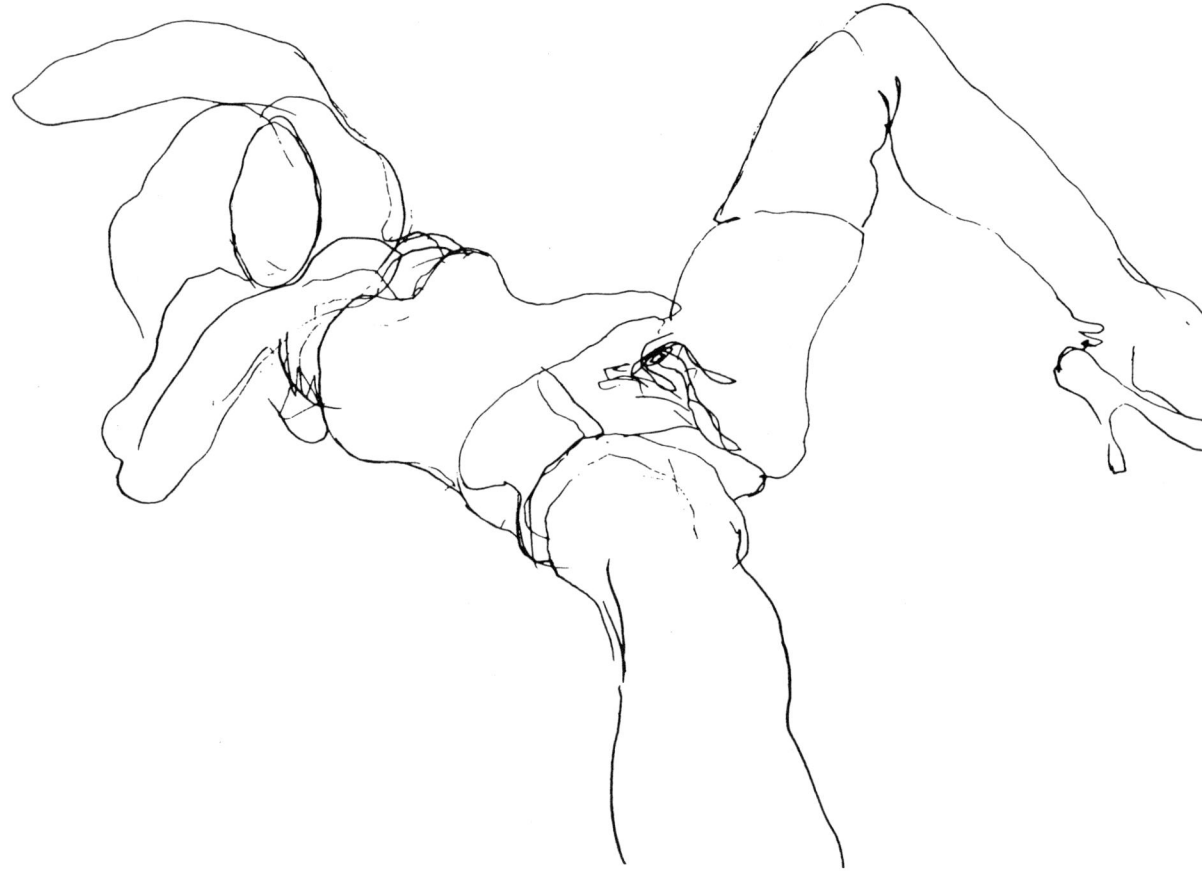

"… so I really got to like it. The strip became a real home for me, the other girls were really nice, they lent me shoes. Helped me … showed me things. I don't copy. I like to be my own person. I think what I do is art, not just gross spreading your legs.

"There's a man that comes to see me a lot and when the lights are down at the finish of my act he reaches out to shake my hand you know, very discreet, he's shy and there's always a ten dollar bill in his hand. He never tries to bother me, or ask me anything. And I get gifts. I got a package with all kinds of Avon cosmetics like creams and powders and lipsticks. Most people are nice. If they really want me then I enjoy that. I think stripping can be evil, you know, sadistic, and still be art. I like to control my audience. Sometimes I think I'm a magnet. I attract evil people. And there's a lot of those kinds of people around. One time this guy asked if he could take me home. He seemed nice so I said sure and we got into his car and I realized that he was going the wrong way, towards dark roads and he stopped the car and started to grab me. I was crying, really scared but what could I do? and I knew it was bad so I said come on big boy slow down take it easy because I was afraid that he would hurt me so I acted, pretended that I was enjoying it and when it was over he drove me close to my street and left me. The cops think that if you are a stripper you're asking for it. I like people too easily. I have to be very careful."

I saw a woman get a tattoo, a small rose etched into the nape of her neck, only to be seen by lovers, and at the edge of her pubic hair, blood butterflies. Woman adorned. Fascination with self. Beyond embellishment. Sheena of the Jungle. Wonderwomen everywhere. Their offerings of nipples like pencil erasers, innocent physical sharings on the streets of summer. Up alleyways, the real women had to compete.

Upstairs, second storey strip parlor built all wrong, the audience is in the dancer's lap. That close, the dancer becomes just another girl, a woman with no clothes, sweat and stretch-marks, tiny webs of veins, everyday life bruises. Perfect distance is needed to measure a vision. I hesitate to place beauty: its hopelessness is the only reality. She risked that distance, making male masturbation motions, huge hard pumping, hissing through a red slashed mouth. As the lights died and she stooped to pick up her things the man in the front row reached through the unfair distance, touched her ankle, and leapt back, stumbling, escaping. The man left, furious, humiliated, ice-cold in the finger tips.

... folding under her, into all the fleshy sweetness, damping down the soft curs with beads that catch the light, gauzy, steamy flashes across the room, the G-string sending messages … it's right on top of things, the true signal of this charged atmosphere, the way revolving mirrored balls focus on motion in those New York second-floor dancehalls. Tom Waits sings: "I'm so horny the crack of dawn better watch out!" We watch it move, winding through the space, nudging at us; awesome light blinds us, inevitable power. The G-string, the ultimate tool of the trade. It encloses the very life of us all, we see ourselves with clarity. The G-string is all our skins looking for work, looking for worry. Women are made so beautifully, they're stylized, the way the flesh flows through muscle and pelvis, hollows, ridges, the G-string formalizing our beginning of understanding, the G-string's arrogance fastens us, the G-string's *dangerous* … sequined patches, triangled sunshine in all the dark bars, patches that can only hurt, haunt, nothing in real life like it, too real.

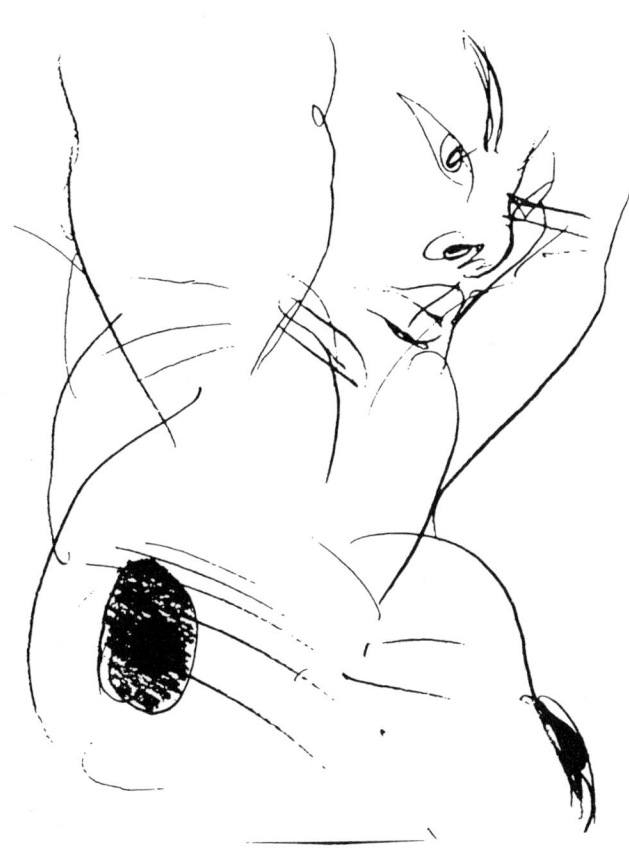

Like all religious experiences, the essential transforms. The High Heel does just that. The Egyptians invented the High Heel, can you imagine the startled glee when women, Nile beauties, walked into a room, their pelvises thrust forward, their backs straight, immediately intraformed into treasures, the High Heel became ikon.

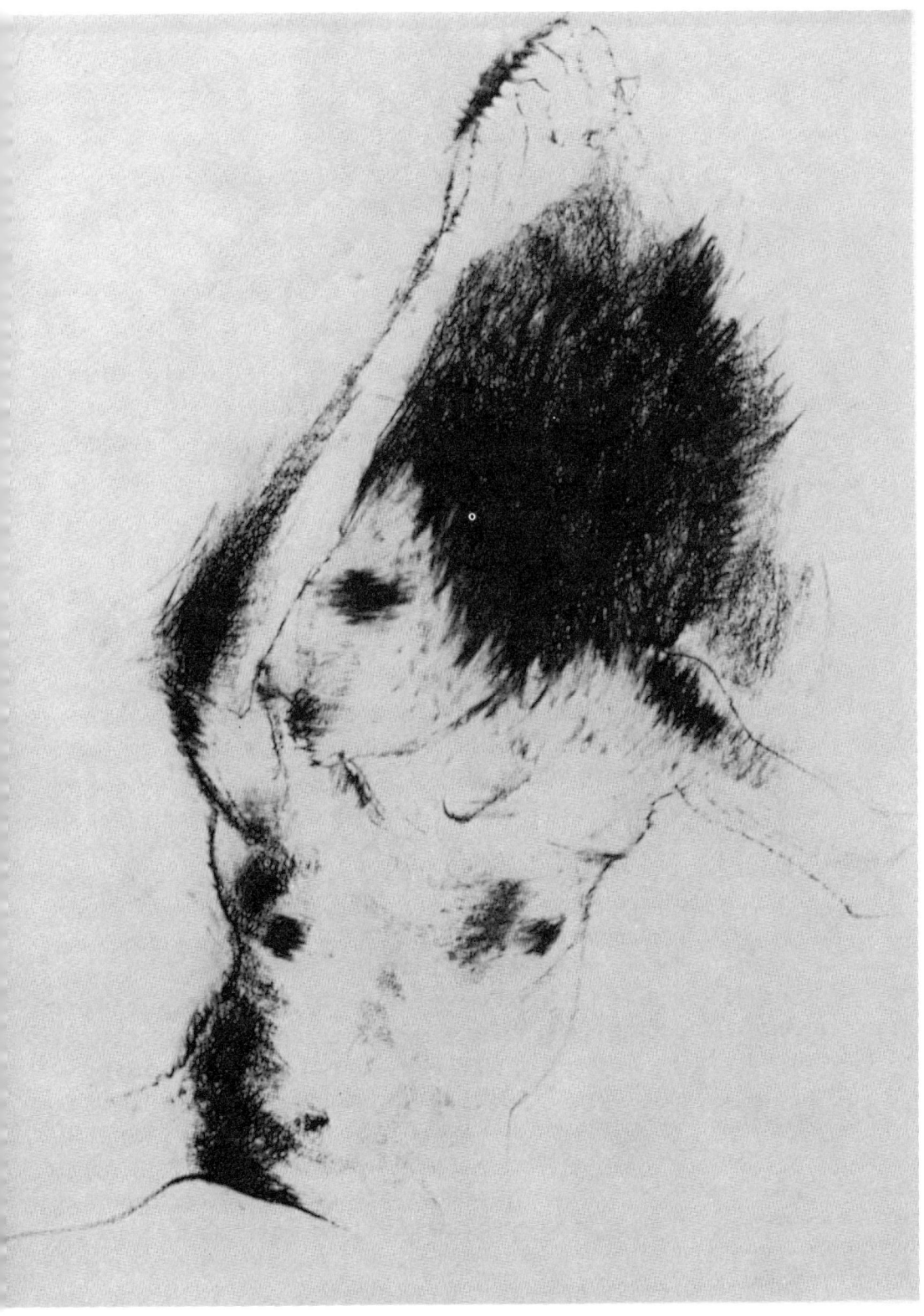

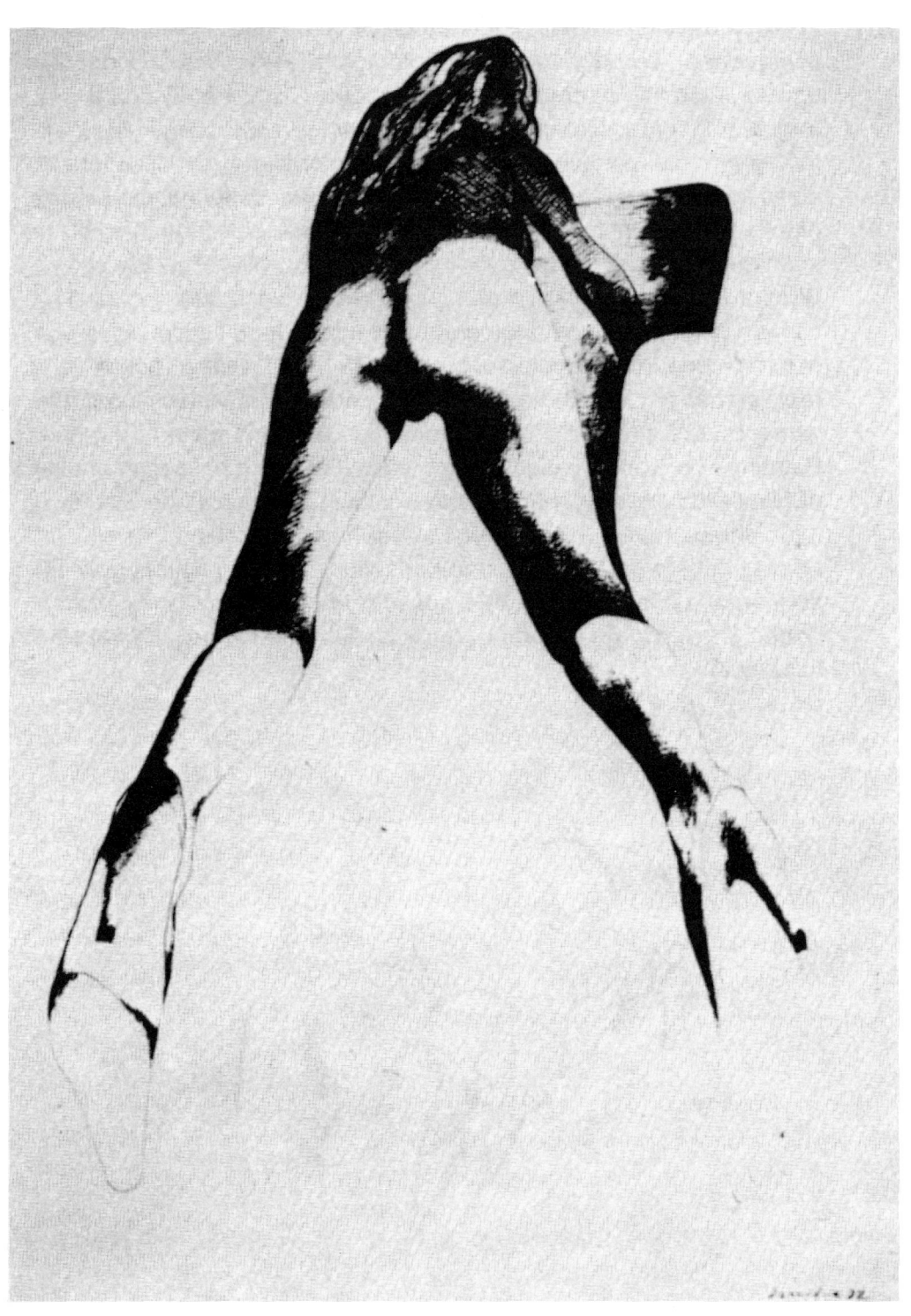

… legs stretched in the night's light like reminders of what I couldn't do. I wonder if paint and charcoal could ever retrace the life of breathing flesh as it articulated its domination of space and time. I looked for working space. Morley Callaghan says the artist keeps looking at the *appearance of things*. De Kooning says that content is just a glimpse, no more. When I was very young I saw a woman get a tattoo on that fleshy plane a woman has on her back just before it turns into a shoulder. *Woman adorned. Fascination with self. Beyond embellishment.* In order to fully understand the thighs of Sheena of the Jungle, you had to see the violence explicit in the ragged edge of her leopardskin loincloth: points on which to build a vision. And the wonderwomen of the strip are good company for glimpse and appearance. So I stay with it. The figure endures.

What this means, to some, is that I am admitting to a certain kind of public failure. The existing conceit in art's academic world says that the figure no longer has a place in modern art. When all is said and done, the figure can be no more than illustration. Giants like De Kooning gave it a good try but he ultimately failed, critics tell you. This attitude places my work outside the mainstream of modern art. I don't know if I'll ever find my way back into an academically acceptable position.

Apathy in the midst of wonderment. All those guys with their righteous statements about art.

I went to New York, immersing myself in the De Koonings, the doorways of fire of Rothko, the rich elegance of Barnett Newman's large canvases filled with color and light. Brutal slashes: I remember reeling before my first Jackson Pollock. Also, to the Follies Burlesk, a seedy bar with a small room in the back for entertainment. I saw the Grecian Goddess there, the first time that I had confirmation of the existence of the "figure," *my* figure, moving in space. The room was walled in mirrors, badly joined. But they made the room seem enormous, and I soon realized that I was not looking at the stage, but at the reflections of the Grecian Goddess in all those mirrors. It was uncanny; she would move through the space of one mirror and then explode into fragments of flesh. I saw her flesh change shape, becoming a true expression of what she was. When guys tell me that the figure is dead, of no purpose, they imply that it was the Rothkos and the Newmans, and especially the Pollocks, that took it away from me; then I know how little they see. Those guys gave me more space to work with, larger eyes, and they taught me a way of making my figures even more vital. Rather than threatening my vision, they enlarged it and made it work.

61

She is best when she's on the stage, held in space, in *in potentia* – waiting to be recreated by the imagination. Not a young girl, but a heroine of sorts.

"You have to understand that, like the men watching me, I fantasize, too. The G-string gives me mystery. I can look into their faces and I can tell if they're interested. I am for *men*. Sometimes the women say nasty things. They're jealous because their man is getting turned on by me. They try to destroy me because they're not satisfied with their own lives. They can't be loose. I'm loose. I'm enjoying myself. I'm doing something that they can only fantasize about. Their laughter isn't the laughter of people enjoying themselves. Their laughter is like knife wounds ..."

Besides the politics of equal opportunity, there is a space, a distance, between men and women that has no culture, only a mysterious emotional life. Within this space compassion lies side by side with violence. It's a strange and devastatingly lonely landscape, the only topography I find worthwhile mining. It's my obsession with this space, this distance, that makes me hold on to the figure.

I tell her she's beautiful.

"Yes, maybe so, but should I be hurt just because I'm beautiful?"

THE WARS

Timothy Findley

1:   All of this happened a long time ago. But not so long ago that everyone who played a part in it is dead. Some can still be met in dark old rooms with nurses in attendance. They look at you and rearrange their thoughts. They say: "I don't remember." The occupants of memory have to be protected from strangers. Ask what happened, they say: "I don't know." Mention Robert Ross – they look away. "He's dead," they tell you. This is not news. "Tell me about the horses," you ask. Sometimes, they weep at this. Other times they say: "That bastard!" Then the nurses nod at you, much as to say – you see? It's best to go away and find your information somewhere else. In the end, the only facts you have are public. Out of these you make what you can, knowing that one thing leads to another. Sometime, someone will forget himself and say too much or else the corner of a picture will reveal the whole. What you have to accept at the outset is this: many men have died like Robert Ross, obscured by violence. Lawrence was hurled against a wall – Scott entombed in ice and wind – Mallory blasted on the face of Everest. Lost. We're told Euripides was killed by dogs – and this is all we know. The flesh was torn and scattered – eaten. Ross was consumed by fire. These are like statements: *"pay attention!"* People can only be found in what they do.

2:   You begin at the archives with photographs. Robert and Rowena – rabbits and wheelchairs – children, dogs and horses. Barbara d'Orsey – the *S.S. Massanabie* – Magdalene Wood. Boxes and boxes of snapshots and portraits; maps and letters; cablegrams and clippings from the papers. All you have to do is sign them out and carry them across the room. Spread over table tops, a whole age lies in fragments underneath the lamps. *The war to end all wars.* All can you can hear is the wristwatch on your arm. Outside, it snows. The dark comes early. The archivist is gazing from her desk. She coughs. The boxes smell of yellow dust. You hold your breath. As the past moves under fingertips, part of it crumbles. Other parts, you know you'll never find. This is what you have.

3:   1915.

The year itself looks sepia and soiled – muddled like its pictures. In the snapshots everyone at first seems timid – lost – irresolute. Boys and men stand squinting at the camera. Women turn away suspicious. They still maintain a public reticence.

Part of what you see you recognize. Here for the first time, the old Edwardian elegance falters. Style is neither this nor that – unless you could say it was 'apologetic.' The men wear caps and shapeless overcoats to work, jamming their hands deep into pockets. Imitation uniforms spring up everywhere: girls wear "middy's" – boys are dressed in sailor suits. Women wear a sort of great coat and flat brimmed hats with rosette badges. Ladies no longer wear their furs; they drape them from their arms with all the foxtail trophies hanging down like scalps. No one smiles. Life is dangerous. Summer induces the parasol – winter the galosh. Some of the photographs are blurred. Even though the figures freeze – the dark machines that fill the roads move on.

Here is the Boys' Brigade with band. Backyard minstrels, got up in cork, bang their tambourines and strut across a lawn on Admiral Road. Every parlor has its piano: here are soldiers, arm in arm and singing: *"Keep Your Head Down, Fritzie Boy!"* Tea-Dance partners do the Castlewalk to orchestras of brass cornets and silver saxophones. Violins have been retired.

This is the age of motorized portation. Over one thousand makes of motorcar can be had. Backyard blacksmiths build them to custom. ASK THE MAN WHO OWNS ONE! Here are families, sitting overdressed in Packards – posed aloof in the backs of Chevrolets and Russell Knights. Everyone, it seems, is journeying around the block. Children vie to blow the horns.

Then something happens. April. Ypres. Six thousand dead and wounded. The war that was meant to end by Christmas might not end till summer. Maybe even fall. This is where the pictures alter – fill up with soldiers – horses – wagons. Everyone is waving either at the soldiers or the cameras. More and more people want to be seen. More and more people want to be remembered. Hundreds – thousands crowd into frame.

Here come the troops down Yonge Street! Women abandon all their former reticence and rush out into the roadway, throwing flowers and waving flags. Here come the 48th Highlanders! Kilts and drums and leopard skins. Boys race after them on bikes. Little girls, whose mouths hang open, hardly dare to follow. Older men remove their hats. There is Sir Sam Hughes standing on the dais, taking the farewell salute. "GOD SAVE THE KING!!!" (a banner). Everywhere you look, trains are pulling out of stations, ships are sailing out of ports. Music drowns the long hurrah. Everyone is focused, now, shading their eyes against the sun. Everyone is watching with an outstretched arm – silenced at the edge of wharves and time.

Robert Ross comes riding straight toward the camera. His hat has fallen off. His hands are knotted to the reins. They bleed. The horse is black and wet and falling. Robert's lips are parted. He leans along the horse's neck. His eyes are blank. There is mud on his cheeks and forehead and his uniform is burning – long, bright tails of flame are streaming out behind him. He leaps through memory without a sound. The archivist sighs. Her eyes are lowered above some book. There is a strand of hair in her mouth. She brushes it aside and turns the page. You lay the fiery image back in your mind and let it rest. You know it will obtrude again and again until you find its meaning – here.

A Band is assembled on the Band Shell – red coats and white gloves. They serenade the crowd with "Soldiers of the Queen." You turn them over – wondering if they'll spill – and you read on the back in the faintest ink in a feminine hand: *"Robert"* But where? You look again and all you see is the crowd. And the Band is still playing – quite undisturbed – and far from spilled. Then you see him: Robert Ross. Standing on the sidelines with pocketed hands – feet apart and narrowed eyes. His hair falls sideways across his forehead. He wears a checkered cap and dark blue suit. He watches with a dubious expression; half admiring – half reluctant to admire. He's old enough to go to war. He hasn't gone. He doubts the validity in all this martialling of men but the doubt is inarticulate. It slammers in his brain. He puts his hand out sideways: turns. He reaches for the wicker back of a wheelchair. "Come on, Rowena. There's still the rest of the park to sit in."

Thomas Ross and Family stand beside a new Ford Truck. The new Ford Truck is parked before the gates RAYMOND/ROSS INDUSTRIES, where farm machinery is made. This picture will appear in the Toronto *Mail and Empire* with a banner headline, stating that the truck is being turned over to the RAYMOND/ROSS Field Surgery Hospital behind the lines in France. Large red crosses adorn its sides. The "family" consists of Mister and Mrs. Ross and three of their children: Robert, Peggy and Stuart; Rowena, the eldest, is not shown. She is never in photographs that are apt to be seen by the public. In fact, she is not much admitted in the presence of a camera. Robert has her picture on his bureau.

Rowena is seated in her scalloped wicker chair with the high, double wheels. She wears a white dress. Her hair is curly and short. Her shoulders are perpetually hunched. Her head is large and adult but her body is that of a ten-year-old child. She is twenty-five years old. She is what is called *hydrocephalic* – which in plain language means she was born with water on the brain. Her expression is lovely and pensive. She wears a wide and colorful sash. In her lap she holds a large white rabbit. Robert told her once, she was the first human being he remembered seeing. He was lying in his crib and, waking from a nap through half-closed eyes, he saw his sister gliding in her chair across the room and coming to rest beside him. She stared at him for a long, long time and he stared back. When she smiled, he thought she was his mother. Later, when he came to realize she couldn't walk and never left the chair, he became her guardian. It was for her he learned to run.

Mother and Miss Davenport, wearing their canteen aprons, stand on the platform at Sunnyside Station handing out chocolate bars to the soldiers who are leaning out of trains. They do this every Thursday afternoon. Robert wishes his mother wouldn't do such things because he's shy and thinks she appears too much in public. But Mrs. Ross is adamant. Such things have to be done ... someone has to do them. The leaders of society are dutybound – and what would people say ...? Etc. Etc. All the while, Miss Davenport is nodding and smiling: agreeing with every word. But not one word of it is true. Mrs. Ross performs her duties Thursday afternoons because of dreams.

65

Here is *Meg – a Patriotic Pony*, draped in bunting, standing in a garden. Her ears lie flat. She is either angry or frightened. Meg is very old. Just at the edge of the picture, Stuart can be seen squinting at the sun. He wears an Indian headdress and he holds a baseball bat.

This is *Peggy Ross with Clinton Brown from Harvard!!!* Nothing in Clinton Brown from Harvard's appearance warrants three exclamation points. He was only one of Peggy's many beaux. Robert is in this picture too, seated on the steps of the South Drive house along with a girl called Heather Lawson. Robert was supposed to be "interested" in Heather Lawson but the fact was it was she who was interested in him. Not that Robert didn't like her – only that he wasn't interested. "Interested" led to marriage and this is what Heather Lawson wanted. So did her parents. Robert was a fine catch for any girl. He was a scholar and an athlete. Besides – he had money.

One summer the Rosses crossed to England on the *S.S. Minnetonka* in order to spend a holiday with the RAYMOND/ROSS British representative, whose name was Mister Hawkins. All through the month of June they languished on the beaches of the Isle of Wight. In late July they came home on the *Minnetonka's* sister ship the *S.S. Minnewanka*. From the decks of this ship, early one morning, one of the Rosses (it was not clear which) – took a photograph of the ocean. Whoever it was, later drew an arrow – pointing to a small white dot on the far horizon. The small white dot can barely be seen. Nothing else is visible but sea and sky. Just above the arrow, written in bold black ink is the question: "WHAT IS THIS?" All too clearly, the small white dot is an iceberg. Why whoever took the picture failed to verify this fact remains a mystery. The thing is dated August 4th but no year is given.

Shuffle these cards and lay them out: this is the hand that Robert Ross was born with. Mister and Mrs. Ross – Peggy and Stuart – rabbits and Rowena. Also a dog named Bimbo and a clipping from the paper, reading: "LONGBOAT WINS THE MARATHON!" Meg and Miss Davenport – Heather Lawson and the iceberg. And Clinton Brown from Harvard, who died a hero's death at the battle for Belleau Wood in June of 1918 – worthy of an exclamation point at last.

This is perhaps a good place to introduce Miss Turner, whose importance lies at the end of this story but whose insights throw some light on its beginnings.

Marian Turner was a nurse in the Great World War and she remembers Robert vividly. It was she who received him and cared for him after he'd been arrested and brought into the hospital at *Bois de Madeleine*. She has given (on tape) the only first-hand account of him we have aside from that of Lady Juliet d'Orsey. Here is part of what Miss Turner has to say. She is over eighty now, but still robust and she speaks with a good ideal of energy, sprinkling her conversation with laughter and offerings of sherry in a wide, green apartment overlooking a park.

"You will understand, from what took place, why I cannot tell you what he looked like. I suppose such things are of interest. Well – of course they are! (LAUGHTER) Everyone wants to know what people look like. Somehow it seems to say so much about a person's possibilities. Do you know what I mean? What I can say is that Lady Barbara d'Orsey was in love with him – and that all her other men were smashing! So I dare say Ross was, too. Anyway, because of what happened I can't remark about the face – but my impression was of someone extremely well made who cared about his body. At least that's my memory of it – the way it was. You get them all mixed up, after so long a time; and every boy they brought to us seemed such a handsome lad. You never hear that any more: *he was such a handsome lad!* But we were always saying so in all the letters we wrote to their families. I guess you saw them all as beautiful because you couldn't bear to see them broken. The human body – well – it's like the mind I guess; terribly impressive till you put it in jeopardy. Then it becomes such a delicate thing – like glass. Robert Ross? Well – it was just so tragic. When you think that nowadays so many people – young people especially – might've known what he was all about. But then ... (PAUSE) My opinion was – he was a hero. Not your everyday Sergeant York or Billy Bishop, mind you! (LAUGHTER) But a hero nonetheless. You see, he did the thing that no one else would even dare to think of doing. And that to me's as good a definition of a "hero" as you'll get. Even when the thing that's done is something of which you disapprove. He was *un homme unique* – and that's much more of a compliment in French than it is in English. Oh, he was ... (PAUSE) ... Fire, you know – there's nothing worse than fire. Even after all I've seen. And the story of the horses is something I'd rather never have known had happened. Oh, I quite understand why you feel it must be told – but ... (MISS TURNER TURNED TO LOOK OUT OF THE WINDOW AT THIS POINT. THERE IS QUITE A LONG PAUSE ON THE TAPE) ... Well. It was the war that was crazy, I guess. Not Robert Ross or what he did. You'll say that's trite, of course. But is it? Looking back, I hardly believe what happened. That the people in that park are there because we all went mad. Yes. He was unique. But you have to be careful, searching his story out. I've been through it all, you know – (LAUGHTER) – the whole of this extraordinary century – and it's not the extraordinary people who've prevailed upon its madness. Quite the opposite. Oh – far from it! It's the *ordinary* men and women who've made us what we are. Monstrous, complacent and mad. Remember that. Even if I do sound a moralizing fool, I'll risk it. After all – I'm pretty old. (LAUGHTER) I could be gone tomorrow! There may not be anybody else who'll say this to you. Everyone's so sophisticated these days they can't stand the hot lights. Eh? Well – I saw both wars. And I'm here to tell you the passions involved were as ordinary as me and my sister Bessie fighting over who's going to cook the dinner. And who won't. (LAUGHTER) Those people in the park – you – me – everyone – the greatest mistake we made was to imagine something magical separated us from Ludendorff and Kitchener and Foch. Our leaders, you see. Well – Churchill and Hitler, for that matter!

(LAUGHTER) Why, such men are just the butcher and the grocer – selling us meat and potatoes across the counter. That's what binds us together. They appeal to our basest instincts. The lowest common denominator. And then we turn around and call them *extraordinary*! (HERE SHE TAPPED THE TABLE, RATTLING THE SHERRY GLASSES) See what I mean? You have to be awfully careful how you define the extraordinary. Especially nowadays. Robert Ross was no Hitler. That was his problem."

4:      Easter was early in 1915. Good Friday fell on April 2nd. It snowed. Robert got off a train that morning in Kingston, Ontario. He carried a brand new suitcase and wore his checkered cap. His raincoat – also new – was of a style that soon would be known as the "The Trench Coat." Its buttons were made of criss-crossed strips of leather and its salient feature was that it was short: short enough for you to wade in water up to your knees.

Robert stood alone to one side, watching the engine from under the eaves of the station. He was watching the stoker feed the flames with rattling shovelfuls of coal. He watched with his hands in his pockets – shoulders hunched and his toes pressed hard against his suitcase. At school he'd been taught that hunching the shoulders was an ungallant posture; still he maintained it while the engine bellowed and hissed. Great clouds of steam billowed out and around its wheels. The *"fire horse"*: that's what the Indians called it. Robert looked to one side from under the peak of his cap, hoping that no one had seen him flinch from the steam or stepping back from the fire. He was wishing they would leave. His shoulders hurt. His arm was sore. There were bruises on his back. He ached. He wanted all the others who had got off the train to depart the station before him. There must have been three dozen – forty or fifty men – all coming down from Toronto together – joining others from as far away as Winnipeg and Saskatoon. Most of them had swaggered up and down the cars like braggarts – smoking cigarettes and drinking out of silver flasks. Robert avoided them all through the journey – wanting to protect the last of his privacy. Now they were drifting away in groups of three and four – joshing and pushing one another – calling out names and throwing snowballs – singing songs.

Robert looked the other way down the platform where he saw three women. Two of them were young and smiling. The other was older and wore a nurse's uniform and cape. The younger ones were dressed in neat blue coats and one of them was watching him. Robert turned away, annoyed and confused. He was shy of girls, just now – distrusting them and wondering why they had to look at you and make you think you wanted them. Only a few weeks ago he had discovered he was not in love with Heather Lawson. Heather had behaved so inexplicably. What did women mean to do with men? At a party – in his own house – she'd told him that someone else was in love with her. Robert was not disturbed by all this at all. What had someone else's being in love with her to do with him? But Heather Lawson wanted him to be disturbed. "All right," Robert said, "who is it? Maybe then I'll be disturbed." (He'd smiled.) "It's Tom

Bryant," Heather said, "and I think you ought to fight." Robert didn't understand. *Bryant*? Who was he? Did Heather Lawson love him? "No." she had said, "of course not." "Then why should I fight him?" Robert had asked. "Because he *loves* me," she said. She spoke as if Robert were stupid. It all made perfect sense to Heather, but Robert thought it was idiotic and said so. Heather wailed out loud at that. Wailed and railed and paled. And fainted. In short – she made "a scene" of the sort then popular in the books of Booth Tarkington. All the guests at Robert's party left. There were even social complications for his parents in the aftermath and Heather said she never, never, never wanted Robert in her sight again. All because he wouldn't fight a man she didn't love and whom he'd never seen.

The matron snapped her fingers and the final cab was hailed. After their luggage had been lashed to the roof, the two young women made for the open door. One, not looking back, got in beside the matron but the other – just for an instant – turned and looked in Robert's direction. He was handsome – no question – even though his ears stuck out a bit too far and his jaw was unfashionably wide in an age of pointed features. Something in the way he stood alone appealed to her. But the matron's hand reached out and the girl was snapped inside like a folded doll and the cab was driven away. Looking back – her expression said "goodbye" and she was gone.

Twenty minutes later, Robert still stood there with his suitcase – immobile. He stood so resolutely still the Station Master came and asked him if he'd missed the train. Robert said no – that he was fine and if there was another cab, he'd hire it. But the Station Master said there were no more cabs. Just the standard quota and these days that was never enough, what with everyone coming and going all hours of every day and any day. The week had no more meaning. Even holy days of abstinence and sober significance like Sundays and Easter, the trains came and went and the people got on and off laughing just as if the world wasn't going to end.

"I suppose you've come down here like all them others to join with the Field Artillery, hunh?" he asked.

"Yes," said Robert.

"Well – I wish you luck, young man. The way they pile 'em in and outa here, it seems to me they're lookin for a long, long war."

"Yes, I guess they are," said Robert.

The Station Master went about his business, slowly making his retreat into the warmth of the Telegraph Office and Robert could see him talking to the Key operator – chucking his thumb in Robert's direction – probably saying: "There's a queer young lad out there who doesn't seem to want to leave ... "

Robert picked up his suitcase and turned away towards the Station Yard. His shoulders ached. The bruises bore the brunt of the shift in weight every time he moved his arms. The yard was wide and wet. An old white dog was walking across the cinders toward the gate. Robert had stood so long, the snow had turned to rain. Off in the town, the Easter Passing Bells began to toll and Robert looked at his Oxford boots and gauged the width and depth of the nearest puddle brimming off the edge of the platform. Staring down expressionless, he watched as his reflection was beaten into submission by the rain. He turned his collar up and pulled the peak of his cap right down to the bridge of his nose. He closed his eyes and took a deep breath. The melting snow began to turn to mist and the mist was filled with rabbits and Rowena and his father and his mother and the whole of his past life – birth and death and childhood. He could breathe them in and breathe them out.

Right to the very last second – hearing an approaching train that might have taken him home – he did not know in which direction he would go: down into the puddle and up to the town or back along the platform. The dog beyond the gate, bedraggled and lost, sat down to watch him. Maybe some decision of its own depended on which way Robert went. Then Robert closed his eyes and made his choice. He stepped down into the puddle and stood there.

How could he move?

Rowena had been buried the day before.

Samuel Beckett

THE CAVE OF NIGHT

John Montague

I
Underside

I have seen the high
vapor trails of the last
destroyers in dream:
I have seen the grey
underside of the moon
creep closer to earth …

II
The Plain of Adoration
from the Irish, 11th century

Here was raised
a high idol of cruel fights:
the Cromm Cruaich –
the King Idol of Erin.

He was their Moloch,
this withered hump of mists,
hulking over every path,
refusing the eternal kingdom.

In a circle stood
four times three idols of stone:
to bitterly enslave his people,
the pivot figure was of gold.

In dark November,
when the two worlds near each other,
he glittered among his subjects,
blood-crusted, insatiable.

To him, without glory,
would they sacrifice their first-born;
with wailing and danger
pouring fresh blood for the Stooped One.

Under his shadow
they cried and mutilated their bodies;
from this worship of dolour
it is called the Plain of Adoration.

Well born Gaels lay prostrate
before his crooked shape until
gross and glittering as a cinema organ
he sank back into his earth.

III
Cave

The rifled honeycomb
of the high-rise hotel
where a wind tunnel moans.
While camouflaged troops
ransack the Falls, race
through huddled streets,
we lie awake, the wide
window washed with rain,
your oval face, and tide
of yellow hair luminous
as you turn to me again
seeking refuge as the
cave of night blooms
with fresh explosions.

IV
All Night

All night spider webs
of nothing. Helpless
to help that helplessness.
Condemned to tread that
treadmill of bitterness.
Distended, drowning fish,
frogs with lions' jaws.
A woman breasted butterfly
copulates with a dying bat.
A pomegranate bursts slowly
between her ladyship's legs.
Her young peep out
with bared teeth:
the eggs of hell
fertilizing the abyss.

Shy skyscrapers incline
together like stilts.
Grain elevators melt.
Cities subside as liners
leave by themselves
all radios playing.
A friendly hand places
a warm bomb under
the community centre
where the last evacuees
are trying a hymn.
Still singing, they
part for limbo, still
trailing their blankets …
Permit the little –

A land I did not seek
to enter. Pure terror.
Ice floes sail past
grandly as battleships.
Blue gashed arctic distances
ache the retina &
the silence grows to
a sparkle of starlight
like sharpened knives.
Lift up your telescope,
old colonel, and learn
to lurch with the penguins!
In the final place
a solitary being begins
its slow dance …

V
Ratonnade

Godoi, godoi, godoi!
Our city burns & so did Troy,
Finic, Finic, marshbirds cry
As bricks assemble a new toy.

　　Godoi, etc.

Humble mousewives crouch in caves,
Monster rats lash their tails,
Cheese grows scarce in Kingdom Come,
Rodents leap to sound of drum.

　　Godoi, etc.

73

Civilisation slips & slides when
Death sails past with ballroom glide:
Tangomaster of the skulls whose
Harvest lies in griefs & rues.

  Godoi, etc.

On small hillsides darkens fire,
Wheel goes up, forgetting tyre,
Grudgery holds its winter court,
Smash and smithereens to report.

  Godoi, etc.

Against such horrors hold a cry,
Sweetness mothers us to die,
Nicens digs its garden patch,
Silence lifts a silver latch.

  Godoi, etc.

Mingle musk love-birds say,
Honey-hiving all the day,
Ears & lips & private parts,
Muffled as the sound of carts.

  Godoi, etc.

Moral is of worsens hours,
Cripple twisting only flowers,
One arm lost, one leg found,
Sad men fall on common ground.

  Godoi!

DEAF TO THE CITY

Marie-Claire Blais

He stood watching the busy traffic in the street from the window of the Hôtel des Voyageurs, wearing the apron he wore at lunchtime when he helped his mother in the restaurant, his face pinched in the sallow light, his restlessness frozen for a moment in meditation, so that he looked at that instant like the very countenance of pain captured by Munch in *The Scream*; like that anonymous figure whose silent cry fills the painter's canvas, Mike rested his heavy head on his frail hands and with his wide-eyed questioning gaze, his pupils enlarged with concern, he challenged the world, or rather the various silhouettes that made up his world at that instant – the people passing by out on the street, his mother, the men she was waiting on at the bar, Tim the Irishman who was standing near him unfolding his newspaper, all the strangers going in and out of the hotel, each and every one of them – just when it seemed as though his quavering, half-open mouth was about to emit an endless scream to remind the indifferent human mass gathered there, crouching or musing over a glass, a sunbeam, or some other scant dose of morning pleasure, that even if it were not a shame to live as they were living, as tranquilly and inconsequentially as flies – although flies had been blessedly spared those human cravings that weigh down so many good and wicked men alike – even if this were not cause for shame, it was scandalous to live and die without ever managing to strip away the damning halo that branded their foreheads with the sentence: "You shall suffer on earth … " It was engraved on all things, Mike thought, even on old Tim's flabby face as he muttered in English, his nose in the paper: *"Do you believe everything you read in the paper, Gloria, do you? Hé, the kid wants to go the movies, hé, a blue movie, Mike, what's the matter with him, Gloria, anyway? They all took their money out, they're crazy …"* Day after day the same sounds came stumbling from the wrinkled, bitter mouth: *"What a bastard he is, hé, what a bastard, take care of your heart, my Gloria, take care of your heart …,"* and Gloria responded to the fetid murmur of the bar with a haughty, ferocious sensuality that would have struck them dead in a single glance if her body had been as hateful as her soul, but her body was bored and gave in, gave in with the softness of her handsome, languorous arms and the curve of the placid, voluptuous breasts she offered up to all, her body yielded despite herself to the torpor, to the somehow unclean fondling of so many fingers, "And that's OK" thought Mike, "just so long as she doesn't start pawing them all over and getting them excited … if it rains Tim will take me to a dirty movie … three orders of spaghetti in the oven, yes, just so long as Mom's hand doesn't slide any lower …" Lethargy, the first caress of the day, Gloria thought, "if you don't like it you don't have to look, Mickey, don't forget your father wasn't just anybody, he was the great Luigi, we'll go to the hospital for

75

your treatment and then we'll take in all the movies you want, *stop it, Tim, you could kiss my royal ass, OK*? Why don't you go fetch me the porno slicks at the corner, na, not for the kid, for me, he don't read much, that one, his head hurts too much … " "How'd it all start?" asked Tim, his lips slobbering against Gloria's face, *"there's always a beginning, hé, always a beginning …"* "It's nothing!" Gloria snapped back, "nothing at all, he's OK, they got rid of his tumor, going to take him all the way to San Francisco on my bike this summer, *shit* won't it be a pleasure not to see your holy mug, you damned Irishman!" "Well, what if his father turned out to be just an ordinary Italian," said Tim, *"or just me, your old lover, just an ass like me, hé?"* "You holding that spaghetti up for Easter, Mike? Get a move on, and wash some cups for coffee while you're at it, what're you standing there like that for with your tongue hanging out?" Mike, with an anguished look, avoided his mother's glance and hid his head in his arms. "It's nothing, mom, nothing. I feel hot." "The doctor told you it's normal to feel hot, that spaghetti's going to be burned to a crisp …" It was a cool day, the street bright with sunshine, and before long the student who ran down from the mountain would break into the street, then the park with his long-limbed weightless flight, and in a moment Mike would be left only with a sense of the perfection of the runner's muscular life, the spirited body dashing forward towards life itself, he would be no more than a long back stiffened by effort and the tight clothes binding it, a scarlet blob about to disappear around the corner, "Tell me now, Tim, what d'ya know about the role of sex in life? Nothing, cause it's up to us women to know about those things … " As for me, I'm a mother, first and foremost a woman and a mother, and mistress all round, or love, if you prefer *my old boy …* " The Irishman's big fist was resting on Gloria's chest, the runner was coming down, still coming down, and he must get a bit winded, Mike thought, the whole city was running out of breath bit by bit, noise and light dilating it, the aroma of coffee was invading the dimly lit kitchen and Mike said to Lucia who was staring at the burned spaghetti, "Hurry up and take care of Jojo and we'll go out, it's a nice day, we can take a walk in the park …" "I don't want to be late for school," Lucia replied, "I'm afraid I'll miss my bus. Why don't you feed her yourself?" "I don't know how," Mike answered. "Just put the spoon in her mouth, see, like this – Mom feeds you stuff that's nothing but juice when you can't swallow! You know who her father is, Mike?" Lucia's tiny shadow went bouncing through the yard and disappeared. "Eat up now," Mike said to Jojo, "then we'll go out in the sun …" but Jojo refused the spoon Mike tried to slip into her mouth, she was laughing and crying at the same time and then all of a sudden a question seemed to fix itself in her black, uncannily knowing eyes. "Do *you* know why I was born," she seemed to ask Mike, "what I'm doing here?" Mike went on feeding her patiently with the kind of dreamy, slightly far-off gentleness that had come over his movements in the past few months. "Let's go play in the park, Jojo … but stay away from the horses, sometimes they get mad if you bother them," the grass was coming up in the park, it was spring, "this summer we'll go to San Francisco" said Mike as he set the child down in a patch of light and warmth, and Jojo immediately began to run every which way with Mike running after her, laughing,

76

laughing because it was nice out at long last and in winter you couldn't see or hear anything when the snow and the wind blinded you, and now, as he went skipping along in the path of his sister's fragile destiny, Mike listened to his heart beating in his chest, "where I'll be next year, maybe I won't hear it any more." Jojo went on laughing, falling down and scrambling to her feet, thinking to scare Mike by hiding behind trees. Mike let her whirl about him, stronger for the kind of glow he felt in her presence, as if not even the mighty, unsightly cathedral that dominated the city could protect the child as he could just by letting the back of his hand brush over her hair, this was life, this was living and the people walking and scurrying around him didn't know it, none of the people spilling out of the subway in groups or emerging from the station and the banks knew it – or were their hearts making as much noise as the furious cascade that seemed to roar in his veins, yes, perhaps ... It was a bright day, but Gloria had forgotten about the electric sign and the red letters sparkled with their nocturnal fire: "*Come as you are, day and night, chez Luigi.*" Tim would come staggering out of the hotel, others would stop in for a beer or a coffee, Gloria had a man in the house but he was bad, Mike thought, she also had dogs to protect her and they were bad too, "but it's better than being alone", he reflected, and the sky was so blue you saw it a lot closer, without fear. "Look, Jojo, the birds are back ..." but the small ball of life wouldn't nestle long in Mike's hands, it drew close only to run off elsewhere, far away, already far away, leaving in its place a waft of perfume, a breath, now it was just a curly head of hair, curly like Gloria's, a big head for a child, thought Mike, a head set atop a bundle of woollen clothes since Gloria hadn't noticed that spring had arrived, and inside this colored package there was life, life that knew how to walk and run unaided towards a goal that didn't yet seem at all obscure although it would cloud over eventually, maybe even the very next day. The runner, Mike thought, must have turned the corner a long time ago, as if sucked up into the blue sky, for it was already time for the girl – he didn't know her, but he had become used to seeing her – to come down the mountain for a cup of coffee, to sit at the bar while Gloria hissed, mocking and impious, in her ear, "Say, love, what's your name again? Judith Langenais ... That's right, you told me yesterday, Judith Lange, Judith Angel; you'll wake up in the gutter one day, all the same, the cappuccino's on the house today cause it does me good to see you, it's a welcome change from Tim, you're a professor, hé, must be tough going sometimes what with the brats you got in schools today ... What d'you teach? Philosophy! Well, then, you ought to be able to answer my question: what's the role of sex in life?" Leaning against a tree while Jojo toyed with some pebbles at his feet, Mike observed the woman, his mother, from a distance, he was steeped in her, in her shamelessness, in her benevolent lewdness, so benevolent for herself and for others; he didn't hate her, he respected her, even loved her sometimes, especially when the weather was nice and you had the illusion of suddenly seeing her face and the eager movements of her features very close up, when the words she pronounced every day resounded in your ears as if they were rising from her entrails, the stream of lewdness that was also Gloria, that was Gloria and nobody else, for it wasn't just any

77

woman who was willing to be called Gloria and to have had a husband murdered in the street, and a bar that might also become a bloody stage from one night to the next, what kind of a life was it after all, being called Gloria and having dyed hair and a sick child, "and others who aren't doing so bad but that's just it, you've got to feed them, all the same the best part of the T-bone's for my dogs in case we're attacked one day, you understand, love? You still haven't answered the sex question, should be a cinch for you, being into that philosophy stuff you should know all about it!" Judith didn't answer, Mike knew Judith never answered Gloria's questions, he had seen her coming down from the street's golden summit, Judith, Judith Lange, the Angel, as his mother called her, although nothing about her made you think of an angel, she walked with her books under her arm, she had a class at two, she taught philosophy, her shiny raincoat was open at the collar and a gold chain glittered on her bare neck, a rather buxom girl, that was how Mike saw her approaching in the distance, first recognizing her head, then her neck that she never covered, not even in winter, and he recalled that when spring came she suddenly seemed lighter, slimmer, as if everything floated around her, maybe it was just the shiver of the air, unlike the runner who flew along with the current of the buildings, of the houses, Judith Lange drew near with a slow, heavy step, her feet sank into the ground and then she came back up towards you, maybe it was her slowness and the invisible weight of her gait, stealthy as a cat's, that stirred the air, she said nothing when Gloria asked her an indiscreet question, only smiled, but Gloria thought she heard her say, "But Gloria, sex is everything, life, death, everything, Gloria." But she never said anything, Mike thought, it was the kindness of her smile that traced on her lips the words Gloria alone could really understand, then Gloria, appeased, would say, "Love, you wouldn't think, seeing me like this behind my cash register, that I had an ancestor who came from Norway like me, she was the first woman doctor received by the Academy … And even me, Gloria, my eldest daughter, Berthe, is studying for the bar, not the alcoholic kind, mind you, no, she's in law school, it's a change for us but the girl's got a heart of stone, won't have anything to do with us, even disowns her father! But I've still got my Mike, my Michel, and I swear you'll see us take off on the bike for San Francisco this summer! They won't keep him at the hospital, he's my little boy, after all. You've got time yet, have another coffee, at your age I was always shacked up with one guy or another, didn't give a damn about school, you see I've had sex on my mind for a pretty long time now …" But maybe Judith Lange wouldn't be coming today, Gloria said Mike pretended to be deaf when she spoke, deaf to her groans of pleasure, to the wrenching sighs of her revolt, deaf to everything, she said, and yet he heard her when she spoke of "life, sex, and death," and again of "sex, death, and life", those words that churned about freely in Gloria's mind and perhaps hers was the only mind in the world that harbored them, thought Mike who wanted to be like Gloria, working late into the night, sometimes seeking out her clients in funeral parlors, she would tell Judith about that, too, some day, sex was Gloria's legend, she would tell it all to Judith one day, but Jojo was living her own life under the tree, the tree Mike was fondling with his moist palms, you could tell when you leaned against it that it was a tree that still had many years of life ahead, Mike thought, yes, the day would come, tonight or tomorrow, it might be fiercely violent or sweetly murderous, the soul just took off, all the souls of the dead were wandering in the sun, looking for someone to understand, someone who would let them into his or her thoughts, even Gloria's thoughts about sex, life, and health, one day Mike would understand everything, everything that was dormant in Gloria, on Judith's lips, the delivered soul went elsewhere, went to all those places to which it had been denied admittance during its joyous but often terrible captivity, and it might be only a short time before Mike's soul would also know that flight, that dance deep within the hearts that were now closed to him. Mike, still leaning against the tree, suddenly forgot about Judith as he noticed three boys in the park lying in the sun, spread out on a bed of grass that seemed to have been made for them at that instant; Jojo had probably run around them, chirping, but the boys, dozing, remained aloof in their wholesome nonchalance, each of them resting his head on the other's leg, and in the moment of unexpected languor in which sleep had caught them off guard, in such a rigid, three-sided pose that one might have taken them for statues, thought Mike, the only thing that still recalled their existence or the fact that they had been alive ten minutes earlier – and they had been, they'd spoken loudly, they'd quarrelled – was a pair of running shoes; one of the shoes that no longer served to walk and run had been separated from its twin, and during the battle that had brought the three boys together the shoe, harassed, molested at the hands of the enemy, tossed up like a ball, had landed close to the tree and Mike, and if in the distance the flash of blue and yellow T-shirts added a bright touch to the triangular tomb the boys seemed to form, only the battered, saddened shoe appeared, as Mike contemplated it, to claim an existence proper; broken, subjugated by its owner, it knew, better than Mike, the boy it had shod and protected against the cold, it had soaked up his joyous and grieving sweat, it had loved, cried, laughed, and suddenly it was just an obsolete thing that would soon be cast aside for another and it lay there, close to Mike who watched it living its final moments of revolt in the sun. Eternal Gloria, celestial Gloria, thought Gloria of herself, she gave all men their bottle, there could be no higher philosophy than the one Gloria dispensed to all, her body's fluids drenching the arid earth where everything one loved would die tomorrow; it was Friday, Judith was having lunch at her parents' house, Madame Langenais was asking her daughter "what she was going to do later on," she was an attentive mother and Judith had every reason to be proud of her, Marianne, Gisèle, and Micheline were wearing their school uniforms "but they're not severe enough," Madame Langenais informed her husband, "the skirts are too short this year ..." and she hardly dared let her gaze slide over her daughters' splendid thighs – the stockings stopped below the knees and all the rest was on display, the healthy, silken flesh and the pleats of the navy blue skirt not quite covering it, Marianne, Gisèle and Micheline would go off to play tennis this afternoon as usual rather than study, and of course, Madame Langenais explained to her husband, their studies took a back seat to everything else, and Judith asked her father if he had been afraid before performing that morning's operation, no, he hadn't been afraid, "strangely," he told Judith, it was afterwards that fear really gripped him, "even when the operation had been successful," the soup was served and Madame Langenais suddenly wondered, as if it were a fact she'd never noticed until this particular Friday, why her daughter had green eyes when nobody else in the family had green eyes, teaching philosophy, it was no career for a woman, what would become of her later on, Good God, she had surgeon's hands like her father, she would rather not know what Judith did with her hands, hands so firm yet delicate, there was no way of knowing anything about Judith since she no longer lived at home, as for Marianne, Gisèle and Micheline one knew just about all there was to know, Madame Langenais still decided what books they read, or practically, but Judith's soul eluded her completely and for a mother there was something obscure in that, an irritating, wilful secret, they had finished eating, Gisèle and Micheline could be heard trying to find their tennis rackets "in their mess of a room," remarked Madame Langenais while Judith silently ground a piece of fruit between her small, cat-like teeth, thought her mother, Marianne went to sit on her father's lap, her knees red and so bare, so bare, she was too big to sit on her father's knees now anyway, at her age, thought Madame Langenais, thinking at the same time about the gardener, she'd have took after that, Judith had asked why Gilbert didn't eat with them and Madame Langenais had firmly replied: "Gilbert prefers eating alone in the kitchen," that's the way things were, she wasn't going to give in to Judith's whims, to that communist, she mused, staring at her with her round eyes, Judith, she had to keep reminding herself that this was her flesh, her blood, Marianne was addressing her father, "you don't know anything, Papa, no, you don't know anything, you told me you knew everything but you don't know anything at all," her father explained that mathematics had changed a lot since his youth but Marianne wasn't listening and Madame Langenais, while carefully watching her family, was casting furtive glances towards the garden where Gilbert was coming and going with a shovel, the tip of his cap just visible beneath the window, social classes no longer existed, a shame, was there a place left on earth where people still respected them, of course everybody has a right to his or her political ideas, but how did Judith spend her nights; the word "night" sprang up like a sudden menace in Madame Langenais' mind, the word was the very essence of insubordination, night, sumptuous night, secret night, no, better to ignore what Judith did at night, the word was so heavy with sighs, with abandonments, and these easy-going girls thought their parents had ceased loving each other, but the night, nights, and all of a sudden Judith had risen and wound her giant arms around her mother's shoulders and Madame Langenais had heard the hissing of her raucous voice in her ear, a voice that was saying, insidious, loving, "Maman, dear Maman, Josephine, I love you in spite of everything ..." Madame Langenais, accustomed to her daughter's affectionate outburst, hadn't budged, the tip of Gilbert's cap could still be seen bobbing up and down beneath the window as he passed, and Madame Langenais was overcome by a kind of sinner's sadness, she realized she'd been lacking in charity, Judith's warm breath against her cheek evoked the latent fault, the fault that was so ancient, irreparable, a habit already, it was too late, even if Judith was a communist, she had no proof of that but where Judith was concerned it was fitting to imagine the worst, she thought, it was already too late to ask Gilbert in to share the family's meals, Madame Langenais had no reason to complain, didn't she have affectionate, maybe over-affectionate daughters – there was Marianne still cuddling up against her father – yes, but how did Judith spend her nights, and Gilbert kept passing back and forth with his shovel, his piles of earth, we'll have beautiful roses this year, Josephine, I love you in spite of everything, the "in spite of everything" ringing in Madame Langenais' ear, there was a rebuke in it or at least a hint of rebuke, Madame Langenais pushed her daughter off gently, saying "I've already told you I don't want you calling me by my name ... not in this house ... ask your father if I'm not right ..." and suddenly, while Judith's arms were still resting on her neck, a young couple Madame Langenais had noticed that morning on her way to the bank came to her mind, they had been waiting at a street corner and suddenly, in an amorous impulse, looking each other over, they had brusquely grasped each other in a long embrace, passionately intertwined right there on the sidewalk where they stood, Marianne's bare knees flashing before her were suddenly confused with the enchanting yet dangerously sensual explosion of the two young people clad in colored shorts, each giving the other, without any particular reason, this entangling of knees and tongues, drowning in broad daylight, they'd yielded to the moment without shame or reproach, each so lost in the other as long as the hypnotic embrace lasted that Madame Langenais had felt herself a witness to their bodies' most intimate movements beneath the transparent, multicolored shorts that offered such scant protection on such a cool morning. Suddenly Judith was no longer there, Madame Langenais was alone in the empty house with its blue drapes, out in the garden, on the mountainside, you could see the whole city, where was Judith now, what was she doing, a class at two, Madame Langenais was going to go out and offer Gilbert a bit of advice, red roses or white roses, Judith's breath was hot, before long the whole city would be in blossom, fragrant, so fragrant, and Mike had dozed off vaguely while his sister played at his feet, he was still standing against the tree, "don't put that poison in your mouth, Jojo ..." old Tim came out of the drugstore with his porno papers under his arm, his old dog trailing after on a rope, Tim and the dog staggering towards their bench under the brotherly hundred-year-old tree that awaited them, the tree, the bench, these were their shores and neither Tim nor his dog noticed Mike, flotsam in the sun, they went on, kept going, they didn't fall, they were walking almost straight, the entire city was feverish with men and sounds but they were still headed for their bench, the old dog was also called Tim and he too was Irish, you could no longer tell which of the two was at the end of the rope, the one with the logger's jacket or the one with tattered fur and unsteady gait, both were hungry but once at the bench they would share the crumbs of the same sandwich, they would watch the women together, their desires coming through in identical fashion, two muzzles dripping with drool, old Tim and his old dog,

81

they were close to Mike now, running out of breath together, but they didn't see him leaning shakily against a tree, you couldn't really buckle under with pain or sadness, you could only give in, give in slightly on such a good day, weighed down by that something, maybe it was ecstasy, the ecstasy of being alive, and suddenly the vision of his mother came back to Mike in the whirl of old Tim and his dog, of the plaid jacket and the haggard dog at the end of the rope, flotsam in the sun, but they were still on their feet and so was he, slackening a tiny bit as he leaned against the tree, the tree that would always be there, tomorrow or later, in rain or snow, Mike saw again his mother, saw old Tim pinching her hip that morning, slipping his shifting hands into Gloria's armpits, so old Tim didn't know that at night Gloria was transformed, that she became for her son something terribly severe, the image of crucifixion, the Mother of Sorrow, that was Gloria, she had a man or several men with her in her room, they were all bad like the five police dogs in the yard, that night she was sleeping with Charlie, "my goddamned hooligan on probation, you don't even know how to make love," she shouted, "leave the door open in case my kid calls me ..." "What did Charlie do, Mom?" "Nothing much, he killed someone one day, he was too young, he doesn't even remember ..." Charlie had killed, maybe he'd kill again that very night, Lucia, Jojo, and Luigi 2 were downstairs, all the people Gloria knew had killed, but it was time to sleep, nothing had been written on sleep, not yet, and sleep, white as a snow field, was calling Mike, come, come, and Mike would not be slow to obey, love and sleep also belonged to those who had killed, Gloria and Charlie would soon sleep just like everybody else, "All the same leave a light on in the hall, just in case he calls me, first time I've ever heard of a guy getting homesick for prison, never saw the likes of it!" Sleep was still as pure as a sheet of blank paper but in the feeble light coming from the hall it seemed as though an unknown, detached hand had come to write on it, yes, a hand was writing by itself, drawing on the wall, the design was imperceptible, the work of an ant, the written expression of the terror that crept along the wall, something was pursuing Mike, hunting him down even when he hid under the sheets, or maybe the devastating parasite was lodged in his own body and it was nothing but his own shadow that he saw on the wall, it was his head, his thronging head that had become a refuge for these larvae; and his heart that usually throbbed so wildy, pounding with fever, was suddenly beating noiselessly, without echo, maybe it wasn't a parasite after all but that formidable She, maybe the Unnameable had just entered his body, and surely this deaf heart, this voiceless heart was no longer his own; and yet, though he heard no sound rising to his lips, his moan too low to be perceptible, it was she after all, Gloria, who now bent heavily over his iron bed, she, Mother of all Sorrow, of the crucified: "Stop screaming, come on, I'm right here ..." and cradled in her breasts, he had watched it all flee, even the ghost of his terror, the hand writing by itself on the wall, the worm of his own destruction nestling into the purity of the night, and his heart had taken up its own rhythm and song once again, "But why do you give your mother such frights?" Not even old Tim who was so proud of being a Catholic knew that the saints were no longer in heaven but among us on earth, in the lightning flash of our pains, he was stretched out on the bench with the panting dog, still holding on to the end of the rope although there was no need to hold the old dog who had been Tim's master for such a long time now, old Tim saw the sky through clouds of alcohol, it wasn't a sky full of angels furious because he'd had too much to drink, it wasn't a sky so blue that it was like blue lake-water passing over his eyes, pained by visions, no, it was the sea, his own country's sea, he only had to dream a bit and he found it again, a pale sea waiting for him on the other side of a pine-covered mountain, then it slipped out of sight and came back again with a tumultuous clamor, his native sea that had thrown him up here on this bench with an aging dog for company, he no longer knew how many years had passed, if he let the dream continue the bench became soft dunes under his back while the sea moved by with perfect, rigid tranquillity, a woman was coming down towards him, Gloria, the woman who had been the village schoolteacher during his childhood in the suburbs of Limerick, a nun hiking up her skirt and leaping over boulders – old Tim's dog had sneezed and the spell was broken, old Tim was back on the bench and would have to wait until tomorrow to find his native sea again, he grumbled, grumbled *"those bastards, those bastards,"* moaning when a boisterous gang of adolescents, trampling the new grass with an insolent, dancing tread, began to bark just for a laugh, "woof woof," tossing the "woof woof" to old Tim and his dog more as a mock homage than as an insult; it so stung the drunkard's delicate soul that he spit with scorn, but then went on barking, "Hi, woof woof," and old Tim began to dream, he was gunning them all down with his rifle, it didn't matter if his hand was a bit shaky and he had no rifle, only Tim's old dog was touched by the music and suddenly light-hearted under his tattered coat he perked up his nose and ears and answered with drawn-out echoes the amused barks which, just this once, had been aimed at him, one had so few laughs with old Tim, they would wind up in the city pound or the poorhouse sooner or later, yes, better enjoy it while it lasts, *"will you shut up, you monster!* said the Irishman, kicking his best friend, *"you bastard, I'll kill you!"* and the dog, surprised, sad again, thought that yes, the city pound or the poorhouse, that was their future, but old Tim had had too much to drink, he was "stiff to the very roots," as Gloria put it, better stop barking, quiet down, submit, since old Tim still held the end of the rope. "All the same, some have it easy, sweet Jesus," muttered Tim, noticing a taxi driver who was taking a nap in his car, "look at that bastard!" He was a thin man and seen in profile he looked like a corpse, as though the solemn stiffness of rigor mortis had allowed him to relax and listen to the call coming in over the radio without slouching in his seat: *"It is an emergency test, only, it is an emergency test, when you hear this sound ... "* then he'd fallen asleep and Tim saw him thus from a distance, with his corpse's profile and the nervous line of a last little smile that persisted, flouting Tim and his dog, the taxi driver telling Tim *"Look how lucky I am, you dog!"* Two images lingered still between the taxi driver's eyelashes, one of a Spanish star – at any rate that was how he imagined her – wiggling her hips on the street corner while waiting for a man, followed by the apparition of a Greek pope, or a person who bore a striking resemblance to a Greek pope with his black tunic and purple

83

bonnet, accompanied by a businessman, nobody knew where they were all going like that, the mysterious convoy of the street coming and going, it doesn't matter, thought the taxi driver, it was time for his nap, the rest of the world was thrashing about in vain in a swamp full of footsteps and sounds; perhaps it was at that very moment that Judith Lange, who was explaining Descartes to her students, suddenly noticed in the college yard, which was otherwise bare and ugly, a lone branch of white lilac trembling at the window, hovering alone as if the wind had blown it off the bush; it was probably an illusion, the yard was ugly and bare, but someone had nevertheless thought to plant the white lilacs that lined the wall, it was Judith who had been blind to their presence for so long, and suddenly the lilacs were alive again in the warm spring sun, and the quavering wind that was a foreboding of summer gales and storms parted the branches of lilac; their white intoxication floating in towards Judith's nostrils so sweet that she put her book aside – it was daylight, a radiant day bathing the students in the classroom and Judith herself in its generous, fragrant light, and silence had hushed the din of life, yet Judith thought of night, nights full of love and all those fragrances, and that light too, but night was when one was apt to give in to despair, "and what did you do last night?" her mother had asked, she had been to see Florence, she was the visitor who broke into lonely nights, but her students to whom she went on explaining Descartes knew nothing about that side of her life, who was this Florence, after all? – a woman she'd met in a train station, a deserted eighteenth-floor apartment in a big city, Florence, a woman alone, where was her husband, where was her son, both dissolved in an ocean of memories, "No, you must not die," Judith had told her, and now the lilac branch seemed to confirm her statement which was suddenly truer than ever, the lilac branch whipped the windowpane, the sun flooded the classroom, springtime, spring, and summer before long, and Florence had not forsaken the joys of life, not yet, not that night, but now it was day again and a dull light fell on her furniture, on the pictures of her husband, of her son, all that wrenching apart of the past frozen on the wall, Judith, a stranger, who was she after all, perhaps nothing more than a dream with which she'd consoled herself, the apartment was deserted once again, inhabited by so many bourgeois victories, Judith had said, maybe she was an anarchist, a revolutionary, inhabited, yes, with treasures, with china, but it was a distressing place since Florence had thought about dying there, Judith Lange, friend of suicides, sister of the inert martyrs of existence, where was she now, Florence wondered, why had she come to save her, for one night, for a few hours, when the fatal act was already stamped on her being, tonight or tomorrow, what was the sense of hanging on, respecting life when she was bound to it by nothing more than a young woman's smile illuminating the night, the apartment was deserted once again, Judith Lange was no longer there, the same nauseating sense of life rose in Florence's breast, and perhaps in thousands of other breasts at that very moment this same sensation was working its way into the thousands of gloomy, silent hearts in spite of the glorious light that flooded the white lilacs in the college yard, into hearts that had already settled into silence as they advanced in their own solitary company towards that eternity of silence of which we know nothing; Florence was already dead, she thought as she cast an indifferent glance at her hands resting on her knees, dead hands resting on icy knees, Judith Lange had tried to warm them between her own but they were no longer fit for the reasonable task of living, how sweet it must be to belong to the community of the living, to love and live as they lived, deliciously and weightlessly; dying was a malady that weighed you down so, it was so heavy that even two frail hands on your knees felt like lead, and wasn't the painful light pouring from the sky spilling all over you and your paleness only to strike you down? This heavy heart was dead, and yet it kept on beating loudly in Florence's chest, it was a knell, a strident wail that nobody heard and it went on repeating, "soon everything will be all over!" but time was passing and nothing was over yet, time was passing even more heavily today than yesterday, it passed with the sudden lulls and flashes of recovery that come to the condemned: that was when Judith's magnetic smile held the night hour at a distance, but the people of death remained close by, they were all gathered just beyond the fragile door, pressing against each other in these attics of time and silence: it was the city of the dead, the great faceless refuge, and if there was also a human presence lithely calling her back to life with warm breath and smiles, it was only Judith, a passer-by of whom Florence knew nothing except that she might never come back, and Judith at that moment noticed a student couple walking under the canopy of white lilacs; they looked like an ordinary boy and girl, perhaps their only asset was the awkward charm of youth as they walked along close to each other, their hands barely touching, and Judith read in their features the desire of love, or love about to blossom even if they themselves were still all shyness and disorder; it was as though the brightness of the white lilacs, the radiant headiness that filled the air had caught them off guard in this uneasy enchantment without their quite realizing it; maybe they were holding their breath, maybe their pulses were slowing down as their eyes searched the other's and yes, perhaps the wind shivering amongst the lilac, this barely perceptible movement of nature, was all that was needed and the boy and girl, separated now by the trembling shyness of their desires, which seemed as they glanced at each other cautiously as impenetrable as a wall, would be united, the slightest breath would suffice and they would find themselves uniting in each other everything which at that moment cut them off from all the rest, Judith would see them embrace during that moment of peace, the luminous veil would close in over them as the veil of death would close in over Florence tonight or tomorrow; but they were shy, the boy made an awkward move that brusquely detached him from his companion and then they disappeared as they had appeared, gentle and magic, and Judith took up her book again, Descartes, Descartes, but they weren't listening, they were all staring at the lilac branch at the window and Judith's body panted with the simple joy of being alive, she felt their gaze, their impatient caresses all around her, life was the only sacred philosophy we had, the words were still ringing in Florence's ears ...

Translated by Carol Dunlop

85

FRANÇOIS MAURIAC

David Annesley

"Z"

René Lagorre

Acrylic on paper, 1978, 5¾″ × 7¼″

ACTION IN NEW FIELDS

S.W. Hayter

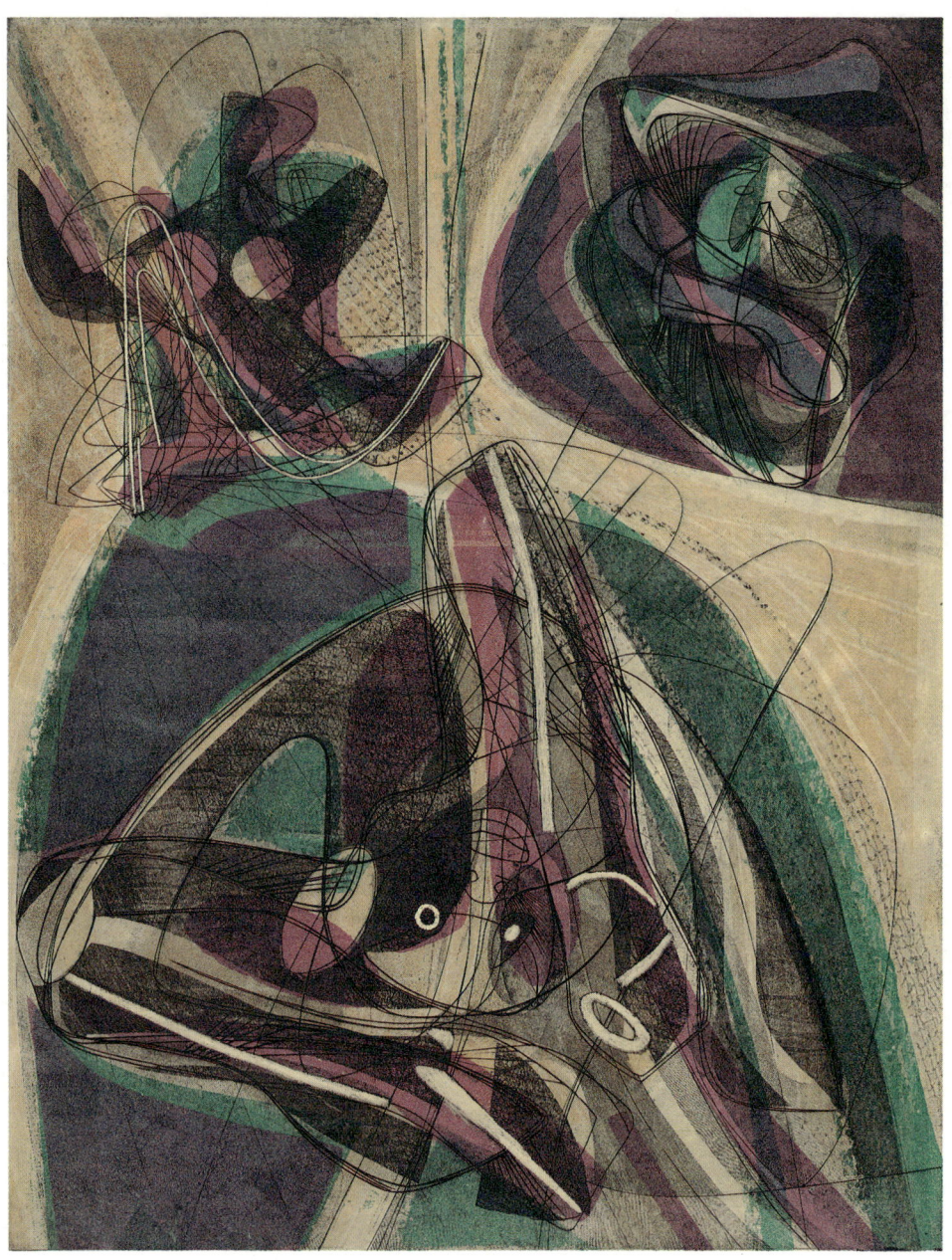

Engraving, 1952–54, 17¼″ × 23¼″

ATLANTIS

John Meredith

Oil on canvas, 1966, 70″ × 70″

HOGG

Barry Callaghan

Oil pastel and pencil on paper, 1976, 9″ × 12″

JOYCE CAROL OATES

David Annesley

Ink drawing on paper, 1972, 36″ × 24″

"UNTITLED"

John Meredith

Oil on canvas, 1970, 6″ × 5′

PLONGEON

S.W. Hayter

Engraving, 1976, 18″ × 23″

"Z"

René Lagorre

Acrylic on paper, 1980, 5¾″ × 7¼″

THE HOGG POEMS:
JUDAS PRIEST

Barry Callaghan

''I was the boss stud, called me
        Bad Blood Jeremiah
Stuck, five-foot-one come four
        in elevator shoes.
I was the Pussy King of Dundas
        Station, I held
the razor hand, had the dedication
        of a man fattening
frogs for snakes. I tell you true,
        I was on the take
every night at nine, almost supine
        with satisfaction
as I checked my action in Le Coq
        D'Or saloon and
Starvin' Marvin's Striperama,
        upper room. Then,
old Stuck got in a jam, cut up
        my Sally Ann
and she took the stand and says,
        that's him, pimp,
purveyor, there's no where you'll
        send him safe enough:
that sucker's Mr. Tough. Well, they
        stuck me in the looney-
bin, going to 'lectric shock me
        back to Doctor Spock,
and maybe Doctor Ded, which is
        what they said, but
never done. Just sat me on my buns
        in solitary, for
three years, and the walls in that room
        sweated tears.
Makes you think, alone with the deadfall
        of your own fear,
there must be more to human affairs than being
        belly-up in despair.
Three years, friends, three in the hole.
        But I'm back,

shifted my gears, and I don't pretend
        to save your soul,
but old Jeremiah Stuck, he's going
        to lay some strange
saving words down, so stick around.
        It beats pot-luck.
Now: — this here's a world of losers
        and winners, and
you know who the sinners are. The poor
        in their pews.
The church is led by those who have
        the bread, while
the priests ration out Christ's compassion,
        and Jesus is
their bag man, collecting dues. But that's
        all a lie,
that's bull. Not one apostle in the gospel
        of good news
had any kind of special pull. Jesus died,
        had himself crucified,
to wrench a new election out of insurrection,
        like when they put
that local hooker to the wall, Magda Lana,
        he said, You got
the big-time reputations, but when you're
        dead, and making
deputations, you'll find thieves on my
        right hand, out
on reprieve. To get my kingdom done,
        I've come to save
the damned, the scum of your society.

        Old Jeremiah Stuck
can tell you, when you reach out, sleepless,
        for the walls
of your hole, and all you touch is the darkness
        of your soul,
you scrutinize how and why a man dies,
        why, when Jesus had him
dead-to-rights, he broke the bread and said,
        eat your fill, Judas,
I know who you're going to kill.
        The question's this,
why's the kiss the ancient invitation to the abyss?
        Well, I've come to see
what above all Jesus knew, that built
        into love is
betrayal. The cock crowed. Peter cried,
        No, I don't know

nothing about that guy, no Sir. Denied him
        Peter did, to save
his skin and then went mewling and puking
        over his sin,
but Jesus called that liar his rock,
        as if the rebuke
and the blessing were one. Not James,
        not John, not Luke,
but the guy who fled, vilified, was
        in the end,
Peter Pontiff, sanctified. So it is,
        those who've done
the worst, the last, shall be first."

        Hogg held up his hand:—
"Hold on my man, old pimp,
        preacher, whoever
the hell you are, I've already gone too far,
        already been wiped,
clean, right off the salvation slate,
        unable to forgive
myself more than my enemies,
        been down in my own
black hole, my soul . . ." "Well," said Stuck,
        "in that case I'm going
to tell you the Judas gospel. Like his Lord,
        not in hatred, but in love,
        he hung himself dead.

        Now what you know
        about Judas is,
he was the juice man taking care of business.
        But see, you got to ask
how he saw his appointed task,
        because the bossman
beside him sipping wine be also
        the Eye in the Sky,
Divine, who knows what we all up to,
        Himself included.
But the genius of Judas perceived the applied
        logic that eluded
the priestly pedagogic, who couldn't believe
        God'd take two legs,
let alone save the dregs by doing a suicide —
        that His benevolent
intention was our subsequent redemption
        since back before
man's invention — but to die he needed
        some fully aware

fall-guy who'd shoulder the sin of suckering Him,
      who'd come on
as the reprobate with all appropriate device
      and signification
for the sacrifice — like silver coin, the kiss,
      intermittent ejaculation of the law, —
because he foresaw that double-dealing
      dealt his life
new meaning — that once he had his own hide hung
      in perfect imitation
      of God's begotten Son,
then he and Jesus would be One, and that is
      what he done
for you and me, shared this complicity
      in death, so we do
draw today deliverance breath, that's why old Stuck
      has come undone,
free, and telling you the essence of all
      be not mendacity
but complicity, for if Judas and Jesus are One,
      if by betrayal
the beautiful is begun, then not only Judas
      be in you,
but Jesus, too. You wear His face no matter
      your disgrace.''

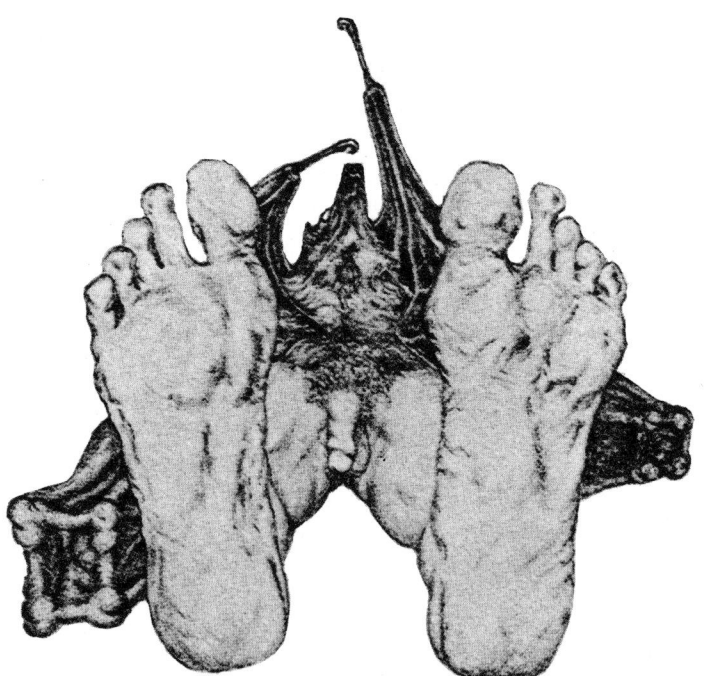

Hogg

Barry Callaghan

HELEN

Yannis Ritsos

(*Even from a distance the wear and tear showed – crumbling walls with fallen plaster; faded window-shutters; the balcony railings rusted. A curtain stirring outside the window on the upper floor, yellowed, frayed at the bottom. When he approached – hesitantly – he found the same sense of desolation in the garden: disorderly plants, voluptuous leaves, unpruned trees; the odd flower choked in the nettles; the waterless fountains, mouldy; lichen on the beautiful statues. An immobile lizard between the breasts of a young Aphrodite, basking in the last rays of the setting sun. How many years had passed! He was so young then – twenty-two? twenty-three? And she? You could never tell – she radiated so much light, it blinded you; it pierced you through – you couldn't tell anymore what she was, if she was, if you were. He rang the doorbell. Standing in the place he once knew so well, now so strangely changed with its unknown entanglement of dark colors, he heard the sound of the bell ringing, solitary. They were slow to answer the door. Someone peered out from the upper window. It wasn't her. A servant, very young. Apparently laughing. She left the window. Still no answer at the door. Afterwards footsteps were heard inside on the stairway. Someone unlocked the door. He went up. A smell of dust, rotten fruit, dried-up slop, urine. Over here. Bedroom. Wardrobe. Metal mirror. Two tottering carved arm-chairs. A small cheap tin table with coffee cups and cigarette butts. And she? No, no impossible! An old, old woman – one, two hundred years old! But five years ago ... Oh no! The bedsheet full of holes. There, unstirring; sitting on the bed; bent over. Only her eyes – larger than ever, autocratic, penetrating, vacant.*)

Yes, yes – it's me. Sit down for a while. Nobody comes around
anymore. I'm starting
to forget how to use words. Anyway, words don't matter. I think
summer's coming,
the curtains are stirring differently – they're – trying to say
    something – such stupidities! One of them
has already flown out of the window, straining to break the rings,
to fly over the trees – maybe as well to haul
the whole house away – but the house resists with all corners
and me along with it, despite the fact that I've felt for months,
liberated
from my dead ones, my own self, and this resistance of mine,
incomprehensible, beyond my will, strange to me, is all I possess –
my wedlock
with this bed, this curtain – is also my fear, as though
my whole body were sustained by the ring with the black stone I
wear on my forefinger

I notice you also have a perplexed, dumbfounded face, distorted
by the slow undulations of black water – now widening, now
     lengthening your face
with yellow streaks. Your hair's writhing upwards
like an upside down Medusa. But then I say: it's only a stone,
a small precious stone. All the blackness contracts, then
dries up and localizes in the smallest possible knot – I feel it
here, just under my throat. And I'm back again
in my room, on my bed, beside my familiar phials
which stare at me, one by one, nodding – only they can help me
for insomnia, fear, memories, forgetfulness, asthma.

Little by little things lost their meaning, became empty; did they ever
perhaps mean anything? – slack, hollow;
we stuffed them with straw and chaff, to give them form,
let them thicken, solidify, stand firmly – the tables, chairs,
the bed we lay on, the words; always hollow
like the cloth sacks, the vendors' burlap bags;
from the outside you can already make out what's inside them,
potatoes, onions, wheat, corn, almonds, or flour.

Sometimes one of them catches on a nail on the stair
or on the prong of an anchor down in the harbor, it rips open,
the flour spills out – a foolish river. The bag empties itself.
The poor gather up the flour in handfuls to make
some pies or gruel. The bag collapses. Someone
picks it up from its two bottom ends; shakes it out in the air;
a cloud of white dust enfolds him; his hair turns white;
especially his eyebrows turn white. The others watch him.
They don't understand a thing; they wait for him to open his mouth,
     to say something.
He doesn't. He folds up the bag into four sections; he leaves
as he is, white, inexplicable, wordless, as though disguised
as a lewd naked man covered with a sheet,
or like a cunning dead man resurrected in his shroud.

I don't know why the dead stay around here without anyone's
     sympathy; I don't know what they want
wandering around the rooms in their best clothes, their best shoes
polished, immaculate, yet noiselessly as though they never touch
     the floor.
They take up space, sprawl wherever they like, in the two rocking
     chairs,
down on the floor, or in the bathroom; they forget and leave the tap
     dripping;
forget the perfumed bars of soap melting in the water. The servants
passing among them, sweeping with the big broom,
don't notice them. Only sometimes, the laughter of a maid
somewhat confined – it doesn't fly up, out of the window,

it's like a bird tied by the leg with a string, which someone is
    pulling downward.

At night I hear the servants moving my big pieces of furniture;
they take them down the stairs – a mirror, held like a stretcher,
reveals the worn-out plaster designs on the ceiling; a windowpane
knocks against the railings – it doesn't break; the old overcoat on
    the coat-rack
raises its empty arms for a moment, slips them back into the
    pockets;
the little wheels of the sofa's legs creak on the floor. I can feel
right here on my elbow the scratching on the wall made by the
    corners of the wardrobe
or the big carved table. What are they going to do with them?
    'Goodbye,' I say
almost mechanically, as though bidding farewell to a visitor who's
    always a stranger. There's only
that vague droning which lingers in the hallway as though from the
    horn
of downfallen hunting lords in the last drops of rain, in a burnt-out-
    forest.
Honestly, so many useless things collected with so much greed
blocked the space – we couldn't move; our knees
knocked against wooden, stony, metallic knees. Oh, we've really
got to grow old, very old, to become just, to reach that
mild impartiality, that sweet lack of interest in comparisons,
judgements,
when it's no longer our lot to take part in anything except this
    quietness.

Not that I don't remember anymore – I do; it's just that the
    memories
are no longer emotional – they can't move us – they're impersonal,
    placid,
clear right into their most bloody corners. Only one of them
still retains some air around it, and breathes.
That late afternoon,
when I was surrounded by the endless shrieks of the wounded,
the mumbled curses of the old men and their wonder of me, amid
the smell of overall death, which, from time to time glittered
on a shield or the tip of a spear or the metope
of a neglected temple or the wheel of a chariot – I went up alone
onto the high walls and strolled around.
                            Alone, utterly alone, between
the Trojans and Achaeans, feeling the wind pressing my fine veils
against me, brushing my nipples, embracing my whole body
both clothed and naked, with only a single wide silver belt
holding my breasts up high –
                    there I was, beautiful, untouched, experienced

101

while my two rivals in love were duelling and the fate of the long war
was being determined –
I didn't even see the strap of Paris' helmet
severed – instead I saw a brightness from its brass,
a circular brightness, as his opponent swung it in rage
around his head – an illumined zero.

                            It wasn't really worth looking at –
the will of the gods had shaped things from the start; and Paris,
divested of his dusty sandals, would soon be in bed,
cleansed by the hands of the goddess, waiting for me, smirking,
pretentiously hiding a false scar on his side with a pink bandage.

I didn't watch anymore; hardly even listened to their war-cries –
I, high up on the walls, over the heads of mortals, airy, carnate,
belonging to no one, needing no one
as though I were (I, independent) absolute Love – free
from the fear of death and time, with a white flower in my hair,
with a flower between my breasts, and another in between my lips
    hiding for me
the smile of freedom.
They could have shot
their arrows at me from either side.
I was an easy target
walking slowly on the walls, completely etched
against the golden crimson of the evening sky.
I kept my eyes closed
to make any hostile gesture easy for them – knowing deeply
that none of them would dare. Their hands trembled with awe
at my beauty and immortality –
(maybe I can elaborate on that:
I didn't fear death because I felt it was so far from me).
Then
I tossed down the two flowers from my hair and breasts – keeping
    the third one
in my mouth – I tossed them down from both sides of the wall
with an absolutely impartial gesture.
Then the men, both within and without,
threw themselves upon each other, enemies and friends, to snatch
the flowers, to offer them to me – my own flowers. I didn't see
anything else after that – only bent backs, as if all of them
were kneeling on the ground, where the sun was drying the blood –
    maybe
they had even crushed the flowers.
I didn't see.
I'd raised my arms
and risen on the tips of my toes, and ascended
letting the third flower also drop from my lips.

All this remains with me still – a sort of consolation, a remote
    justification, and perhaps
this will remain, I hope, somewhere in the world – a momentary
    freedom,
illusory too of course – a game of our luck and our ignorance. In
    precisely
that position (as I recall), the sculptors worked on
my last statues; they're still out there in the garden;
you must have seen them when you came in. Sometimes I also
    (when the servants are in good spirits
and hold me by my arms to take me to that chair
in front of the window), I also can see them. They glow in the
    sunlight. A white heat
wafts from the marble right up here. I won't dwell on it any
    longer.
It tires me out too after awhile. I'd rather watch a part of the
    street
where two or three kids play with a rag ball, or some girl
lowers a basket on a rope from the balcony across the way.
Sometimes the servants forget I'm there. They don't come to put
    me back in bed.
I stay all night gazing at an old bicycle, propped up
in front of the lit window of a new candy store,
until the lights go out, or I fall asleep on the window-sill.
    Every now
and then I think that a star wakes me, falling through space
like the saliva from a toothless, slack mouth of an old man.
Now
it's been ages since they've taken me to the window. I stay here in bed
sitting up or lying down – I can handle that. To pass the time
I grasp my face – an unfamiliar face – touch it, feel it, count
the hairs, the wrinkles, the warts – who's inside
this face?
Something acrid rises in my throat – nausea and fear,
a silly fear, my God, that even the nausea might be lost. Stay
    for awhile –
a little light's coming through the window – they must have lit the
    street lamps.

*(She stopped talking. Her head fell back. She might have been asleep. The other
person got up. He didn't say Good-night. Darkness had already come. As he went
out into the corridor, he felt the servants glued to the wall, eavesdropping. Motionless. He went down the stairs as though into a deep well, with the feeling that he
wouldn't find any exit – any door. His fingers, contracted, searched for the
doorknob. He even imagined that his hands were two birds gasping for want of air,
yet knowing at the same time that this was no more than the expression of self-pity
which we usually compare with vague fear. Suddenly voices were heard from
upstairs. The electric lights were turned on in the corridor, on the stairs, in the
rooms. He went up again. Now he was sure. The woman was sitting on the bed*

with her elbow propped up on the tin table, her cheek resting in her palm. The servants were noisily going in and out. Somebody was making a phone call in the hall. The women in the neighborhood rushed in 'Ah, ah,' they cried, as they hid things under their dresses. Another phone call. Already the police were coming up. They sent the servants and the women away, but the neighbors had time to grab the bird cages with the canaries, some flower pots with exotic plants, a transistor, an electric heater. One of them grabbed a gold picture frame. They put the dead woman onto a stretcher. The person in charge sealed up the house – 'until the rightful owners are found,' he said – although he knew there weren't any. The house would stay like that, sealed up for forty days, and after, its possessions – as many as were saved – would be auctioned off for the public good. 'To the morgue,' he said to the driver. The covered car went off. Everything suddenly disappeared. Total silence. He was alone. He turned and looked around. The moon had risen. The statues in the garden were dimly lit – her statues, solitary, beside the trees, outside of the closed house. And a silent, deceitful moon. Where could he go now?)

May-August, 1970

Translated by Gwendolyn MacEwen and Nikos Tsingos

THE QUEEN OF SHEBA

Pierre Jean Jouve

The Queen of Sheba

The Queen of Sheba wears a green diadem.
Is it for love, shame, or loving shame?
It's one of the marvels she owned
When she died to an angel's trumpet.
A blast of wind.

•

She allows me an ecstatic smile
She gives me kisses, strange and false,
She swims among my animals, the watching fish
She makes airy flights with her limbs.

Longs legs & hair. This woman is a born diver,
More imperceptibly than nature she settles like a rose
At the bottom of the sea's garden.

•

A twirl on her rose stockings
An embroidered belt red at her waist
Provocative, she waits

Lean and naked a second
After rolling small tight
Pants slowly down her thighs

Breasts, two swarthy pears,
Shoulders sloping to magnificent arms,
But, better than all, her stomach

Pit proferring an enormous tuft,
Pungent and black, like a sin
Only admiration can crush.

The feminine fur lies lower still.
Lord you have seen my guilty eye
Slither there. So the jungle bird
Falls to the alligator, its laughing jaws.

The dreaming tropics, its streams, the ripeness
Of paradise, music's primal themes.

•

Begin at the pool's bottom
Where words thicken, obscene and cold.

Shudder of the horse of death!
He submits to the temptation of the black mouth
Hidden beneath the enamelled face,
The game of curtains, mingled legs, embrace.

•

It's true I have never, never prayed
Said the tall lady with the slim waist
But let him have my breasts, my belly, my youth
And see if he isn't satisfied.

•

She sucks, kisses, wears out and awakes.
When I am finally broken, she flies off,
Blowing my precious memories out –
A trail of blue bubbles.

How much man suspects the mouth he adores
But there was ecstasy there that he still pursues
And vitality. He longs for the smell,
The taste, the color of women's bodies,
Their flexibility, their faithlessness,
Chaste death smiling through their nacreous bodies
And afterwards that sadness
Which he knows too well.

•

A marvellous beast parades by,
Always wounded, his inner thigh,
A wound of fresh and flowing blood,
I felt him lure me into solitude.

The stag is born from our most blatant actions
Inhumanity discovered in its distress
The heat blazing in the side of icebergs
The torrent reascending its rocky cliff

The stag is born of the back streets
Of self, the sweetness of slaying the father,
Erotic secrets with our sister,
Laurels & love excrement smeared.

The stag appears in the street
Between the cash register and the gutter
Unrecognisable under the sodium lamps
Where even the sky is full of menace.

Translated by John Montague

NUESCAPES

Michel Lambeth

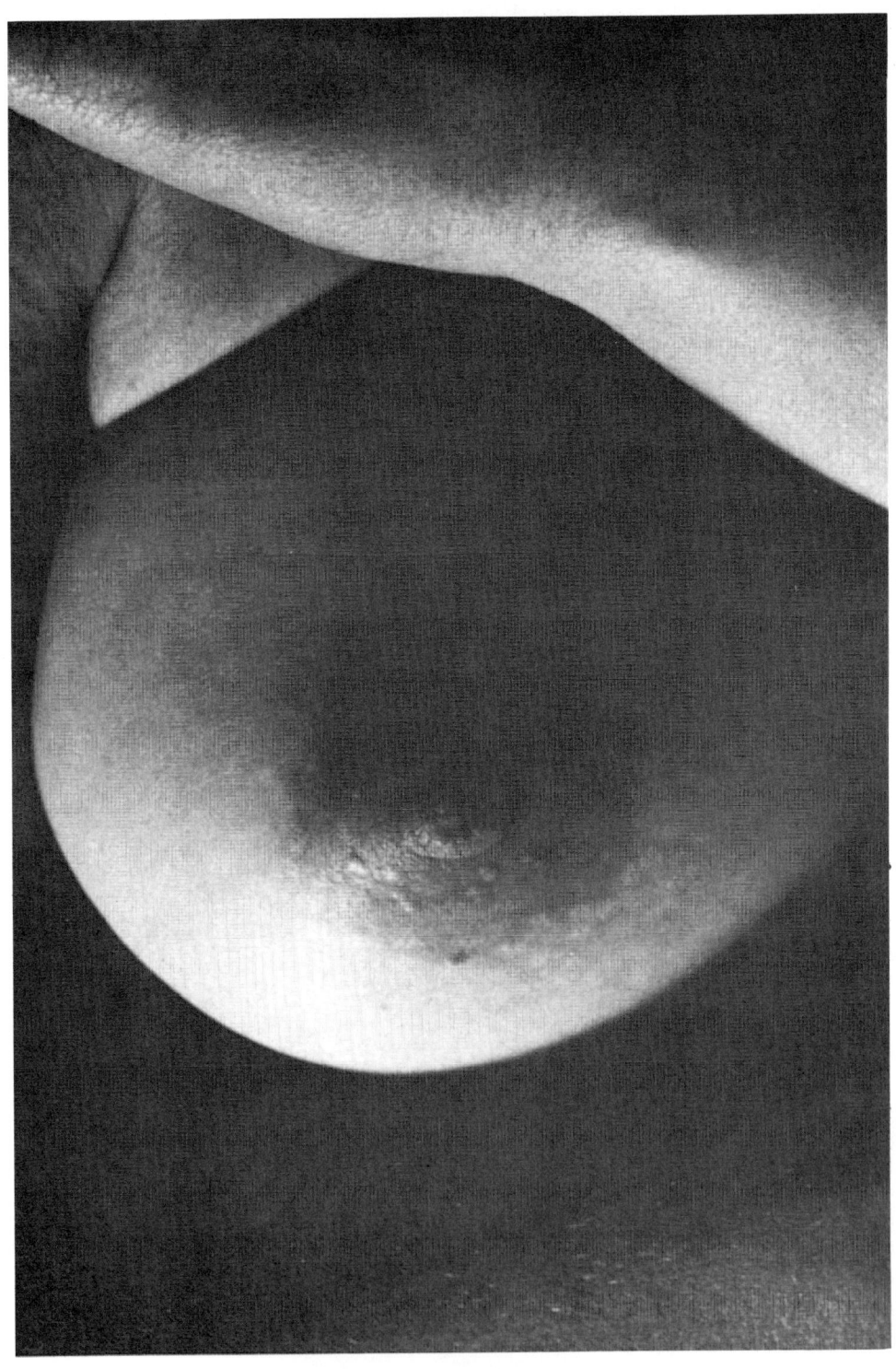

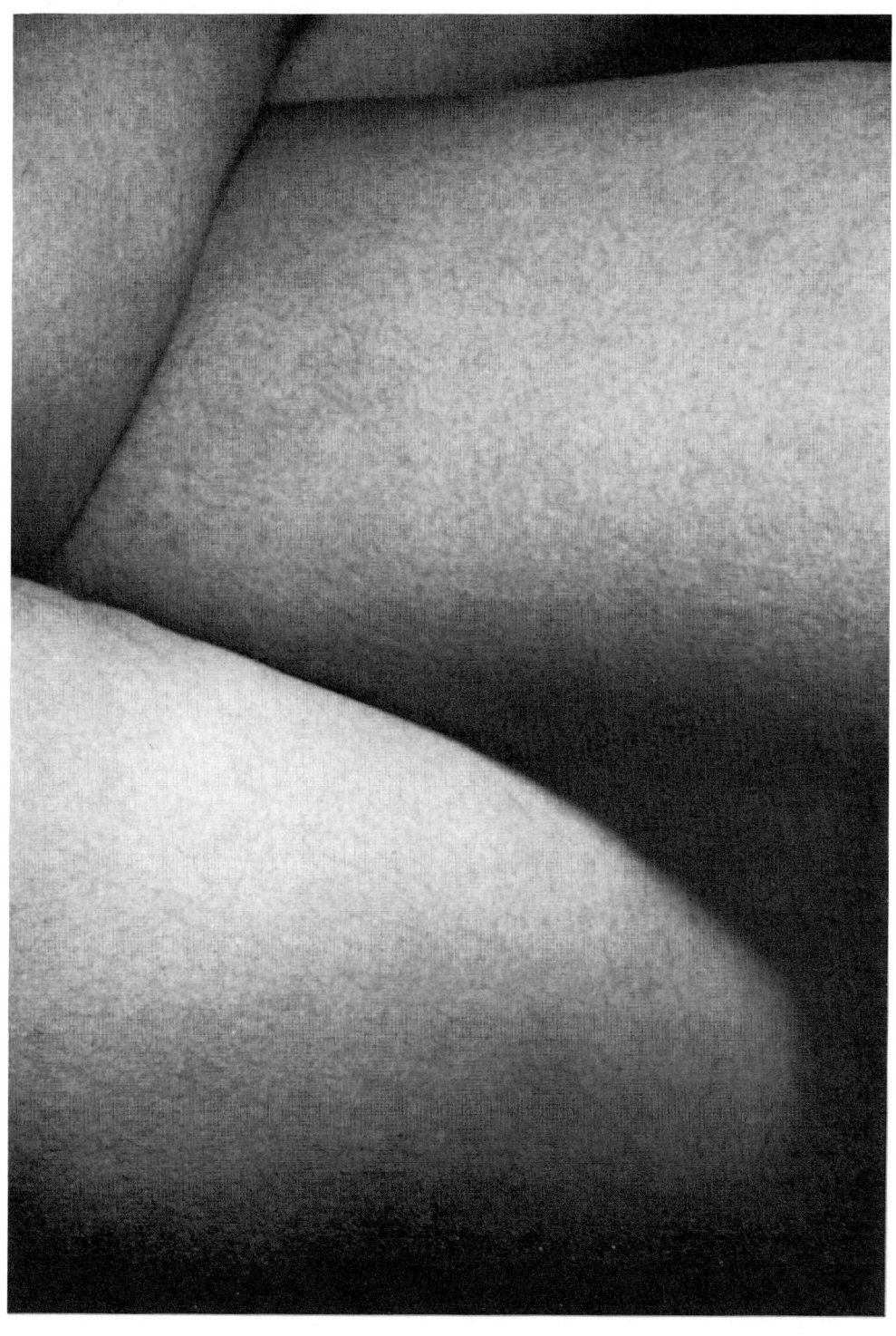

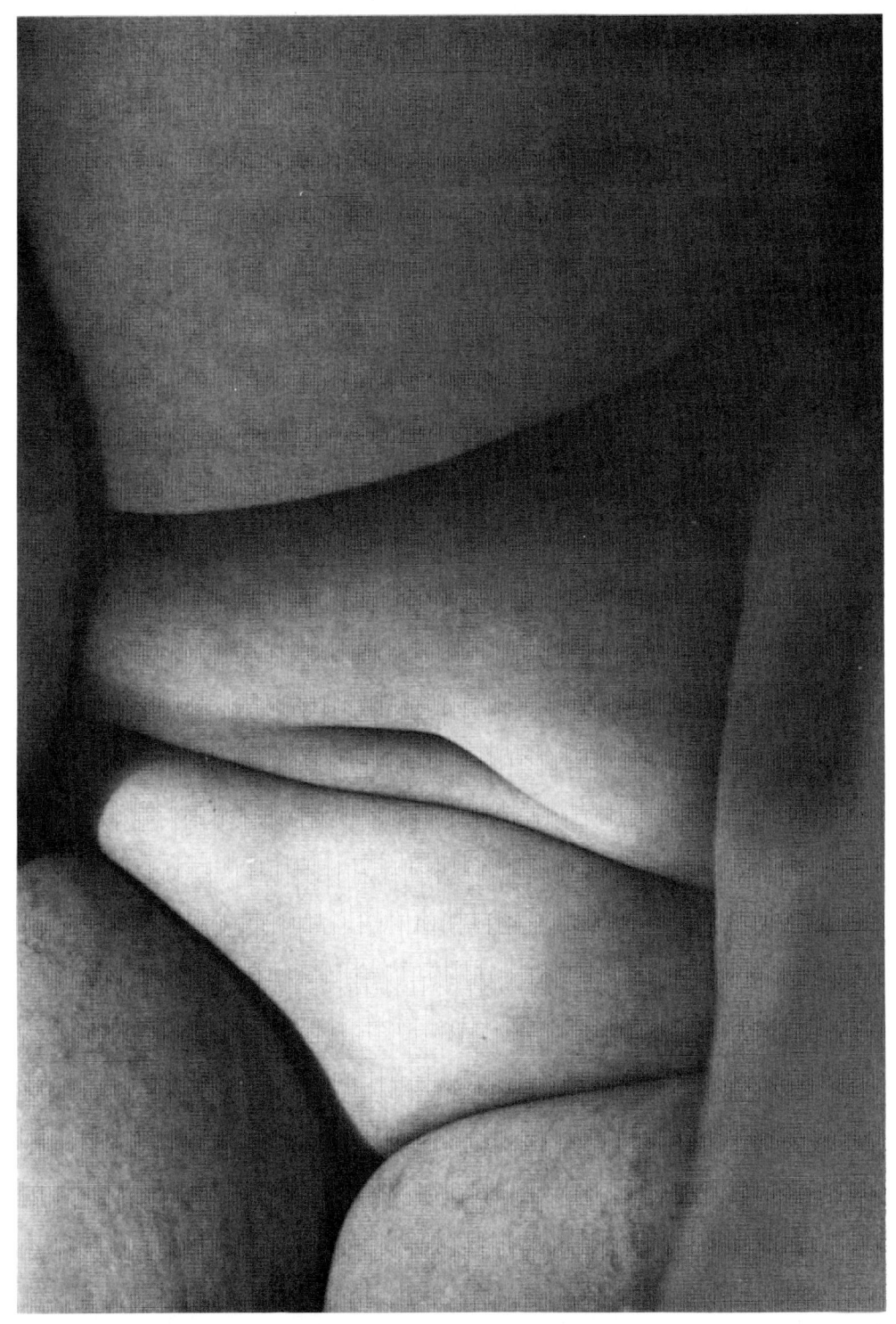

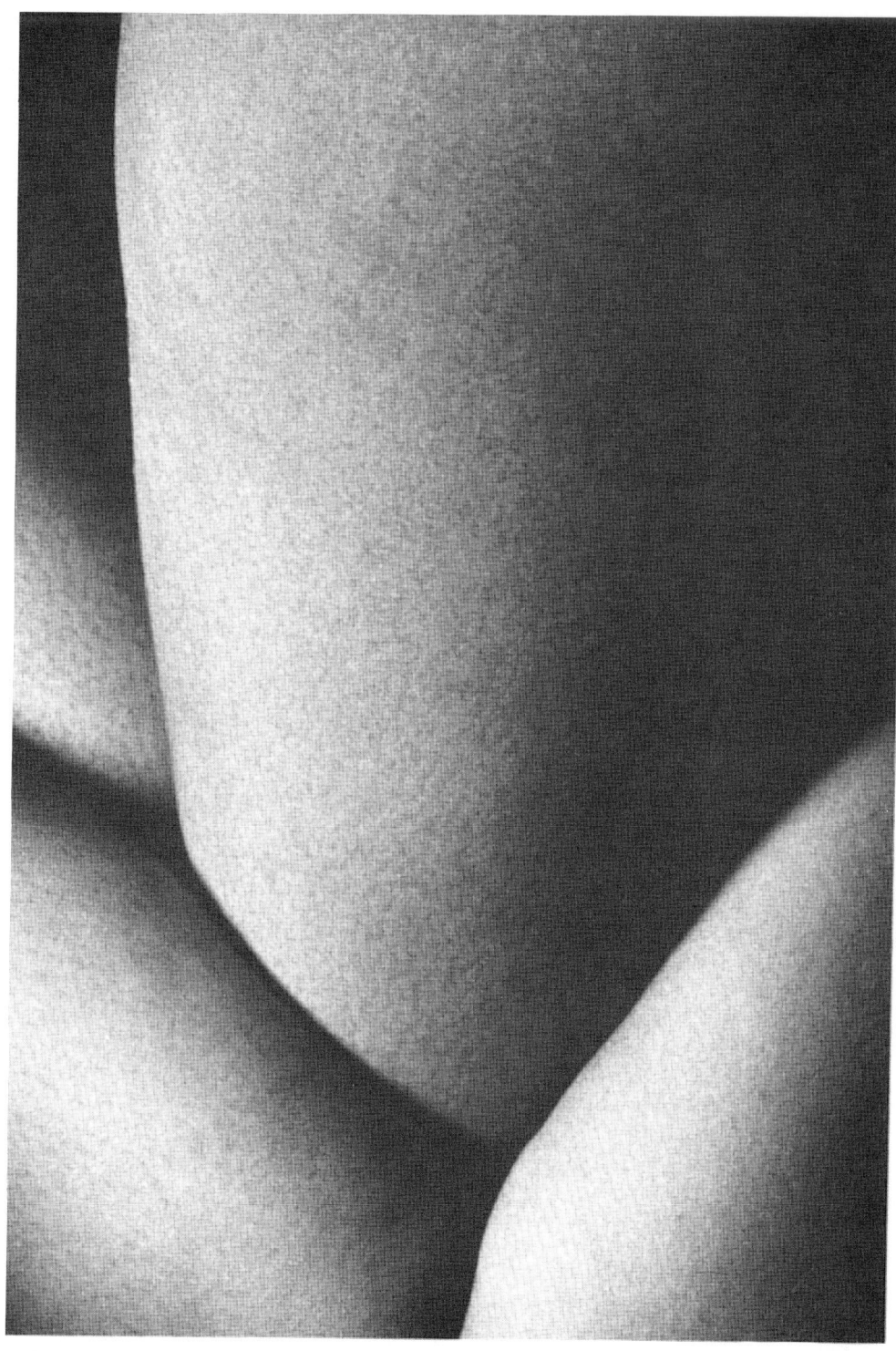

THE KEY

Robert Zend

The End.

FOOTNOTE ON THE CONCEPTION OF THE SHORT STORY ENTITLED "THE KEY".

Whenever we returned (from a walk, or a bookstore, or the University, or a restaurant, or the library, or the cemetery) to the apartment house in which he lives, Borges took the key out of his pocket, opened the door and, invariably stopping between the half-opened door and the door frame, started to speak about keys. The first time he said: "Isn't it fascinating that a small piece of metal like this can open a huge building like this?" I replied: "Similarly, the prick, a small piece of flesh that can open the body and the soul of a woman ... " Another time he said: "One key, you see, but it isn't one key, you can have duplicates made of it so that many different people can open the same house with it ..." Still another time he said: "I am fascinated with the idea of the Key, I think it was the greatest invention in man's history, not the telephone, not the airplane ..." So, during our last conversation (the eighth within the week), I asked: "During your whole life you seem to have been fascinated with the idea of the Labyrinth and you have been writing about all sorts of Labyrinths, like the mythological one in which the Minotaur lived, or Labyrinths stretching through space and time, or the Labyrinth of the human mind which tries, in vain, to comprehend that other Labyrinth, that of the Universe, and you also wrote about the Labyrinth of the infinite sand in the Sahara and Labyrinthian castles and gardens built by emperors ..."

"Yes," Borges nodded, "because I find it particularly intriguing that someone builds a Labyrinth in order to get lost in it ..."

"And you are also fascinated with the idea of the Key. Have you ever thought of combining the two and writing a short story about a key which opens a Labyrinth?"

Borges seemed astonished. "No! I have never thought of that! Very interesting. A short story about a man's search for the key to the Labyrinth. Yes!"

I became excited: "He is searching for the key so that he could enter the Labyrinth in order to get lost in it …"

"Yes," Borges continued, "and do you know how I would end the story? The man never finds the key, but when he dies, in the moment of his death, he realizes that his search for the key was futile because the Labyrinth was his own life …"

"But," I barged in, "the search for the key made him wander in many lands and made him meet many people and made him study many books and made him learn many languages, so while his search *for the key* was futile, as you say, the search *itself* was not futile because through it he did enter the Labyrinth of his life because the search was the key!"

"Well,"Borges smiled, "a new short story! Thank you very much!"

"Will you write it?" I asked with sparkling eyes.

"Yes, I might. But no. You should write it. I give it you. After all, it is your story, isn't it?"

"No, no, no!" I said, "it is your story! I would be very happy if you wrote it. I wouldn't steal it …"

"Look," Borges said, sliding his palm over the edges of the table, "it doesn't matter who writes it, you, or me, or you and me together. I am sitting at this side of the table, you at that side, certain elements of the story came from this side, others from that side …"

"It should be written by the *Table!*" I said.

"It *is* written by the Table," Borges said and laughed.

FOOTNOTE ON THE MISCARRIAGE OF THE SHORT STORY ENTITLED "THE KEY".

After this last conversation with Borges, a cloud of inspiration descended on me and kept my mind enshrouded. A voice, independent from my will, talked in my head incessantly, dictating startling-new-beautiful thoughts, sentences, half-sentences, expressions, adjectives, and I obediently recorded everything immediately no matter where I happened to be when it spoke, walking on the streets of Buenos Aires, sitting on park benches or in sidewalk cafés, and once, while I was falling asleep, it even pushed me out of my bed.

Before my departure from Argentina – since my suitcases were too many and too heavy to carry – I mailed all my books and notes and tapes to myself in Toronto. At the time of present writing, this shipment has still not arrived.

However, a few days after my return, on a certain Tuesday morning, while visiting the Editor of this literary quarterly, with the purpose of correcting the galleys of my short stories entitled "A Bunch of Proses," I was complaining about the unbearable slowness of the mail from Argentina which prevented me from writing another prose piece to follow and conclude those which I had just corrected. He seemed to be interested, so I told him how the idea of this piece was conceived by Borges and me, and asked him if he wanted me to write the short story, entitled "The Key," as soon as my notes arrived.

"No," he said, "I am not interested in the story about the key to the Labyrinth, but you can write the story of Borges and Zend inventing the story of the key to the Labyrinth, as you just told me."

I thought for a moment. "Hm. I never thought that the story about the story could be a story. This, actually, is your idea. Should it be written then by Borges and Zend and you?"

The Editor laughed: "As you wish. After all, it is your story, isn't it?"

I found his idea quite inspiring, so upon returning home, I grabbed a pen and, without hesitation, I wrote down the story of how the story, entitled "The Key," was conceived (by Borges and me) and received (by the Editor). This second version was a straightforward narrative, it started with the sentence, "Whenever we returned ..." and ended with the Editor saying to me: "After all, it is your story, isn't it?" Having finished writing it, I read it aloud to myself, I liked it, so I read it aloud to myself again, I liked it even more, so I called the Editor on the phone and read it to him. He sounded somewhat disturbed by the ending of my story involving him (in that version I used his name instead of calling him the Editor) and he said: "I don't think that you should use my name."

"You're wrong (I said) because it is not you but me who is writing about you since my story would be incomplete without you, and anyway, don't forget that after all, it is my story, isn't it?" We laughed. "You know what?" (I added) I will not end the story two hours ago, that is, as I've read it to you now on the phone, but I will end it with my saying to you, 'isn't it?' just a sentence ago. So I will include your protesting and my refuting your protesting, and ..."

"And you will entitle it, 'Isn't it?' as first said by Borges, then by me, then by you ..." the Editor said, and I felt a bit lost.

"Maybe I should write a series of footnotes without a story and entitle it 'Feetnotes' ..."

"It's getting too confusing (the Editor said), but try it, anyway, and we'll see ..."

When I hung up the receiver, suddenly I saw the shape of the third version of my story clearly projected on the inner screen of my mind.

When trying to understand abstract ideas, I cannot help simplifying them into structures. Everybody, more or less, does it: doodles drawn during a lecture or a conversation subconsciously reflect the visual model of how the listener *sees* what is said. With me, this process has always been extremely conscious. In elementary school, for instance, when the teacher explained to us that every composition must have an introduction, a treatment and a conclusion, I immediately saw in my mind this tripartite form:

Ever since, if I hear someone talking about linear stories, I visualize them:

Therefore, Boccaccio's Decamerone, a linear story about ten people, each telling ten linear stories in the course of ten days (altogether 101 linear stories), looks to me like:

Whereas A Thousand and One Nights, another chest-of-drawers story, a world of Eastern magic, with its convoluted framework, containing stories within stories, rather looks like this:

The Divine Comedy, Dante's epic consisting of 3 parts, each part containing 33 cantos, each canto written in 3-line stanzas, takes this shape in my mind:

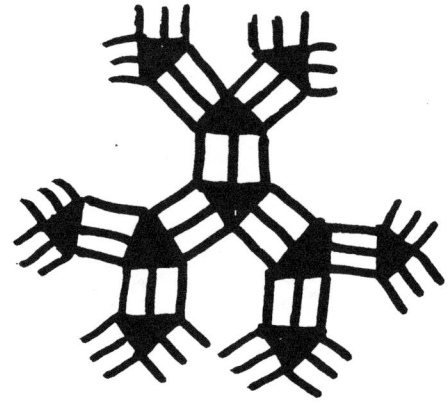

I see the intricate plots of Shakespearean-tragedy, with the colliding emotions of its heroes, most of whom die sooner or later, something like this:

Pirandello's stories are based on the games inherent in the number Two, mirrors and parallels and shadows and portraits and alteregos, and their plots usually end with a new start, making a spiral out of a circle:

Ionesco is full with unexpected flashes of wit, seemingly fragmentary, but based on a closed and wholesome (perhaps morbid) wisdom:

Proust seems to me an unwinding spool of unbeginning and unending memories:

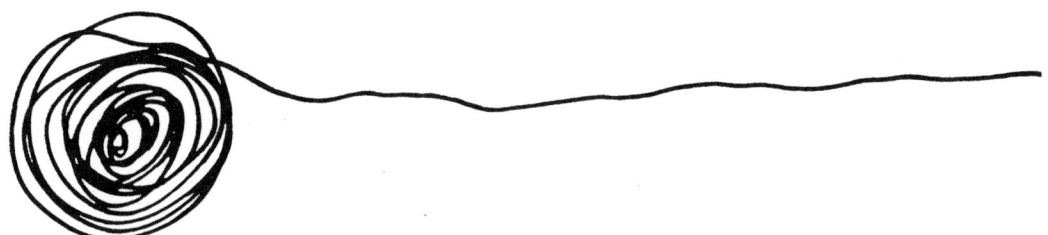

Joyce is a multilinear story flowing at the same time on many levels like a super-Bach fugue:

Updike tells a story in a linear way, but his line constantly zig-zags among the Joycean levels:

Borges' 'forma mentis' I see as a huge and beautiful (both ancient modern) city, in which every avenue branches out into many directions, thus each one is connected with all the rest:

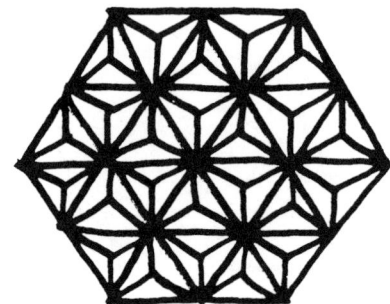

After I hung up the receiver, realizing that what I wanted to write is not the story entitled "The Key", it isn't even the story of the conception of the story entitled "The Key", but it is the story of the conception of the story of the conception of the story, entitled "The Key", I suddenly visualized Escher's three-dimensional triangle, the optical illusion of which can dazzle only on two-dimensional paper (it is impossible to sculpt it):

Cover with your finger any of the angles, there is nothing wrong with the other two:

  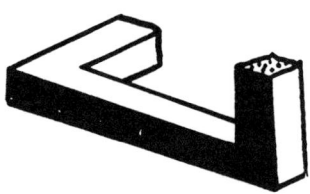

only the third (no matter which) angle makes the other two impossible:

118

And this was the form into which I attempted to translate the *form* of my originally linear story, entitled "The Key", in this present (third) version.

FOOTNOTE ON FOOTNOTES.

Writing footnotes as organic parts of a fiction is not my innovation, I am merely imitating Jorge Luis Borges who imitates DeQuincey who probably also … Borges openly imitates innumerable writers innumerable times since he doesn't believe in originality – everything was said and done before, he thinks. This is quite an original philosophy of writing, at least nowadays: in the Middle Ages it wouldn't have been. Thus, although writing footnotes on footnotes had been done, yet writing footnotes following a blank page had not been done, and I consider this to be my innovation in this present piece of writing: however, it is possible that I do so only due to my lack of cultural awareness.

Beside the two reasons I brought up so far for leaving the original story unwritten (the slowness of the mail and the Editor's disinterest in it), the third and deeper reason is that, although Borges and I invented it together and he encouraged me to write it alone and did not object to our writing it together, still, the hard fact is that our common story *is* unwritten as yet, so consequently, the only proper way of writing it as a collaboration is unwriting it as a collaboration, which idea is respectfully expressed by the blank space following our names.

My fourth reason for writing a story by not writing a story – and this became clear to me after the writing, so it must have been unconscious during it – is that I feel now, having written the story in this way, that I made the reader wander through/ and get lost in/ a Labyrinth, that of my style, thus he is forced to search for the key to understand what he is reading, and during this process he, himself, becomes the hero of the unwritten story, grasping its essence not by reading it, but by filling it in and identifying with it.

But my fifth – and main – unconscious reason for writing a story through a Labyrinth of footnotes was perhaps to practise the Borgesian style (so often compared to Escher's art), not to avoid it, but to live through it, for if I am under his influence now, as I am, it would be unhealthy and futile to deny it or to pretend not to be. The only honest and fruitful way to deal with this influence, it seems to me, is to go through it and absorb it and make it part of me and then go ahead. So, although this piece of writing seems to make a mockery or a caricature of a certain aspect of Borges' style, what it really amounts to is but a humble study of it, or a rather unsuccessful experiment in trying to dissolve my former self in his (as he dissolved his in others) and to do it openly. I have no reason whatsoever to hide it since I consider him one of my spiritual fathers not only after knowing his works, but even before that.

FINAL FOOTNOTE.

The shipment from Buenos Aires finally arrived! I've read through my beautiful notes and realize that I must abandon at once the Editor's plans for my story. That voice, independent from my will, is talking to me again and I cannot help but record its words:

THE KEY

By Robert Zend

Once upon a time there lived a man who

OBJECTS

Jean Benoît

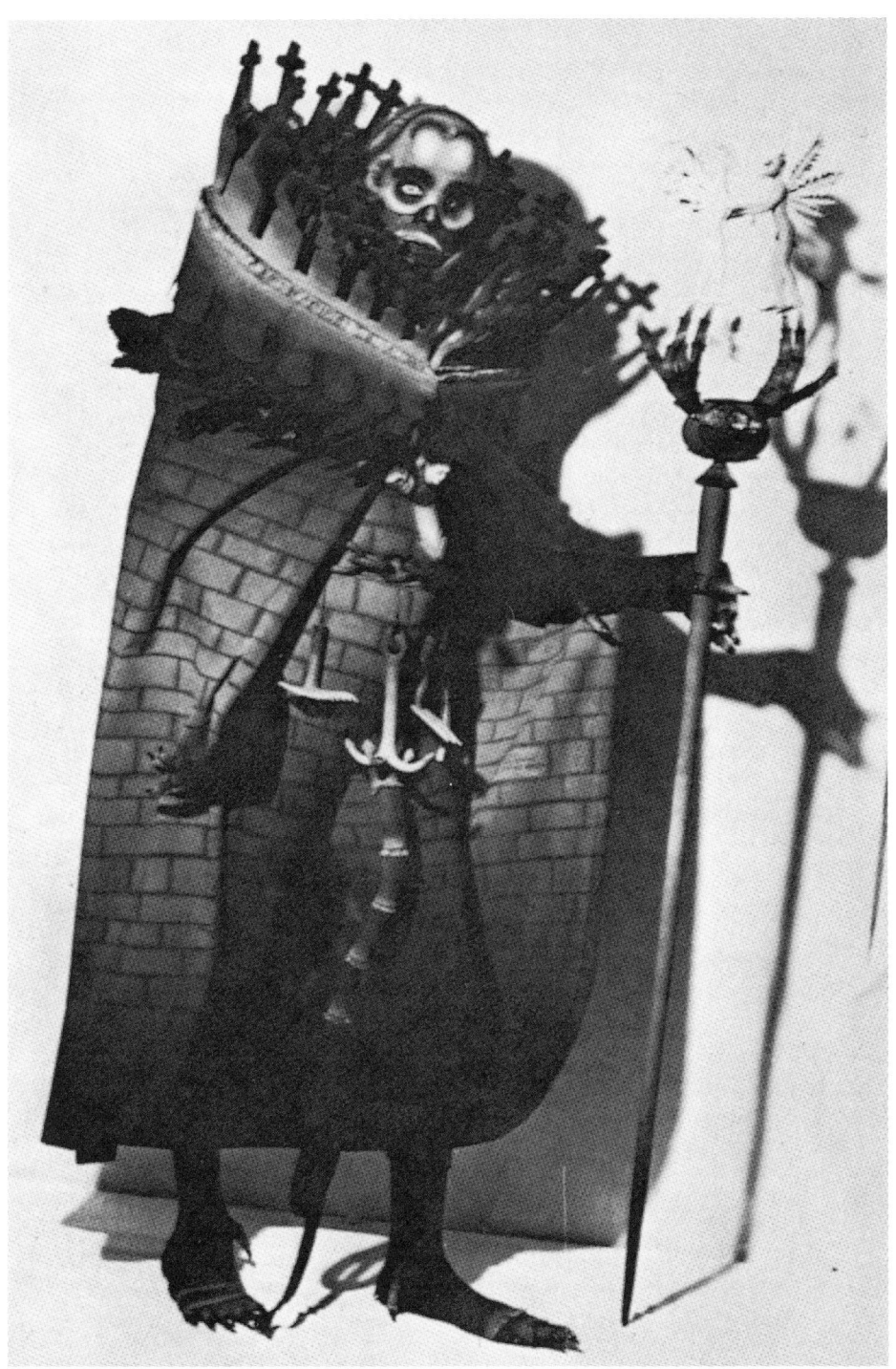

MAKE WAY for the Marquis de Sade, "large as life" and reinvested with all his potency by Jean Benoît.

André Breton

THE NECROPHILIAC (Homage to Sergeant Bertrand)
Collection P. Langlois

Description of the costume:
On the shoulders, a large "collerette" made of thirtynine tombstones, plus a family vault engraved with the names of heroines from all ages: Louise Labé, Ninon de Lenclos, Pauline Borghese, Jeanne Duval, etc. Hanging from this macabre collar, about twenty black birds — the crows of Van Gough's last painting. A large cape like a canopy used to adorn churches for funerals. Lower down, it flares out and thus looks like an undertaker's cloak. Seen from the back it is more like a priest's chasuble. A large cross is depicted on the back, within this a large coffin holding the head of a woman, this head itself formed by two linked skulls with cat's eyes. Below it, this inscription: DEATH, LIFE LIES IN WAIT FOR YOU. Moulded by tights, the body carries the pattern of a classic cemetery wall. Around the waist, a heavy chain holding all the tools of the grave-digger's trade — and around the neck, a phallic pendant inscribed: "Hommage to Sergeant Bertrand" (who was, as everybody knows, the most famous necrophile of all time). On the hands and feet, claws from the great ant-eater. The penis uncoils and droops to the ground like an animal's tail. In the right hand, a large scepter whose pommel is made of a giant spider lying on its back and, balanced on the end of its claws, two people, male and female, looking at each other and holding more small spiders on a thread. The face is made up in the same lurid manner as the rest of the costume and the head is covered with a mortuary mask of which the crown has the same streaks in the design and the same velvety texture as a moth. The only colours to be seen on the entire costume (which is grey and looks somewhat like the light of dawn) are provided by my eyes and the inside of my red-tinted mouth.

Jean Benoît

"The omnipotence of love never shows itself more strongly than in deviation."
Freud

"This body was the first one on which I gave myself over to indecent acts. I cannot define what I felt at that moment, anything one might feel with a live woman is nothing in comparison."
Sergeant Bertrand, giving evidence at his trial.

OBJECT TO CONTAIN LES CHAMPS MAGNETIQUES
André Breton and Philippe Soupault

... in a way, this work is a rendering of the "image" of my personal convictions concerning automatism. André Breton's thoughts on the subject are still authoritative. If in Point du jour (1934) he admitted that "the history of automatic writing is one of continuous misfortune," he nonetheless confined in his Entretiens (1952) how much automatism "was still dear" to him. The same applied to painting with this one difference: that the painters, supposedly, had shamelessly, commercially, exploited automatism. And so it was in a rather fine fury that I opened up the skull to see for myself how this pretty mechanism could have jammed at the very moment such a generous "idea" was formulated – was suggested to it – and out came, as you can see, a toad, one of Alfred Jarry's "totemic" animals.

Jean Benoît

The four "active" characters were made from a mixture of bones from guinea hens and rabbits. For the largest – the equivalent to a man six feet tall – I chose a large rabbit and a fat guinea hen; the reverse for the characters supposed to be about five feet tall. Thus I recreate an anatomy which could be coupled with nature's, in spite of the difference in scale. Also, if you look carefully you will see that the musculature of the toad's paws was "suggested" to me by chicken's beaks. The monkey, on the other hand, was fashioned with the aid of toad and chicken bones. The old woman's skull actually belonged to a thirteen-year-old girl, etc., etc. As you can imagine . . . this little "alchemy" is a source of great satisfaction to me, and helps me create a world entirely my own.

OBJECT TO CONTAIN A MUMMIFIED HEAD (Mundurucu Tribe, The Amazon)
Collection P. Langlois

Among the perversions cultivated by Jean Benoît the most fertile of late have been fetishistic tendencies, and it is to these tendencies we owe the monumental containers, true cenotaphs, in which he has enclosed various rare books. It is a remarkable fact that Benoît's fetishism expresses itself actively on objects which do not belong to him. Isn't there some incompatibility between the spirit of possession and the creative forms of fetishism? That, at least, is what we might gather from the reliquary that Benoît has just constructed for a Mundurucu trophy belonging to Pierre Langlois. But in reality a non-possessive fetishism, by the laws of nature, verges on necrophilia. Ever since she left the enormous forests where she was born, not far from Rio Tapajos, this very beautiful child who almost miraculously transmits her uneasy humour to us, was forced to constantly travel exposed to the eyes of dogs. But Langlois and Benoît were united in a common devotion, they shared the same jealous fervour. It's never too late to be loved.

Vincent Bounoure

... My work is a lot like a taxidermist's, with this difference: here the animal is completely recreated from all sorts of pieces — bones, teeth and claws of rodents, beetles' carapaces (from the Amazon), leather and fur (Astrakan). Incidentally, I find my "artist's materials" at a knacker's whose yard is way out in the suburbs. He gets dead animals from the zoos.

Jean Benoît

126

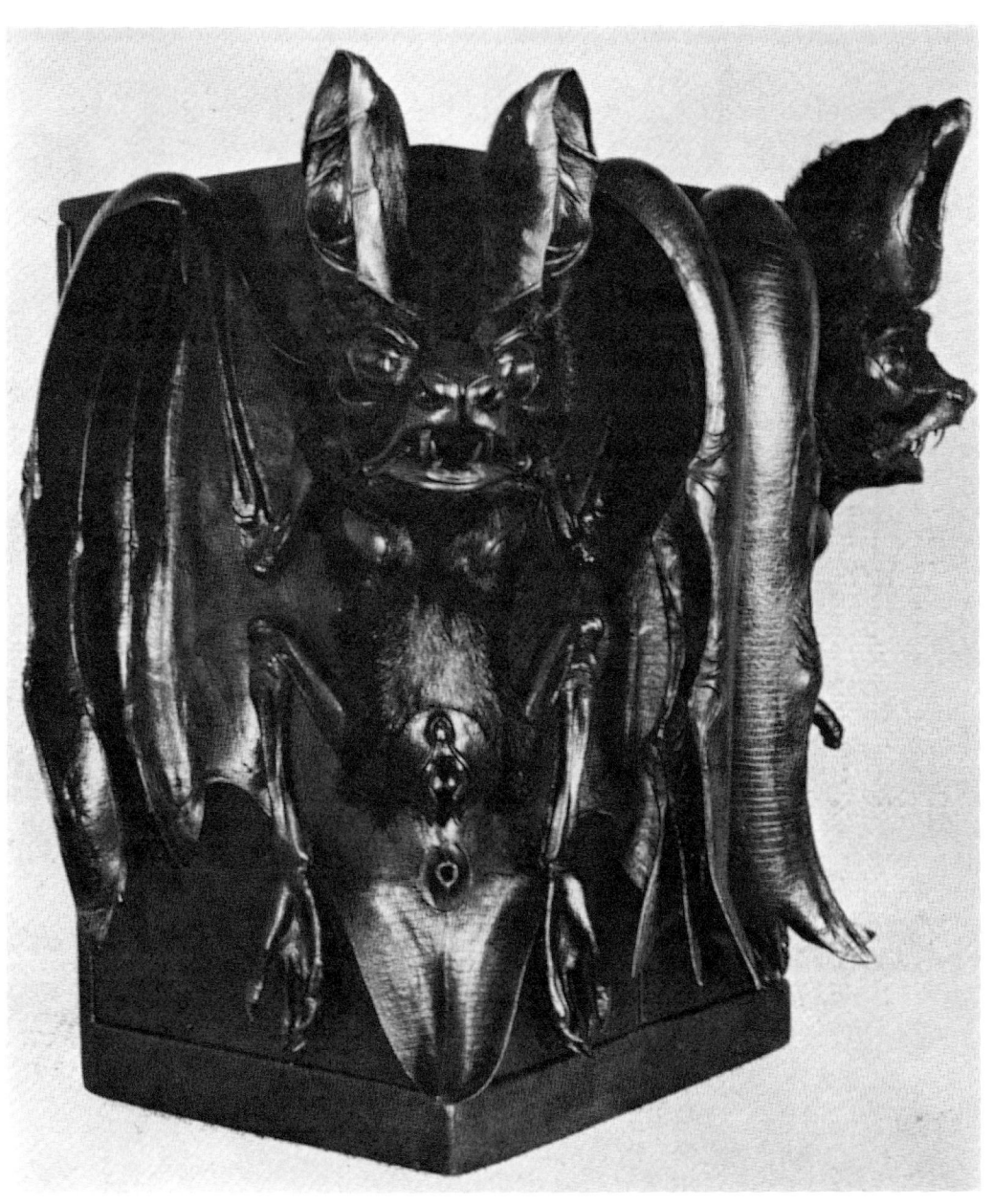

LIGHT MUSIC

Derek Mahon

1. Architecture

Twinkletoes in the ballroom,
light music in space.

2. History

The blinking puddles
reflected daylong
twilights of misery.

Smoke rose in silence
to the low sky.

3. Negatives

Gulls in a rain-dark cornfield,
crows on a sunlit sea.

4. Portrush

Tedium of sand and sea
then at the white rocks
a little girl fleetingly
blazer and ankle socks.

5. Donegal

The vast clouds migrate
above turf-stacks
and a dangling gate.

A tiny bike squeaks
into the wind.

6. North Sea

The terminal light of beaches,
pebbles speckled with oil,
old tins at the tide-line
where a gull blinks on a pole.

7. Rory

He leads me into
a grainy twilight
of old photographs.

The sun is behind us,
his shadow in mine.

8. Twilight
A stone at the roadside
watches snow fall
on the silent gate-lodge.

Later the gate shuts
with a clanging of bars;
the stone is one with the stars.

9. Mozart

The Clarinet Concerto
in A,K. 622;
the second movement.

Turn it up
so they can hear
on the other planets.

10. Morphology

Beans and foetuses,
brains and cauliflowers;
in a shaft of sunlight
a dust of stars.

11. Come In

The steel regrets the lock,
a word will open the rock,
the wood awaits your knock.

12. October

The fields dark under
a gunmetal sky
and one farm shining
in a patch of sunlight
as if singled out
for benediction.

13. Elpenor

Edacity in the palace
and in the sandy timber
of my crumbling monument,
its lengthening shadow
pointing towards home.

14. Revelation

A color the fish know
we do not know so
long have we been ashore.

When that color
shines in the rainbow
there will be no more sea.

15. Flying

A wand of sunlight
touches the rush-hour
like the finger of heaven.

A land of cumulus
seen from above
is the life to come.

TRUE ROMANCES

Margaret Atwood

i)

When I knew them they were an ordinary couple, she smiled and laughed a lot, she was a physiotherapist I think, and there was nothing wrong with him either, that you could see, except he was a little, you know. That summer they went on a vacation together, they always went on their vacation together, to Europe, that was back when you could still afford it. Everyone thinks he cut her up and put her in four green plastic garbage bags and left them in garbage cans around the city, or maybe not in cans, do they have cans there? In Barcelona, except I know it wasn't in Barcelona. He said they'd gone to Paris, and one day she just went out for a walk and never came back, but the landlady, in Barcelona or wherever it was, says she saw him back at the flat or whatever it was they'd rented, after the day he said they'd gone to wherever. And the bags with her in them were in Barcelona, not Paris. So they're there and he's here and naturally they want him to go over, for questioning they say, and naturally he won't. He says he doesn't need the distress all over again. I'll bet. I saw him in the supermarket last week. He was holding an eggplant and he said, *aubergine*, it's a much better word, don't you think? He was running his fingers over the purple skin. He hasn't changed a bit.

ii)

A long time ago I was desperately in love. Desperately is what I mean, in fact you could leave out the love and still get a good picture. He felt the same way and the strange thing was, neither of us could understand a word the other said. Because of this we used to throw dishes at one another, to attract each other's attention, I suppose; we used to shout. For some reason they were always his dishes. Once I ran into his kitchen and cut a hole in my arm with his kitchen scissors, not a very big hole, so he could see there was real blood inside, but he didn't understand that either. It isn't sex that's the problem, it's language. Or maybe love makes you deaf, not blind, because now we go out to dinner every once in a while and we can understand each other perfectly, we tell jokes and we laugh at them, we really think they're funny. We never used to think any of it was funny. I look at him and I can't believe we once threw dishes at each other, but we did. I can remember which plates, which cups, which glasses, and which ones broke.

iii)

My friend called me on the telephone and said, I'm going to kill myself. Why? I said. He's left me, she said. I have nothing to live for. All right, I said, how are you going to do it? Pills? No, she said, that would make me sick. If it doesn't work, I mean. I can't stand having my stomach pumped out, it's humiliating. Well, a gun then, I said. Think of the mess, she said. it's indelible, and I hate loud noises. Hanging, I said. You look so awful, she said. You could say the same of drowning, I said. Well, I guess that's that, she said, but what am I going to do, now that he's left me and I have nothing to live for? Who told you it has to be for anything? I said. But were you living for him when he was there? No, she said. I was living in spite of him, I was living against him. Then you should say, I have nothing to live against, I said. It's the same thing, isn't it? She said. I said No.

iv)

Most people in that country don't eat eggs, she told me, they can't afford to; if they're lucky enough to have a chicken that lays eggs they sell the eggs. There is no such thing as *inside*, there's no such thing as *I*. The landscape is continuous, it flows through whatever passes for houses there, dried mud in and out, famine in and out, there is only *we*. That's why they can kill so many of us and not make any difference. To make a difference they would have to kill all of us. They cut off the hands and heads to prevent identification but they cannot prevent it. Everyone knows who has been shot and thrown into the sea, who has been beaten, which man or woman has been methodically raped, which left to starve and burn in a pit under the noon sun. It's bright there and clear, you can see a long way.

As for my lover, she told me, we had to separate. None of us can afford to live with just one other. You get careless, you forget how much you want to live, you start making bargains with yourself, you become dangerous to others. That kind of love is a weapon they can use against you. Among those of us who still have heads and hands there are no marriages.

v)

I don't think about you as much as I ought to, I don't have to, you're there whether I think about you or not. Many people aren't.

When I do think about you it's not what you'd expect. I don't want to be with you: most of the time that would be an interruption, for both of us. I like to consider you going about your routine. I think about you getting up, brushing your teeth, having breakfast. I vary the breakfasts, though I don't devise anything too fanciful for you, I stick to cornflakes, orange juice, eggs, things like that. No strawberries out of season. I find it soothing to think about you eating these mundane and in fact somewhat austere breakfasts. It makes me feel safe.

But why should you go on eating breakfast at the same time, in the same way, day after day, just so I will be able to feel safe? You're contented enough, true, but there must be more. I'm getting around to that. One of these mornings, when you reach the bottom of your cup, coffee or tea, it could be neither, you will look and there will be a severed finger, blood-less, anonymous, a little signal of death sent to you from the foreign country where they grow such things. Or you will glance down at your egg, four minutes, sitting in its dish white and as yet uncracked and serene as ever, and sunlight will be coming out of it. But on second thought your coffee cup will be vacant and the egg, when you finally close your eyes and slice it open blindly with the edge of your spoon, will have nothing in it that is not ordinarily there. Then you will know that at last I have imagined you perfectly.

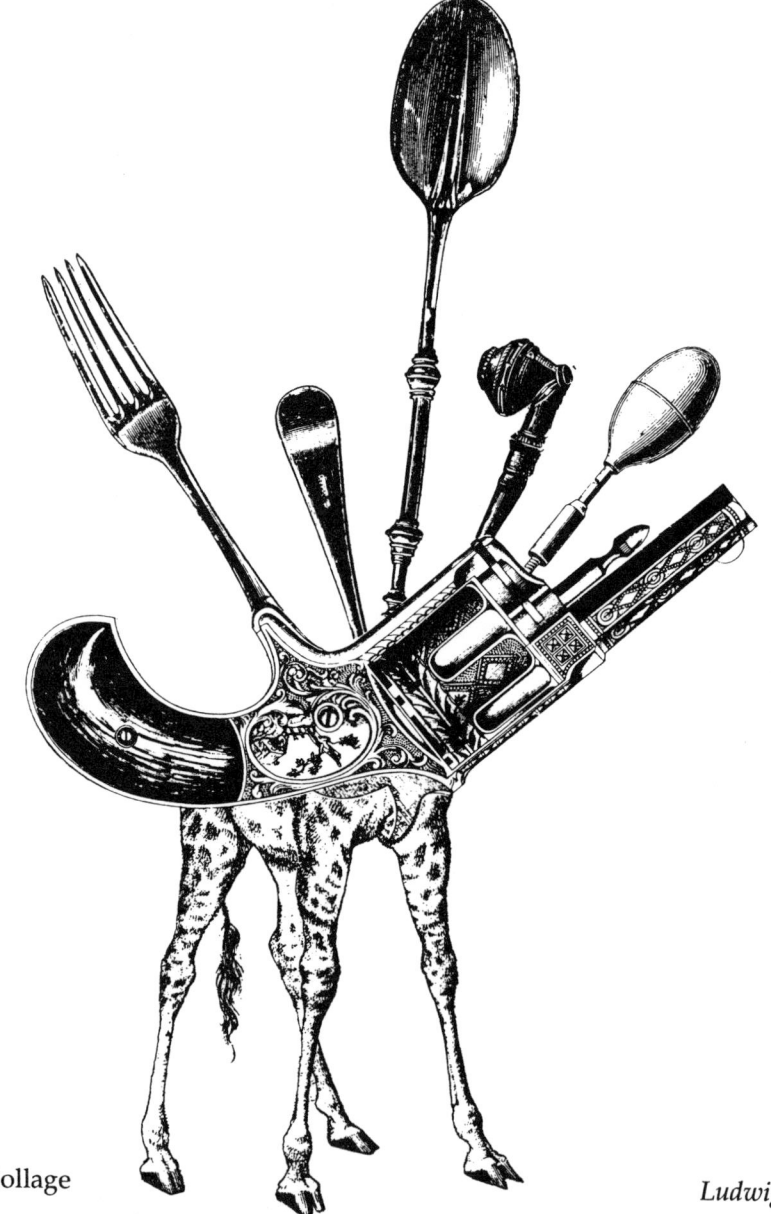

Collage

Ludwig Zeller

PAPA BOSS

Jacques Ferron

3

Your dinner went to your head. The sky mirrored the blue of your plate, and again the sacrificial baby birds came to life in your eyes blinded by the scales of everyday perception. How could you help but be fooled? You imagined that the sun, becoming an egg, shed its white to concentrate on being yellow. When you did that, you were distorting reality. And you were wrong too, later, when you thought it was a cloud you saw crossing the sky, reaching the top level of the terraced slope. Seen from your window, it gave the slope a natural perspective and it breathed life into the whole world, through your mouth. Albumen, water vapor, not at all! It was an angel, plain and simple.

The very top terraced level, recently opaque green and now a dappled brown which was turning to mauve and violet, consisted of a clump of large trees more or less consecrated to God, in the back yard of a convent. He let himself fall onto the roof of the convent, bounced back into the air and came down again much closer to you, on the gable of the two-storey house in the next street on the other side of the main road. At that moment, the scales fell from your eyes.

He was standing still, with his wings folded and his head tipped a little back, leaning against the wings. He was dressed in feathers and white linen, with brown hair and a big nose. You weren't surprised. An angel on the gable of a house, what could be more natural in November? You were in your husband's place, and the glass of the window melted into the clear air. The gentle warmth of the heater rose On-High, and in exchange an angel came down. The gable where he rested was right on the road from heaven. The two-storey house belonged to a judge. Somebody once told you his name, but you had forgotten it — Simonette or Dorion, with Eric or Amédée for a first name. At first, you thought naively that the angel had come to counsel him and you were wrong again. You had too high an opinion of judges and in your humility, in your tranquil indifference, you weren't in any way awaiting annunciation. But suddenly the angel will leap.

He will go across the street to the bungalow below. Its yard ends in a hedge of Chinese Elms and abuts against the yard just raked. From the simple, almost flat roof of this bungalow, he jumps to the hedge and from the hedge into the yard, which he crosses with mincing steps. It's done in an instant, and he has already gone into the landlord's flat. You will rub your eyes, but you have not been dreaming. It was possible to be mistaken when he was beginning his long descent to earth because he was still high, and far away, and because the eggs, sunny side up, had gone to your head

135

and shown you a reflection of the sky as cocks see it from steeple-tops. But there was no mistaking him when he was on the gable. You recognized him for what he was: a plain handsome angel, with wings folded, quite content to jump and walk, obviously a pure spirit since the Chinese Elm hedge supported him. In any case, it was not Mister G. Pelletier going into his house, finished with his leaves, his rake on his shoulder.

No, you weren't dreaming. You believe your eyes, you believe as we are told to believe, with a brand-new faith which glories in you even before you feel the glory yourself, like a sparkling cider just before you get the kick. You say to yourself, calmly, impartially, as if you were reading an official report, you say: 'Look at that! an angel has come to visit the landlord.' And then the cider begins to sparkle, your heart bubbles, and you are happy from too much good fortune, even if the visit is not your concern. You are happy for Mister G. Pelletier. He worked so hard all his life, that man, and his wife was such a good housekeeper, they deserve to have an angel come down from the sky to congratulate them. And besides, you think that if there's an angel for the landlords, it's a good sign for the tenants. Maybe they'll have one too, just a tiny one; nothing flashy, a sort of butterfly, but still an angel, just as civilized as the other, who won't ask for money, and who will only want to shake hands: *'How do you do?'* A gentle angel, not intimidating, even though angels always speak English, and you will reply, simply, *'Very well, thank you.'*

That's what you were thinking. Rejoicing, flipping your thoughts from one side to the other, and you would have gone on, saying more and more flattering and agreeable things to yourself, if you hadn't been interrupted by a knock on the door ... What! you mean you weren't expecting it? All the same. It was bound to happen: old man Pelletier wouldn't flub a chance to do the honors, to show his guest his life's work, from top to bottom, and his guest trailing after, polite and condescending, his great wings quivering, tucked up and unhappy. It was a miracle that nobody had knocked before now.

4

You got the main things done and then went on to details, with accomplished care (and it didn't take that long), so that the flat gleamed spick-and-span with order, ready for any angel from heaven, even this one, who, instead of coming straight down, decided to come by way of domestic interiors such as Flemish masters had used in their Annunciation scenes. As yet, they hadn't come to visit you, and you took full advantage of the miracle. If woman attains perfection through good housekeeping — and that's what they say, and it's very likely — then you weren't far from perfect, or at least you had improved yourself a lot. Now they could knock, you wanted nothing better than to answer the door.

But you wouldn't want the bedroom in a painting. Your husband was sleeping there and you didn't dare disturb him. He lacked piety, he had no pity, even for himself, so how could he have pity for priests or even vicars? He was a hard man, bitter and unbelieving, even mean in a way, like all unbelievers, like all husbands who only know how to groan through the mouths of their wives. Better to keep him out of the picture, hide him, forget him. That was the only way for you to retrieve your virginity. You were ready with a smile, a pout, a consent on your lips. But good God, what was the matter with them? Why didn't they knock?

You were ready, but for what? Ready to consent to what? You scarcely knew, and didn't care much about being told. To cheat on your husband? Yes, maybe. One thing was sure: you wouldn't let your husband come between you and the angel. What an affront to God that would be! A poor angel, already sheepish about his big wings, and your sneering husband who would shower him with insults, call him a joker, something left over from Halloween, a retarded antique, a simpleton. No, you didn't want that. The marriage bedroom must remain sealed like a tomb.

Still nobody came. But again, that was no miracle, there was no mystery to that, because they were inspecting the basement, that's all. Madame Pelletier had intervened and was showing them her preserves, enough for two floods. So your wait wasn't over, puuh! so much the better. 'So much the better!' you said: you had time to take a bath. There was no conscious liturgical consideration, just a sort of return to the primitive ritual demanding that every ceremony be preceded by ablution. You let the water run, you got undressed. In such an orderly and clean house your nudity wasn't indecent. You got into the bath. Standing up, the water came above your ankles; sitting, above your navel. It was warm, bountiful water, perhaps holy. Bending your knees, you sank up to your neck, to your chin. The only parts still aerial were your head, your lower thighs and doubtless, also, the tops of your legs on the opposite slope of your knees. The rest of your body bathed in another element. With each breath your breasts rose to break the surface, appearing and disappearing. They were the reefs, you were the tide. One of your hands floated over your belly, and the sea-urchin between your thighs was silky-soft. You felt miraculously good, on the verge of letting yourself dissolve, but only on the verge, that's all. There were things to do. But then, after a while you were bored, and sort of disillusioned.

Figuring your chances of being visited by the angel, you had forgotten to reckon your neighbors on the same floor, the in-laws of the landlord. They were so quiet, they just rocked in their rocking chairs. They were called Louis and Délima Barnèche, and their ages laid end-to-end made a century and a half. They came from the Kamouraska hills, glad to be here, certain they wouldn't be going back. There they were, on the other side of the partition, and their presence had thrown out your calculations ... With chubby cheeks and a sly look, they rocked and said nothing, letting autumn look after preparations for winter, with no fear of the cold, and yet how they used to shiver! They used to work like dogs, but now they rocked, that's all they did. They had worked themselves out. They had been unloved, weaned early, poorly nursed. They had had many children, and gave what had been given, which was not much: the art of living on nothing and fearing everything. Now autumn was going to bring them the sweet warmth of winter, and old age had already left them enough to eat even in the grave. Finally, they could rest and rock, not to keep from

137

screaming, but only for the pleasure of rocking. They had begun again from scratch. They said nothing because they didn't know how to talk yet. Sleeping away the day in their chairs, the night in their beds, they made no sound. They digested. The oil heater kept an even heat in the house. They were back in the womb and they would not be driven out again except on their way to heaven. Assured of salvation, they were already enjoying eternal bliss, with chubby cheeks and a sly look. An annunciation was no longer possible because everything that might have been announced had already happened. They were rocking the Messiah. They had a right to a visit. After the normal pleasantries, the son-in-law would say to the angel: 'On the other side of the partition is an apartment the same size and the same plan as this, except that the three rooms on the right here, are on the left there. We can go back downstairs now.'

You stayed in the tub. The water was still warm. You weren't feeling so good any more, neither good nor bad. You weren't waiting for anyone any more. You had stayed for nothing ... for nothing, or so you thought. In the water up to your chin you looked straight ahead between your knees and the angel appeared.

5

He was standing at right angles to you. It would have been embarassing (you hadn't soaped yourself and the water was still clear) if he had stared at you the way you were staring at him, in the position you were in, from where he was on the other side of the sea-urchin between your thighs. But he was covering his face, it was the only decent thing to do. Still, you were intimidated. You were hardly breathing and your breasts no longer rose out of the water. He alone emerged and he didn't go back in. It wasn't from the flow of the tide, nor a sudden germination of the sea-urchin, or any other sea food. No doubt about it, he was an angel, though you weren't sure which one of you was supposed to be hidden by his veil. He was wearing a robe of white linen and the wings already mentioned, still folded. His robe was so long it covered his feet or maybe he had no feet. The robe was very loose and he was very thin. Maybe he had no body, at least up to his shoulders, but at that height a hand came out of his sleeves, not a young hand, twice your age. The hand was holding a kind of veil in front of his face and the other was elsewhere, perhaps behind his back. Above the veil you could see the crown of his bald head, and, on the opposite side of the hand holding the veil, an ear lying close to the temple, well formed, a little pointed, a kind of puny ear, topped with a little tuft of hair.

You stayed calm. The angel didn't have to say, 'Fear not, Madame.' You didn't move. You only knew you were going to be disappointed, and you weren't surprised, unworthy as you were of the grace of God. You knew the angel wasn't Catholic, but you had no idea who might have sent him, since you knew nothing about inferior theologies or redemptorist teachings, or about Papa Boss and his Quebec Voodoo. All the same, you had dreamed of a quite different message, about a love which passeth all love.

138

For ten years, you had been tired in the monotony, tired in all your sets of silent lips, tired even in your caruncles though you still could make the cock strut. He hurt your belly with his spurs. In the darkness of your nave you sighed after another steeple, one not topped with a weathercock who gnashed his teeth. Your past ecstasies, due to inexperience, seemed farther and farther away. You wanted to attain a higher virginity which would be the fruit of the flower, practice made perfect. You had called forth an angel, there in front of you, on the edge of the bathtub, a questionable angel, well endowed with wings but non-flying, with the pate and the hand of a sixty-year-old property owner, an angel who hid his spurs as if he were ashamed of them, one of those cocks who struts no more, no matter how the lips might pray, no matter how swollen the caruncles. You were naked, you were still beautiful, you were barely thirty. The angel said to you:

— Hail to thee Madame. I am not looking at you, but I am positive your virtues are many. Let me inform you that you are blessed among women.

—Thank you, sir, for that greeting. I appreciate it very much. Would you mind repeating it?

The angel did so.

—Thank you, sir. I shall remember and repeat it to myself for ever more.

He still hid his face.

— But why don't you uncover your face?

—Then I would uncover you, madame, and you are exposed enough already. Besides, that's not what I came for. Papa Boss has sent me to announce that he will cover you with his shadow.

And he added:

— Blessed art thou among women.

— What will I get out of that, sir?

—That which is to be gotten from the greatest compliment of all.

— Which is nothing at all.

The angel shuddered. He raised the veil that covered his face so that you could only see the top of his receded hairline. By so doing, he exposed his neck and Adam's apple.

— It's not even a compliment, sir: how could I not be blessed among women? Who do I know besides myself? Anybody can see that every woman, left to herself, would think the same, and you could tell her what you told me and never go wrong. She'll believe you while the others won't hear a thing about it.

The angel didn't answer. As he sought to swallow his saliva, his Adam's apple rolled between the top of his robe and the bottom of his veil. He wasn't disconcerted, but just annoyed, asking himself if maybe you hadn't played him for a pigeon, whose wings could have been your raised knees. Why had he appeared to you? To catch you in your bath, stark naked, nothing more. And here you were talking back to him, taking the words right out of his mouth. He came for the fun of frightening you, and you hadn't even budged a thigh. He'd come, finally, to bring you the word of Papa Boss and you didn't seem ready to accept, arguing over a formula you knew had stood the test of use through the centuries. He couldn't think of anything else to say.

139

You asked him:

— Who, sir, is Papa Boss?

He nodded his head, rather quickly, both relieved and condescending. Now everything was clear: you didn't know who Papa Boss was. His Adam's apple quit bobbing and he made ready to answer you ... Suddenly you sat up in the bathtub, furious and out of patience. Crouched in the swirling, slopping water, you screamed in his face that you didn't want to hear about it.

—That Papa Boss of yours, he doesn't exist!

— And me, Madame, do I exist?

— You exist with great difficulty, sir.

— It doesn't matter how I exist. If I exist, Papa Boss exists, because I am sent from him.

That made sense.

— Who is Papa Boss, sir?

— Madame, I will not say that he is King of the world and God of the country. Another shall follow after me, who shall instruct you.

— We'll see.

— You will see, Madame. He will come sooner than you think. Now, know that you need Papa Boss and Papa Boss needs you.

You didn't seem convinced. So the angel added:

— Anyway, you already know all this, otherwise you wouldn't be waiting for me.

— You, sir, are not what I was waiting for.

— You were waiting for an angel unspecified and I came, therefore You were waiting for me.

That made sense.

— Who is Papa Boss, sir?

—The capital gain of life, a clear profit out of each and every existence, the eternal quintessence of mortal capital.

— You don't say!

— You are nothing but a loss, Madame, and it's on your loss that Papa Boss gains. You are the increase of his profit. In exchange, and if so desiring, he may reinvest in you. He is good fortune. Believe in him, and you can win.

— Win what, sir?

— Anything, Madame, as in the lottery. You can win no matter where, win no matter whom. Everybody wants to win. Don't you see? Papa Boss is the wealth of the poor, the All-Powerful of the powerless. I will tell you more, Madame, and then you will understand why you waited for me. By the intercession of Papa Boss we can still talk of love, in spite of limp old age. No, don't object! He is the moving spirit behind a marvelous mutual fund. From his holding company he sees the needs of each man.

— Does he truly exist, sir?

— His angels have come down to earth, Madame.

You pouted and kept quiet out of politeness. Papa Boss didn't seem like such a big-time creator to you. More like maybe he slapped his angels together out of used parts. That's why this one hid his face, not because he was modest. He even resembled the landlord a little, in fact you'd swear to it, judging from the hand, the ear and the bald head.

The water was cold, so you got out of the tub. You dried yourself, put on your housecoat, and then turned around.

— Peekaboo, it's me!

You were right, it was the landlord, Mr. G. Pelletier. There he was in front of you, standing in an angel suit like a crazy old fool.

— Mister Gérard Pelletier!

— No, Gérald, Gérald like in Géraldine.

You remembered your wild laughter and so did he. He bowed his head.

— What about Papa Boss?

He looked you in the eye.

— Don't be fooled by appearances, Madame, I am not Gérald Pelletier.

— Who are you then?

— I am the angel of Papa Boss.

And as he had appeared he disappeared. You stood there puzzled. He reappeared:

— Excuse me, Madame, I forgot to say that your prayer has been answered.

— By whom?

— By Papa Boss.

Once more he vanished before you could ask what prayer he meant.

6

All the steam had fled from the bathroom, leaving only the mirror misted over. But the fog was so thick that standing close, only a few feet from yourself, even the outline of your body was blurred. Maybe the mirror had hidden the angel's exit. Mirrors have always been mysterious passageways. We look into them from inside ourselves, to see the apparition of our outside appearances. A ghost opens a door for all others. But the open door can also close after such an escape. What if he is there when you wipe the mirror?

You wiped the mirror. Not escape, but a young woman approaching. She stood close to you, on the other side of the still damp and dripping window. You looked at her, she looked at you. You were aware of each other, but did she see you as you saw her? The door was still closed. Like the mirror itself, her eyes hid what you had hoped to find, the secret passage.

You smiled at this young woman. She smiled back. You stuck out your tongue and she replied in kind. She mimicked you, to refuse replying, leaving you ignorant of yourself. You pouted and she passed that back. But then, maybe you were the mimic. In fact, you'd have trouble explaining to her why she impressed you so much. Often, the appearance of a face was only a mask for her. How could you see her? You hardly knew her! Did she get to know herself better so she could understand who you were, and so provide you with a truer self-portrait? When the young woman gave a sad smile you knew that sometimes she thought like you. That

141

made you happy and her face became happy. She was almost a sister, an unknown woman with whom you shared the same soul. And you didn't dare ask her any questions, because your curiosity worried you, made you a little ashamed. What heart-break, if you'd found out that you seemed more different to her than she to you.

In fact, it's possible, from the depths of a mirror, to perceive ourselves in a quite other than normal light. And it's possible, as you had just found out, that such a misapprehension can have its own consequences. Take the angel that appeared to you and the confusion he found himself in, looking like the landlord, so much so that he had to hide his face. Individual existences and physical differences didn't help at all, given the fact that he and the landlord were a match-set, if not duplicates. The confusion arose because they were two aspects of the same person. The relationship between them, before a sundering both actual and incredible, was no different than what you had with this young woman. And out of this came your fear of being too curious, as well as your shame; since we do not know how to love ourselves we often search for ourselves.

In the everyday process of life, the physical and the spiritual unite like the colors of a rainbow melt together in the clear air. Just as a prism can separate the colors of the rainbow, a mirror, by means of a double vision, can divide the physical and the spiritual. The effects are, however, short-lived. The mirror sets the marvelous free, but itself remains behind. Under its own momentum, the marvelous forges ahead, while, little by little, the spiritual breaks away from the physical to finally become, under certain conditions, free-floating.

That's what happened to Mr. G. Pelletier. Just like you, just like everybody, he had looked in the mirror. There are mirrors all over the place and nobody worries about them, and then one day it so happens that, while looking at ourselves we begin to reflect and find ourselves caught between two reflections, one real, the other an illusion; and it just so happens that Papa Boss gets into the act, we get confused, we mix up the two reflections and can't tell them apart any more. What happened to Mr. G. Pelletier happens to us.

Looking in his mirror he saw himself as a landlord and, in fact, it was as a landlord that you saw him, a little later, from the kitchen window, down in the yard covered with dead leaves, carefully raking, in his landlord way. That's how he saw himself and that's how he stayed. From inside the mirror, however, his reflection saw him differently, saw him as an angel and not as a landlord. Soon this case of diplopia grew worse. It was no longer a question of bringing a double image into focus through a simple adjustment, but of differentiated doubles unable to re-enter each other, and so find their lost identity. Everything was set, waiting for the final touch, the complete split. It was Papa Boss who was waiting for this moment, to slip in behind the mirror.

He breathes on the reflection of Mr. G. Pelletier, the reflection becomes a ghost, and the ghost can talk. He says to Mr. G. Pelletier:

— Gérald, you're an angel.

And Mr. G. Pelletier heard what his ghost said to him. He had no time to lose, he had to turn his back to the mirror, it was his last chance to prevent that split between the physical and the spiritual, to outwit Papa Boss and keep his reflection. Otherwise, Papa Boss is going to lay hold of it and so add to his band of angels.

— Gérald, you're an angel.

The voice didn't make him jump. He knew it came from the mirror, from himself, though he had not opened his mouth. He was surprised, and a little flattered.

— Oh come on, an angel? That's impossible.

He looks at himself again and knows perfectly well that he's a landlord. Perhaps it's because he's so sure that he doesn't get excited. But the ghost has no doubt about what he sees. He sees an angel.

Far from turning away, Mr. G. Pelletier does not move, spellbound before the baleful mirror, which begins to vibrate. Lightning-quick, an imperceptible blade of light cuts across, slices, and the physical and the spiritual have been sundered. Mr. G. Pelletier, landlord, is exactly the same, he's certainly that. Meanwhile, on the other side of the mirror, the angel moves off into the distance. He will return as the angel from Papa Boss who appeared to you.

Mr. G. Pelletier, landlord, had a whole yard to rake. Now was the time for it. November already, and the leaves fallen from the poplars, some yellow, some brown, even a few still green. So he went to fetch his rake. Had he looked in his mirror once more, he would have seen no one.

13

The angel was waiting for you in the bathroom. You pretended not to see him, having come for the bidet, not for him. As you were washing away the pollution, a sentence from scriptures came to mind: 'An evil man is better than a tempting woman, for the woman covers the man with shame and reproach.' You wondered what the man covered the woman with. The angel said to you: 'Fear nothing, Madame.'

— Why should I be afraid of you? I knew you were there; I saw you when I came in.

— You have found grace with Papa Boss.

—That's not so hard with your Papa Boss. Even dogs do it.

— And, behold, thou shalt conceive in thy womb, Madame, and bring forth a son.

— A son who shall be called Jesus, right?

— You can name him whatever you want, Madame. To us, it is of no consequence. But he shall be great, that I can tell you for sure.

— He shall reign over the house of Jacob for ever, and of his Kingdom there shall be no end.

— One can be great a lot easier than that, Madame.

— Get out of here! Go on!

He made a deep bow and disappeared.

— Deformed child! A monster!

But, far from being indignant, little by little you calmed down. Your misgivings were about to take shape and you shut your eyes, to watch the beasts parade by, and it was at the serpent that you finally stopped. He mounted you by throwing his coils around your body and when he had reached your eyes you were entrapped: it was the handsome face of the gardener's son swaying in front of you. At that moment the angel reappeared. You said to him:

— I am the servant of your lord, Sir: let my fate be as you say.

The angel replied:

— Madame, your consent was not required. The most you could do was pray, and you did, and your prayer has been answered. It was for a great favor that you asked, an exception to the rule. By granting you that favor, Papa Boss wanted to reveal his omnipotence.

You didn't understand, and he continued:

— You were lacking your medical card. That card is indispensable: we need to key-punch it in the machine.

— Machine, Sir?

— Yes, Madame, the machine, amazing instrument of truth and hygiene, inspected each day by an engineer and architect; blessed by four pastors, three priests and two lay preachers; and sworn in by Judge Dorion.

— Isn't he the judge in the two-storey house and gable roof that I can see from my kitchen window?

— Yes, Madame, but he might be called Simonette, too, with the first names Frédi, Eric or Amédée, who knows? It doesn't matter, because he's a certified judge and his swearings-in carry all necessary Civil Code guarantees.

— Is that so?

— Yes, Madame. After all those precautions you can bet the machine is reliable.

— I believe it.

— Insert your medical card, the machine goes click, she goes clack, she goes biff-bam and gives you back your card with all conjunctions possible, the only authorized ones.

— Authorized for what, Sir?

— But Madame, why do we conjoin? You're overplaying this Annunciation! I'm an angel, after all! One conjoin, to joins and one joins for the purpose of profitable, scientific, sanctified and legal fornication, always keeping in mind genetical prognostication!

— But why are you telling me about this machine? I don't have a medical card.

— All the same, you have conceived.

— Without the machine?

—Through the omnipotence of Papa Boss. You are the exception, Madame, which doesn't mean that you can't profit from the machine-provided advantages. Genetical prognostication, there's the rub in this love business. The foretelling of mental retardation, congenital blindness, convulsions and certain other problems including delinquency. Thanks to genetical prognostication we can bring forth in the world consumers more talented at consumption and yet still good citizens. Do you have any idea what a social break-through that represents? And each day we improve. All we must do is eliminate glaucoma, retinal blastoma, microthalmia, neuro-ectodermic dysplasia, Huntington's chorea, albinism, Tay-Sachs disease, daltonism, mongolism, to list only a few afflictions, not counting the Chinese whose extermination cannot be far off. We proceed in various ways. The value of finger and palm prints has been emphasized by Dr. Uchida of the Winnipeg Children's hospital, one of the authorities in this field, who has for years been giving medical counsel by mail. It's useful to know the blood type ... Yours is, Madame?

— Unfortunately, I'm not sure.

— Well, it doesn't really matter: it's useful only for determining paternity. As for the sex of the child, that can be found by investigation of the Barr bodies. We have special techniques that reveal the chromosomal scale. Blood samples are taken from parents and grandparents, if possible, to discover mitoses with diminution, translocations, or trisomes. This method is especially recommended when the first-born suffers from Downs' syndrome. As for cleft palates, they correspond with the Dh trisome, yet are also seen in completely normal children. Empirically, if the parents are not affected, the risk is 0.4 percent, increasing to 2 percent if one of them is affected, and to 13 percent if both are. The same figures apply for other congenital defects. Malformations of the central nervous system, however, occur once in 200 births, according to our insurance companies. I mention insurance companies especially because in the Papa Boss Empire everything is interconnected: insurance and medicine, foot-races and rockets, atomic fall-out and day-care centres, finance and religion. So you see, Madame, Papa Boss represents a return to simplicity.

— I don't doubt it, I don't doubt it.

— And what a Godsend stillborn children are! Study of their chromosomes has contributed enormously to our knowledge of lethal genes. Exigetical examination of deletions, translocations and multiple autosomes opens the way, through congenital anomalies, to a new conception of life.

— And deformed children?

— Less interesting. The same with freaks. They can be improved by corrective surgery.

— And monsters, Sir?

— We are studying them, Madame. And we do what we can to keep them alive as long as possible, though they age with exceeding rapidity. No doubt the secret of their particularism resides in the sexual organs of their procreators. Recently, a number of allusions have been made in medicine to the age of the father; and in medicine, such allusions prepare the way for the scalpel. Circumcision at birth, castration at thirty. And after that? In the U.S. of A. they're already making prostheses.

— Already?

— Yes, Madame.

— I would have been one of the last women to ...

145

— Madame, I am able to hide nothing from you: in the implied ratio of ages, that is to say, 1 to 3 and 1 to 30, yes, you would have been the last.

You fell on your knees:

'My soul glorifies the Lord and my spirit thrills with the joy of Papa Boss because he has deigned to look down on my lowliness ...'

When you arose, the angel had no more wings, no scarf, no linen robe. He had given way to the landlord, Mr Gérald Pelletier, nude as a dew-worm, his rood upright.

— Ah, Gérard!

— No, he said: Gérald, Gérald, as in Géraldine. One for thirty. You had lowered the ratio from a third to a half, and you stood there transported; it was the Holy Spirit again, not just an ache in your pit. Two snakes climbed your body in spiral unison until they reached your eyes, your lips, two images of that same beloved face. Ah, God's mouth, what a kiss! Then two hands each placed themselves on one of your shoulders, and you were aware that the angel was before you once more, linen robe, wings, and all else. Had you made love with him?

Reading your thoughts, he nodded no with his head. So then you pouted: what was he, some kind of peeping tom? But his face was sad, his big nose sheepish. You took pity on him. After all, you had plenty of pity to go around. You had pity for his double, for his father-in-law, for his mother-in-law, for his fat wife, you had pity for the county of Kamouraska, the high parts and low parts, you had pity for the whole world.

— And your husband?

Your husband you had completely forgotten. In the circumstances ... and anyway, you can never think of everything! All the same, you would have preferred not forgetting, especially this one time when he had left you alone, asleep like a deaf man in the bedroom at the front, easy to get along with for once!

You smiled: forgotten? A little, a lot, but not entirely! Your pity had gone out to him too: wasn't he part of the whole world?

Translated by Ray Ellenwood

COMING OF AGE

Susan Musgrave

The pit at midnight
crusty with snow
like day-old bread pudding

and Giffey the outlaw
giving a sermon about sin

right down there
in a preacher's black gown

only his cock and his
cloven hoof peeping out a little.

The chalk pit where
Giffey would show us his stump.
We used to line up for him,
undaunted by his obscene gestures.

And show him *our* proud bodies.

All nine of us, nubile and
cheeky, dancing just out of his
reach

and old Giffey getting all creamy
and churned up
with each of us worrying and wriggling
like that.

We were so quick
we teased him until he came,
blasting off into the moonlight
for all the world to watch.

Then he would cry
and we thought he was crazy,
not daring to come close or
touch, not near enough for
comfort.

We were the peaty source of his
darkness, with our lies and our smiles
and stories about our lives.
For there were no blessings in our cold
eyes, only cruelty, and more of that for
our youth.

At night I would dream of
giving myself to him,
being drilled into the dirt,
cursing and carrying on like
old Giffey himself when his
wormy thing wouldn't get hard.

I saw myself kneeling below him,
opening myself before him,
lying open beneath him

tightening and tempting

until one night he never
came anymore.

We were haunted and stripped
naked at last, eager for
whatever unpleasantness he would
permit

anxious for all his ungainliness:

he never came.

Colder than ever in that chalk
pit tracing circles with our toes

we crept home finally to our
clean beds, long past the usual
hour, completed and alone.

THE CIRCUS

Tibor Déry

The children were bored. It was a stifling, hot, and dusty Sunday afternoon. The children's bare feet sank ankle-deep into the dust of the great courtyard enclosed by the flour mill to the left and the house on the right. Their eyebrows were grey with dust, and when they spat, dust grated in their teeth.

"What should we play now?" asked Manci. She was sitting on the porch steps staring at the dust in front of her. The other children hung lazily around her, standing first on one leg and then on the other; they were silent. Kalman, the watchmaker's son wiped dust off his glasses with a large walnut leaf.

The house belonged to them now. The chief miller had left for Pest; his wife had gone to the farm to visit grandmother who was gravely ill. The mill was at a standstill. A Sunday stillness hung over the street outside; not even barking dogs could be heard. Traffic had been suspended since noon when a Catholic priest had passed the house, bells of the altar-boys growing louder, then dying away in the dense village silence. If anyone went down the street, the cloud of dust balling up behind him as it drifted toward the board fence betrayed his presence no matter how noiselessly he ambled along. All along the street, houses were shuttered against the burning sun, which drove everyone indoors. Only the mill yard was full of children and dogs.

"What should we play?" asked Manci.

They were all alone in the house. They could tear it down, or, if they felt like it, burn it to the ground. There were nine or ten little children and older ones from the neighborhood, as well as Manci, the 14-year-old daughter of the chief miller and her twin brother Gyula. Until nightfall when their mother came home, nobody would know if they had axed every piece of furniture in the house or drowned every hen. But for the time being, they were sitting quietly, standing about in the dust eyeing each other.

"What should we play?" asked Manci. "Now we can play anything."

She had large grey eyes whose cold and sleepy stare flustered even some adults as she fixed them with her languidly searching gaze. Not even her mother had ever seen her cry, except from impotent rage. She bore every punishment in silence. But once when she was ten years old, at a taunt from her father, she had grabbed the kitchen knife on the table and with all her strength plunged it into the palm of her hand. The scar was visible to this day. This summer for the first time she sat alone in the yard underneath the mulberry tree and with her sleepy cold eyes she stared at the yard bathed in moonlight until her mother chased her off to bed.

"What should we play?"

149

The children were silent.

"We can play anything we want."

"Let's pretend we're having an Olympics," said Pista Deli, the son of the neighbor, a fairly prosperous peasant. A hot-blooded child with a short neck and red face, famous because he would soundly trounce even much older children if they dared look askance at his shortness. He had not yet tried his strength against Gyula, the chief miller's son who was the same age.

"Olympics?" said a girl's thin voice. "It's too hot."

"It'll be hot in Rome, too."

"No, let's not," said Dezso Trenka, the stonemason's son who lived next door "Besides, it's boring".

Pista Deli turned toward Manci sitting on the porch steps. She fixed her large, brooding, cold grey eyes on him, looked at him for a while, then shook her head.

"Let's play doctor," said another girl.

"That'll be all right. The patient will die."

"Then we'll bury him."

"Where?"

Again they looked at Manci. The young girl's ivory neck and reddish-brown hair were impervious to the sun. Her face had only a faint pinkish glow below her long, tightly combed hair. And young bespectacled Kalman, scrawny son of the local watchmaker, stood behind the girl, leaning on one of the porch columns and studying the downy nape of her neck in rapt absorption; then a minute later, turning pale, he tore his gaze from her. It was obvious, even from behind, that the girl had nixed the idea.

"Let's play grocer's," said someone.

"Let's play ball."

"Let's play Tarzan."

Manci said nothing "Let's play Tarzan," repeated a boy's voice. The young girl shook her head. "Today we can play anything," she said impatiently "even something special."

"Let's give the brood-hen a bath."

"Let's go up to the attic."

The children grew silent. They stared ahead blankly, downcast. Three spotted dogs were lying side by side in the shade of the mulberry tree. One scrambled to its feet, circled the others, then threw itself on its side, tongue lolling, and sighed.

Young Kalman with the glasses stepped down from the porch, taking a deep breath. "Let's start the mill," he said with lowered eyes. "If we get it started, we can grind 20 sacks full."

"What for?"

Kalman blushed and said nothing. The girl looked disdainfully at the silent children. "You're all stupid," she said quietly to the dust at her feet. "You can't find anything to do."

"Go to hell!" said Pista Deli. "Don't you tell us what to do!"

Manci got up, slowly and lazily stretched herself. She smiled and shrugged her shoulders. "Where are you going?" asked Piri Trenka, alarmed. "Wait! I'm coming with you."

"You don't have to," said Manci without turning around. Her legs, covered only to the knees by the short cotton cambric skirt, were girlishly round and as white as her arms and neck. "I'm going inside to read."

Although Busan, largest of the three dogs, was lying with his hindside to the porch, he raised his head and looked back. He pondered for a moment, then got up and, tail wagging, set off after the girl. At this moment, the sharp cracking of a whip was heard from the other end of the porch, short and hard like a gunshot. "You're staying here!" said Gyula, the head miller's son, and again he cracked his short-handled, leather-thonged whip. It was impossible to tell whether the command was meant for his sister or the dog. Both stopped. "You're idiots," said the boy, turning his pale face with the great blaze of red hair toward the children. "Idiots."

"Who's an idiot?" asked Pista Deli.

"You're one too."

The squat, short-necked child bowed his head; blood rushed to his forehead. "Why am I an idiot?" he said in a muffled voice.

"Ask your Papa," said Gyula, smiling disdainfully and squinting. He turned his long freckled face toward the sun. "Manci is right. If I weren't here, no one would know what to do."

"I know," said Pista Deli.

He turned and started for the gate. With his disproportionately wide back, short legs and arms, he seemed shorter than he really was. Gyula waited till he reached the gate. "Wait, idiot!" he shouted after him in his rather thin, rasping voice "I need you, come back!"

Pista Deli stopped, but did not turn around. The other children listened silently without moving. On the porch, Manci was also standing with her back to the group, only her head turned out of curiosity.

"Come back!" said Gyula. "I've found something to do." The circus game the gang was going to play for the first time required every hand, every head. The oppressive heat seemed to suddenly give way; unseen sweat poured down the high-spirited children's backs. Mozsi Beck, the poultry contractor's son, ran home with two companions to fetch empty chicken coops in which to put the menagerie. "Hey, bring your little brother too!" shouted Gyula. "Your youngest brother!"

"Why him?' said Mozsi Beck, "he still wets his pants."

"Just bring him!"

"What for?"

"He'll be the ape," said Gyula.

They had to get a handcart, at least two of them, to transport the menagerie. Dezso brought a little trap-like two-wheeled handcart from home; assistants had to help bring it over. Pista Deli stole rabbits from the courtyards, complete with pens whenever possible. If he couldn't find pens, he brought them naked under his coat; they were put in Beck's chicken coops. There were plenty of cats, dogs, even pigeons in the mill yard. But it wouldn't hurt to add one or two. The mill yard wearily on the verge of slumber a moment ago, in an eye-wink roused itself from dusty summer sleep and man and beast began to whirl around the leader, Gyula, like electrons. The initial excited shouting was succeeded by the tense

151

silence of creative work, broken only by the joyous yelping of dogs thrown into confusion and rushing about in every direction. Young Kalman leaned against the porch, and wiped his glasses.

"What did you bring from home?"

"Nothing," said Kalman.

In the village one seldom came across suitable raw materials for a circus in the household of the watchmaker's widow. Gyula, sinking his hands into his pants pockets, looked the thin, round-shouldered boy up and down scornfully.

"Go help Pista Deli!"

"No."

"Why not?"

"I don't want to," said Kalman.

Blinking, Gyula turned his long, freckled face toward the sun. "I can't hear you. Speak up!"

"I don't want to," repeated Kalman.

"You don't want to?" asked Gyula, incredulous in a sing-song. "You don't want to. What do you mean you don't want to? I don't understand. I said, go help Pista Deli."

He raised his whip and slashed it into the dust, exactly an inch from Kalman's naked toes. A tiny round cloud of dust rose suddenly in its wake. The boy with the glasses involuntarily stepped back.

"Stop jumping!" said Gyula. "What are you jumping for? I tell you, go help Pista Deli."

The boy with glasses, his face pale, stared at the tiny cloud of dust whirling at his feet.

"Well, what are you going to do?" asked Gyula and his face was still full of surprise.

"He can't go," said Manci, behind his back at this moment. "I need Kalman."

"What for?"

Rather than answer, the girl laughed softly. She had a clear, bell-like laugh. The thick crystal vase that her father had taken in the war from an Arrow-Cross member's house, a man who'd fled the country, rang with the sound of her laughter. Gyula looked at his sister and screwed up his face.

"You need him?"

"What of it?"

Gyula stood for a moment longer, then turned without a word and walked away.

"Are you coming?"

"I'm coming," said Kalman, his ears burning. The young girl had already turned around; she could not see the boy's enraptured look beneath his self-conscious glasses.

"Oh what a fine game it will be!"

"Yes," said Kalman. "What do you need me for?"

"Oh, they'll be delicious," shouted the girl. "We'll eat heaps of cold, sweet melons."

Kalman quickened his pace. "What do you need me for?"

The girl laughed. "For all kinds of things. Don't you want to come?"

"Yes."

"Then why do you ask?"

Suddenly she shot off. The dust her feet stirred rose toward her tiny waist like a long, light train. Reaching the porch, she turned and waited for the boy striding along slowly and manfully.

"Or don't you want to come?" she said, fixing her coldly pensive, sleepy gaze on the boy's face.

"Now what do we do?" asked the boy.

In the room darkened by the shuttered windows, Piri Trenka knelt in front of the bottom drawer of the large dresser and cautiously lifted the heavy cool sheets and eiderdown cases placed one on top of the other. The plank floor was covered with linoleum; two rows of preserve jars stood on the dresser top, half their contents dried up. The air was cool, musty and made one shiver with pleasure. Kalman had never been in this room before.

"Not there!" said Manci. "There's nothing there."

Even in the gloomy room it was apparent that his face was flushed with excitement. Piri Trenka's groping hands were shaking, her tousled black hair kept falling into her sweating forehead.

"I tell you, there's nothing there."

"Well, where then?"

"In the wardrobe. Maybe on the top drawer."

"Can I help?" asked Kalman, who had visibly drawn courage from Piri Trenka's presence "What should I look for?"

"As a matter of fact, I'm going to be a bride," said Manci, opening the wardrobe. "There's a bride in every circus; she rides a black horse and leads the procession. The groom follows her on horseback or on foot. Then come the animals and the clowns."

Kalman swallowed hard.

"What am I going to be?" he asked after a while.

"I don't know yet. Do you want to be a clown?"

"No," said Kalman firmly.

"You don't want to be the groom, do you?"

The girl laughed a thin laugh. Her eyes sparkled in the gloom. Piri Trenka giggled. "All right, we'll see," said Manci. "Now come here and take down Papa's linen suit. This will be Gyula's because the ringmaster always wears a white suit."

Kalman was allowed to stay in the room, but he had to face the wall while Manci changed. Among her mother's things, she could not find a white dress to serve as a wedding gown. She had to make do with a grey silk dress for which they dug up a little white lace collar from the top drawer of the dresser. Piri Trenka pinned the dress up all around because it was too long. While Kalman stared at the stains on the white-washed wall, the young girls were whispering ceaselessly behind his back. From time to time, a suppressed, titillating giggle would burst from the cloud of whispers, tickle his neck and make it break out into goose-bumps. The clomping of shoes could be heard on the linoleum. A pair of white stockings and old-fashioned high-heeled black leather pumps from the dresser turned up on the young girl's white feet, of course, after a thorough foot washing.

"Don't you turn around!" shrieked Piri Trenka.

"I won't," said Kalman standing stiffly beside the wall with burning red ears.

They ransacked the house for a bridal veil in vain; finally they had to make do with the dirty tulle curtain that Piri Trenka pinned with a few wire hairpins to Manci's reddish-brown curls. But when the bride in the grey silk dress, with the curtain on her head reaching to her waist and her loudly thumping patent-leather shoes slipping off her feet, finally marched onto the porch with shining eyes, there was such a hullaballoo raging in the mill yard that no one noticed her enchanting presence; even less Kalman's wide-brimmed black felt hat emblem of his rank as groom, which, though it was stuffed with straw, kept slipping over his ears.

Now fifteen or twenty children were rushing about in the yard beneath the burning sun, screaming at the top of their lungs, red faces shiny with sweat. Three handcarts stood in front of the rusty fly-wheel leaning against the wall of the mill. The two-wheeled street barrow which Dezso Trenka had surreptitiously sneaked out of his father's house was behind the carts. In the corner of the courtyard, where three or four old millstones were lying about in burnt-out yellow grass, chicken coops and wicker baskets and larger goose pens were piling up; with tireless zeal, Mozsi Beck and his pals had transported them from the poultry contractor's courtyard. Also, on the millstone slabs the other indispensable parapher-nalia of the circus were gathered together – ropes, chains, a box of red minium paint, a washbasin, cooking-pots and lids, wooden spoons, a sausage stuffer and a large brass trumpet glittering like gold that a mem-ber of the volunteer fire department band had, unbeknownst to him, donated to the circus.

Gyula, in his blindingly white linen suit, stood whip in hand on the well-curb and directed troop movements. A pair of dogs had already been harnessed to the handcarts and most of the members of the menagerie were in place. A large red cat was huddled in one of the cages bearing this sign: LION, BE CAREFUL: HE BITES! BEWARE OF LION!

Two large white rabbits posing as polar bears were lying on their stomachs in a small wicker basket, restlessly twitching their noses. There were plenty of birds of prey, eagles, vultures and falcons, exactly as many chickens, geese, ducks as the children could carry to the mill yard. A parrot was screeching in a frenzy of joy above the tiger. The most splendid specimen of the menagerie the anthropoid ape, was at that moment, being led by hand toward the ringmaster by Mozsi Beck when Manci, Kalman and Piri Trenka stepped onto the porch.

"Undress him!" said Gyula appraising the flawless superb specimen.

"But he's only wearing these drawers," said Mozsi Beck.

"Those too!"

Mozsi Beck looked ahead, frowning, a worried look on his face. "What are you going to do with him?"

"Nothing," said Gyula. "We'll lock him up in a cage and we'll put him on exhibit."

154

"That's not a good idea!"

Pista Deli laughed so hard he had to hold his sides. "Why isn't it a good idea?"

"He'll cry," said Mozsi Beck.

"So?"

"Why should my little brother be the ape?" said Mozsi Beck. "There's lots of little kids around here. I brought ten cages for the circus."

Gyula impatiently cracked his whip. "What are you haggling for! Everybody brings what they have. If you don't like it, you can go to hell."

Pista Deli guffawed with laughter. Even his neck turned red.

"What are you laughing at?" said Gyula. "It's not funny. Grab him and take off his clothes. We're going to put him in this cage."

They had left the largest wicker cage empty for the ape. Pista Deli jerked the little black pants off the child, then picked him up under the arms and lowered him into the cage through the narrow opening of the lid. All the *artistes* and other employees of the circus gathered around the cage; having heard news of the recent acquisition they yelled wildly and watched the spectacle. The ape stood up to his armpits in the cage, motionless, clutching the willow twigs of the lid, and mutely he ran his astonished, frightened eyes over the screaming crowd. His tiny, pale face was twisted with fright, but he did not cry.

"Oh! He won't fit," said Piri Trenka.

"Of course he'll fit! All he has to do is pull in his neck."

Manci arranged her bridal veil, which kept slipping onto her nose. With an unconscious, wan smile on her face, her eyes were shining.

"He won't fit if he sits down," said a boy's voice. "Only if he lies down curled up."

Kalman was standing behind Manci. "This should not be allowed," he said surprised and indignant.

The girl kept staring at the cage.

"Do you hear, Manci?"

"Be quiet," said the girl without turning around. "Be quiet!"

Pista Deli clutched the ape, still half-protruding from the cage, and pushed him down by the shoulders. "Sit down," he shouted in his ear as if he were deaf. "Squat down, don't you understand? Damn you, sit down!"

"Slap him!" yelled a voice from behind. "Then he'll sit down."

The excitement spread to the dogs. Busan began to howl, a long-drawn-out sound like a wolf. A smaller dog named Didujka who could not free himself from his harness emitted ear-splitting yelps and threw his body to and fro like an epileptic. The two dogs harnessed in front of the second cart also barked and growled in alarm. The eagles and vultures in the cage were gabbling mightily. The lion, its hair on end, stared out into the dust with round green eyes.

The sun had long passed its zenith by the time the procession got underway. Though inside the courtyard it had provided an edifying spectacle, it reached full splendor only when it could unfold its entire length on the street in thick clouds of dust. Andris Kiss the herald, led the way. His naked upper body had been smeared from neck to navel with dazzling red

155

minium paint. With the gleaming brass trumpet raised to his lips and his father's fireman's hat on his head, he looked like an archangel. On either side of him, a step or two behind, followed drummers who accompanied the trumpet air by beating rhythmically on pots hung around their necks. Meanwhile, they strained their throats carrying out their duties as town criers. At the sound of their voices, the gates opened and filled and along the length of the street, more and more children, as from a frayed string of pearls, twirled on both sides of the procession.

A few steps behind the herald, the ringmaster marched alone in his blindingly white suit, cracking his whip. He was wearing white lady's gloves and a woman's straw hat, an attached wide red silk ribbon hanging down to his shoulders. The bride followed him, also alone in the procession. Unfortunately, her sleek bay steed had gone lame so she had to wobble in the dust on foot. She stepped along with downcast eyes, befitting a bride, looking neither right nor left. Directly behind her, barely a few steps away, marched Kalman the bridegroom, his glasses glittering bravely under his huge black hat. Unfortunately, apart from his dignified bearing and triumphant look, no clear outward sign indicated his status as bridegroom.

Following the vanguard came vehicles, interspersed here and there with an *artiste* walking by himself. Here, the noise and dust were greatest. The dogs pulling vehicles were barking vociferously; birds of prey were crying and crowing; the personnel designated to care for the lion, tiger and polar bears were yelling at the top of their lungs. Heading the line was the little two-wheeled street barrow carrying Eszti Bodor, the fortune-teller, hanging onto the sides of the cart with both hands. She was dressed in a flour sack held together under her arms by a thick rope; her head was covered with a large black silk scarf. Four short assistants pushed the heavy cart.

"What's this?" asked the onlookers.

"This is Robinson, the world-famous fortune-teller," shouted the herald who marched beside the cart, waving a national flag above his head. "She tells fortunes night and day and she'll tell your fortune for only ten cents. A week ago she stated the score of the Hungarian-English game, six to three, and she prophesied the flood. This is Robinson, the world-famous fortune-teller."

The news of the circus far preceded its coming. Old women stood before the gates, shaking their heads disapprovingly and shutting smaller children up in the house. Older girls ran out into the street and, giggling, they watched the pack of children growing more and more enthusiastic marching down the middle of the road. "Of course, it's that chief miller's boy who put them up to it," said a woman, "That brat should be given a good lickin'."

"The girl's the villain," said another woman. "She's the one that stirs them up."

"That's the one!"

"She'll be a great whore someday, that one will!" said the first woman watching the girl in the white veil.

The head of the procession had already turned onto Rakoczi street when the sound of the bugle suddenly faded away. One wheel of the fortune-teller's cart turned into the ditch with a great thud and Pythia swayed back and forth in the cart. The geese shut up in the crates gaggled piteously as they cooked in the merciless sun.

"They should never have been left alone!"

"The head miller went up to Pest. I saw him at the station this morning. His wife went to the farm to see her desperately ill mother."

Behind the fortune-teller's cart marched Pista Deli. His chest was thrust out and he was swinging his torso stripped to the waist and flexing his arm muscles, showing them off as boxers do. Around his neck he wore a rusty well-chain that he could break in two with one yank. Unfortunately, the terrifying rattle of the chain was muffled by the howls of the caged wild beasts. Behind him in a separate cart pulled by two dogs, the greatest attraction of the circus approached, the anthropomorphic ape. Hiding his face in his arms, legs drawn up to his belly, the thin brown body lay motionless in the cage.

"Hey, Laci," shouted a country lad leaning on one of the gates. "What's in that cage?"

"An ape."

"What's its name?"

"Ape."

"But what's its real name?"

"It doesn't have a real name " said a little girl. The young fellow laughed. "Have you ever seen a cart push the horses?"

Standing in the middle of the street, the children looked at each other. As a matter of fact, the dogs were not really pulling the cart; on the contrary, to make the cart go at all they had to be pushed by their behinds. But this was so only in reality and reality doesn't count.

"These are good horses!" shouted Sanyi Brio, one of the cart pushers, pertly. "These are good pulling horses. I can barely hold the cart back so they don't run off with it."

The band marched next to the ape cage. Two children on both sides of the cage were using pot lids as crashing cymbals. Two more were carrying a large enamel washbasin on which a third child was drumming as hard as he could with a sausage stuffer, disregarding pieces of enamel flying around. Members of the band who were not so adept at music kept the rhythm by beating on pots and pans or trumpeting into funnels.

When a pack of gypsy children on one of the street corners attached themselves to the procession, the ringmaster beckoned to a drummer in front of him.

"Run back, Peter," he ordered him, "and tell the men to keep an eye on the gypsies or else they'll steal the eagles and vultures from the cages."

"What eagles?"

"Idiot!"

"Oh, I understand," said the drummer.

"I will whip anyone to a pulp who dares steal anything," said the ringmaster, turning his long freckled face and fiery red hair covered by a little straw hat. He glared severely at the messenger. "Then get back to your place immediately."

"I'm going," said the boy "Shouldn't we pass the hat?"

157

The ringmaster gave him a withering look. "Whoever dares to beg," he shouted in his thin, rasping, adolescent's voice, "will be expelled from the procession. And then I will whip him bloody" he added for greater emphasis while he pulled up his white pants with both hands since, in spite of the tight belt, they were continually slipping down to his bare feet. "Come on, move!"

Mozsi Beck marched beside the ape cage. Hangdog, he looked neither right nor left, his ears standing out from his head were burning red from shame. Beside him, one of the acrobats, who had taken a wide red velvet ribbon from the head miller's dresser and tied it around his neck as an emblem of his craft was uttering cries and turning cart wheels. A seven- or eight-year-old little girl whirled around her own axis until she got dizzy and laughing uproariously, fell headlong into the dust.

The more the troupe advanced, the more easily and enthusiastically it showed off feats and stunts before the wonderstruck audience lining the length of the street. It almost seemed as if the *artistes* were infected with genuine enthusiasm beyond professional skill, and now they were performing difficult and highly responsible work for the sake of the game, as it were, free of charge. When they'd set off, they had timidly sidestepped the council president's wagon and the trotting cow tied behind it. However, by the time they reached the school, they very nearly trampled Kalman Tapodi, the old cowherd of the Petofi Collective Farm who, unsuspecting and defenceless, rode his bicycle toward them down the middle of the road. A few men, pushing wheelbarrows on their way back to the threshing machine after Sunday rest, shook their heads as they drew over to the side of the road to avoid the procession which was growing by leaps and bounds, having absorbed half the village children.

Mozsi Beck, walking beside the ape cage, suddenly broke into a run and passing the strong man, the carriage of the fortune-teller, the Bridegroom and the Bride, ran up to the ringmaster.

"Gyula," he panted, "we have to take the child out of the cage."

"Address me as ringmaster."

Mozsi Beck's face twitched nervously.

"Don't you hear?"

"Ringmaster, sir," said Mozsi Beck. "We have to let the child out of the cage."

"I don't know what you're talking about. What child?"

"Well, the child."

"I don't hear you. Which child?" repeated the ringmaster.

"The ape," said Mozsi Beck, having pondered a while.

The ringmaster looked him up and down without saying a word. "How dare you step out of line!" he shouted, knitting his brows sternly. "Get out! Go back to your place, on the double."

In the heat of the discussion, both children had unconsciously slowed down and the bride and groom walking behind caught up with them. "What's the matter with you?" asked Manci.

"We have to let the child out of the cage," said Mozsi Beck. "Which child" asked Manci, fixing her lazily pensive eyes on the boy's face.

"The ape," pleaded Mozsi Beck.

"Why?"

"He's crying."

There was a silence for a moment.

"He's crying?" asked Manci.

"His whole body is shaking," said Mozsi Beck. "Even his legs are trembling."

The girl's large grey eyes immediately filled with tears. "Poor little ape," she said softly to herself. "I've never seen an ape cry."

"Get back to your place," said the ringmaster, lashing his whip in front of Mozsi Beck's feet. "If you don't take your place immediately "I'll hit you in the face. About face!"

The boy jumped back and raised his trembling hands protectively "That not an ape; he's a child," he said, deathly pale. "He must be taken out of the cage!"

"What did you say?" asked the ringmaster.

"That's not an ape," said the boy defiantly. "My little brother is not an ape."

Gyula raised his whip and struck Mozsi Beck. Calculating the blow, the leather thong whistled in front of the child's face and struck his naked neck. Mozsi Beck cried out in pain, helplessly clutching his naked neck. Again Gyula raised his whip. But before he could strike, Mozsi Beck turned and ran off crying loudly.

"Still, the child should be released!" said Kalman the Groom.

Meanwhile, the fortune-teller's cart and Pista Deli, the strong man walking behind her, caught up to the ringmaster's group. In front, the herald with his minium-red torso and golden archangel's trumpet also stopped and turned around, and the two drummers stopped drumming. The procession piled up.

"We must release the child!" said Kalman slowly, firmly, turning his pale bespectacled face toward the ringmaster. "A human being should not be shut up in a cage!"

The ringmaster was occupied with his pants; owing to the sudden movements they had slipped down again. Kalman looked at Manci standing beside him. The girl was smiling mysteriously.

"What are you interfering for?" said Gyula. "You all should have stayed in Auschwitz. Now, come on, everybody go back to your places. Let's go!"

Kalman shook his head. "No. First, release the child!"

"It's none of your business!" shouted the ringmaster, and snatching his whip from under his arm, he whirled it in a wide circle above his head. "Back to your place!"

"First, release the child!" said Kalman in a trembling voice. "I'm not going back until you let him out."

"You're not going?"

Unblinking, the two boys stared at each other. Gyula was taller by a head than the young bespectacled boy; his grey eyes were colder, his muscles more resolute. If it came to a fight, he could obviously make short work of his opponent. Kalman was deathly pale, his knees shaking. He looked at Manci. The young girl with her mysterious smile fixed her dreamy lazy eyes on his face.

159

"Manci?" said Kalman, swallowing hard. His mouth was full of dust, his back bathed in sweat. He looked at the young girl, who nodded imperceptibly.

"Release the child, Gyula!" said Kalman. "You must not lock a human being in a cage!"

All the children had gathered around the opponents. There was such a silence that even the last row could hear a little girl's excited whisper. Gyula glanced around at the silently waiting children. "Everyone back to their places!" he shouted, and smiling scornfully, he raised his whip. Those standing up front flinched and moved back. The circle widened, thinned out and began to disperse.

"What are you waiting for?" asked Gyula maliciously of the bespectacled boy standing before him. Suddenly he lashed his whip at Kalman's feet and the thick dust puffed up in a dense little cloud over Kalman's naked toes. Kalman looked around. The others were slinking away. Only Manci was still beside him, standing a few steps away. Obviously, the command didn't affect her. Pista Deli's broad, indifferent back was visible as he slowly ambled by the fortune-teller's cart.

"Release the child!" said Kalman, swallowing hard, his head lowered as though trying to protect his glasses from the raised whip. "I'm not leaving until you release him."

A wagon stopped unnoticed on the side of the road, directly beside them; the dust and the excitement had swallowed the rumbling wheels. A tall woman dressed in black was sitting in the back of the wagon on a plank.

"Gyula!" whispered Manci, covering her face with her hands. "It's Mama!"

The boy suddenly lowered his raised whip and turned around. Shoulders hunched, blinking in fright, he looked at the wagon enveloped in the dense cloud of dust. "Get on!" said the woman sitting on the wagon. Her eyes were red with weeping. She glanced quickly at the grey silk bridal gown, the white linen suit, then turned away without a word. The two children huddled around her feet in the straw and the wagon set off. None said a word. Instead of the high-laced shoes she'd been wearing when she left home, grandma's loose, comfortable slipper was flopping on their mother's aching, swollen foot. Manci stared at it for a while with wide eyes, then suddenly burst into tears.

"Did she die?" she asked sobbing.

She loved her grandmother even more than her parents. Gyula too grew pale; all his freckles stood out on his face. The wagon rumbled by the disintegrating circus procession leaving the monkey cage lingering behind, the sobbing ape sitting beside it in the dust; then, in a few moments, it turned into the mill yard.

Translated by Elizabeth Csicsery-Rónay

CARNAC

Guillevic

Sea on the edge of nothing
Mingling with nothing

To better perceive the sky,
The beaches, the rocks,

To better receive them.

*

Woman dressed in skin
Who moulds our hands,

Without the sea in your eyes,
Without that sea taste we seize in you,

You wouldn't overflow
The volume of rooms.

*

The sea, a nothingness
Which longs to be the sea

Which longs to lend itself
Terrestial attributes

And the drive she
Derives from the wind.

I played on the stone
My stares, my fingers

And mingling with the sea,
Riding out on the sea,
Returning by sea,

I believed in the answering stone.

They're not all in the sea,
On the shores of the sea,
Those rocks.

But those a long way away,
Straggling over the fields,

Have a more profound lassitude,
Near the edge of confession

*

Don't trust seaweed: the sea
Sought refuge there from itself,
Consistency and shape.

The unraveling there
Might ravel the sea.

*

Will we never play,
If only for an hour,
A few minutes,
Solemn ocean,

Without your preening
As if preoccupied elsewhere?

*

I'd like to like you more,
Unconfinable sea,

The pools you spread out
Into the salt marshes.

There I saw you asleep
Alongside other glooms.

*

Nearly the same at first
As the open sea,

From pool to pool
Your water thickens

And ends by nourishing
The kinds of green
We find in fountains.

*

There you are a-swarm
But at least I can see.

*

From your cleft
In the rocks of Por en Dro
Out into the open sea, the horizon,

I've tracked you upstream
All the way to the salt marshes

Where I didn't know whether to cry,
Possessing no more of you than these mounds of white salt.

*

Before you were there,
Clinging to the salt,

I saw you so often,
Confined to pools,

Return to the setting sun
The homage of calm waters.

*

But you know full well that we like you,
That those who've left you

Find you in the harvest,
Look for you in the grass,
Listen for you in the stone,
Unseizable.

*

You look at the sea
And search for eyes.

163

You look into eyes
And see the sea.

*

At Carnac, behind the sea,
Death touches us, exhaling
As far as the fig trees.

They stand in the air,
The dead bones.

The cemetery and the dolmens
Somehow soothing.

*

Ageless sea
With no wound to heal,
Without a belly, apparently.

Church of Carnac
Like a
Hollowed rock

Furnished
To banish fear.

*

There were poor houses
And poor people.
This couldn't be
A time
For the living.

The people dwelt there like menhirs,
They'd been there a long time.
They didn't go and stare at the sea,
They listened.

From the sea to the menhirs,
From the menhirs to the sea,

The same road, contrary winds,
And the sea wind
Full of fratricide.

*

Behind the menhirs
Yet another wind
On woods and fields

Earth with less sand,
Green and leaden

Perhaps it was
From here that the sea
Became an open eye.

It bears little resemblance
A whole body and its eye.

*

You represent something
In the notion of God,
Water no longer water,
Power deprived of hands, instruments,

Weight without function
For which time doesn't exist.

*

Often to occupy yourself
You come calling us
Towards the peace in your hollow.

*

To ponder your deeps
You look after them poorly
Or perhaps you encourage
Those monsters who penetrate
The place of our nightmares.

*

Be fair: if you weren't there
What would space
And the rocks be?

165

Your fear of not being
Makes you imitate the beasts
And your fear of missing
The movement of beasts,
Their alarm, their cries,
Makes you magnify them.
Sometimes you moan
Like nobody's business.

*

To the right, between the town
And the beach, there was a fountain
Perpetually
Rewinding time.

*

The girl who came
Would also be the sea,
The sea amidst the earth.

The day would be bountiful,
Space and us, accomplices.

We would learn
To not always part.

*

We would have power
And not use it.
We would be full
Of what we possessed.

*

A presence then, never too heavy,
With you surrounding us
Composing our world,

Since time limits itself
To the dimensions of what we possess.

She had a face
One of those faces
Open and closed on
The calm of the world.

In her eyes I shared
In the ocean depths, its struggle
Towards a tolerable light.
She had the smile of a seagull.
She encircles me.

In her clashed the dreams
Of low stone walls,
Potent herbs,
Sea shimmers,
Herds on the moors.

Around her a trembling
Like the lichen
On dolmens and menhirs.
She lived underneath,
Called me, leaned on
What we give to each other.
Our days fatal and gay.

So it follows death is dead
And I am living
So that death keeps
A distance from the shore,

Ocean, you ask yourself
Such questions.

Translated by John Montague

THE NIGHT THE RABBIT CHEWED MY HAIR OFF

Ruth Andrishak

My father once said that if I had as many pricks sticking out of me — as was stuck into me, I'd look like a porcupine. My father really knew how to hurt a guy.

Uncle Si is always happy — a fine old Indian. The first time I met him — I'd gone to his sugar shack (he called it) with his nephew — and he said and I'm your Uncle Si — and after that he was. I went to his place for years. I'd sit back in a chair — put my feet up on a case of beer, fire burning in the old cook stove, lots of time to fuel for the lamp, just a bitch smoking (string in a can of lard). The men would jig (chase the rabbit they called it — when just men dance), Uncle Si plays the fiddle fine and there'd always be another Indian or half breed that played a guitar or a fiddle too.

Uncle Si was married to a white woman and had about six kids. He was working on the C.N. branch in Elk Point, section foreman — when he started going deaf. He'd see his family's lips moving and figure they were talking about him — and at work the same thing would happen with the crew — or he wouldn't hear a train coming. Everyone thought he was going nuts and so did he — and he started drinking. In time he found out what was wrong and got a hearing aid but by then his wife had left him and the railroad demoted him to labour. When I met him I got him to go to the doctor because I knew of a new operation for certain kinds of deafness — and a few years before this operation would have worked but it was too late now.

Uncle Si always gives his money to his family and friends (and Indians have lots of each) so he's always broke. For two years he claimed a couple of sons as dependents when they were working — and the government charged him $1,800 in back taxes. He doesn't quite understand why because his sons were still dependent on him — they sure took his money — but he paid it back out of his $450 a month wage. He lives in St. Paul now in a $30 a month room and works and drinks for company at night. He'd like a permanent woman again. Uncle Si plays for dances on the reserve once in a while — you can tell when he has a dance to play for — you see him packing his T.V. down the street to the pawn shop to get his fiddle out of hock. Whenever I meet Uncle Si we go for a beer and the last time he was laughing like always and said he had T.B. and would be going to the sanitorium for at least a year. And the government could take care of him — about $1,800 worth anyway.

Judy was eighteen, beautiful, and not even pregnant. She went to school in Elk Point. One night last January her girl friend and her talked about what it would be like to be dead. They said who they would have for pall bearers, if they had a funeral. The next day Judy didn't go to school. She took a twenty-two and walked one half mile from home to the river, put the gun to her head and shot herself. About an hour later a man out ski-dooing thought he saw a jacket lying in the snow and found her. She lived another couple of days, but never regained consciousness, and died when they tried to take the bullet from her brain. My brother Brian was one of the boys she had told her friend she wanted for a pall bearer. He didn't even know her that well, but I guess she just figured he had a bit of a soul to understand her. Most of the town was as cold to her in death as that cold forty degree below clear day she went down in the snow with a steel barrel against her beautiful head.

Dirty Liz is a mess when she's drunk — and Dirty Liz is always drunk. In this great age of panti-hose and fortrel tops — she still wears a garter belt — so one stocking is twisted and full of snags and runs, and the other is undone and hanging over her worn shoe. Her see-through nylon blouse has beer and coffee stains and bits of food all over. And the front is smeared with the dirty paws of the local Elk Point alkies. You can see the raggy bra, one strap broken revealing a stringy, leathery breast. Hair is a mess of Toni-ed frizzed split ends. Black pores in her punched nose. Bad horsey teeth. Pidgeon-toed, and knock-kneed as hell. And though she's not tall or fat — her heavy bones belong to an ox. You look at her and think — there's an example of what people have in mind when they say morons should be sterilized. For what did her Ukranian peasant mother rut with to produce that miserable hunk of meat. Dirty Liz is one ugly broad.

Once after the bar closed — we were going to Uncle Si's — to finish the party. Tommy was kind of funny drunk, and picked up Dirty Liz to carry over the plank that was over the ditch on the path to Uncle Si's. It had rained for days, and it was muddy and black as hell, and you could hear the water roaring beneath the board — cold and wild from the north — for it was the middle of spring. Tommy got half way across the board before he slipped and dumped Dirty Liz into that ditch right out of sight. You couldn't see two feet ahead anyway. So — the men put down the beer they were carrying and we all ran along the ditch slipping and laughing in the mud till we found Dirty Liz and pulled her out. Uncle Si got the lamp lit and built a fire, and wrapped Diny Liz in a blanket and gave her a beer. And Dirty Liz got drunker, and we had a good time, and said it was lucky Dirty Liz had so much alcohol in her blood — it acted as an anti-freeze. A normal person would be sick.

And once Tommy went to see Bernie (Dirty Liz was living with him then) and he walked right into the middle of the kitchen with tons of mud on his boots. And then looked down and saw the floor was spotless, and was embarrassed because it showed that he didn't think that Dirty Liz could possibly have a clean floor.

Once Bernie and Pete (Bernie's one-armed brother) helped Cameron with the cattle. They had just got the steers into the new steel pole corral, and were sitting in the truck — drinking beer and congratulating themselves on putting out — when this one rangy black bugger jumped the fence and hit back over the prairie. Cameron hollered get that steer Dirty Liz and she downed that beer so smooth, and jumped out of the truck and hit the ground running. First she just kind of loped off behind the steer, and then she picked up speed and was flying. No shoes on — just those big bohunk slabs of flesh pounding the prairie — leaping over badger holes — going strong. The steer was heading north, so Dirty Liz angled north east to head it off, catching up with him till they were running side by side. And then the steer turned and she was right with it — herding it back — running for the sheer joy of running. As they neared the corral Dirty Liz threw her arm around the steer's neck, and they kept going till they crashed right into that new steel corral. And they both fell panting and foaming into the dust. Dirty Liz was still sitting next to the steer when Cameron and Bernie and Pete came up in the truck. They saw that the fence and the steer were O.K., and gave Dirty Liz a beer, and told her how good she could run. Must have learned how from running after tricks on Ninety-seventh Street. Cameron told the story every time he was in the Dewberry Bar for months after about how Dirty Liz ran that black bugger a couple of miles — just aflying over the prairie. And right back — smack dab into that new steel corral. Everybody always laughed.

Who were you Dirty Liz when you ran so fast with the hard-brittle prairie cutting into your flesh? Leaping, flying, running, did your soul try to run out of that ugly body, that only the meanest of Gods would condemn anyone with? Were you free at last from the hassel of the cat calls, dirty propositions for a drink of cheap wine, the memory of a child taken from you by the government, were you at last one with the land, sky and animals — did you belong? No wonder you drink Dirty Liz, and I'll try not to laugh anymore Dirty Liz.

The first time I saw Mrs. Dumont she was peeking around the corner of the door frame of their old log cabin. Mrs. Dumont had no teeth and her hooked nose looked like it was trying to get into her mouth. Her thick pale hair was dirty — looked like a rabbit had chewed it off. A too-short man's T-shirt revealed the outline of her saggy breast which rested on her gut. Half of this stuck out where her shirt ended and her plain brown cotton skirt started. She was barefoot and a couple of kids peered out from behind her legs, which they were holding on to. A bunch more stood back in the yard, some hers and some relations had dropped off, all bug-eyed at a stranger. Tommy, Jerry (his cousin) and I had all ridden up on our horses, and this is my mother said Tommy, and I realized why Tommy was no raving beauty.

Tommy's dad was Sam Dumont, a big good-looking half-breed with black curly hair and a Clark Gable mustache, a descendant of Gabriel Dumont, Louis Riel's friend. Everyone in Elk Point said he was good for nothing but breeding kids. One night he got drunk and stayed at Johnson's, just a few miles out of Elk Point. In the middle of the night he got up, fell through the hole in the upstairs floor to the main floor below (they had a ladder to use but I guess he forgot) and broke his neck. He lived about three weeks. I felt bad about it because Tommy took it hard, but my dad said the only good Indian was a dead one.

Mrs. Dumont moved to Elk Point and Mrs. McDonald, the school vice-principal, bought her some teeth. Mrs. Dumont went to normal school that summer, brushed up on her teaching and has taught in Elk Point the last ten years. A very good teacher, very liberal in her thinking and one of the few teachers that has a genuine liking for kids.

She is on the library board, church board, teaches Sunday school, helps with the Elk Point Bugle Band and heads the committee for Elk Point's annual Ati Yak Days — their annual small version of Edmonton's Klondike Days. Mrs. Dumont is well liked and respected, mom's best friend, and between them they practically run the town.

I use to have a beauty parlor in Elk Point and you know how women start talking when you work on their heads. I once had a woman tell me all about her affair with a doctor and ask what she should do about it. I've never seen her before or since. Anyway Mrs. Dumont and I were talking and she told me how her dad had brought his family from England to homestead by Frog Lake Reserve. They were fairly well to do in England, and her father was a big shot in the government there or here, I didn't quite remember. When she started going with Sam, her dad wanted to send her back to England until she got over him, but she wouldn't go, and married Sam. Then she spoke of when Sam broke his neck and they let her live in the hospital. She slept in a bed next to his, so that she could take care of him constantly. She would try to feed him and talk to him, and pray to him, and how he died. And she got a sad look and said I wish he'd never got hurt, my happiest time of my life was with him. Everyone thinks lucky Mrs. Dumont, that fine lady at last has teeth and is out of the bush. Most say the best thing that ever happened to her was when Sam fell through the floor and broke his neck.

Shorty is really a good person in his heart — he's about the best I know. He doesn't try to manipulate anyone — he's honest in his business dealings — with him a handshake is as good as a contract. He's smart — can fix any machine but figures reading books too much can be bad for you — no one reads much in that country. He doesn't like to see anyone abuse an animal and can live in the bush — he knows his fishing and hunting.

But farming went all to hell for him a few years ago and he started drinking bad — he said to sit there and listen to other people's problems — made his not seem so bad — but it was bad for us, because it got to be an everyday thing. One drunk lasted sixteen days when you live with a man like that — you count.

Once when I went to his brother's house for a pail of water — Shorty was drinking there and tried to pull me in the kitchen for a drink. I pushed him away and spilled his glass of whisky. He said after some went in his face and that made him mad. He grabbed me outside and kicked and hit me till he laid on the ground panting and said if he could get up he'd kill me. I looked at him and wanted to kick his head in but knew then he'd sure get up — so I went in the house. Later he came in and laid down on the couch and went to sleep and a couple of hours later he woke up and said

171

I suppose you're mad at me — and we went to the bar. The next day he joked to the boys about having to slap the old lady around but didn't hurt her none.

A couple of summers ago the crop looked good and he said if we pull this off we'll have her made and then it hailed three times — flooded and then the Bertha Army worms set in. He said God must of heard him and hated him.

We left in the fall to look for work with dishes, clothes, ski-doo, cat and sacks of vegetables piled in the panel truck. We went to Edmonton and Calgary — but it wasn't easy and I had to get the kid in school so went back to mom's. While travelling it turned cold and ruined all those damn vegetables — a lousy summer's work. I got a job styling hair in St. Paul — twenty-five miles away — and Shorty got work in Swan Hills.

Tommy Dumont was my friend, for a long time we rode that country as kids — and later we'd bomb around in his old car and drink beer with our friends on those long Saturday nights. He's been dead since January 26, 1965, so I don't think of him that much now. He was hurt on an oil rig up north and died a couple of days later. After I wrote to Jean and said in my young stupidity — Tommy is alive — as long as when I see something or do something and think of him and tell him about it — he's alive. So maybe for awhile he was — but finally the nothing little things of every day made me quit. Death is really hard to accept the first couple of times. I'd walk through the bush at night — sometimes I could hardly see ahead of me but I knew the country well. The wind would blow and I'd run — and it would blow faster and I'd run faster — searching for the Why — maybe through the next field or by the creek — down the train track over and over that prairie. I was the puppy who runs from one bush to the next — sniffing one scent then the other — working himself into a frenzy — running — back and forth forgetting what he was originally looking for. In time I forgot the question. Now I feel hard (tough) towards it — and yet accept it more without ever finding out why — maybe that's the answer — don't ask the question.

Tommy was a half-breed — my dad and brother said the only good Indian was a dead one and mom said it was too bad but I shouldn't hang around people like that anyway.

I was in Dewberry Bar the night the eighteen-year-olds could start coming in. Six kids came up from Vermilion — forty miles away — strangers. They sat there — trying to look like they'd always sat in bars — nervous a bit — but smiling and talking to each other. They must have felt a little big — sitting with the local cowboys and farmers — now they could see what it was going to be like to be grown-up. Maybe school tomorrow — but tonight they were men. But their hair was long over their ears. Everything was cool till one of them went to the can and on his way out — took down a funny little sign that hung over the door — looked at it, smiled and put it back. One of the Dewberry men said — nobody can touch that sign and hit the kid. Then more got up — taking on the other boys. These were tough — thirty- to forty-year-old men. The bar tender didn't break up the fight — just threw it outside. The kids tried to get to their car — but they had to fight all the way. The people that weren't fighting grabbed a glass of beer and went out to watch. There's a lot of fights there — but nobody tires of a good fight.

Everyone the next day said that was the most fun they had since before the Indians could come in the bar. In those days a half-breed with a bar card — showing he could buy beer legally would go in the bar and get it for his Indian buddies. Sometimes the white guys would chase them out of town, run them into the ditch, beat the hell out of them and take their beer and women. Now those were the good old days — but last night was fun too.

I met the McGrew boys — John, Patty and Mickey at Uncle Si's years back — they're what people have in mind when they say wild as an Irishman. They all play the fiddle and jig — and Mickey was so good — he represented Alberta in Canada's fiddle contest in Nova Scotia once. Patty is about forty-five and Mickey around thirty-eight now — they live with their parents on the farm. John, a little older, lives a few miles away on his farm — he at least got around to marrying which is probably unfortunate for all involved. They used to go with their old man and get in the bar and stay for days. And they only lived six miles away. But I guess the old lady was a real tyrant when they drank — so every night when the bar closed they figured they best not go home and anger ma in this shape — but would hit out first thing in the morning. And then first thing in the morning — they would decide — well just one little beer to steady the nerves and — they said by the time they got around to getting home ma was so glad to see somebody — they had outstayed her anger.

The old man is too old to booze now — so the boys go on their own. They've all been in so many crack-ups that if you drive with one of them in your car — you can't go over thirty — they are so paranoid. So when a bar closes they can't go home — might crash or the cops will get them — and in the morning they need one little drink to steady their nerves.

Shorty was on a tear with them last winter in St. Paul when he was supposed to be working in Swan Hills. After the third day he phoned me up at Elk Point — he knew I was coming up there to work so he said bring his underwear and his hard hat he'd forgotten and he'd go to work that night. It was forty-five degrees below that morning — a bright, frozen-solid day — no way my car would start. I was late so didn't bother finding a bag for his stuff — and took off for the highway half a mile away. I laughed at the picture I cut — trucking alone carrying a bright yellow hard hat and long johns. I went to Ollies garage and told them to ask for a ride for me — but it looked like nothing would be moving all morning. A few trucks came down the road — and I ran out and stuck out my thumb — but all I got was instant frostbite. Then a funny little French priest came sliding all over the road in his Volvo — coming from Frog Lake. He drove like God was with him and I was sure he was — on his side of the car. I figured if we slid into the ditch — I'd be totally wiped out but the priest and God would be fine — but we made it. I walked into the hotel and up the stairs where the McGrews peeked around the corner at the top of the stairway and giggled like leprechauns. Shorty was in a little room that the chambermaids keep their cleaning crap in — drinking beer with the two old chambermaids. One wouldn't go to bed with him because her husband was serving beer downstairs — and the other — I don't know — maybe her arthritis was acting up. I gave him his stuff and went to work and at noon I went back to his room and asked him to stop drinking — and then I just cried — and the McGrews grinned and squirmed in their chairs and Shorty winked at them. A few days later Shorty went back to work — he'd been there five days — the McGrews stayed ten. They were always afraid to drive.

I'd seen them everyday when Shorty was with them and a couple of nights I'd stayed. We'd sit in the bar — with other welfare alkies — smokey — dirty — smelly — a couple bullshitting — most arguing and someone sleeping with saliva running out the corner of his mouth. In the morning they'd all compare how sick they were — they have beer and a cigarette and wait for the vendors to open for a dollar bottle of wine. At noon they'd manage to get some soup down and sometimes it stayed. Around two they would start feeling good and the bullshit would start. The stories — the sayings each one had heard it all a hundred times — if one had dropped dead the other could have finished the story for him. Christ — I could have. By evening they had drunk themselves into a half-sober depression or were asleep. They never ever chase women — they weren't queer just scared of them. Nothing eventful would happen — the only thing they could talk about days later to their friends would be that they were on a ten day drunk in St. Paul — that's it.

A neighbour had stopped in to see the McGrew boys after they'd been gone from home five days — actually had stopped in to give them a drink — but saw the old lady needed help with the livestock and she's in her eighties. The pigs were eating the dead ones and starting on each other— the cattle were suffering — and a few late summer calves had died. I was glad to hear they went out of livestock this summer. Now if they'd get their mother a phone.

Saturday, June 26/65 — I kept thinking six months since Tommy had died — all that rainy day, the kind you just feel like sitting in the bar and losing your mind. I'd broken my collar bone when I rolled my car a couple of weeks ago — so wasn't working in the beauty parlor. Victor (Tommy's brother), Irvin, Marvin and I had a few beer and decided that night we'd get honked. I went home and soon after mom came in — all upset — she had seen a horrible accident on the highway half a mile south of Elk Point. Two cars head on — bodies on the road. Tough — but always happening somewhere — and then a little later I heard it was Marvin. He'd gotten in with a friend who'd had a few beer and can't handle one. We were with him once when he drank two lousy bottles — blacked out and hit a snow bank. Marvin should have remembered. This guy drove up the highway once — ninety miles an hour — went half a mile — turned back to town and then did it again. This can be one of the main thrills in a small town — to retards. The next time he hit the other car — killing the mother and

174

hurting the two small kids and father — Marvin was killed too. It was a long time ago — but I remember going to where it happened with Marvin's family. Telling his little brother and sister to stay in the car — but the little boy ran out on the highway and started hollering wow he'd found a doll that belonged to one of the hurt kids — all excited. And his stunned mother — who had been in the bar all afternoon — kept saying — someone told me Marvin was hurt. And Marvin's stepfather's tired sad eyes — knowing that this was just another incident to send his wife back to the mental hospital.

The night after the funeral I was sleeping in Marvin's bed with his sister, I heard Marvin calling my name. I opened my eyes and he was there — kneeling a couple of feet from the bed — outlined against the windows from the street light. I looked at him for a minute and then closed my eyes and said go away Marvin — I can't talk to you yet — I'm sorry but I'm scared. And his sister woke up and said I heard Marvin. Yes, I know I said, I know.

Three weeks later my brother was driving his friend and a couple of girls home from a dance and rolled his car down a hill — him and the two girls were O.K. but his friend was thrown through the back window and the car fell on him — killing him.

A couple of days later my brother said now I know what it's like and put his arms around me and cried — and I cried too — to see him hurt and I cried for his dead friend and mine.

I lived in a tent last year from May till September — when we came to Calgary. It seems funny now when I think about it — getting up — putting on warm clothes making a fire — eating breakfast — looking out over some lake — then into the tent — putting on my hot pants — jumping into the car and bombing away to work — some sixty miles away. Making like a hair stylist all day — then driving back — fishing for supper. I quit work at the end of June and Lance was out of school so he lived with us then — usually had his friend with him for company — and our german shepherd who hated to be out in the rain — and it rains a lot at the lakes — so the tent was fairly crowded at times. It was hard but it was good — the best summer I've had for a long time. It's the best part of going back now.

Everyone says marriage isn't easy — you have to keep working at it. But in time the broken promises — the lies to each other and especially yourself — the plans — dreams you had — falling away — exposing the hopelessness — the nothingness — it just seems too much to bother with. And yet you stay together — because to admit all of this — is to admit that what you thought you saw in the other person didn't exist. And it didn't really — one never really falls in love with another person as he is — but when attracted to someone — see into him all the qualities you want to see — and are blind to the other facts that don't go along with your ideals. You hold onto your dream person to love rather than admit he never was. Or maybe I'm just afraid to be alone with nothing — scared to go through all of this again. But I'm so tired of working at my marriage.

I was thirty — April third — Shorty had come down a few days before to permanently leave me again and then stuck around. That afternoon after school we took a mickey and went out to get willow bark for dying wool. We drank out in the bush and it was like being home — looking at those combined fields and willow bushes. And Shorty said we could never break up and he'd quit drinking so much and be better and we drank to that.

We went to bed early and sat and drank and talked till late. Shorty told me things about his life and I understood him again — he told about working day after day on the old tractor when he was a kid — until he'd be ready to fall off — and he'd cry because he was so tired. And finally he started a little ritual of getting off the tractor every day at lunch break and flipping a coin and asking God — was his life worth it — was there meaning to this — and heads God said yes — and tails — no — but he got enough yes's to go on with hope. And of fishing this winter — and wondering could we make it and asking God if I was his woman — and flipping a coin.

We talked of everything and then got onto the cruelties of man versus animals — I'm always for the animals — but he had good points and I wrote them down as he said it after— for example — wolves in a pack — take down more game than they can eat — so hamstring the hind quarters eating the animals alive — keeping the meat fresh — and how he's seen dogs do the same to pigs in a pen and then sit around laughing — because they're not hungry — just bloodthirsty — and how skunks and weasels get at chickens sucking their blood out — as they slowly die. I've seen this a lot too. But he was talking how one day him and Bernie Garner were walking home from school when they heard this squeak in the bush — a fuckin' garter snake had swallowed a frog he said — so — (and he pauses for a good swig of whisky here) so we promptly kill the snake and cut it open and the frog jumped out — hopped away — but it was poked full of holes and spouting blood where the teeth had cut its skin. (I thought this was funny.)

Maureen's birthday is the day before mine so the next day we were comparing them — she had champagne— I had whisky. She went out for dinner — I had a hamburger at Peter's. She got skiis — I got F-all. She got feeling quite high and there so did I. I don't know if her husband told her about snakes and frogs or not.

All the people from that country are basically good — but most have had hard lives — and their parents did — so a toughness is bred into them. It's the country harsh — you sweat and curse and pray to pull off that bumper crop and often as not — the heat gets it or it floods or it gets diseased or bugs and then the whole mess is snowed on and in the spring you fight like hell to get what's let off — so you can start all over. The women work the hardest — besides helping the men they have chores and big families and gardens.

They're a community bound by their everyday problems and don't say anything about one of them — they're pretty well all related somehow. Because of phones now if Ma Ewen's potatoes were frost bit last night or

176

one of Hein's heifers died giving birth to twins — everyone knows the next morning.

Some give up to booze — but that's a boozing country so it's accepted — but if you're too different in any other way — watch out and get out.

Yet — then again — they sure do some crazy things. Once in a while some farmer will get so mad while he's working that he'll shoot his combine or tractor full of buck-shot. Sometimes they shoot themselves or each other instead. And a few have taken gopher poison. Some Indians have died from drinking rubbing alcohol or hair spray. We go through a lot of people.

Sigamo's big sow had broken through the ice on the slough and couldn't get out. So Sigamo walked out on the ice to save her — he was just about to her when he broke through too. So he waded out to her — it was above his waist — must have been fairly cold. So by the time he got to her he was so mad — he held her under the water till she drowned. Sigamo goes through a lot of animals.

HEY — MY MAN

There are three people living in my body, and at times it gets a little crowded. Two argue all the time, and at times I just laugh — but at other times they just about drive me nuts, and I tell them to shut-up, especially if it's three in the morning, and I'm trying to sleep.

Those two have my body's life planned out — and if they don't wreck it by the time I'm thirty it will be amazing.

My body loves you — but it will never get free from them — they have its life planned out for the next hundred years. One part of your body loves me. How many people in you are holding it back?

When a hundred years are up — we'll have to let those two get together. Maybe that's the best.

My man wrote me a valentine note on a napkin. It was a good evening and I kept it, it meant a lot to me. I pressed it into a book of poems. Tonight I was reading the poems and the napkin fell out, folded so I didn't see the writing. I went to the can and used my napkin, then I saw the writing. I could have cried so I laughed.

Once I had a valentine note from my man, it really meant a lot to me.

Once I had my man — now that really meant a lot to me!

But I went to the can... no, I just have a hard time not wrecking things.

I'm home from school — tired and feeling so good. I'm lucky to be here — living in Calgary and going to school. A spirit must be looking after me. And I stretch and smile at the walls. Life is so easy now — just my brother and myself to take care of. So easy that I feel guilty. I look at my work on the walls — not great — but I know that in time it will be O.K. Such beautiful good days.

Today my man and I went to an automatic car wash. It was really scarey going through — water pouring at the windows and big rushing machines pushing from all sides. You couldn't see the other end. I hate it when I can't see the other end. I was really glad my man was with me. It was like the time my kid and I were at the fair, and we went through a House of Horrors in a dirty sticky little cart. It was ninety above outside, and about one hundred and thirty above inside. I crunched down in that cart as far as I could and closed my eyes and covered my head with my hands. Lance, my kid, kept hollering for me to look — but no way was I going to. And about one hundred hours later he said he could see daylight — the other end — so I took one peek. Today wasn't that bad. Scarey — but I kept my eyes open — and my man was with me — it's a beautiful day — but that sure was a bad nightmare last night.

A thousand men had walked into my body with heavy boots covered with filth and nails, ripping and tearing until only raw dead flesh was left.

I used to have waking nightmares that I was tied to a tree and snakes were crawling into me — and then that seemed kind and I no longer feared it because in reality it could be so much worse.

I heard of love so beautiful that no one could describe it. And I looked at their faces and hated them and thought — contented cows — what do you know — you are nothing for nothing makes you happy.

And then my man said — you're not ugly — Oh you're not ugly inside. And I looked up from my stumbling words and saw sincerity in his eyes. And he put love into my older-than-me womb — and I felt.

My man went north — I knew he'd go soon — so was prepared for missing him. I knew he had to go — he likes to be alone in the bush. He paints and reads and lives off the land. He's very self-contained and needs no one and can handle God real easy. I'm glad to be alone too — love makes you give too much.

He left me so many things — showed me bookstores and concerts and talked mainly — showing me you can talk and love and don't need booze — Kindness — just nice thoughtful kindness. I used to always pick up a book of poems in the bookstore and read it — and one day he bought it for me — the book always opened on this page
—catch and hold love
   sooner catch and hold the wind
   tightly in closed hands
   breaking definition.
Two young guys live in his house now — and at first I couldn't stand to go in it — it was so much like him and yet different — new smells — new thoughts — unseen peoples present.

Someday I'll go north — and I'll find my man again. It might be Shorty — but if it's not — I'll find my man.

Once my baby jack rabbit sat on my pillow all night and chewed my long hair off in enough patches that I had to cut the rest. I'd look stupid with three long strands hanging. Anyone else had done it — I'd have killed them — but you can't get that mad at a baby jack rabbit.

The moral of the story is don't drink beer before you go to bed with baby jack rabbits or anything else from that bush. Hair is not the only thing I lost. Hell — that was one of my better nights. He did leave eight rabbit turds on my pillow.

178

FAMILY ALBUM

Louis de Niverville

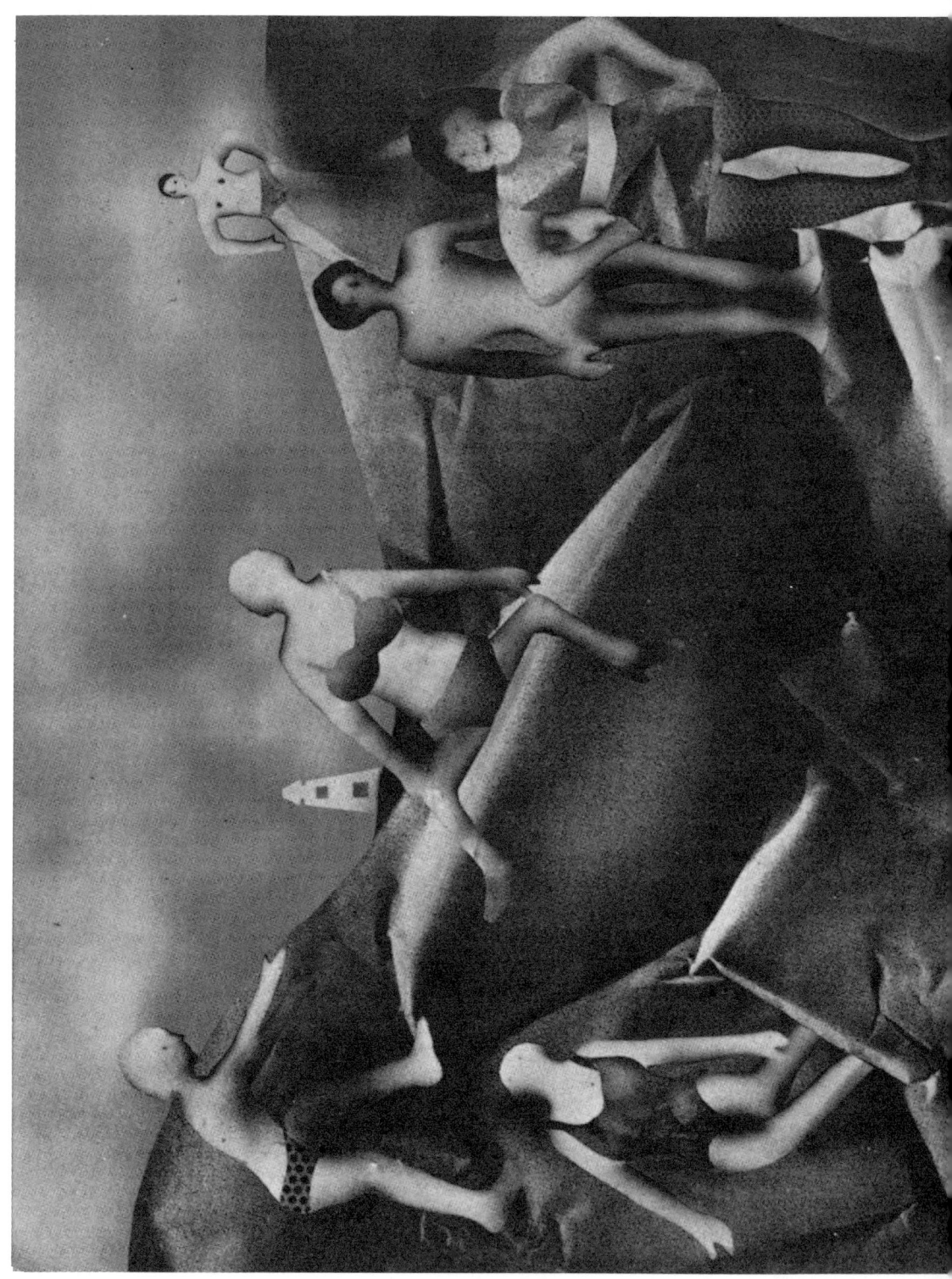

185

HUNTING LES ANGLAIS

Roch Carrier

There was a spattering of applause. Bottles rolled across the floor. Dorval opened another case. The Marchessault children threaded through adult legs, arguing over the bottles. Bottle-caps went flying. Dorval threw a bottle to the end of the hallway and you could see the shine of the Nigger's skin as he moved to catch it.

"Follow me," said Dorval.

His tone made it an order. He went to the window and his tenants gathered around him. One of La Marchessault's breasts was squashed against his shoulder. Barnabé kicked his children to get them closer to Dorval; Dupont-la-France said, "All the same, night-time in Montreal just isn't like night-time in Paris"; the Laterreur Brothers had an arm around each other's waist, very polite; Cowboy was quietly singing an obscene song into La Vieille's ear.

"Before you," said Dorval, "you have the skyscrapers. That's where capitalism lives. Listen."

Dupont-la-France shrugged his shoulders.

"Listen. Do you hear a voice?"

"No," they said, a bit disturbed.

"You don't hear a voice? But you follow all its orders like a bunch of goddamn slaves!"

They looked at each other, insulted.

"It's the voice of capitalism."

Doubt thickened the veil that alcohol had already drawn over their eyes.

He stretched out his arm and offered to the future the bottle he was holding, then brought it to his mouth. His gesture was copied unanimously. The beer gurgled down into gullets whose thirst would never be quenched.

"What language does it talk, the voice of capitalism?" asked Dorval.

"English."

"Baby American Jesus," Strangler suddenly remembered, his hand still holding Killer's. "We forgot all about our fight."

"We're all going with the Laterreur Brothers."

When they had all jumped into the old Packard it fell to its knees like an overburdened donkey. Cowboy, sitting on somebody's knees, tickled his guitar:

>   Un canadien errant
>   Tried eating an *Anglais*;
>   But then it made him sick
>   And gave him the diarr-ea-ay.

Dorval came hopping along with his cast and his crutch, trying to catch up with the others and get a hold on the Packard. He finally got onto the running-board. Everyone but the Nigger was piled inside like beans in a can, while Dupont-la-France clung to the car, holding onto his beret, and several of the Marchessault children shouted insults at everybody. Dorval twirled his crutch, shouting as they passed the buildings:

"*Maudits Anglais!*"

The bottles of beer that hadn't been emptied flew from mouth to mouth. The Laterreur Brothers weren't drinking. Suddenly pale, they were busy trying to revive the fire of violence within them in time for the fight.

"*Baptême!*" Dorval was amazed. "Even the beer we drink is English!"

But he didn't spit it out.

The Laterreur Brothers, blinded by the spotlights directed at the ring, couldn't see the assembled crowd, but they heard it breathing and moving and shouting all around them. Dorval's tenants shouted and waved to encourage them.

"Don't be afraid; we're with you!"

In the brouhaha Killer and Strangler could make out the shrill voice of Dupont-la-France.

"If they try to hurt ya bite the bastards!"

This in the harsh little voice of La Vielle. The Laterreur Brothers held back their smiles so as not to spoil their mean appearance. They weren't alone now in the centre of the rumbling swarming crowd. The MC grabbed the microphone.

"On my left, the honor of Québec, the ancestral genius of French-Canadian strength, weighing in at 597 pounds of solid muscle: the Laterreur Brothers!"

Applause.

"On my right, from Canada, weighing 609, the undisputed Canadian champions from one Atlantic to the other: the Gorgeous Glasscos."

A hail of insults, boos and threats reverberated through the arena to the ring.

The fate of the Québecois race was in the hands of the Laterreur Brothers. In their biceps 300 years of history trembled. And in their heads, Dorval's theory resounded with the rhythm of a crazy clock:

"*Résistance! Résistance!*"

At the referee's signal the Laterreur Brothers leaped, as one, onto the Gorgeous Glasscos. Blind and furious tanks. The Canadian combatants received them in their arms, carried them like babies to the ropes and let them drop to the floor of the arena: two bags of garbage. They no longer heard the voice of history. The fate of the Québecois race was lying in blood-red jerseys, fat hairy legs spread apart.

It was not until later that the Laterreur Brothers found enough strength to open their eyes. They had been taken away in the Packard. Marchessault was at the wheel, Hildegarde was sitting on Killer's lap, caressing Strangler's chest and Dorval was standing on the runningboard surrounded by humiliated children and shouting blasphemies:

"*Mes Christ! Mes Ciboires! Mes Baptême! Mes Vierge! Mes Jésus!* You won a battle but we're going to win the war"

The air slapped at his face and whistled past his ears; Dorval felt strong. If he had wanted to, he could have pushed back the wall of buildings that hid the sky from him. The Laterreur's defeat brought back the memory of a slap on his face, and his heart was far away, being trampled on in an unknown room somewhere by that whore Mignonne Fleury.

"Résistance!"

The Packard, parked in front of Dorval's house, emptied silently. The humiliated tenants were eager to get back to their flats. In the heavy silence, lights appeared at several windows.

"Look," said Dorval. "The city's standing up in its own shit. See the English capitalists' skyscrapers? They're coming down on us. We're gonna be buried. All us little guys are gonna be wiped out."

"We've got to resist," said La Vieille. "Nobody's gonna bury me till I'm nailed inside my coffin."

Killer Laterreur was holding Strangler's aching head. "In our contract with the Georgeous Glasscos it was written out specifically that we were supposed to win the fight."

"The Glasscos are *Anglais* and *Anglais* don't respect contracts," said Hildegarde.

"Go on and argue if you want," said Barnabé, "me, I'm going to study. Construction starts soon and when I finish my correspondence course I'll be a qualified man with a trade and a job and a salary. I'll be a *man*."

"At last!" Hildegarde sighed. "I'll be sleeping with a man that's got a job and a diploma."

"Dupont," Dorval ordered, "pass out the beer!"

He was applauded as loudly as the Laterreur Brothers before their fight.

"Tonight," he went on, "we were all humiliated along with the Laterreurs."

They nodded their heads in agreement, not yet daring to use words to record the true facts.

"But that insult is nothing compared with what's waiting for us. When the skyscrapers come down this far …"

Convinced that the moment was serious they pressed around Dorval, drinking in his words as avidly as his beer. He explained his new tactic: better attack than be attacked. So, attack. But who? He did not immediately name the enemy.

"Who? Spit out his name! Who?"

The chorus of tenants exclaimed:

"Les Anglais!"

The Nigger's door slammed. Dorval passed around more beer. Then he gave the signal for the attack:

"The hunt is on. You know how the government gives a bounty to wolf-hunters: they buy ears by the pair. Well, I personally will give a special bounty to any of you that brings me back a pair of *Anglais* ears and I'll give the women an extra little premium in kind!"

Hildegarde Marchessault chortled; Barnabé objected:

"My future is in studying."

"The future," Dorval interjected, "is being decided today."

Barnabé tore himself away from his book, Cowboy picked up his guitar and the Laterréur Brothers were already far away.

"Don't forget: one ear doesn't count. I want the whole pair."

They scattered in the night, sniffing out the paths that would lead them past some *Anglais.* They hurried towards the city, along streets and lanes where it would be easy to spot an *Anglais* among the mixture of cars and pedestrians, pull him into a dark corner and twist his ears, saying: "If I hurt you it's because your great-great-great-great-grandfather stole my country and I'm going to get it back one of these days."

It was so dark in their lane: Strangler Laterreur squeezed Killer's hand affectionately to give him courage. A pale light was seeping out of some heavily curtained windows. The Laterreur Brothers walked more slowly. Each door, darker than the night, was like a gulf plastered with threatening shadows. Someone was walking behind them. They heard no sound, not even breathing, only a silence that weighed against their backs as heavily as a stare. Killer pressed Strangler's hand. The ring had taught them the power of a ruse: they turned around abruptly, their big bears' paws ready to strike. A man was following them.

"Do you speak English?" Killer roared.

"Yes."

The man had whispered, his throat knotted with fear. The Laterreur Brothers came crashing down on him as they had not managed to do to the Canadian fighters in the ring. They crushed the little man to the ground under the weight of their triumphant bellies.

"It's easy," said Killer.

"We nabbed our *Anglais* already," said Strangler.

A muffled voice that seemed to come from below the pavement was squealing:

"Hang goong apoon floon na ni noon!"

"Mama!" Strangler exclaimed. "It's an *Anglais* from China!"

The street was suddenly alight. The Laterreur Brothers stood up.

"The police!"

They cleared out, pursed by a police car, its revolving red light whipping at the black wall. The little man hopped along behind them, waving a threatening fist.

"Hai anakoong alaloon shan tikoo han ban ting doon dong ding!"

In another lane La Vieille, ambushed in a recess in a wall, was waiting for her *Anglais.* It was one of those lanes where the kids won't tolerate a single unbroken street-light. La Vieille was anxious.

"No *Anglais* ain't coming to a dark corner like this one. It's a hole for French Canadians."

Standing close to the wall, La Vieille became shadow and silence. Far away in the night the city was snoring. La Vieille was on the lookout. Her heart was beating much too loud in her old breast and her old bones; it was beating as it had when she was a young girl and she could hear her fiancé's footsteps on the balcony. Someone all in black was coming through the night. His heels tapped feverishly against the road. He was already facing La Vieille, who stuck her head out of the shadow.

189

"Hey," she called out in French, "do you speak English?"

"Yes."

La Vieille took an excessively youthful leap and threw herself onto the passerby. Stammering a lament that was incomprehensible but almost caressing, the passerby, in an attempt to defend himself, lifted La Vieille's skirt, causing her to be raised up into the air and vigorously brought back to earth again. Suddenly she felt such a potent strength penetrating between her thighs that she spread her arms, proclaiming, *"Vive l'Angleterre!"* The passerby put her down on the road, moved around on top of her, groaned, shouted: "Confiteor Deo omnipotenti."

Suddenly, as though lacerated by a heavy whip, he exclaimed, "Deus, miserere nobis!"

La Vieille opened her eyes but she could not see the face that was breathing above her own; she thought that if all the *Anglais* were like this one she could spend the whole night hunting them.

"Are you a real *Anglais*?" she whispered.

The passerby pressed her breast and went away intoning, "Kyrie eleison!"

La Vieille wanted to call back her prey but she didn't speak English. She returned to her hiding-place.

"That was a real *Anglais*. He just talked English. He had nice English manners too. Gentle."

The passerby, a winged angel in his nocturnal joy, had flown away. La Vieille couldn't see him stop under a street-light to check the long row of buttons on his seminarian's soutane.

Dorval was limping along a street that he knew very well, toward a whorehouse he had never visited before. He went in and drank a beer.

"Jos, I got an urge to screw England. Have you got an *Anglaise*, a real one, built like a plum pudding?"

The barman made a telephone call in English.

"Number 28's expecting you."

Dorval picked up his crutch, climbed up the stairs and knocked at the door of number 28.

"Come in, my love."

He pushed the door open. Throwing out his chest, slinging his crutch over his shoulder and stiffening his legs he said:

"Good night, madam."

This *Anglaise* wouldn't escape his net. Of course he wouldn't bring a pair of ears back from his escapade but he would be able to tell how he'd sunk the Québécois tool that was starting to shine in his trousers into the body of an *Anglaise*; he would describe in loving detail how the beautiful *Anglaise* had writhed on the mattress, how she had been paralyzed by his caresses, how she had wept under his delicious torture, pleading in the agony of her pleasure but begging Dorval not to put an end to the punishment, imploring him to plunge deeper, more furiously, shouting that he took her breath away and begging him to put out the fire that was consuming her. Ah! how Dorval would tell the story of his hunt!

"Children, I'm going to tell you the story of a chase that's far from chaste, ha ha!"

190

Ah! this *maudite Anglaise* was going to learn something about Québécois domination.

"Get undressed," said the voice.

Dorval couldn't see anyone but he could hear garters snapping behind a screen. He moved forward.

"You give me twenty bucks before. If you want me completely naked it's twenty-five."

"*Baptême*, even in a whorehouse we get screwed by the *Anglaise!*"

At the same time his proud, well-tempered sword of honor was tearing a hole through his trousers. He reflected that it was always easier for French Canadians to give than to ask.

"If you want me completely naked it's free," Dorval.

"I don't like beggars in my bed."

Dorval threw twenty-five dollars onto the bed. The girl left her screen without looking at her customer. She picked up the bills, unfolded them, smoothed them out and put them into a bag that she then replaced under the mattress. Then she dropped onto the bed. Dorval shot forward like someone about to pillage Ali Baba's cave:

"Dorval!"

"Mignonne Fleury!"

She was standing on the bed, leaving the bedside lamp. Her nostrils were flaming like an angry dragon's. Dorval hid his sex with one hand; with the other he searched for his crutch, unable to stand up on just one leg.

"But I asked for an *Anglaise.*"

"Whoremonger! Rapist! Help!"

He moved the hand that was hiding his sex and, using his crutch, he walked towards Mignonne.

"Since you pass yourself off as an *Anglaise* I'll give you the little treatment I was saving for her."

He dropped the crutch and hurled himself at Mignonne, using his good foot.

"Goddammit woman – I love you."

The bedside lamp came crashing down on his head and the bulb smashed into electric crumbs that crackled around him in the total darkness. Dorval had grabbed a leg. His hand recognized the beginning of the calf.

"Mignonne Fleury, you're as cold as steel, but goddamn you I'm going to turn you into red-hot iron!"

"Help!"

Dorval realized that he was holding not one of Mignonne Fleury's legs but a bed-post. He groped around in the dark, found his crutch and ran to the window. He could no longer see Mignonne Fleury who had disappeared into the night as though it were the folds of a curtain.

"Mignonne Fleury, I love you! I love Mignonne Fleury!"

The night replied with a woman's laughter. He heard her footsteps tumbling down the fire-escape. Leaning on his crutch and furiously clenching his toes in their cast he ran down the stairs as though he were plunging into the void.

"Rape!"

191

Mignonne's steps resounded on the iron stairs, lower down.

"I love you!"

Suddenly he was stunned as though something hard had hit him: it was the beam of a searchlight. He remembered that he was naked, wearing nothing but the cast on his foot.

"I'm bare naked. Turn that off, goddammit!"

"Get down outta there or we'll bring you down by the balls!"

"Christ! When the whores don't want it the cops come running. What manners." *Monsieur le Curé.*

"No insults! We're the law."

At the end of the same lane, Hildegarde and Barnabé Marchessault heard the screaming of tires and sirens, but the police car didn't disturb their *Anglais*-hunt. They advanced slowly, he skinny, she waddling in her fat, both holding their breath, taking a hundred precautions as though the night had leaves and branches. Ahead of them there were voices speaking English. A man and a woman were holding each other so close that they made one round shadow in the night. The man said something and the woman burst out in a laugh that was not French-Canadian. Then their round shadow divided; the woman escaped, laughing, and the man, who was also laughing, went off on the other side of the street.

"My heart's dancing a jig; listen" said Hildegarde.

"Shut your trap if you want me to hear anything!"

Hildegarde took Barnabé's hand and pressed it against her heart, into the soft flesh of her enormous teat. He whispered, "Tease!"

"Impotent!"

Barnabé withdrew his hand.

"I'm attacking," said Hildegarde.

"Wait for your orders," said Barnabé in a voice like a general's. "We'll divide the catch: I take the woman, you take the man."

In the back pocket of his pants Barnabé was carrying, as he always did, the hammer that had been given to him along with a screwdriver as free accessories for his correspondence course. He held out the hammer to his wife.

"Take this. The *Anglais* have hard heads. Don't hit too hard or you'll bust the hammer."

They divided their forces. Hildegarde made her way among the heaped-up garbage cans and accumulated piles of rubbish. Barnabé wove among the cars in a parking lot. A lighted window here and there prevented the darkness from being total. Wings were quivering in Hildegarde's back. This game of hunting *Anglais* was the funniest thing – as funny as ... Hildegarde didn't want to think about that when she was hunting. What a man, that Dorval, who had invented the *Anglais*-hunt! Hit an *Anglais*! Her pleasure reeked of sacrilege.

Barnabé picked up a stray brick. Obviously he wouldn't bring the ears of the *Anglaise* back to Dorval. Dorval always went too far. He'd just bring him a trophy from the hunt: her underpants or her brassiere.

Sitting astride the fence Barnabé scrutinized the night with its spots of light. The *Anglaise* was coming. He jumped off the fence, ran to hide under a staircase and waited, stuck against the wall.

Hildegarde walked close to the wall, trying to make herself invisible in the night. She could distinguish the dark shape of the *Anglais* just a few steps away from her.

Barnabé was clinging to the wall, invisible. He was so close to the *Anglaise*. His hair was standing on end.

"Do you speak English?" he asked, grasping his brick firmly.

The *Anglaise* raised her arm very high and Barnabé was struck by a hammer. He fell down at Hildegarde's feet. She got to her knees to contemplate her prey. Just as she recognized Barnabé a weakened hand, armed with a brick, split open her forehead.

The *Anglais* couple, walking along the street, found Hildegarde and Barnabé Marchessault moaning, their faces all bloody.

"Help! Help!" cried the *Anglaise*, in tears.

Three streets away there was a neon sign with just a few letters illuminated, but connoisseurs could tell that they designated the Taverne Alberta. Dupont-la-France had always expressed profound disgust for these smoky rooms where the drinkers always made the same grunting noises, whether they were talking, laughing or belching. English sounds brushed past his ears. His search for game had led him to the Taverne Alberta: he stood in the doorway listening, then went in, analysed the battle sites and went to a corner where the people were speaking English.

"Bring me a glass of draft," he ordered, "very cold and not too strong. And no head, please."

"Son of a bitch, it's a Frenchman. Boys! We got a goddamn Frog here," announced Giguère the proprietor.

"It's my turn," said the waiter, bring Dupont two drafts.

"Guys, let's drink to the honor of France!"

Dupont raised his glass, drank a mouthful with a grimace and put the glass back on the table, but the others were still drinking. To conform with the folkways of the country, Dupont swallowed another mouthful. The others were still drinking. Finally he managed to drain his glass like everyone else.

"Please stand drinks all around," said a big man who seemed to be talking in his sleep.

Several glasses were raised in Dupont's honor, and so as not to look effeminate, he drained his in one gulp.

"Hey you, big guy, if you're with RCA Victor you can buy a round; I'm with the CNR so I can buy one too." He switched to English. "I am able to pay for as much beer as you can. Okay? Understand?"

Glasses piled up on Dupont-la-France's table and he felt obliged to drink them in order not to be discourteous. He was even polite.

"I've travelled all over Europe and I've never tasted such good beer. It's the champagne of beers."

"You're too fucking polite; you can't be a real Frenchman."

"I've been French as far back as our ancestors the Gauls who drank beer like pigs!"

Dupont was dizzy. He felt as though he were looking at his companions from the top of the Eiffel Tower.

"I went to France," said one of the drinkers, in English. All his teeth were gold and he was missing an arm. "I know France very well. I went with the Army. To the Queen, salute!"

Beer glasses were raised high in the air. Only a few separatist arms stayed on the table. Dupont, because he was an immigrant, had to outdo the others. He presented two arms and two glasses to the Queen.

"What the hell are you doing here in Canada?" asked Giguère the proprietor.

Dupont was as full of beer as a barrel. Opening his mouth to reply he had the impression that the beer was running out.

"I came to hunt. Bang bang! You know."

"A hunter!"

Dupont drank again.

"What are you hunting for?" In English.

"*Anglais*. English. I am hunting *Anglais*, you know. I collect their ears. English ears, you know?"

"You goddamn Frenchman, get out. And don't ever stick your nose in my tavern again," said Giguère.

"Get out of here!" in English.

"*Maudit Français*, don't go stirring up trouble here in our free country."

Several hands seized Dupont-la-France and threw him outside. The shock of his landing on the sidewalk burst the barrel of beer and he urinated in torn trousers. Dupont was still; he was sleeping like a child in the gentle warmth of his bed France.

Meanwhile Cowboy was sitting on the doorstep of the Toronto Dominion Bank, grumbling at Dorval's childish game. From time to time, to punctuate the sentiments he was expressing, he would pluck a string on his guitar.

"The *Anglais* have never stopped me from singing (do mi sol do). It's true what Dorval says though, they own the skyscrapers (do). It's true their skyscrapers come all the way down the hill and they're gonna crush us (la si re). But at least they're airconditioned (do si fa si fa). It's better than the stink of dead rats in the wall (do). The *Anglais* never stopped a French Canadian from singing what he wanted (do). Because they don't understand a goddamn word!

> I sing to kill time
> That I got on my hands.
> And when I see an *Anglais*
> I sing; Go to hell
> *Maudit Anglais*."

Cowboy was abstaining from the Anglais-hunt and his decision was irrevocable. He got up and slung his guitar over his shoulder. The soundbox struck against the glass door. The strings quivered. Had he broken their guitar? He examined it. Nothing. It hadn't been hurt and the glass door was intact, but the burglar alarm had gone off.

That was why some policemen took him to Station 10-12, to the common bird-cage where he found Dorval and all his tenants, even La Vieille who, after she had been raped by a seminarian she thought was English because he spoke Latin, had gone to give thanks to God for her great joy. But she had been unable to leave the church without taking as a souvenir the lily at the feet of the Virgin.

Everyone knew Mignonne Fleury. The policemen greeted her respectfully. She was the first to be invited to leave the common cell. Dorval watched her parade down a corridor where greetings came pouring out the open doorways. Her bottom, quivering under her tight dress, shimmered like sunlight in this cellar where the city stowed away its rejects. Dorval began a harangue.

"There's no justice in this goddamn capitalist country. I'm telling you a woman's behind is stronger than the truth. That's what makes the law. That's what determines the course of justice."

"Shut your trap. We're trying to sleep."

"We don't give a shit about you and your behinds!"

In the morning the cage door was opened but the hunters of *Anglais* ears did not leave. They were detained, interrogated, not given any food. They had been caught in the act of terrorism, but no one had found any weapons or subversive literature or explosives on them.

"We were just having fun," Dorval pleaded.

"The Revolution," said one of the inspectors who was sucking on a candy for his digestive problems, "is not a game."

"We just wanted a laugh, *Monsieur la police.*"

"You wanted to cut off ears for a laugh?"

"Yes, Monsieur la police. Me, I say a free country is a country where you can laugh."

"Cutting ears off poor harmless *Anglais* that already have enough trouble trying to understand our language – you call that funny?"

"The *Anglais* capitalists take our houses and our land. Taking their ears, it's the least we can do, *Monsieur la police.*"

"And what about order and harmony and national unity?"

"If order means that little kids have to get down on their hands and knees and kiss capitalist asses, me, I say let's have disorder! Vive la Révolution!"

"Don't try to intimidate the Enquirer, you big son of a bitch. You're in a free country, okay, big guy, but you're still in jail! Terrorist, earstealer, raper of innocent girls, insulter of the law!"

"Don't try to intimidate the prisoner, *Monsieur la police.*"

During these difficult moments of human incomprehension Dorval told himself that wars could indeed break out between different peoples if brothers who spoke the same language couldn't manage to understand each other. One thing gave him some comfort, though: the thought of the little garden he and his tenants had worked and planted together. Sometimes he felt so attached to his garden that he wanted to stay in jail for days so that when he came out he could see the green plants sticking out of the newly alive earth.

The enquiry lasted for three days, at the end of which the patriotic ear-hunters were set free. They piled triumphantly into a taxi and when they were near their house they noticed a fleet of bulldozers levelling their garden.

Translated by Sheila Fischman

195

THREE POEMS

Breyten Breytenbach

Dung-Beetle

Anyone here ever seen a white beetle?

Neither have I

But it's a terrible creature
Like a missionary in Africa
with helmet and dark glasses

White beetles live in bright rooms: camouflage
Scampering lumps of sunlight on the wall
Up,
Beware the white beetle with its sting its poison flask

Keep your eye peeled, do be sure
to look carefully under your bed at night

Not With The Pen But With The Machine-Gun

What should I tell you John-Jesus of Nazareth
I white African featherless fowl
I never naked
how should I lay my barren land upon your mind
you who have also foretold your trail
in whose sake the crucified toll in the winds of hills
worse: in whose name those of the night
are webbed in the spittle of the spider's arse
I'm talking of course of order and civilization?

Should I tell of
hospital beds where experiments are performed on children
every season the wheat is reaped anew
pale cadavers sucking at the black heart in the agony of death
red poppies swaying on the slopes
the individual blue with talking splinted in every mirror
the summer honey tastes of lavender
a black man withdraws into the bitterness of his own hut
the body of the cicada is green
cicadas don't know about the black man

the white man knows only the sun
knows nothing of black or of man
what would the black man know of cicadas
and what should I tell the black man of you?

Of humility Manjohn of Nazareth
of what humility
except that I shall never really know
neither be allowed to say again
that this cup must be taken from me
the humility
not to disown but to despise
not to betray but to destroy
to write in white on white
King of the Jews and the Kaffirs the Baboons?

Will I, then, humbly, Jesusjohn Man of Nazareth
inherit this fertile carcass of the world
I white African featherless fowl
I never exposed or bare
I as black as an unuttered word
of coming and becoming

Untitled

The following poem was written immediately after the poet had been sentenced to 9 years imprisonment on 26th November, 1975, and just before he was led off to the cells

May the trees remain green
and the stars white
and may there always be men
able to look one another in the eye
without shame
for life is as long as a single breath
and the stars of that Other Place
are dark

Translated by André Brink

AN EXCERPT FROM
A LESSON FROM ALOES

Athol Fugard

Characters

Piet Bezuidenhout   An Afrikaner, in his mid-forties.

Gladys   His wife, the same age.

Steve Daniels   His friend, a Colored man, the same age.

The action of the play moves between two areas representing the backyard and the bedroom of a small house in Algoa park, Port Elizabeth.

ACT ONE

Scene One

(The backyard. It is cluttered with a collection of Aloes in a variety of tins of all shapes and sizes. There is a gate with a nameboard: Xanadu.
Piet, seated at a garden table with an Aloe in front of him, is studying a small field-book on the plants. He is wearing short trousers, no shirt, and sandals without socks. Spectacles.
Gladys, behind sunglasses, sits very still on a garden bench.
Time: late afternoon)

Piet
(Reading from the book) "... small, glaucous leaves, erect or incurved ... " *(studies the specimen in front of him then back to the book)* "Tuberculate-based ..." *(turns to the glossary at the back of the book)* Tuberculate ... "Having knobby or warty excrescences." *(back to the entry he was reading)* "Tuberculate-based soft prickles on both surfaces." *(He holds the book at arm's length for a comparison between the illustration and his plant. He shakes his head)* No. That's not it. *(The book is closed, the spectacles come off. He gets up quietly, the Aloe in his hands, and looks at Gladys)*

Gladys
(Without moving) I'm awake.

Piet
Well my dear, we have a stranger in our midst. Aloe Anonymous! Because that is what it is until I know its name. I've been through my book twice, page by page, but there is nothing that looks quite like it. I don't think I can

allow myself to believe I've discovered a new species. That would be something! I'd name it after you my dear. Hail Aloe Gladysiensis! Sounds rather good doesn't it. *(The other Aloes)* Hail Ferox! And you Aristata ... Arborescence ... Ciliaris ... all hail! Members of the most noble order of Eastern Cape Aloes. An impressive array of names isn't it. And knowing them is important. It makes me feel that little bit more at home in my world. And yet, as little Juliet once said: What's in a name? That which we call a rose by any other name would smell as sweet. *(These lines, and all his other quotations, although delivered with a heavy Afrikaans accent, are said with a sincere appreciation of the words involved. He thinks about those he has just quoted)* Alas, it's not as simple as that, is it. Or what do you think?

Gladys
Are you talking to me?

Piet
Who else?

Gladys
The aloes ... or yourself. I'm never sure these days.

Piet
Names are more than just labels. *(He sits beside her on the bench)* Petrus Jacobus Bezuidenhout. *(A little smile)* So, would Petrus, were he not Petrus called, retain that dear perfection which he owes without that title?

Gladys
What are you talking about?

Piet
The balcony scene. Where the little lady laments Romeo's name. I was just thinking about mine, trying to hear it as others do.

Gladys
And?

Piet
Nothing ... except that when other men say Piet Bezuidenhout it is me they are talking about. Yes! That is what's in a name. My face, my story in mine as much as theirs is in Romeo and Juliet. 'Then deny thy father and refuse thy name.' Hell! I don't know about those Italians but that's a hard one for an Afrikaner. No. For better of for worse I will remain positively identified as Petrus Jacobus Bezuidenhout, species: Afrikaner, habitat: Algoa Park, Port Elizabeth ... and accept the consequences. *(He looks at his wrist watch)*

Gladys
What is the time now?

Piet
Just on four o'clock.

Gladys
It's passing very slowly isn't it.

Piet
Yes it is. The sun is as lazy as us this afternoon.

Gladys
(*Shaking her head*) It's because we're waiting.

Piet
Let me get you something to read.

Gladys
I'm alright.

Piet
I've got today's paper inside.

Gladys
Stop fussing, Peter. I've learnt how to sit and wait. When must we expect them?

Piet
I didn't fix a definite time. I just said: Supper. So what do you think? Half-past six? Seven? They won't be too late because of the children. If we start to get ready at five we should be alright. Everything under control in the kitchen?

Gladys
Yes.

Piet
Then relax my dear. Enjoy the sunshine.

Gladys
I'm perfectly relaxed.

Piet
Good.

Gladys
You're the one who can't keep still.

Piet
(*At the garden table where we first saw him*) Just tidying up my mess.

Gladys

I hope I'm not getting too much sun.

Piet

No danger of that on an autumn afternoon. This is the start of our gentle time Gladys ... our season of mists and mellow fruitfulness, close bosom friend of the maturing sun. On the farm there was almost a sense of the veld sighing with relief when autumn finally set in. We certainly did. Man and animal. Months of grace while we waited for the first rains.

Gladys

My skin can't take it. I learnt that lesson when I was a little girl.

Piet

Sunburn.

Gladys

Yes. A holiday somewhere with my mother and father. On the very first day I picked up too much sun on the beach and that was the end of it. My mother dabbed me all over with calomille lotion to sooth the pain. I can remember looking at myself in the mirror ... a frightened little white ghost. Mommy was terrified that I was going to end up with a brown skin. But she needn't have worried. It all peeled away and there I was the same as before.

Piet

The voortrekker women had the same problem. That's where the old white bonnet comes from. Protection.

Gladys

I think it was Cape Town. Not that it made any difference where I was. All I remember of the outside world was standing at a window and watching the dogs in the street go berserk when the dirtboys came to empty the bins. Heavens! What a terrible commotion that was. A big grey lorry with its mountain of rubbish, the blackmen banging on its side and shouting, the dogs going for them savagely ... *(Breaking out of her reverie)* I think I need my sunhat.

Piet

Don't move *(To the backdoor)* Where is it?

Gladys

In the bedroom. *(Piet exits into the house – the bedroom – and returns a few seconds later with the sunhat)*

Piet

Here you are. *(Gladys watches him)* Anything wrong?

Gladys
Did I put away my diary?

Piet
I didn't notice. (*After a moment's hesitation Gladys exits abruptly into the house – the bedroom. She unlocks a dressing table drawer and takes out her personal diary. She looks around the room and then hides it under the mattress on the bed. She steadies herself and returns to Piet*)

Gladys
Safe and sound.

Piet
I'll never interfere with it my dear.

Gladys
I know that!

Piet
So, where was I? Yes, our nameless friend. (*The unidentified Aloe*) I'll have to wait for it to flower. That makes identification much easier. And it will! It's got no choice. I've put it in a tin, so it needs me now. A little neglect on my side and it will be into a drought as fearsome as anything out there in the veld. If plants had feelings this would be as bad as keeping animals in cages. It's the roots that upset me. Even with all my care and attention they are still going to crawl around inside this little tin and tie themselves into knots looking for the space creation intended for them.

Gladys
(*Obviously not listening to him*) And you are quite certain they're bringing the children.

Piet
Yes. I very definitely made it an invitation to the whole family. It's high time we saw our godson again. Children grow fast at his age. And little Lucille should be quite the young lady by now.

Gladys
How many of them are there again?

Piet
Steve and Mavis, the three girls, little Pietertjie and then the two of us. Eight all told. It will be quite a party. Have we got enough to feed the hungry hordes?

Gladys
(*Betraying a nervousness*) More than enough. That's not going to be the problem.

Piet

Then what is? *(Gladys doesn't answer)* They're not strangers Gladys. It's Steve and his family.

Gladys

It's a big family.

Piet

We've had them all here before and you coped splendidly.

Gladys

That was some time ago. I'm out of practice remember. I know what's going to happen. You and Steven will end up in a corner talking politics all night and I'll be left with the rest of them trying to make polite conversation. I can't even remember their names, Peter!

Piet

Mavis, Lucille, Charmaine ...

Gladys

And then that little boy ...!

Piet

Yes I know. Little Pietertjie can get a bit boisterous at times, but don't worry my dear. Steven knows how to handle him. You must admit the girls are well behaved. You always admired their manners remember. Please and thank you and speak when you're spoken to. Please relax my dear. You won't have any trouble.

Gladys

Well ... you can't deny we are going to be crowded.

Piet

Yes I do. Observe. *(Placing two tables in front of the garden bench)* The Festive Board! *(Positioning chairs. He works hard at trying to allay Gladys' anxieties)* The Lord and Lady of the Manor ... our two honored guests ... and then in descending order of age ... Lucille, Charmaine, Beryl and Little Pietertjie. *(Gladys studies the seating arrangement in silence)* Does that look crowded?

Gladys

No.

Piet

Then what's the matter?

Gladys

You've got the little boy next to me.

Piet

Because Steve is sitting there and I thought … Alright, alright! We'll change it around. Pietertjie here and then Beryl, Charmaine and Lucille next to you. How's that?

Gladys

Thank you. It's not that I don't like children …

Piet

Say no more my dear. I understand. *(Surveys the table)* We mustn't forget your brass candlesticks. That was an inspired thought. Al fresco and candlelight. It's going to look very good. Continental!

Gladys

Don't expect too much from me. I can only manage cold meats and salads.

Piet

Have we got a little pudding?

Gladys

Yes. Jelly and custard. I've tried my best Peter!

Piet

I know that my dear. I was just thinking of the children.

Gladys

If you want the menu it's assorted cold meats … ham, brawn and polony … three salads … potato mayonnaise …

Piet

What could be better? A cold buffet! It's going to be a warm evening. I must remember to chill the wine. *(Looks at his wristwatch)*

Gladys

(Anxiously) Is it time?

Piet

No, not yet.

Gladys

How much longer?

Piet

Let's try to forget it my dear and enjoy what's left of the afternoon. That's why it's passing slowly. We're flattering time with too much attention.

Gladys

You can't exactly blame us. They'll be our first visitors since I've been back. *(She waits for Piet to respond. He doesn't)* You do realize that don't you?

204

Piet

Yes, now that you mention it. All the more reason for a celebration.

Gladys

I won't have any trouble finding something to write in my diary tonight. "At last! Other people! Just when it was beginning to feel as if Peter and I were the last two left in the world, Steven and his family came to supper."

Piet

(*Back with his unidentified Aloe*) So … What I'll do is make some notes and go to the library and sit down with Gilbert Westacott Reynolds. 'The Aloes of South Africa.' A formidable prospect! Five hundred and sixteen big pages of small print … and that is not counting General Smuts' Foreword. A lifetime's work so that ignoramusses like myself can point to an Aloe and say its name. And make no mistake about it … I want to. So … let us attempt a sketch. What is that makes knowing them so important?

Gladys

Aloes?

Piet

No, their names. Just names in general, yours, mine … anything! There's a lot of mystery in them isn't there.

Gladys

Peter and Gladys Bezuidenhout, 27 Kraaibos Street, Algoa Park. It sounds very ordinary to me.

Piet

Because it's your own. Familiarity has bred contempt. I can remember very clearly how when we first met, 'Gladys Adams' was a name to conjure with.

Gladys

Oh come Peter!

Piet

It's the truth my dear. How did you feel about mine?

Gladys

I liked it. Very much. It was certainly much longer than anything I'd hoped for. I thought it had a strong earthy sound …

Piet

Yes, it has got that. Bezuidenhout! Origin: Dutch. The first one arrived in 1695.

Gladys

But to be quite frank I wasn't sure that Gladys went with it.

Piet

Really? Gladys Bezuidenhout. Sounds alright to me.

Gladys

Familiarity has bred contempt Peter.

Piet

Touché! But it goes even deeper than that. What's the first thing we give a child when it's born? A name. Or when strangers meet, what is the first thing they do? Exchange names. According to the Bible that was the very first thing Adam did in Eden. He named his world. "And whatsoever Adam called every living creature, that was the name thereof." No. There is no rest for me until I've identified this.

Gladys

Can I see it? *(He passes her the Aloe)*

Piet

(His field book) This is the nearest I could get to it. Aloe Humilis. But it's not right, is it.

Gladys

They all look alike to me. Thorns and fat fleshy leaves.

Piet

Of course. The distinguishing characteristics of the genus, the family being Liliacae. Protection against grazing animals and the storage of moisture during periods of drought. But what species! There's the rub.

Gladys

Do any of them have any scent?

Piet

No. That they don't have. But the old people used to make a purgative from the bitter juice of the leaves. And they are mentioned in the Bible.

Gladys

Really Peter! That doesn't help them. Purgatives and the Bible! It only makes it worse.

Piet

How do you mean?

Gladys

Well they're not very pretty plants you know. Is there a good word for something you can't and don't want to touch? That would describe them.

Piet

A rose has also got its thorns.

Gladys

There's no comparison! They've got a lovely scent, they're pretty to look at and so many beautiful colors. But these ... *(She pushes the aloe away)* No thank you.

Piet

(Looking around at his collection) This is not fair to them. An Aloe isn't seen to its best advantage in a jam tin in a little backyard. They need space. The open veld with purple mountains in the distance. This one ... Arboresence ... I think it is possibly my favorite ... we had one on the farm growing around a goat kraal. Eight, ten foot high and so thick a chicken couldn't push its way through. You should have seen that when it was flowering. A veritable forest of scarlet spikes with the little suikerbekkies ... honey birds ... sucking up the nectar. Or even old Ferox, with all its thorns! A hillside covered with them in bloom!
"Damp clods with corn may thank the showers
But when the desert boulder flowers
No common buds unfold.
A glory, such as from scant seed
The thirsty rocks suffice to breed
Out of the rainless glare."
Roy Campbell. He understood them. And remember it's a defiant glory. Gladys. That veld is a hard world. They and the thorn trees were just about the only things still alive in it when I finally packed up the old truck and left the farm. Four years of drought but they were flowering once again. I'm ashamed to say it but I resented them for that. It's a small soul that resents a flower, but I suppose mine was when I drove away and saw them there in the veld, surviving where I had failed.

Gladys

Is that the price of survival in this country? Thorns and bitterness.

Piet

For the Aloe it is. Maybe there's some sort of lesson for us there.

Gladys

What do you mean?

Piet

We need survival mechanisms as well.

Gladys

Speak for yourself Peter. I'm a human being not a ... prickly pear.
(Piet stares at her appalled) What's the matter?

Piet

The prickly pear isn't an Aloe, Gladys.

Gladys

Please Peter …!

Piet

It's not even indigenous my dear. The jointed cactus is a declared weed.

Gladys

This conversation is upsetting me Peter.

Piet

Sorry my dear. What have I said?

Gladys

We've already had droughts, prickly pears and despair. I suppose we'll be into politics next and the blackman's misery. I'm not exaggerating Peter. That is what a converation with you has become … a catalogue of South African disasters. And you never stop! You seem to have a perverse need to dwell on what is cruel and ugly about this country. Is there nothing gentle in your world?

Piet

Is it really as bad as that?

Gladys

Yes it is. And don't make me feel guilty for saying it. *(The Aloes)* Look at them! Is that what you hope for? To be like one of them. That's not the only possibility in life you know. If that's what your expectations have shrunk to it's your business, but God has not planted me in a jam tin. He might have cursed you Afrikaners but not the whole human race. I want to live my life, not just survive it. I know I'm in this backyard with them but *that* is not going to happen to me.

Piet

I … *(Helpless gesture)* … what can I say? I'm sorry you don't like them.

Gladys

Don't like them! It's worse than that Peter. *(He looks at her)* I'm going to be very honest with you. They frighten me. Yes. Thorns and bitterness? I'm afraid there's more than that to them. They're turgid with violence, like everything else in this country. And they're trying to pass it on to me.

Piet

(Carefully) What do you mean my dear?

Gladys

Don't worry. I won't let it happen. I won't! *(Pause)*

Piet

(Trying to break the mood) Well … *(Looks at his wristwatch)* Time to get ready. They'll be here soon.

Gladys

(Fear) Who?

Piet

Steve and Mavis. *(Pause)*

Gladys

Yes of course. *(Hands to her face)* I think I have picked up too much sun you know. I feel quite flushed. I wonder if we've got any calomille lotion. *(She exits into the house leaving Piet alone)*

SOWETO AND HILLBROW

David Goldblatt

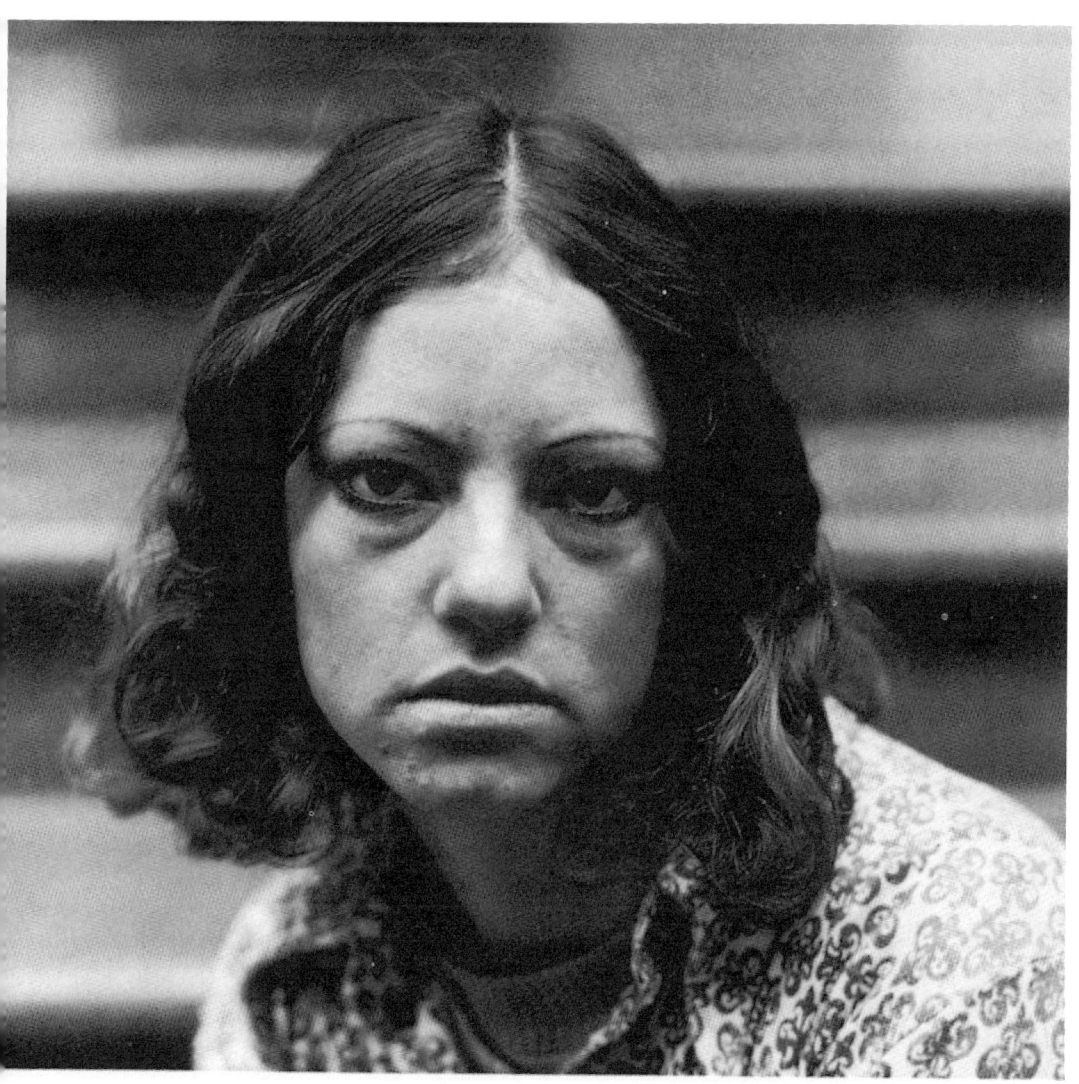

AN EXCERPT FROM
THE ART OF THE SELF
ESSAYS À PROPOS *STEPS*

Jerzy Kosinski

... If sin is any act which prevents the self from functioning freely, the greatest sources of sin are those formerly protective agencies like society and religion. The original sense of "creative" becomes completely reversed; now the only possible creative act, the independent act of choice and self-enhancement, seems to be the destructive act — as in Sade. In *Crime and Punishment* Raskolnikov kills for the sake of independence, and in contemporary literature Genet's criminality exemplifies the doctrine. Perversion, defined as any act or practice or viewpoint which subverts procreation in the physical sense, is esteemed as a gesture of freedom, in that it negates the creative-procreative impulse. In perversion, the negation of "the creative" becomes literal — an acting out of a more fundamental negation; an example of this is the murder which Caligula attempts when faced with the knowledge that "men die and they are not happy" (Camus, *Caligula*). In this, murder is the ultimate negation, for it genuinely devolves a thing from a human being.

When one can accept the unchanging definitive statement "men die and they are not happy," the indifference of the universe is inescapable. Man dies because the human condition both wills it and allows it. The definitive act of defiance and of superiority over the human condition is to defeat Nature with her own weapon, is to bring about death at will (truly, one's *last will*).

For the protagonist of *Steps* suicide is an act of the present. In performing it a man chooses to escape from his future and from his past, thus overcoming the knowledge that he will die.

By suicide, he takes over a natural function. To die in nature's time is to accede to a denial of man's dignity: to die in one's own time is to affirm that dignity. Man has the power to choose — it is his comfort in the face of the predictable.

In committing suicide, the man makes himself historical (that is, people can and must preface their statements about him with "he was"). He is transferring the burden of his past onto the shoulders of the world, onto history.

But even in self-destruction, his shadow outlives him. He imposes on other people the necessity for remembering and for judging him, for summarizing him as a character. He creates the means to outlive himself.

218

Sade's vision is theatrical because he reduces the other person to his most basic characteristics. He shows only those facets which advance his own intended action. Sade *behaves in scenes*, each with its own specific result. The other person, then, becomes a function of his purpose. Automatically, the other person is the stage onto which Sade projects a form of his past. In this way he acts out the self, obtains a kind of purgation derived from the scene which does not last beyond the scene's physical duration. Thus Sade must act again and again — without lasting satisfaction, without the true recognition of having discarded the forms of his past. In forcing history to summarize him in a word, he has obliterated his self, but has marked his survivors with chosen forms of his past, with his particular shadow.

For the protagonist of *Steps* memories carry no emotions: they exist as incidents, as concise dramas. He does not remember (*i.e.* experience) his past emotion or pain. He can recall his response to a specific incident in the past — a movement of the mind, a physical reaction — but he cannot re-experience the pain or the emotion proper which produced this response.

For the protagonist of *Steps* emotions have no memories: they exist only in the present. When he reads emotion into memory, he is acting in the present, spontaneously filling in the structures of the drama with feeling (this is similar to what one does when engrossed in a play or in music). Thus he is revisiting the present.

A speculative aside: memories have no emotions, and emotions have no memories. Perhaps that is why the Nazis were compelled to create emotive memories in order to hold the German people within the strictures of the past and make spontaneous present action impossible. Their purpose was to create a crippled group past and maintain it in an almost frozen state.

A direct way to achieve such a situation was to create an emotionally recalled enemy. Such an enemy had to be easily identifiable — and have certain stereotyped characteristics — thus heightening the emotions. In purging an "unhealthy" mass element, a nation was really attempting to purge the unhealthy (the unacceptable) in itself. This selected group served as a screen on which one could project one's own individually crippled past. This was acting out a sheer transference.

Does a man's commission of a crime take for granted his commitment of himself to it? Or is guilt a choice after the fact? Does a time come when a man judges himself? What makes a man guilty in his own eyes?

Do the Germans feel guilt? Have they ever chosen to admit to themselves the crimes they committed? The Nazi actions, unlike Meursault's killing of the Arab in *L'Etranger*, were not totally gratuitous: they were planned and carried out, premeditated in the extreme. The case of the Nazis accepting the crime is not merely that of accepting the black humor of an indifferent universe. Bending to the will of a totally gratuitous circumstance is not the same as choosing guilt. If the Germans as a nation accept a communal guilt, they do not necessarily as individuals accept a personal one. Communal guilt still leaves the individual innocent.

Deliberately to choose as a victim an individual or a group with a definable past to eliminate spontaneity from murder, surpasses in its impersonality even ritual killing, since it is devoid of emotion. Rational murder is the ultimate anti-theatre. Theatre implies *agon*, a struggle between two forces; it is essentially two-sided because it depicts the struggle within an intimate relationship. Massacre, then, is also ultimate anti-theatre; the holocaust (one-sided horror) is contrary to the ultimate theatre, to truly emotional killing.

Whereas ritual murder at least implies the superiority of the murderer — the priority of the persecutor over the persecuted — mass murder on the scale of the holocaust dissolves this distinction in the bureaucracy. Bureaucracy entails levels of routine, duties to be performed, patterns which preclude passion. Hannah Arendt's term, "the banality of evil," is apt; mass acting out is usually devoid of drama.

When the boy in *Steps* kills the children, he is performing a drama at the level of a relationship with a stranger. He selects only those facets of the individual which suit his action. Thus the victims are never personalities but characters, pure attributes. They are the means to an end, and (as the boy perceives them) they carry that end in themselves. They are children of certain parents — indispensable to him because they can be killed and because their deaths will produce the desired effect on both the killer and the parents. They are simply the instruments of revenge, not intimately enough involved with the boy to make their murder a crime of passion. They serve a specific purpose, however; the crime defines them lucidly enough to make their deaths take on the character of ritual murder.

Perhaps these murders satisfy the murderer's sense of self and gain for him an increased solidity, a temporary freedom, a previously unreachable equality, and at the same time an absolute superiority. These are rituals of drama, just as Sade's erotic situations are ritual acts and dramas. The boundaries between acting and acting out are obliterated.

Shakespeare's works can be cited. Iago's actions upon Othello, although they seem simple compared with the complex murder they provoke, make him an equal of the Moor, and ultimately his superior. His actions force Othello to bear Iago's forms of the past so completely that the Moor identifies himself with Iago. Iago has estranged himself from the relationship; he has projected himself so wholly upon the Moor that, although the play in the early stages is about Iago, the later stages are about Othello, who has adopted Iago's *persona*.

Murder is an act of intimacy, a potent bond between killer and victim, in which the killer — at the moment of the act — acknowledges the victim's capitulation and thus his own superiority. In literal murder, as well as in the symbolic killing of the other in an intimate relationship, the act of murder is an act of total commitment, and the very instant the deed is done, the murderer acknowledges his withdrawal in the purest sense.

In the symbiotic relationship subject and object are mutually dependent and sadistic-masochistic roles are interchanged. *Commedia Erudite* treated the master-servant relation as comic, introducing the clever servant who leads his master by the nose and directs the machinations of the intrigue. The *Commedia dell'Arte* carries this inversion further, making Harlequin the hero while Pantaleone, the master, is cast as the fool. In Elizabethan and French neo-classic drama the servant or the parasite drains and subjects the master. Today, the basis of horror is often the theft of the self, the fear of having one's identity overshadowed. This is most frightening when the thief is the former object — in the symbiotic relationship — the employee, the servant, the outcast, the intruder from a lower class.

In sado-masochism there is a lack of acknowledgement of the self by the other. This relation, more than hate, is the true opposite of love, for if love is the dual acknowledgment of two selves, sado-masochism denies them totally. In *Steps*, in the incident of the man who possesses a woman without her knowing who he is, her making love to him disaffirms even his self.

Contemporary writers often portray the temptation of self-denial in the symbol of bourgeois man, tantalized by the prospects of self-surrender and his craving for ritual situations. In their view the bourgeois self is so caught up in abstract existence, so barely possessed of itself, so diseased, that it is continually tempted to relinquish itself altogether and to let the remnants of its social awareness wither away. Large segments of western literature are a history of varied forms of malaise. The disease motif in a contemporary work is often built up around a wasting illness — like consumption, as is the case in *Steps*. For Camus a plague symbolizes sickness in society. Sartre declares that nausea, a preliminary to disease, is the only possible response to the contingencies of life. The dwarfishness and the deformity of Günter Grass's narrator in *The Tin Drum* makes palpable the *Angst* and spiritual malaise of the sick society in which he lives. And the "fictional-nonfictional" violence of so many contemporary American novels gives access to the dark desires, the fantasies and the frustration that live just below the surface.

In *Steps*, the sanatorium episode profiles the curious symbolic mating of the professionally healthy (the ski instructors) and the chronically unhealthy (the tubercular patients). In embracing the diseased, the instructors embrace the primordial human predicament. They manifest the intrinsic relationship of the erotic and the heinous, of sex and death.

Hence the motivation of the ski instructors is basically sadistic and that of the patients is masochistic. Within the act, the ski instructors are the subjects. They "understand" — they recognize the object and define the functions to be performed. But they understand little of "love", which, one supposes, is the attempt to be simultaneously subject and object, and is the willing relinquishment of the single subject to a new subject created from two single ones, each subject enhanced into one heightened self.

The judge-penitent in Camus' *La Chute* acts out perfectly the sado-masochistic fantasy: only those who have sinned against themselves are qualified to pronounce judgment. For once the sin against the self is recognized as such, once the sin is objectified and ceases to be an intrinsic and inseparable part of the self one has chosen in favor of the self, made a judgment, and chosen, as in Sartre, for all men. Making the judgment of sin is the one possible way of becoming a judge. As in the Book of Job, "I only am escaped alone to tell thee." Thus the judge-penitent becomes the high priest of the self, of the fulfilled individuality. Thus Sade is perceiving the sins he had committed against himself for others' benefit and decides to live fully as himself, for himself, and can therefore preach the doctrine of the judge-penitent.

An obsession, a compulsion, is the self's love affair with itself. The bond is strongly erotic; obsessions — vice, alcoholism, compulsive eating, drug addiction, etc. — all provide their victims with sensual pleasure. Rilke wrote: "To be loved means to be consumed. To love is to give light with inexhaustible oil. To be loved is to pass away. To love is to endure." These maxims apply perfectly to the obsessed and to their obsessions. In the archetypal religious obsessions — the mystic's craving for God, the cases of diabolical possession — the obsessions are expressed in openly sexual imagery and visions take on direct or symbolic sexual forms.

To the photographer in *Steps* the nurse is an image of youth and purity. To her, he is a thing, he possesses the limited function of an object, interchangeable with another object performing the same function, with the atavistic creature she tends. The photographer is the thing which completes her gesture. But since he has created her, in the sense of creating an image of her, she is as much a part of his self, as much in control of him, as alcoholism is of an alcoholic. And so in his submission to this obsession he becomes an object.

In admitting his obsession, an addict is objectifying it, separating himself from it, and is thus able to comment upon it and upon its relationship to himself. Since the self is in the superior position of commenting upon its involvements, the obsession no longer objectifies the self. The addict can then choose and does choose, in pronouncing for or against continuing his involvement with the obsession. The obsession thus becomes a thing.

In *Steps* the incident of the caged woman is ordered by a progression of images from the literal cage to the legal cage to the religious cage. The priest is imprisoned in the conflict arising between the systems imposed on him. The woman's madness is also a cage, as is her being set aside by the village, her relegation to a secret place.

The treatment by the villagers of the woman in the cage is the communal acting out of an obsession. To primitive people, feelings and obsessions — of anguish and fear — can be personified and acted out on a social level in dances, ritual, religion.

The men who visit and possess the caged woman are releasing obsessions. And as is the case with a ritual, they function in partial secrecy; they are the interpreters of the mystery, the hierophants; they are superior, they are the chosen few.

It is ironic that the woman is unbaptized and thus excluded from the Church. It is ironic, because the priest is obviously confronted here with something older than Catholicism.

"Hell is other people" (Sartre). Hell is the inability to escape from others who prove and prove again to you that you are as they see you. Hell is also the inability to be alone, to see yourself as your self sees you. Both convert the subjectivity of the other into a menacing object and originate the sado-masochistic struggle to impose our will on another more dominantly than he can impose his will on us. At stake is the retention of the dominant position. This enables one to pronounce judgment, for only the subject can judge; the object can only be chosen. To choose is to constitute individuality, even when the alternatives are externally or gratuitously imposed, as in Camus' *L'Etranger*. Meursault murders by chance, but he learns he must choose his murdering, must embrace what he is and live it fully. So he hopes the crowd will jeer and spit at him when he is executed — he will have fulfilled himself.

In a time of crumbling systems the protagonist of *Steps* searches for symbols and finds that what is offered him is paper-thin. Pushing against them, he resembles a clown jumping through paper hoops. Thrown back on himself and spared the chilly comfort of power structures, he seeks traditions and finds only his own brief heritages, those which he has experienced in an instant and will retain all his life. But this wisdom mocks his courage.

And his own traditions, he soon learns are only sensory recollections, fragments of events, and his personality is a kaleidoscope in which the same reflecting specks appear again and again, but in such different patterns that he himself rarely recognizes them. The whole of his legacy is his consciousness, the fiction which begins and ends with itself. And the stories he tells: how can any of them be more than autobiographical, or less than that? But how can it be autobiographical when he possesses only a bare sense of himself, and when that sense is only perceptible as the most subtle of nuances lurking beneath the reality in which he believes he lives.

For him, to reach back through a particularly painful past for an age of innocence, for the self which, he feels, is waiting for discovery behind the blocked memories preceding his traumas, is to immerse himself in the heart of the trauma itself. To discard forgetting is to be harrowed by the past; it is to expose raw nerve ends and disrupt the benign haziness of present memories. This process, for instance, when it is channeled into a narrative arouses in the hearer a response similar to that evoked by action-painting: an identification with the aspects of personality strewn and spattered throughout the story. In *Steps* the protagonist is communicated as an aggregate of memory and emotion which marks and scores the novel. Characters and events stand not so much as figurations in a fictive reality but rather as stimuli triggering a hyper-personal, hyper-psychic series of responses in the reader.

Psychoanalysis claims in the context of the present to examine the crippled past in order to frame that past more clearly and thus create a more comprehensible present. Here again we see the analogizing of past and future. This attitude is an evasion. It considers the present as a function of the past and of the future — not as an independent entity. It supposes that we require being reminded.

We speak of a comic vision or a tragic vision, but this is not the property of the world in which the artist lives but rather of the world he creates — of those fragments of experience he selects without conscious choice, of the sense of self he chooses to bring up from the depths. Certainly, even in life, incidents are sad or funny. The comic exists really, as does the disastrous and possibly, the tragic. But life is not so pure as to lay down incident after incident in a single vein; life has no structure, only frontiers. But a work of art can be funny or sad, and its structure offers a point of entry into life.

There is a kind of grotesque — that of dreams and surrealism — in which symbols rationally unrelated in subject, tone, and emotional content are lured together into a collage which the mind comprehends on a subconscious level. Here, again, the work produces in us responses we cannot normally summon up; the aroused emotions take us by surprise, bringing to the surface truths which lie beneath.

Displacing particular images, shifting them into contexts with which they are not normally associated, makes us aware of another reality in the midst of our commonplace one. Bosch was a master of this kind of grotesque. By placing sexual scenes in settings which require religious ones and *vice versa* he displayed the exaggerated, the twisted, the strange subconscious links which bind the mind. The result is a dream-like, nightmarish reality which shocks, astonishes, and is easily accessible. In truth, its familiarity and its power to stun are fused. The grotesque is the language of the emotions which silently provoke our actions. Hence the subversive quality of art.

Art is an autonomous reality. A work of art governs its own time, which is always in play with the external flow of time provided by the spectator. The literary image implies a domination of the dimensions, of empirical space-time, which is impossible in life as we live it. In Wilde's *Dorian Grey* the time of art and the time of life are reversed — the portrait ages, the living subject of the portrait does not and instead obeys artistic time, never aging, never changing. The *avant garde* attempts to acquire a sense of time and of self in which past, present and future are nearly simultaneous. It suggests that novelty depends on spontaneity, the element of unfamiliarity, of surprise. Surprise is instantaneous, and the familiar is the habitual. Habit and routine are stultifying and the *avant garde* seeks an acknowledgment that art and life have changed places: when our lives are too "real" (mundane, ordered, predictable), we seek excitement and release in "fiction". Now, the *avant garde* claims, our lives become themselves like fictions — hence the literature, the art, the cinema must supply the truly real, truly felt experience. This is a phenomenon of mass-culture, along with ubiquitous reportage aiming for spontaneity (which nonetheless becomes history the moment it appears) for an "objective" fact-based fiction. But fiction is nothing else but the enacted fantasy, the imagination's own form.

Natural symbolism presupposes the omnipotence of nature and is a throwback to a primitive period when man existed in a more direct relationship with nature. The world was alive with magical presences then, and the gods were immanent in natural forces — in the sun and in the trees and in the stones. This was a period preceding organized religion, if religion is a means of approaching the otherwise unapproachable and marks the moment when the gods or god became supernatural.

In the pre-religious period the world was only man and nature. Man existed as a community in the face of nature; the awareness of himself as an individual did not ensue. It is only when the gods begin to grow distant and earth and heaven become separate worlds that the concept of the self arises.

The feeling of magic, the sense of community, can be conjured up and nature as incantation still survives. Natural symbolism invokes incantatory nature and serves for a moment to create a community response, producing a sense which antedates the individual response.

Natural symbolism also employs macrocosmic analogies. Incantatory nature is mystical, omnipotent, something unknown and sacred. When a natural analogy is made, the thing compared is immeasurably strengthened, it becomes microcosm.

With the death of Man and the birth of collective and mechanized society, faith loses its meaning. In the face of faith lost and in a universe unmasked in its indifference, collective values must be enforced as the true representatives of belief. But these collective values are mementoes of the god-fearing society, and they weigh on the individual. The protagonist of *Steps* is aware of this and to him the most meaningful and fulfilling gesture is negative; it is aimed against the collective and is a movement towards the solitude within which the self can display its reality. Perhaps that is why he looks for the true gesture outside society, going to the edge of despair, to the outsider, to the pariah, to his journey in *Steps*.

Centuries before Freud, Sophocles pictured the human effort to unify the unconscious and conscious, but in *Oepidus* the only blocks against regression are external. History moves inward; the struggles that occur between the external and the internal move inward. Modern art becomes hyperpersonal or else repeats its familiar disinterested message in the undercharged but accessible images of universal misery expressing the individual's difficulty in functioning in a system.

Jung suggests that there had once been a wholeness of the conscious and the unconscious, a unification of public and private appearances. Although Jung is referring to a real primordial mentality, to a naive abundance of involuntary thought, we find this unity most vividly symbolized in the arts preceding the Jacobean period. When this unity occurs, myth is potent, and tragedy takes place. In saying that tragedy is the imitation of an action, Aristotle implies this wholeness. Today, though, with the public mask and the dream of private action so dissociated, we see from a distance, more and more clearly, the period of synthesis. But we see that for us neurosis has replaced the myth. This is why so much of modern fiction bears a certain universality, an allegorical intent: the collective consciousness and any individual collection of consciousness have been radically detached. Jung's definition of the use of myth as a type of self-therapy is easily corroborated in modern fiction which abounds in myths and reworked classical motifs. The purpose of these motifs is thus not so gratuitous as it seems.

When creation falls from the active to the gestural mode, it exhibits a resurgence of mythic motifs, which, like incantations, is an attempt to reassemble the last active unity. But it often achieves only a Pavlovian response, the true opposite of the primal spontaneity.

The myth and the ritual serve a structural rather than an active function. Literature has pre-empted the functions of both. But myths — even dead and moribund ones — still have evocative power and still exist in our thoughts. As tradition is continually attacked in art, myths exist to be broken. Literature seeks to describe what is, and, in the process, to do away with what is not or what is no longer.

From this function of literature arises the necessity for the subversive, for subversion makes its points by indirection; the most seductive and insinuating attack is the indirect one. Formerly, the wanderer returned home safely, wiser from what he had learned in his journeys. Now the wanderer returns safely, but his wisdom is disquieting and he has only affirmed what he has all along suspected. He discovers that his quest in search of inner life is a symbol for something lost or untouched by him. The modern wanderer travels in an empty universe as solitary as that which lies behind his own self: "... I would have stayed in my seat with my eyes closed, all strength and passion gone, my mind as quiescent as a coat rack under a forgotten hat, and I would have remained there, timeless, unmeasured, unjudged, bothering no one, suspended forever between my past and my future." (*Steps*)

ARIADNE

R. Murray Schafer

SCENE 9

AT ONCE I FOUND MYSELF IN ANOTHER WORLD, FOR I WAS IN WHAT APPEARED TO BE A CLUB OR DISCOTHEQUE. I STOOD IN THE FOYER.
    TO MY RIGHT WAS A HAT-CHECK GIRL, WHO EVEN NOW WAS EXTENDING AN ARM TO TAKE MY CRUMPLED RAIN-COAT.

TO MY LEFT, THROUGH A WIDE ARCHWAY, I COULD SEE PEOPLE DANCING TO THE SOUNDS OF A JAZZ BAND. MANY OF THE DANCERS WERE MASKED.

I WAITED FOR A MOMENT UNTIL MY EYES GREW ACCUSTOMED TO THE LIGHT INSIDE THE CLUB, THEN I WENT IN AND TOOK A SEAT AT A TABLE NEAR THE DOORWAY.

HATS, COATS, UMBRELLAS, VALISES.

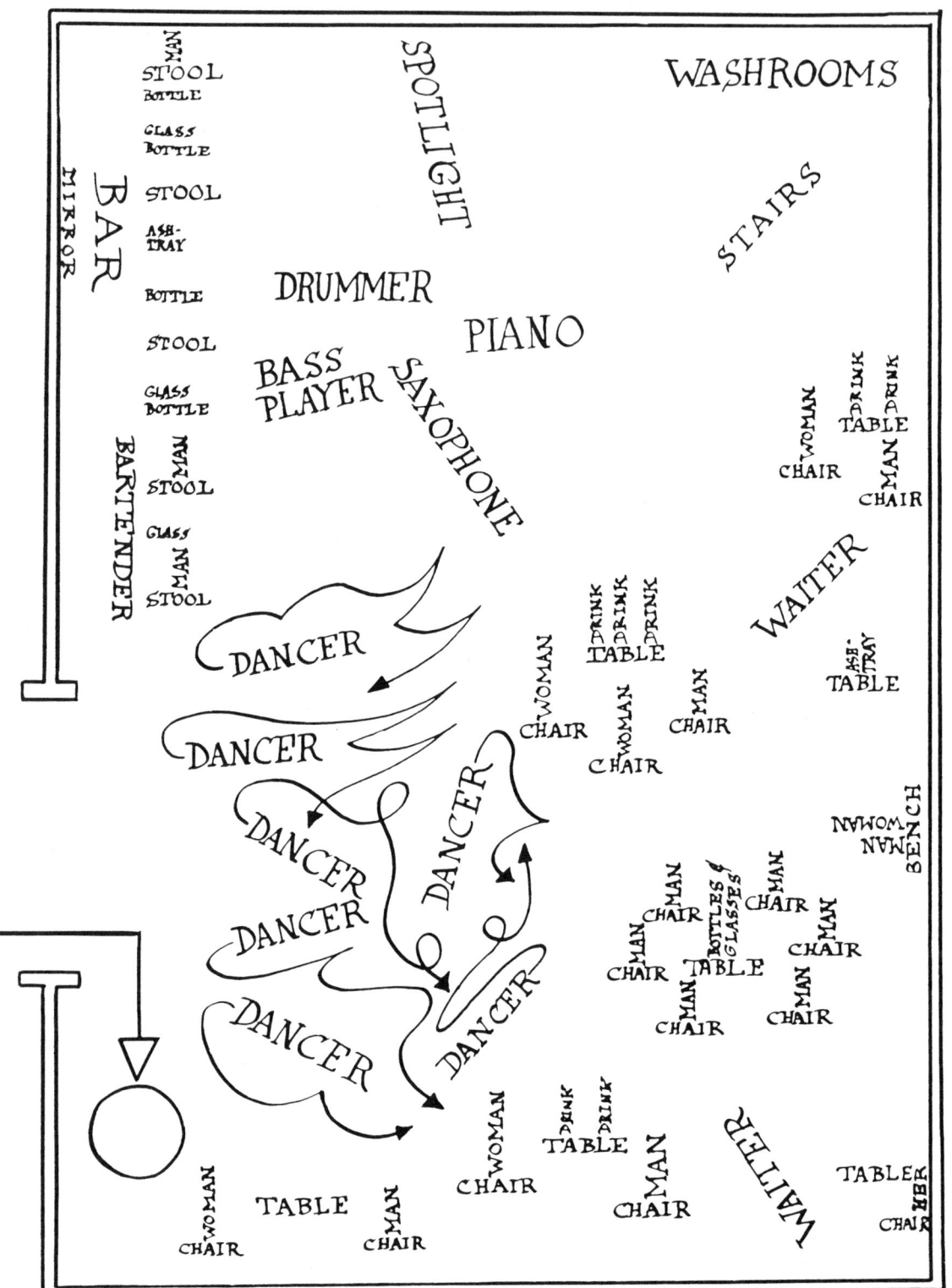

DANCER

DANCER

DANCER

DANCER

DANCER

DANCER

DANCER

THE
DANCERS
SPUN BEFORE
MY TABLE. I
STUDIED THEIR
MOVEMENTS.
IT WAS AS
IF THEY WERE
WRITING SEC-
RET MESSAGES
ACROSS THE
FLOOR.

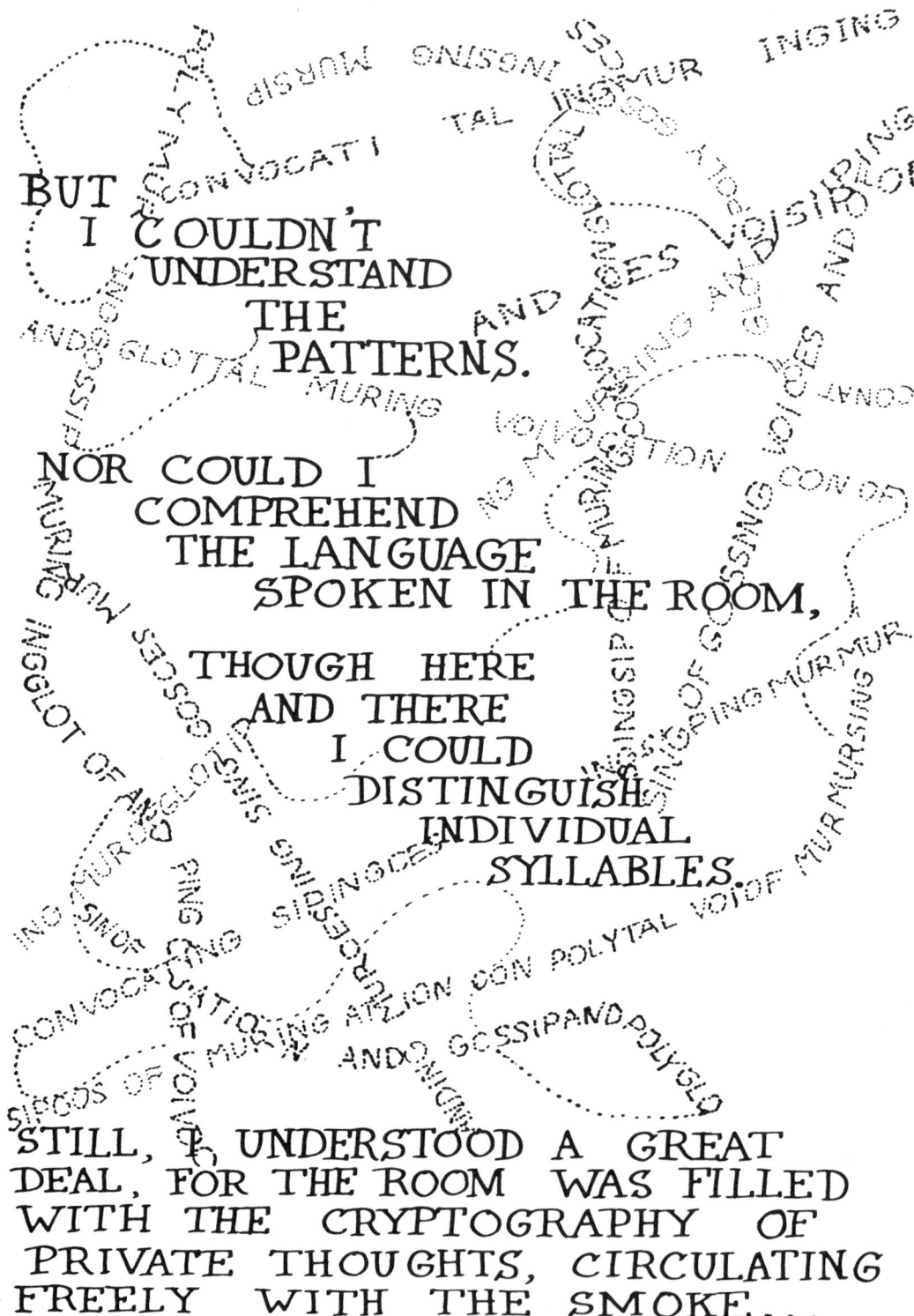

BUT
I COULDN'T
UNDERSTAND
THE
PATTERNS.

NOR COULD I
COMPREHEND
THE LANGUAGE
SPOKEN IN THE ROOM,

THOUGH HERE
AND THERE
I COULD
DISTINGUISH
INDIVIDUAL
SYLLABLES.

STILL, I UNDERSTOOD A GREAT
DEAL, FOR THE ROOM WAS FILLED
WITH THE CRYPTOGRAPHY OF
PRIVATE THOUGHTS, CIRCULATING
FREELY WITH THE SMOKE...

THE BAND HAD STOPPED PLAYING AND
THE DANCERS HAD RETURNED
TO THEIR SEATS. AS THE
WAITER PASSED BY I
ORDERED A DRINK AND
BEGAN TO LOOK
AROUND,
RIGHT,
LEFT, UP
ABOUT.
THE WAITER
RETURNED
WITH MY DRINK
AND MOVED AWAY.
IT WAS THEN THAT
I SAW HER
FOR THE FIRST
TIME, ALONE
AT A TABLE IN
THE CORNER,
WEARING A
CARNIVAL
MASK OF
A SIX
YEAR
OLD
GIRL.

Scene 12

She laughed  as we passed out the door into the cool night air.

"Do you have a name?" I asked after a while.

SHE DID NOT ANSWER SO I TRIED TO GUESS:

IT WAS NO USE SO I TRIED ANOTHER METHOD:

JE T'AI DEMANDÉ TON NOM... 
∧ᵒ,/ ⊃∨ Ξ, SHE REPLIED.

T

S

T

R

H

H

E

A

D

I

E

N

T

T

R

U

S

E

S

T

H

S

c

I

N

o

T

E

H

N

M

N

S

E

T

S

S

A

E

L

E

V

V

T

o

M

R

R

H

F

E

o

A

E

N

M

... AND THE FLIGHT OF THE FLAME WAS IN HER HAIR

SHE WAS PURE MELODY:

239

SOMETIMES WE SPENT WHOLE DAYS...

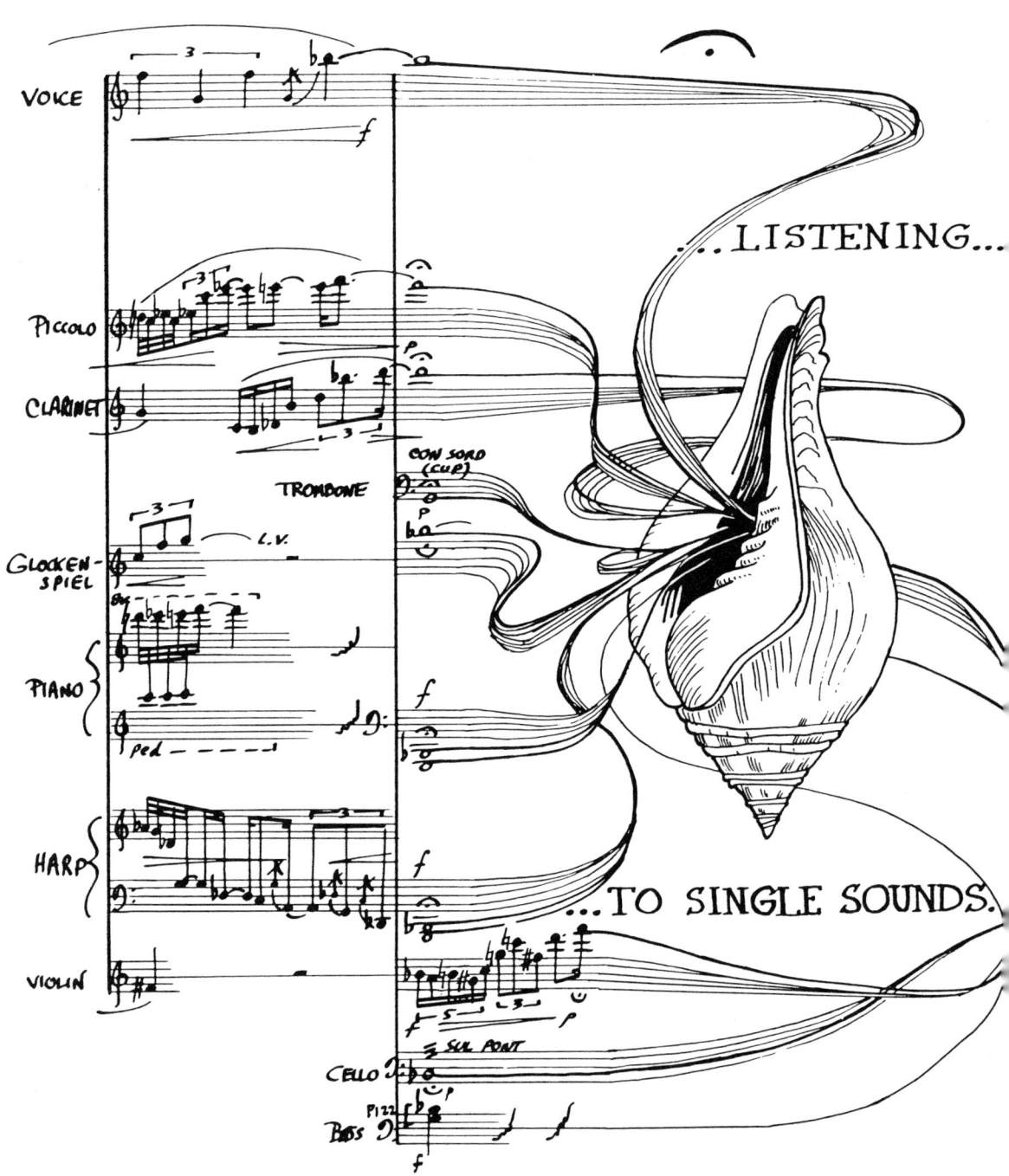

SOMETIMES WE SPENT WHOLE DAYS
REPEATING ONE WORD, GRADUALLY
REVEALING NEW ASPECTS OF ITS
MEANING...

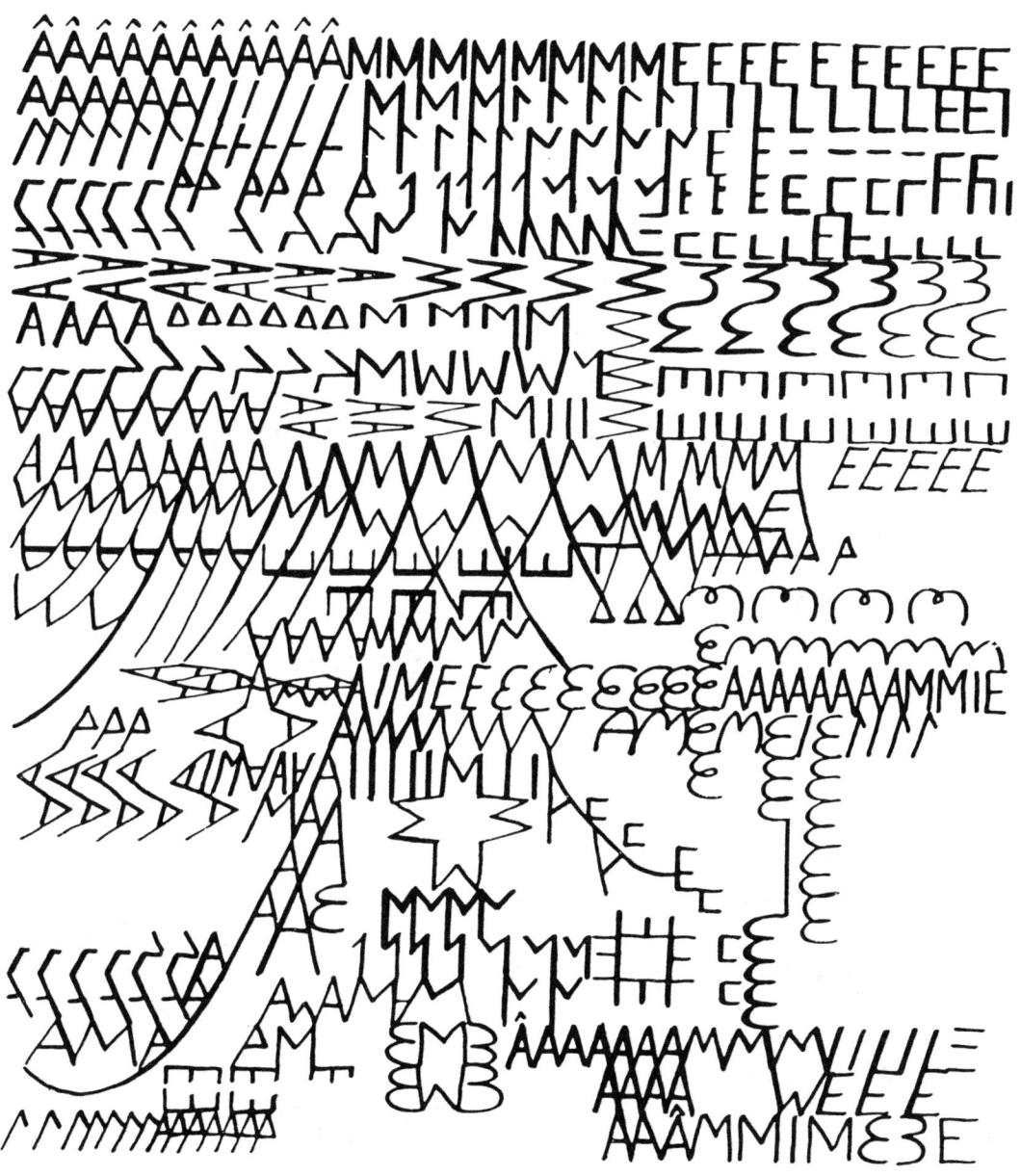

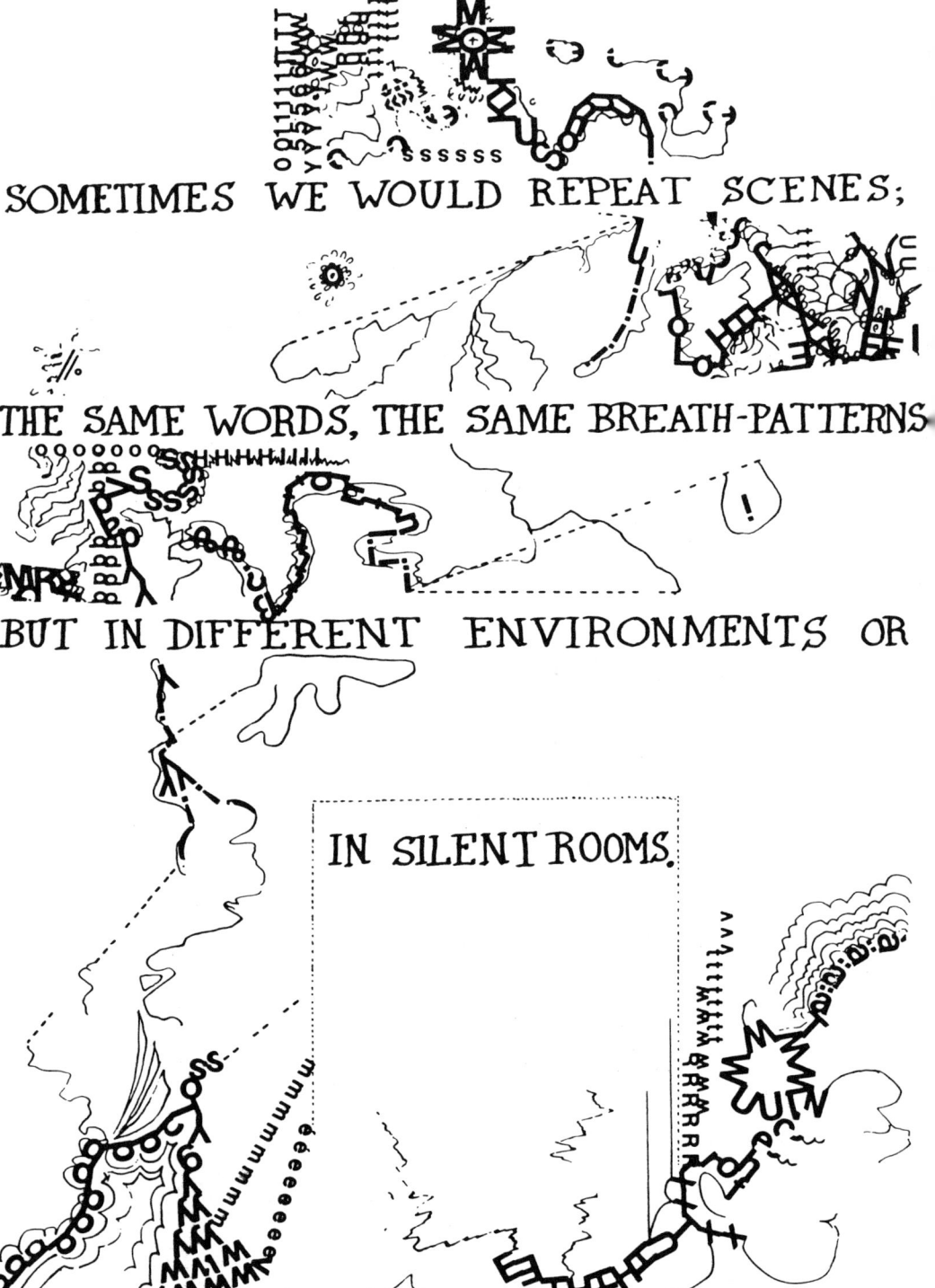

SOMETIMES WE WOULD REPEAT SCENES;

THE SAME WORDS, THE SAME BREATH-PATTERNS

BUT IN DIFFERENT ENVIRONMENTS OR

IN SILENT ROOMS.

242

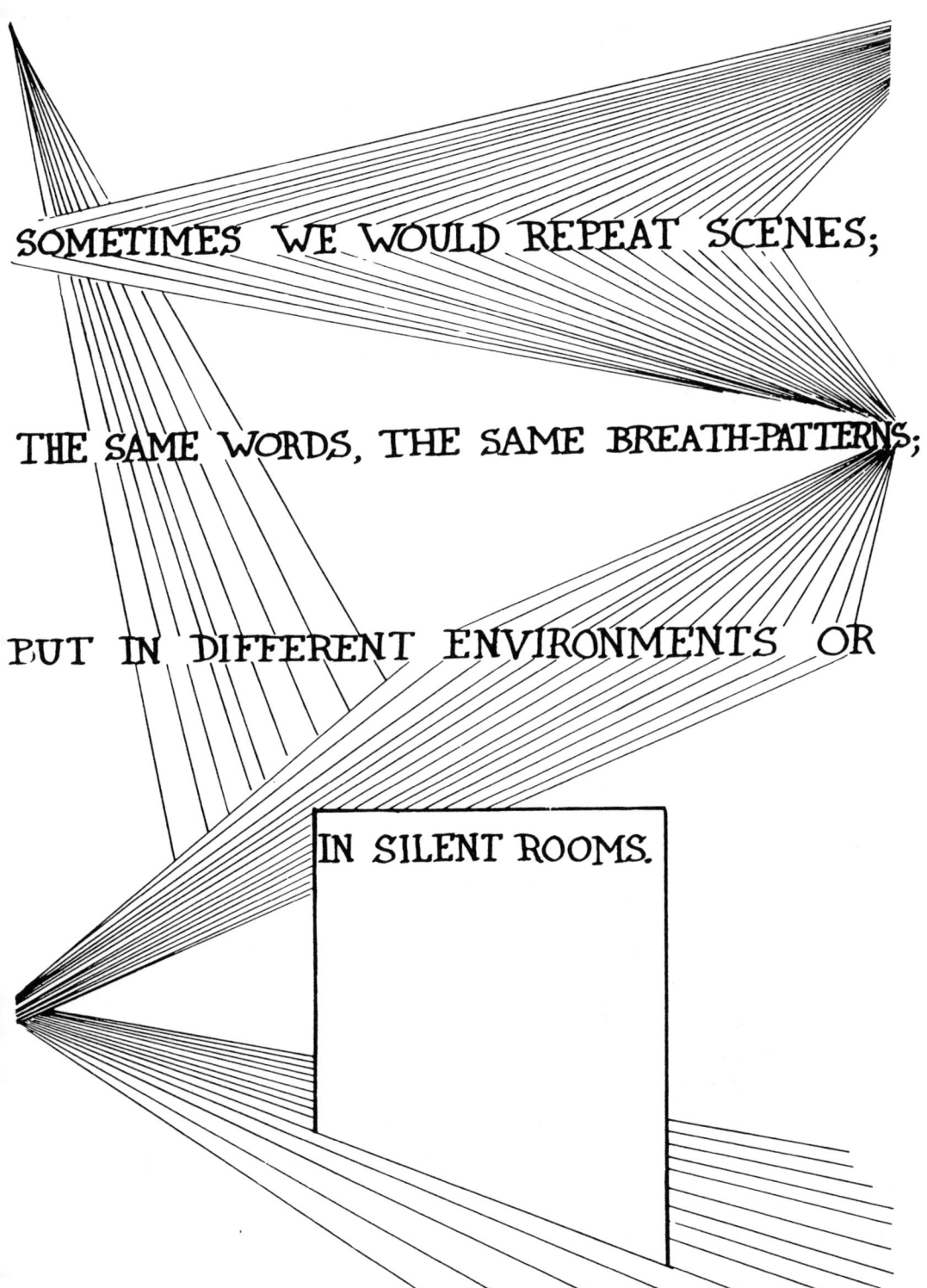

SOMETIMES WE WOULD REPEAT SCENES;

THE SAME WORDS, THE SAME BREATH-PATTERNS;

PUT IN DIFFERENT ENVIRONMENTS OR

IN SILENT ROOMS.

SOMETIMES WE WOULD REPEAT SCENES;

THE SAME WORDS, THE SAME BREATH-PATTERNS;

BUT IN DIFFERENT ENVIRONMENTS OR

IN SILENT ROOMS.

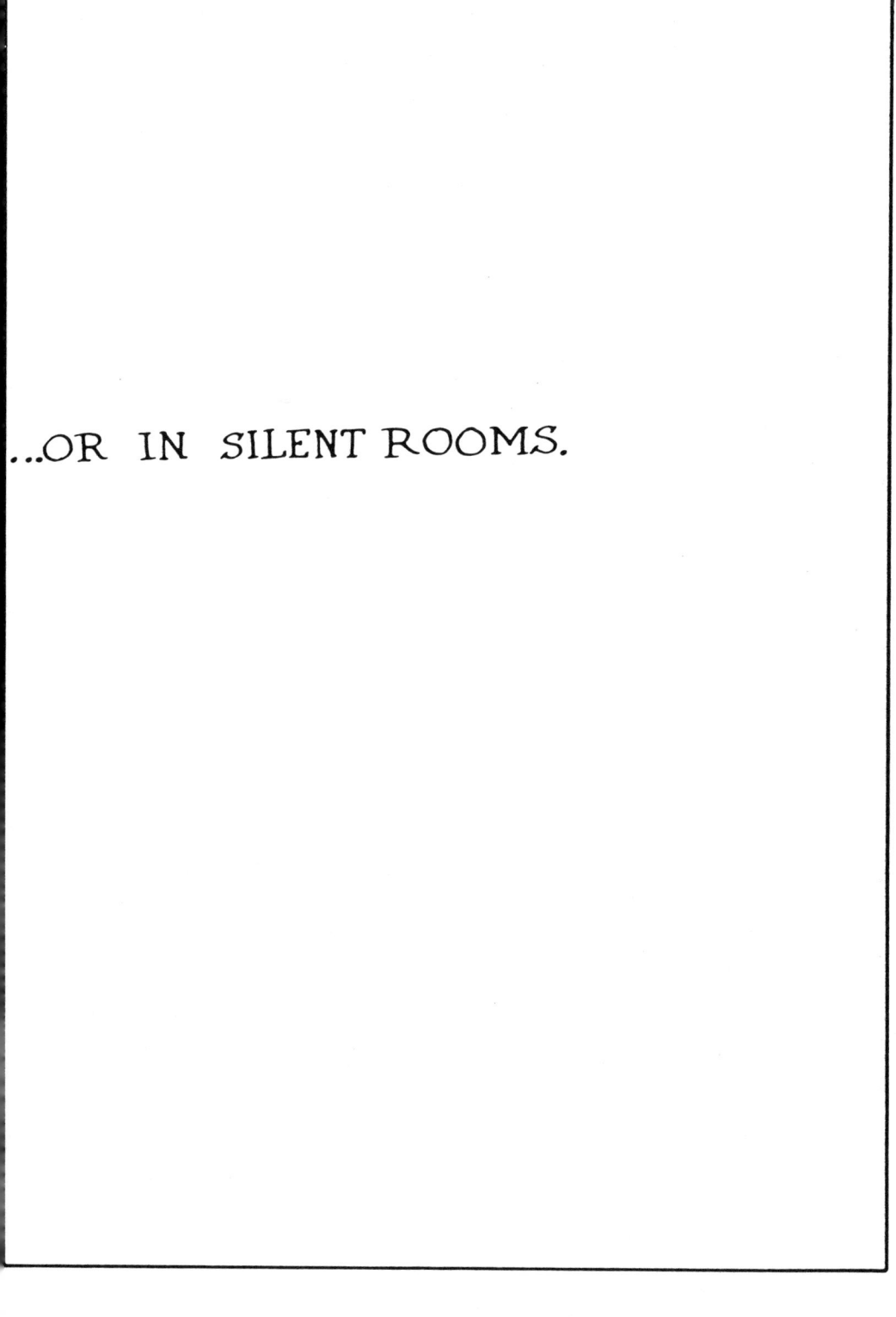

...OR IN SILENT ROOMS.

THE METERMAN, CALIBAN, AND THEN MR. JONES: PART ONE

Morley Callaghan

A gust of cold night wind blew heavy rain drops against Julien Jones' face. As he walked up Yonge Street, he was caught in a shower that became half snow, half rain. Julien, an imposing fastidious figure of a man of forty who walked with a lordly ease, turned up his coat collar, looking around in distress. He was wearing his new expensive velour hat, and his flowing camel's hair coat. He had a red cashmere scarf which looked good when his overcoat was open, hanging softly red against his double-breasted dark suit.

Along the street loafers and pimps and gawking hopeful young men were ducking into the doorways of shops, doorways with sleazy books in the windows, or stands selling sizzling soyabean hamburgers. The cold shower swept them off the street, into the doorways and bars. It was no neighborhood for a man with a distinguished air. Julien Jones stepped unhappily into the Golden Door, a bar and lounge. Only a cold wet sleety rain could have driven Julien to this place. He went in.

He sat on a stool at the end of the oaken bar, glancing around calmly, having no interest in whether anyone had noticed him. Sheppard Crook, the manager, who had a bald head and a tuxedo which he wore every night, though no one else who entered the place ever wore one, was behind the bar. He glanced at Julien, recognizing him. Sheppard Crook liked to lunch uptown, at the Provencal. He liked to lunch alone, as if, when alone, he could be at ease and gallant with himself. He had once eaten at a table next to Julien's, and had been irritated by the man's public exhuberance, as if no one else mattered, as if only his well-being were at stake, and so he had listened to hear his name. Julien Jones. He knew all about the Martel & Jones Agency. In a way, he realized afterwards, he envied the man's commanding aloofness. Now he went to speak, frowned, and decided to let Heinz the barman get Julien his drink. Sheppard Crook didn't like the way Julien looked the place over. Julien, he thought, could only be slumming, but Crook thought his Golden Door was a good place, the only neighborly joint on the strip.

The patrons at the tables could call out to each other, or do a little singing together. It was the only place that had an imported expensive act, like the comic stripper; and once a week a surprise local act. Edmond J. Debuke handled the local girls. They always sat with him, like this one in the mink coat was doing. Sheppard Crook said to little Heinz, his bar-keep, "She's in here like she thinks she's in a washroom and doesn't want to go on. She'd better be good."

"She looks real good," Heinz said.

"I said to her 'I'll take your coat.'"

"What did she say?"

"She said 'No you won't take my coat.'"

"Maybe she uses it in her act, Shep."

"Don't call me Shep."

"Where did Debuke get her?" Julien Jones asked, as if there were no reason why he shouldn't overhear and then enter their conversation.

"Edmond J. Debuke," Heinz said. "That's him. The club foot. We call him Daboot. He's got a whole stable of those broads."

"Leave it to Daboot," Sheppard Crook said. "If she lets Daboot down he'll take her out in the lane," and then he caught Debuke's eye. They exchanged smiles.

The girl and Debuke were only a few feet from Julien Jones. The manager made an OK motion with his fingers as Debuke leaned across the table. The girl drew back, eying him coolly. "Okay, Miss Delury. So it isn't the Waldorf. It doesn't matter where the hell it is if it's a tryout spot. Audiences are all the same. Whether it's a beer parlor or a strip joint or the Plaza, there's always someone on the lookout for a new face. Right at the start we might as well see if you've got it."

"Don't worry, I've got it, Mr. Debuke."

"How do you know you've got it?"

"It's in your face, Mr. Debuke."

"Call me Eddie."

"Oh, you're too old."

"Some of my girls call me old Eddie."

"I'll call you Caliban."

"Who's Caliban?"

"A talent scout I read about."

"Caliban, eh?" And then stroking his chin thoughtfully, "I get the impression you look down your nose at me. No? It's all right. It gives your mouth a sensual pout," and he leaned closer: "Your teeth – I like the little overbite. It's nice. A sensual pout on the face of a snotty little dame is very good. Makes a man wonder ... " Her eyes had gone to his club foot, and then thoughtfully to her own spiked heel, then she glanced at the entrance. Julien Jones wondered if she had decided to walk out. There was sudden animal vitality in Debuke's face; it seemed to fascinate her. "Trust me about an audience, Miss Delury," he said. "I know what sells to an audience," and he chuckled. "You should hear me at funerals. I'm in demand. No matter who the poor son of a bitch is, I can get his friends crying. Hey, come on."

The lounge lights had dimmed; the tired little waiter, Frankie Cline, standing by the piano, announced, "Making her first appearance in our great city, Miss Ellen Delury," and he sat down at the piano.

As the spotlight picked her up at the table, she stiffened, startled; then with a natural ease, she sauntered up to the little platform. She was slim, and about five foot four. Her long straight black hair was parted in the middle. Her simple black dress was cut rather high at the throat. Suddenly she smiled, and the smile had all the assurance of her own distinction. She began to half-talk, half-sing. It was all in the phrasing. The style might have been effective in a good supper club. It was wrong for the Golden Door. She got some polite applause, but it was expectant applause. They were all sure they were being teased – the little black dress, the distinguished air. Then, there were impatient murmurs. Someone laughed raucously. The laugh came from a thin little man at a table near the piano. He yelled, "It's all a tease. All right, honey, take it off." These cries flustered her, and she faltered. Her words got twisted.

Julien Jones took out a long thin cigar, the flaming match lit up his face. The match light attracted the manager. "So that's the little lady who turned up her nose at this place," he said. "Well, maybe she needs a little help." He left the bar, vanished into the shadows. A minute later he appeared out of the wing and stood behind her in the spotlight while she continued with her performance. The manager made helpless gestures to the audience, pretending he didn't know what to do with her, and suddenly she turned, staring at him blankly. Backing away, he made loud clucking noises, a comedian now. In an elaborate gesture of managerial shame he put both hands over his face as if weeping and suddenly he dropped his hands; he had a bright dazzling great clown's smile. As the girl froze beside him, he shot out his hand, got hold, of the front of her dress and yanked. You could hear the cloth rip. The one violent pull tore the dress right down to her waist, it tore away her brassiere too. The dress hung around her like broken petals, and while she stood stunned, the light was on her bare breasts. On the strip at that time there were dozens of topless girls on stages, but this girl's full breasts seemed to come shockingly close, and Sheppard Crook had his hands up like a delighted boy who had opened a magic box. There was sudden yelling, and happy applause. The girl had jerked her head back, motionless, in such a way that the audience was silent. Everything was very still in the blaze of wild, savage beauty in her face.

Julien Jones got off his stool, and he stood hushed and wondering, lifted out of himself. Then the girl swung her fist and hit Sheppard Crook on the mouth. Flecks of blood appeared at the corner of his mouth. But he kept his head; he was still on stage, he could clown. Reeling back, he lurched around drunkenly. The little waiter at the piano, whose mouth had hung open, grew inspired. He began to play waltz time while Sheppard Crook lurched around, and he kept on playing while Ellen, grabbing at her dress, rushed through the tables. The audience burst into applause; a good surprising act.

When Ellen reached her table where Debuke stood applauding wildly, she grabbed her purse, then at her mink coat, which was draped over the chair. "Honey, honey," Debuke said, beaming as held onto the coat. "We got something. This can be big."

"Oh, you little bastard," she said. She tried to grab her coat from him. He held on: he got it away from her. The lights coming on bewildered her and she came dashing by the bar and on out to the street.

Julien hurried after her. The sidewalk had dried and Ellen, her dress gathered around her, was running up the brightly lit street, and then she ducked around a corner. When Julien reached her she was trying to knot strips of the dress around her neck. The purse held in one hand made it difficult.

"Go home, Miss," he said calmly. "Go home. I'll get you a taxi."

"You go to hell," she said fiercely.

"Julien Jones – let me get a cab."

"Screw you," she said. Then put off by his gentle concern she said, "They've got my coat."

"I'll get it," he said. "Here," and he took off his camel's hair coat and draped it around her. Her suspicious eyes made him smile. "Just stay right here, take it easy," he said, and left her. He didn't hurry. Entering the Golden Door, he went directly to the table near the end of the bar. The coat was folded over the chair. To the left, six tables away, Edmond Debuke talked enthusiastically to the little waiter, Frankie Cline, who glowed with importance. "Hey look," Frankie said. Calmly picking up the coat, Julien walked away with it. "Hey, Shep," Debuke called. The manager, who had come to the cash register, would not turn, not until Debuke more respectfully called "Sheppard." Then the manager said to Julien, who was passing him, "Now look here, mister, Daboot has something to say about this." But Julien, in his expensive dark suit, the red scarf hanging loose over his shoulder, and big with contempt, said dryly, "Miss Delury seems to have forgotten her coat."

"You'd better talk to Daboot," the manager said. Debuke came limping toward them. Julien went out without bothering to look back. Outside he heard the club foot come thumping on the pavement behind him. He turned the corner. There, in the doorway, Ellen waited, the camel's hair coat wrapped warmly around her.

"Here you are," he said with a little laugh, because she seemed to be trying to hide from him in his own coat. He lifted it from her shoulder, her own coat on his other arm. "Look out!" she cried. Debuke came out of the corner light, his dark face brightly fierce. "Hey, you," he said grimly. "She's my action. Nobody hustles my action."

"Beat it, creep," Julien said.

"I'm Edmond J. Debuke, you hear?"

"On your way, Debuke."

"Not this time," Debuke said. "I give my life around here to finding action like her. I dig into alleys and sinholes and stinking washrooms. A guy like you sees a buck in it and tries to steal it. Well, she's under contract to Edmond J. Debuke. And get this – whistle on this corner and you're dead. Now come on, Miss Delury," and he grabbed Ellen's arm. "You pig," she cried, "get your hands off me," and she swung at him with her purse.

Julien grabbed him by the collar, whipping it back over his shoulders, snapping the button at the front of the coat, half pinning his arms, and then he swung him around and sent him spinning against the corner lamppost. Julien stooped to pick up the fur coat that had dropped from his arm.

While Julien was bending over, Debuke came off the lamppost, charging at him, his head down like a bull, and Julien, straightening, laughed, cocking his right, measuring him. But, just as he went to swing, Debuke, in a good feint, stopped short and lashed out at Julien's leg with his heavily booted club foot. The boot caught him on the knee. His leg buckled. Then it wasn't there; he half spun on one foot, then lurched and fell. While he rolled over Debuke looked down on him and then kicked him on the head. "You thief," he yelled. Picking up the fur coat he turned imperiously on Ellen. "If you want this coat, honey, you come back and ask for it in a real nice way," and then, his shoulders back, the coat on his arm, he went limping proudly down the street.

"Miss ..." Julien called. A terrible pressure on his head, a dull weight getting heavier, bringing the street light down closer and closer to him, scared him. "Miss ... he called. But his eyes, when she bent over him, frightened her and she looked around, ready to run, to get away. Reluctantly she turned back to him, hesitated, and then said, "You should get a to a hospital. I'll get a cop."

"Help me up," he whispered.

She helped him. He had been lying on his beautiful new hat. Stunned though he was, he pointed at the hat. She picked it up and put it on his head. Then he staggered dizzily to the wall of the building where he stood on one foot, leaning back heavily, his eyes closed. A long-haired man in a leather coat who was passing with a stringy-haired girl in blue jeans, looked at Ellen in the big camel's hair coat, holding the swaying man up against the wall, and they laughed. "Thanks, Miss Delury," Julien whispered. He couldn't stop trembling. "Get a taxi, not a cop."

"Can you stand here?"

"I think so," he said, and with only one eye open – he saw double when he used both eyes – he followed her and thought crazily that he was watching a girl in a beautiful long cape dancing around out in the middle of the road. Then she came and took his arm and helped him hobble to the taxi. "He fell and hurt his leg," she explained to the driver. "Just a few blocks away," Julien mumbled, lying back in the cab.

"The Centurion apartments. The big one, Jarvis street." Then he whispered to her, "Mustn't black out –" When the cab stopped at the apartment house, she took some dollars from her purse and gave them to the driver. "Can you help him in? Please?" She thought she would let the driver look after him. But, as if remembering she had his coat on, she got out too, and helped the driver lead him into the lobby. At the elevator she asked, "Are you sure you'll be all right now?" He said, "Sure," and held her arm tightly. She got into the elevator with him "Thirty-third floor," he said. "Then I'm all right." But she went along the carpeted corridor. She took the key from his hand and opened the door and led him in.

It was a large apartment with a thick golden rug. The window drapes were blue and the cut velvet couch was a lime shade. An old carved desk was in the corner. She led him to the couch where he fell on his back. "Ah, home, I made it," he said with a long sigh and closed his eyes, but he knew she stood looking down at him. Then he felt her fingers running through his black hair, feeling for the huge welt on his head. When he opened his eyes he saw blood on her fingers. "It's an awful bump. It should be bathed and cleaned," she said, and she half-whispered, "I don't know." He knew she was torn, really wanting to get away. "Well, are there any pins around here?" she asked, letting the overcoat fall open. "Over there, the desk,"? he mumbled. The heavy pressure on the top of his head had not lifted, he was afraid it would get worse, that he would pass out. With one eye he followed her over to the desk. She took her time in a cool examination of the material on the desk; it was stage stuff, old clippings, movie material. "Hey," he called anxiously, for she seemed to be drifting further away and might soon vanish. "In the bedroom. The closet. Sweaters. Take one." His heart was pounding in nervous expectation of a sudden blackness and he didn't want her to be left there alone with his blackness: then the relief of hearing her in his bedroom. A pause, and he realized she was standing beside him in a brown sweater that flopped around her.

"You know what they used to call that?" he asked.

"What?"

"A sloppy-joe."

"They still do," she said. "Where's the bathroom and some towels?"

She came back with a wet towel. It was soaked with cold water. It felt good. "Got to keep talking." he muttered apologetically. "Just keep talking. I like your voice."

"I haven't said anything."

"I'll keep talking."

"It's all right with me," she said.

The heavy pressure on his head was lifting: it was such a beautiful feeling and suddenly he had a head, just his own head, and he was trembling with relief. He raised himself: "It's like feeling my brains coming together," and he groaned. "Now I've just got a headache. Get me a Scotch, there's Scotch in the kitchen."

"Should you drink?"

"I need a drink. When you need a drink that's when you drink."

She went into the kitchen, got a glass and the bottle and poured him a big drink. He gulped it down; it shook him; he sat up suddenly, looking around as if realizing who he was and what had happened to him. "God almighty," he moaned in astonishment. "What was I doing in that crummy joint, to end up lying in the gutter? Some club-footed thug. Lying there in my good suit. Where's my hat? It's outrageous." His rage made him want to stand up. "I'll find him. I'll beat him to a pulp. I'll break his legs, I'll break his head," and he did try to stand. But he had only one leg, and falling back he thought his head would burst. "You have a drink," he whispered.

"No thanks."

"All right," he said wearily, "now you can go home."

"No, I can't."

"Why not?"

"Not without my coat."

"Look, in the closet, there's a raincoat. Take it."

"You don't understand. That's my mother's mink coat."

"You mother's mink."

251

"She's was sick in bed. If she goes out tomorrow she'll go to put it on and …"

"I'll get the coat."

"When?"

"Well, not now," he said, trying to grin. "Just leave it to me." Satisfied that he had said something that would make her stay, he lay back and turned his head to the wall. He heard her moving around, and then she sat down, and in the silence he was sure she was working out some way to get her coat. "Tell me about yourself," he said, turning. "What do you do?"

"You mean to pass the time? Receptionist in a very upper-crust dentist's office," she said. "He's got three chairs, right in a row."

"Don't they all?"

"The whole day he hops from one to the other, working three people at the same time. He gets rich but he gets worn out and at the end of the day he wants to sit in the middle chair and look at my legs."

"Just look?"

"Since he met my father. He's too unhappy to do anything but look."

"How'd your father put him off?"

"He thinks my father looks down on him"

"What does your father do?"

"He has a position with the gas company," she said, and turning away, she drifted into a kind of a daydream, held by it till she broke suddenly into a bitter laugh. Half to herself, she said, "How could I have been such a little fool? I really can't believe it. I've been around in some little revues, this and that, and one night Debuke was there, nosing around I suppose, and he said I'd be suitable …"

"Suitable!" he scoffed. "A suitable hooker. Dear God, you can't be such a dummy."

"Are you sore at me?"

"Oh hell –"

"It's funny," she said, troubled. "I don't seem to mind you being sore. Look, Debuke doesn't matter. I've just been in a restless mood these days."

"Maybe I'm the dummy," he said. "I knew you, right away, I really did, up on that stage when you came to life, that fierce dignity. I'm not kidding. I was so moved and not wanting it to end. That was the awful thing, the moment of your humiliation, that's it, that was when I came alive, the way I saw you. It's incredible now to think of a hustler like Debuke anywhere near you."

Upset, she waited, then drawn to him, and apologetic, she came and sat down beside him. "Look, maybe everyone has a night when everything seems all wrong in your life. You feel that something is passing you by and you want to cry out. So there is this Debuke! I knew he was just an animal. I called him Caliban! Might just as well have called him Cucumber for all he knew. I thought I could handle him. I thought he might just be a step on the way."

"To where?"

"How did I know?"

"Maybe you knew one thing, Ellen," he said gently. "Maybe you knew you were tired of having it easy with your nice friends. Maybe you felt it was time to get on any old white horse and ride into the hills."

"You're amusing," she said with a kind of detachment, her arms folded.

"Maybe so but it'd do a girl like you good, working the joints," he said. "That's if you want to learn how to walk across a stage."

"Don't worry," she said. "I'll walk across a stage. Look, what are you anyway?"

"A guy with a broken head."

"You got all that movie stuff on your desk ..."

"I was a director."

"And now?"

"Talent."

"Oh dear God, another one," she said disdainfully. "I'm up to my eyes in talent hunters. Head hunters. All I want is that coat so I can get back home."

"That's a lie," he said, stretched out with his eyes closed. "Nice girls shouldn't tell lies. Think of your days ahead in purgatory, the scars on your mortal soul." The drink had done bad things to his head, the bed was shifting, but he held on. "A mortal soul flown out the window," he said, and then he lay moaning to himself, "Darkness da dum dum. Darkness da dum above. And in my heart the deep unending ache of love." He laughed awkwardly at himself because he didn't know why he wanted to say those things to her, to himself. "Back home eh? In a pig's left ear," he said loudly.

"You don't know me."

"Yes I do."

"What do you know?"

"About you flying the coop," and strange flashes of light before his eyes made him fear he was losing his sight.

She sat down beside him. Her hand came to his forehead as if she thought she would find him feverish. Her hand felt wonderfully cool, and he took it and squeezed it and let his fingers run back and forward over her wrist till she drew her hand away. "Don't," she said.

"It's a little thing."

"You're making it something else."

"In my condition? Oh, lady."

"So why can't I get back home?" she asked.

"Not while you have this thing."

"What thing?"

His face was still turned to the wall. "You lose it, even a little, may be it goes forever. I can't lose it. Not while I feel the way I do. I'm no loser. Not yet. Hey, listen lady. I'll tell you something."

"Yeah?"

"I'm a believing man. Life is a lovely mystery, still is, long after I took to the hills."

"What hills?"

He tried to sit up. "Didn't I tell you I flew the coop. Me too. The seminary out there on the bluffs. Not many left there now. God's looking around for missing priests and they're all out in the hills. The night before my vows,

God the years that've gone under the bridge, I was walking along the bluffs, listening to the lake. Maybe you shouldn't listen to the lake – never listen to the lake water if you want to stay still – and I made my way down the bluffs to the shoreline, and from along the shore I could see the blaze of city lights. I don't know. There by the water I felt I could never be a priest and hold the world close enough. Some strange sacramental thing would never touch me. Something in people, a spark, magic, it comes out in some people. I'd felt it in the theatre. This warm spark, maybe it's an ancient religious thing. Anyway, I walked along the shore, walking for miles, right into the city. And here I am, Quaint, eh?"

"Didn't your people come after you?"

"They sure did," he said. Lying on his back, he stared up at the ceiling. "Kind men, good earnest friends, always. I was the son who'd fled his father's house."

"I think you're a little drunk."

He thought he was falling asleep, then he mumbled to her because he knew she was bending over him, listening, "Stuffed with life. That's me! Starving but stuffed, women, pot, dreams. Nothing's bad, nothing's good, nothing! Everything's in the making." His words seemed to hold her in the chair beside him. That was good. "A long time ago, long time ago," he whispered.

"You'll go back," she said.

"Not me. Maybe you, but not me." And he went to sit up again.

"Sure you will," she said cynically. "The prodigal son and all that. They'll make a big thing of it."

"Lady," he began, and he swung his legs off the bed. He felt dizzy. He helped himself to another drink. His face was burning, his eyes so wild and lonely that she went to put her hand out to him, but she drew back, watching his eyes, and he laughed, shaking his head. "I'm probably one of the few people who understands that damn old parable" he said. "No one else knows, no sir, not about our little son who fled his father's coop and finally went home, and sure there was all that tribal hoopla because they knew the wandering boy knew where his bread was buttered. Come on, Ellen," he said solemnly, "you know why he went back. He was a loser. A real loser. That poor guy, going broke and knocking himself out, then he quit. And you know why he quit, Ellen? There was no one around to love. Nothing to lift him up, so he took the easy route, went home. A loser if ever there was one. And you think that's going to be me?" and he laughed mockingly.

"Right now you're full of wild talk," she said. "I don't know who you are, and why should I? Why should I want to?" She walked slowly over to the desk.

"Why aren't you a director?"

"Blacklisted."

"Who blacklisted you?"

"Mr. Forest."

"Who's Mr. Forest?"

"Early in the game I headed for California, and one night I met a producer in a bar and he liked me and we used to talk about oriental philosophy, and he gave me a job and one day in an office he introduced me to Forest. Owns a chain of theatres, distributing companies, and he's crazy about star-making. My producer-friend told him I had a talent for handling women. A sympathy. Oh, I was the fair-haired boy, the one guy who could tell when a girl had that mysterious little light in her eyes."

"Too bad you're still not the fair-haired boy," she said.

"Ambitious. That's good," he muttered and closed his eyes, then was afraid to keep them closed. "The old bastard," he mumbled. "Owns everyone who comes near him and understands no one he owns. Always uneasy about me, my priestly sympathy, that's what he called it. The girls like it." Then his mind began to wander feverishly. Frightened, he spoke rapidly. "Now I can't get the old bastard out of my mind," and he smiled. "Know what his hobby is? Playing the saxophone. Gets all his hunches about plastics and electronics from God. Maybe he is God. But he knows what people always want to see. Someone who can make you feel the world isn't all crap."

For the first time she laughed, a husky laugh. It startled him and he tried to sit up. "Don't laugh," he said.

"You better lie back," she said.

"Yeah, I'd better."

"That's right," she said, then she pondered. "You haven't told me why he had you blacklisted."

"Oh well," He said. "I found the girl he married. He thinks I slept with her."

"Isn't he sure?"

"I don't think so."

"Well, did you?"

"I'm not sure myself. It was a long party," he said sighing. "Anyway he hated her feeling for me."

"Just bringing out the girl's talent, I suppose," she said sardonically. "I don't see how the man could shut you out of everything."

"Look, the word goes out that I'm not to be trusted. Soon people forget why you're not to be trusted. Since a lot of money goes into a picture why take a chance on a man who's supposed to be a trouble maker?" But she was brooding over him and her eyes hurt him. "Have a little charity," he said. "A man gets lonely."

"I've heard that story."

"Not from me," he said. "There's a story, and we're in it. Felt it when you bent over me. Whether you like it or not, you're in my story now." Silent, a little flush on her face, she stood lost in thought.

"I couldn't take that," she said vehemently. "I'd go after him. If he didn't call it off I'd kill him," and the expression he had seen on her face when the manager had torn her dress was there again.

"Oh, I'm right about you," he said. "Dead right," but now he was fighting a drowsiness too warm and soothing to frighten him. "Do I look like I'm starving?", he murmured. "Got a partner who's an old hand, a great old hand. Between us we got the Caribbean casino clubs locked up. Big in the Caribbean. And I still know all the big moustaches in New York." He tried to grin. "It's in the cards that I make it back."

255

"How?"

"Oh, he'll come running."

"You're drunk …"

Sighing, he whispered, "Look, don't leave me. I shouldn't be left alone."

He heard her say gently, a little ironically. "Maybe it's the priest in you …" Her voice was soothing him to sleep, so warm he didn't care what she was saying. "A big boss in the sky somewhere." There was a strange sad sympathy in her voice. "You're not out in the hills far from home. You're a jailbird, Julien Jones, thinking you're working on a key that'll let you walk out when you want to." And he muttered, "Sure, sure, sure," wanting the words to flow on while he sank into sleep. He thought he was dreaming. She was looking down at him, then she began to take her clothes off, she kicked off her shoes, then she lay down beside him and drew him warmly against her.

Head   *Mario Mascarelli*

AN EXCERPT FROM
SNOW

Ascher/Straus

I

SNOW IS SIFTING

more and more heavily down the nine bright squares, three across, three down, ash grey or mother-of-pearl, of her dormer windows. Monica wonders, momentarily, if this will be a heavy snowfall. Then thinks: because she's asked the question the snowfall is bound to be light. Two weeks ago or three she hadn't had any idea it was going to snow. And a good foot and a half filled up all the empty spaces of life.

I

THE SNOW SIFTS HEAVILY

but almost imperceptibly against the bright boxes of industrial mother-of-pearl cloud or ash, probably cigarette. Lost in sifting from box to box, perhaps caught like clear or cloudy grey plastic in the dry branches in the lower panes of the left hand window, Monica doesn't hear the bell ring. (Snowed under?) On the phonograph, piano is playing with clarinet: thoughtful flights toward, timid turns away from the atonal, the discontinuous, the silent, a sort of ride in a horse drawn sleigh, behind two or four magnificent pink-grey horses, through a distant, vanished region of consciousness: the smooth pastures of snow, the double blue shadows of the runners behind you, a tale to be told, a melody that must be returned to, variations, development, a familiar thread of narrative, a life, but still: a feeling as if you were hearing your own broken voice, or as if someone else were listening to you, a few strange, stammering sounds, long pauses in which the voice can be heard not speaking, longing for speech, someone you can see clearly, sitting on a small persian rug, a woman with red highlights in her brown hair, working a complex instrument of reproduction that has yet to be invented.

I

LOST IN SIFTING

or listening to piano and clarinet, she fails to hear:
     bell ringing
     car horn blowing
     human shouting
     night falling

I

AIR MOVES

in vast, fragmented masses. Vision is impossible. Night is blue with cold, houselights as good as blacked out. The storm lasts the night, and by morning houses and cars are muffled. Housewives are troubled by lack of escape routes from their burrows. Housewife A, for example, cannot, absolutely cannot open her back door and it flashes in on her off the snow that if someone were to break in through the front she can't get out the back, even though the back door leads to nothing more than a small, second story porch, a 15 or 20 foot jump to the narrow flagstone "terrace" or small frozen back garden.

I

SNOW PACKS IN AUTOS

and emotions. The ice pack raises rather than reduces the patient's fever. The snow is knee high in some places up to the thigh: it doesn't help it hinders.

I

STEAMY SHADOWS

in the bright shadows or reflections of windows on rugs and chairs.

I

MONICA HEARS FOOTSTEPS

and a churning of low voices, say in the deep stairwell, its twilight blue, its yellow, its brown, its compressed layers of daylight and midnight traversed by mahogany diagonal banisters, below her door. Someone raps lightly at the door and calls Monica's name.

I

LEILA X'S VOICE

is allowed by Monica to become "Leila X":

olive green wool toque or ample
beret

with pom-pom

blond hair
profile: drops of snow melting on the

lashes

258

                        long bluegrey coat
                        red (sweater)/white (blouse)
                        showing
out at the throat

                        tan cotton slacks
                        white socks
                        blue slippers

Monica is glad or says that she's glad to see Leila: talk about anything but the "duet" (or is it the "sonata"?) she's struggling to put on paper. Leila, as usual, talks about her mother. Something about ma's case: hard to believe it will all be settled a week from Thursday, after so many years of delay. Story of the landlord, the fire, the furniture, etc.: repeated, remembered or merely supposed.

"That soon?"

Behind this false expression of genuine surprise, Monica may be weighing the loss of a day's writing against the gain of a day's tunnelling into X family life. (How "deep" does she want to go? An illusion to think one can remain an observer: one plays a role no matter what. Drawn in through the eyes, if nothing else.)

Leila says that ma's friend, the pianist, Marthe B., knew the furniture well and will testify to ma's sanding, scraping, rubbing with linseed, etc., etc.

I

ICICLES

lengthen to shorten, blaze to disappear.

I

A SENSE OF MELANCHOLY

seems to be called for by: dark skies and falling snow. A familiar sense of melancholy, a bottomless shallow blue well, begins to collect in Housewife B2 with the first snowflake, the second footprint, the fourth auto track, the tenth flurry, the hundredth rattle of the storm windows, etc. Days later, when it begins to thaw, it only feels worse. "As if it were spring." Leaning out the window she feels that the air is sweet, the thigh-deep mass is melting into fragrant steam: "every blue shadow a flowering branch of vapor."

I

MAKE A LIST

of ways it might be possible for you to hear the following "tale." For example:

1) your old friend has just come from a great distance to pay you a visit

259

it's snowing and you sit on the royal blue rug of the large room (your own or someone else's?) talking and talking

memories

a sort of map of ambiguous regions the lives of others or stories attached to more or less familiar names broken lines drawn between these names and here and there beneath this quite palpable horizontal plane a vertical extension a well of language allusions and so on

who is it you or your old friend who says or thinks 'just like Priscilla Lane and Anne Dvorak' (or is it 'Ann Sheridan and Ella Raines' or)

words

you feel that dark stains ought to appear on the enormous blotting pad of the rug

2) your name is Monica and a friend, one of those friends who drops in every 6 months or so and tells 100 stories in 2 hours, say someone named Leila X, is sitting on the orange three-legged stool in your green studio: she's just told you the story of the woman (a cousin of Leila's you've never heard of or an "old highschool chum" named Agnes) who was killed just like this driving on an icy sidestreet in Forest Hills or someplace like that when a crane dropped a load of cinder blocks or sandbags through the roof of her late model auto, a brown Dart or yellow Fury, she isn't sure: now she asks you if you remember Anna or is it Rosemarie or Tanya:

3) in order for you to overhear the story on a bus how many other events, propositions, stories, etc. are necessary:

let's see:

a) you wake up in actual place only you can propose: only you know (might know, might begin to know, might remember, might forget, etc.) for example what exactly what objects are on the second and third shelves of one or another familiar enclosure for chance, interior presence of strange, compressed models of "the World," and so one, what titles of what texts with their stories and information can be read off in order or at random on the dark bottom shelf of the bookcase, etc., what light falls through the tremendous or tiny window, etc. etc.

a₁) one morning I wake up for example to find snow on the ground: not a sign last night, when I fell asleep, but nevertheless, there it is: snow – sleep: snow is still falling outside my dormer windows, no matter what I do I can't seem to wake up, etc.: cream cheese pancakes, black currant jam, Bokar the coffee with heated cream for breakfast, while reading perhaps: "the interlude begins with a brief duet between the celesta and cello. Other instruments creep into the polyphony and among them the piano, which soars up in a solo of paroxysmic trills. It is accompanied for a few measures by percussion instruments; then, at the moment of a cymbal crash, makes way for a brief violin cadenza, before returning to challenge, as it were, its stringed rival, finally drowning it out completely," and so on: snow continues to fall: yellow streetlamps: or simply "a strange lack of lucidity, as if it were night": and so on

b) everything that happens in the street, say walking through slush and water up to the calf, on the way to the bus stop

catalogue of *everything* (everything) seen heard etc. from the moment you step out the door to the moment you enter the bus, with the next-to-the-last item supplied by "me": old woman in skyblue stocking cap, that is, bluer than any sky, more natural than anything in nature, hand knit fiction that nevertheless warms the head, hears someone call out from a distance of 20 yards or so, "IT'S BEGINNING TO THAW OUT!", and slips on a patch of ice that corresponds exactly with the first G in the word BEGINNING

c) memories of what you did or didn't see out the window while riding on the bus and listening to the story or stories being told in front of you, memories you have "now" if you didn't "then":

1st possible memory: on the blue bridge: snow on red clay: as if they were building a new road

2nd possible memory: a solid block of orange snow ("second interior canvas"?)

3rd possible memory: sun but not a drop of snow is melting: a brilliant glaze (resemblances 1–15): frozen footsteps (that lead from "you" toward "me," from "me" toward "you," from "you or "me" toward "it", across what "bridge"): margin of frozen mounds, blue snow rocks, etc.

4th possible memory: as if it were giving off heat: you see a woman in brown mouton, dark blue wool seaman's cap, red highlights in the wavy masses of chestnut brown hair, sitting on a grey wooden porch with pen and paper, surrounded by snow: how does she do it: now is when it says (we say) "as if it were giving off heat": gathering warmth from a few grains of light in the snow, few grains of snow in the ice

5th possible memory: do you remember something that appears "later" or "in the distance," do you recall a "unit" that hasn't appeared yet, may never appear, etc., while riding, listening, daydreaming, and so on: Audrey Hepburn sitting on a pale blue windowsill or window seat in a white dress or gown, watching the parade of soldiers (red + white + gold) marching off to fight Napoleon in the opening scene of *War and Peace* (how much snow?), and saying: "it's so unfair   men are the *only* ones allowed to have any *fun!*"

6th possible memory: blue air is frozen: penetrates whose thin gloves: yours, woman in 4th memory, mine?

7th possible memory: lefthand window of two third storey roominghouse windows you see for precisely 5.5 seconds from at least 11 different angles: venetian blinds down 4/5: within the square of the venetian blinds you see a sort of bluish shadow: frame of white: bottom bar of the frame might be a shadow or the interior of a room: inside the frame a white rectangle: within the white rectangle a lateral pencil line: space ("nothing"?) between the slats or: remainder of the window surface glazed with a yellow glare of muddled reflections: map of THE WORLD: possibility of a tall brown object toward the right that looks very much like

8th impossible memory: the dark figure in the gas station (the figure in the dark gas station) moving toward the car that's pulled up to the locked pump

9th impossible memory: moving along rapidly: how many frozen roads, paths, highways, pavements etc. within the simultaneous grid of real fictions, nothing less real than anything else, family sitting in blue television light behind the window, clothesline, with its white shirts and towels, discarded magazines with their interior miles of text, voice through telephone recounting the plot of *The Worst Woman in Paris*, man in blazing orange hat, that radiates for 200 miles or so, etc., etc.: nothing more real than anything else, each thing a shared invention: snow that looks like ice: fired in the oven: a ceramic glaze

      10th memory: everything else

      d) describe in catalogue form (with or without making a special effort, "paying attention," and so on) the two women seated exactly where in relation to you, who are talking (say in electronically amplified stage whispers) and who tell the infinitely explained tale of the borrowed blue comb that immediately precedes, follows or surrounds the STORY OF THE WOMAN IN THE PARKING LOT or whatever other heading you later attach to the tale that may have already begun to follow

   4) a story you could have heard but didn't

      a story you *could not* have heard (but did?) for x/11 obvious reasons in *A Woman's Face* with Joan Crawford and Melvin Douglas, in *Hold Back the Dawn* with Charles Boyer neither, not even in some forgotten or edited moment of the 4 hour technicolor version of *War and Peace*

   5) a memory of your own: that is: real unreality of something that actually happened once-upon-a-time but which you now must relate to others or to yourself as *if* it had happened

   6) precisely the same as or utterly different from the 10th memory

      Story That Follows, Precedes, Is Embedded
      In (Second, Third, Fourth, Etc. Interior
      Canvas?) How Many Other Stories, Story of
      The Blue Comb, Story Of Last Night's Dream
      Told In An Airmail Letter From Stockholm
      Or Cairo, And So On

She says: Annemarie met Cunningham through Lucy.

Do you remember "Lucy"? Or do you say, exactly because you don't remember Lucy, but have a certain longing to have known someone named Lucy, an old chum, particularly because you're reminiscing with Priscilla on the soft blue rug of the borrowed house: oh sure, Lucy, she moved into our neighborhood in the senior year of high school, she and Annemarie were like this.

Gus Cunningham: the great love of Annemarie's life. They used to drive to different parking lots. "I first made love to Gus Cunningham in an A & P parking lot."

Still, Annemarie would have liked to go out to a film or to dinner or something like that. But Cunningham said he couldn't. "I'm afraid for my life, Annemarie." Seems Cunningham had gotten a girl pregnant in a little town called Wolf Hollow or Beaver Falls or is it Lime Lake or Loon Lake or Orange Lake or Swan Lake or Blue Mountain Lake, or in Pleasant Valley or Hopewell Junction. Now he can't be seen in public. If the father or one of the brothers sees him with another woman they'll kill him. He figures they're watching all the restaurants and movie theaters in New York, with his luck they'll spot him the first time he sets foot in Uncle John's Bar, The Court Cafe, The Blue Danube, The Ballroom, or "The World" movie house.

Annemarie felt that if they weren't going to go to movies or restaurants, it was time to have intercourse. "Everyone else seems to be doing it."

Cunningham said he didn't believe in it. Didn't think it was proper outside of marriage.

So Annemarie used to give Cunningham blow jobs.

You feel the need to make the following rough summary: In other words, for months or years, Annemarie and Gus would meet x times a week, they'd drive to some supermarket, park in the dark parking lot, now and again they'd go to the vast parking lots out at the public beaches, say in Rockaway or Atlantic Beach, and Annemarie would give Gus Cunnigham a blow job.

Yes. "Next comes the story, 'the inevitable story,' of Jeffrey or Leroy or Al." Annemarie meets a man she doesn't love and marries him, has a boring life, as if on purpose, in order to cherish unbelievable memories of Gus Cunningham she can share with her friends, say late at night over the telephone, when her husband is away on business, etc. (Is this another method that ought to be added to the list of possible methods of hearing the story of Annemarie and Gus? Try to remember if you have a friend named Annemarie or Lucy, if you have a *yearning* to have a friend named Annemarie or Lucy, etc.)

After 8 or 10 years with Malcolm or John, they separate, Annemarie moves back to her old neighborhood.

One day the phone rings. "Remember me? It's Gus Cunningham!" "Of course I remember you, Gus! Did you really think I could forget ('could *ever* forget')?" "It's incredible, I can't believe it! I called your mother just like this, out of curiosity: I say, 'How's Annemarie doing, is she ok?' 'What do you mean, Gus, don't you know? Annemarie is back in the neighborhood. She's separated from Walter ...' Can you imagine? It must have been an inspiration!" Annemarie's heart is pounding, "after all these years," etc.

They meet.

Cunningham drives to the tremendous parking lot out at Riis Park on the Rockaway peninsula. Perhaps Cunningham has chosen this particular lot for the occasion: sentimental memories, the low, uncluttered horizon, the handsome bath house, the border of evergreens, the vast, snowy field that helps enclose them in the warm interior ...

Without a word of introduction he starts to pull off his pants.

"Gus, what are you doing?"

He says that he still doesn't believe in intercourse outside marriage.

Does Annemarie give him a blow job or not?

Is it lighthearted, a happy reunion? Does she throw up? Does she scream and try to tear his skin off when it dawns on her that etc? Does she go home and swallow 2 dozen meprobamate tablets? Or do they both cry in the dark auto, parked in the center of the vast snow-covered parking lot, when they discover that, miraculously, they're still in love, after all these years. And so on ....

TREATISE ON WHITE AND TINCTURE

Robert Marteau

Stasis,
no fluttering. No scuffling,
no moon in the boxwood,
no wind. Who can say mist is green
before dawn? In the well, what reflecting cloud?
No gosling in the bulrushes,
no egg, no mother,
no water.

Inverse of eight,
a verging water-lily never seen.
The eagle had not yet flown.
No rend in the wave
from flute or reed.

The source of breath
abides in the absent mouth.
No wash-house paddle or name
moves the unmoved mover.

Contravene the ovum
in the lee of sighs.
Don't christen the blind worm
until the animus of animation
and the desert cuppola
determine its identity,
anticipating Eve's arrival
at the swirling serpent's font.

Vehement seas invite
no forked male,
no arrow inseminates
the surge of insoluble salt.
No tuft at the blowhole,
no plunge where the skein
trembles.

Nothing's alike, axis or beam,
when nothing is equal, all is weightless,
except the future's
palpable shadow in the pans,
settled stakes
in the scales.

The volatile sphere
unfolds unencumbered, boundless,
Ocean without succoring cove,
yet sometimes temples
refurbish their future
music.

With one wave
this fish pond, where no eel
spawns, swells so much the broadening
ring breaks beyond the border
memory will mark for death
if the shattering reversal
returns.

Within the sphere,
the same wave clears the crest.
Though its motion is immutable
a prefigured tutelage
lies broken in the other's image.

When there's neither scale,
nor hourglass, sand, mire, nor marsh,
how can swirling itself
settle into a nest
of peat?

Fire
in the low combes of the Vendées!
Suddenly this tang of apple
and the tree erect in the lap of the world
while still waters counterpoise moons
and coronary branches bloom.

Come, Venus,
unravel your hair in the river,
beached by a shell somewhere
beyond contemplation.
A love-knot, only you can untie it
so that desire aroused in a murmur
may measure the tree.

Translated by Barry Callaghan

THE T.E. LAWRENCE POEMS

Gwendolyn MacEwen

The Water-Bearer

On a hill in Carcemish which is in Mesapotamia, which is
    Between-The-Rivers,
We dug up the bones and artifacts of ancient strangers,
You and your donkey lugging buckets of water
    back and forth over many thousands of years,
While I made notes about absolutely everything, and
    wrote long letters home.

You watered the mules and camels and nothing was ever
Too petty or tiresome that you couldn't make mad and
    silly fun of it;
    everything admired you.
The animals admired you because you had a splendid
    disregard for man that even they
    could not achieve. And a dark and mighty love
That only they could achieve.

When it was too hot, we swam, and then the river
Released us and found its way back home.

They called you Darkness because your skin was fair;
I gave you a camera and taught you how to explore
    the darkness that lived behind light;
You said you would take pictures of the whole world.

Water-bearer, you gave everything and asked nothing
    in return. We dreamed that one day
    the ghosts of your ancestors would arise
    and tell to us wonderful Hittite secrets;
But we did not know what was to come, we had forgotten
    that your name meant also
    the darkness of water before Creation
Or that you would one day drown in the dark water
Of your own lungs.

I loved you, I believe. It was before the horror.

Naked People

Do you really like naked women? I asked my sculptor
    friend.
They express so little.
I've never thought twice or even
Once of a naked woman. Does that mean I'm abnormal, or
A unicorn who's strayed among sheep, and what on earth
Does *that* mean?

Kurdish ladies with awful thin lips once ripped almost all
    my clothes off, outside Carcemish
    and giggling, felt me up all over.
I wonder if they found me beautiful. Their jewellery
Was blue and silver. I wore no jewels.
I carved you naked in limestone for the roof of the house
In Carcemish, but your nakedness only made you
    more secret and inviolable than before.
For a while I thought the stone would contain you, but
    nothing contained you, not even
The bold bright clothes you wore, not even the whole
Width of the sky, and the length of the bright river.

It was as though you assumed
    the world for a while;
Then it fell still, naked and chill and wondering.

Excavating in Egypt

Nobody knows how cold the nights can get in a land
Where sun is lord of the morning. It comes at you
    like a sword, the cold, and lays its side
    along your ribs;
there the flat steel sings
And you shiver under it, waiting for the dawn.

By day in Kafr Ammar we found trinkets of a people
Who lived there before the pharaohs, – odd jewels
    and sad little things that could have been
    gods, or toys;
    whatever they were, one played with them.

By night we grew fearful of these things; as the air
    grew more and more chill
    we gathered them up and returned to the tents,
    smelling of a thousand sweet, pungent spices,
Having wrapped ourselves in the funeral-cloths of the dead.

Solar Wind

for Ali

I did not choose Arabia.
It chose me.
The shabby money that the desert offered us
Bought lies, bought victory.

But I could drown in your mighty eyes, Ali.

I have not been in the water since Aqaba.
I take baths, though, hot ones, scalding me.

We carried these knapsacks of mighty secrets
which mean war,
the bundles of rotting money,
the green figs, the lies.

My various parts burn one by one
from the elbows to the knees.
I have been burning since the day I was born.

Know me, I dare you, know me.

In the white light of these deserts
The villages predict each other –
They are districts of the mind.

The man who served us sheep and rice at dusk
Was blind.

SEVEN LAMENTS FOR THE FALLEN IN THE WAR

Yehuda Amichai

1.

Mr. Beringer, whose son
fell by the Canal, which
was dug by strangers
for ships to pass through the desert,
is passing me at the Jaffa gate;

He has become very thin; has lost
his son's weight.
Therefore he is floating lightly
through the alleys
getting entangled in my heart
like driftwood.

2.

As a child he mashed potatoes
into golden puree.
After that one dies.

The living child has to be
cleaned after it returns from play.
But for the dead man
earth and sand are clear water
in which forever
he'll cleanse his flesh and purify.

3.

The monument of the unknown soldier,
beyond, on the enemy's side.
A good target marker for the gunners
of future wars.

Or the war monument in London,
Hyde Park Corner, decorated

like a rich, splendid cake: one more
soldier raising head and rifle,
one more gun, another eagle, another
angel made of stone.

Whipped cream of a big marble flag
is poured over it all
with expert hand.

But the sugarcoated too-red
cherries
were eaten up already
by the gourmet of hearts. Amen.

4.

I found an old Text Book of animals,
Brehm, second volume, birds:
Description, in sweet language, of the lives
of crows, swallows and jays. A lot of mistakes
in gothic printing, but a lot of love: "Our
feathered friends," "emigrate to warmer
countries." "Nest, dotted egg, soft plumage,
the nightingale, "prophets of spring"
The Red-Breasted Robin.

Year of printing 1913, Germany
on the eve of the war which became
the eve of all my wars.

My good friend, who died in my arms and in his blood
in the sands of *Ashdod, 1948, in June.

Oh, my friend,
red breasted.

5.

Dicky was hit,
like the water tower at **Yad Mordecai
was hit. A hole in his belly. Everything
poured out of him.

*Asdod – A major battle in the Israeli war of Independence
**Yad Mordecai – a kibbutz in the south

But he has remained thus, standing
in the landscape of my memory,
like the water tower at Yad Mordecai.
Not far from there he fell,
a little to the north, near *Houleikat.

6.

Is all of this sorrow? I don't know.
I was standing in the cemetery, wearing
camouflage clothes of the living:
brown trousers and a shirt yellow as the sun.
Cemeteries are cheap and very undemanding.
Even waste-baskets are small, just
to hold thin wrapping paper of bought flowers,
Cemeteries are a well behaved and disciplined thing.

"and I shall never forget you" thus written
on a little ceramic plate, in French.

I don't know who is it, that shall never forget
he is even more unknown than the dead.
Is all of this sorrow? I think
so: "May you be comforted by the building of the land."

How much more can one build the land
to catch up in this terrible three cornered contest
between comfort and building and death?

Yes, all this is sorrow. But leave
a little love burning, always
like in a sleeping baby's room, a little bulb,
without it knowing what the light is
and where it comes from. Yet it gives
a little feeling of security and silent love.

7.

Memorial day for the War-dead. Add now
the grief of all your losses to their grief,
even of a woman that has left you. Mix
sorrow with sorrow, like time-saving history
which stacks holiday and sacrifice and mourning
on one day for easy convenient memory.

*Houleikat – a battle field in the south

271

Oh, sweet world soaked, like bread
in sweet milk for the terrible toothless God.
"Behind all this some great happiness is hiding"
No use to weep inside and to scream outside.
Behind all this perhaps some great happiness is hiding.

Memorial day. Bitter salt is dressed up
as a little girl with flowers.
The streets are cordoned off with ropes,
for the marching together of the living and the dead.
Children with a grief not their own march slowly,
like stepping over broken glass.

The flautist's mouth will stay like that for many days,
A dead soldier swims above little heads
with the swimming movements of the dead
with the ancient error the dead have
about the place of the living water.

A flag loses contact with reality and flies off
A shop window is decorated with
dresses of beautiful women, in blue and white,
And everything in three languages:
Hebrew, Arabic and Death.

A great and royal animal is dying
all through the night under the jasmin
tree with a constant stare at the world.

A man whose son died in the war walks in the street
like a woman with a dead embryo in her womb,
"Behind all this some great happiness is hiding."

Translated by the author and Ted Hughes

SPELLS OF FURY

Michel Beaulieu

8

shipwreck and eyes adrift
burnt rope between teeth
founder you founder in the tackling of words
in this slow cry burrowing sideways into
the exquisite warmth of your womb
you load your shoulders with a shawl of mist
and only water betrays blood by its color
your damp feet soak up sand
when uneasy you watch the sea the sea the sea

9

that the tangent so briefly meets the circle
you were taught long ago in geometry books
you did not know the meaning of objects
that men resemble them despite appearances
with the pitiless hammer of their fists
driving nails into everything
time teaches too early what is forgotten too quickly
the meaning of veins lacking intrinsic meaning
and that the sea devours her vessels

13

so much rain so much rain and our bodies
riveted to the gesture of being but shadows
behind the cardboard of walls and codes
we were told of crosses on space
of scratches across the face
in his own tongue he recounted the legend
we listened in a crumpling of clothes
the day bent its back over the day
curtailing this voice where time trembles

17

you weighed little on my hand
hardly the flutter of a bird on wing
a loaf of bread in the centre of the table
an apple rolling towards the floor
not much on the hand but blood
you clasped in your frozen fingers
in you laughter the glimpse of a drowned girl
in the arms and shoulders splinters
bits of straw on the fire's braids

21

shores fill his brow
when his hand stretches over the apple orchard
does he still know the meaning of the knife piercing
at the precise spot between the ribs
where the heart beats and pumps its blood
does he still know that everything comes
from beams thrown across the ice
the island caught in the vice of currents
sound gorging his body with glitter

26

in the end you quiver at the heart of colors
where drowsy shadows attack you
they emerge with a taste of ashes
if you open the curtain onto the penumbra
a moving lamp plays in the pane
and the world shudders with embers between your lashes
my space my tender offer my impetuous beach
the old wound flows along the thorn
when darkly you founder pinned to my back

27

lamps compasses aside
look at the frightening meaning of our coordinates
when you bend to the last inclination
there you are ripe from fires and dusts
attacked by glimmers fusing from yourf fingers
water streams in the veins of bricks
in aromas where the lover lies in ambush
you rise everywhere between equinoxes
and perched high you contemplate the space beyond

Translated by Arlette Francière

274

AN EXCERPT FROM
WHITE BITING DOG

Judith Thompson

The Characters

Cape

A very handsome silky young man who could seduce almost anybody in twenty minutes. He is *compulsively* seductive, extremely charming and manipulative. He thinks and speaks very quickly, changing mental gears constantly and with great alacrity. He seems to be flirting with everyone he talks to. He even flirts with the audience while telling them the most terrible things about himself. Mid to late twenties.

Glidden

The kind of man others refer to as "lightweight." He is kind, loves to play pranks and wants desperately for his life to be like a Norman Rockwell painting. He is dying of a disease contracted from the constant handling of sphagnum moss – gardening was one of his chief pleasures. In the last few years he has realized that people constantly patronize him and he fights this. Without his wife he has no reason to live. Late fifties or early sixties.

Pony

Her clothing should express her directness: natural fabrics, simply walking shoes, subdued colors, no prints, nice lines. Clothes are for comfort, but are always neat. Her hair should be out of her face, but should not bring attention to itself. She is deeply ethical. Anywhere from twenty to thirty-five or so.

Lomia

She is not knowingly campy and is not a performer. She is obsessed with her physical being. She is often very shy and girlish as well as nasty and powerful. She is buffeted by sensation. Her words are out before the thought is clear in her head; she thinks *as* she speaks. Her clothes should *not* conform to the stereotype of a flamboyant woman. Forty-five to fifty-five.

Pascal

He was brilliant at physics and at chess. He strives to approach the world and every thought freshly. He spends all his time thinking about experience. His costume and hair should reflect this. He can be of any color or ethnicity. Twenty to thirty.

Author's Note:

The wall to GLIDDEN's room must be transparent. Three hard baseballs are on the set.

The Opening of Act Two
GLIDDEN, dressed up in a tux, has set the table beautifully. He is holding up a fork in each hand, and is very excited.

Glidden
Funny how my ... little trick worked. I-I first learned to do it when I was seven years old and my best buddy Tommy fell out of our tree and the next the next day I was sent-sent to Ashbury where-where my feet were always cold and I was called "Figface" and had to sleep in wet sheets and missing Mummy and Grace so ... fiercely – that's when I learned to-to always ... expect the worst. Start-start with little things, see, expect there to be no hot water, not to find your socks, then move up to dinner expect only dog food, expect to have bloody nightmares then a merely "bad" dream, is really quite good! Look forward to nothing, and backward to nothing and it's all ... okay. Like a nice train ride. So I ... yes, I ... expected my wife to leave me, a beautiful woman like that? I used to run home at lunch every day just to see if she was still there. Do you think I expected that heaven to last? That heaven of phoning up from work at five o'clock. And saying "Darl, I'm through! Shall I pick something up on the way home?" And her saying "Yes pooch, a loaf of brown." No-no she had to escape that – she had to escape being – bored. I was – boring. Of course she left. I certainly NEVER ever expected her to come back!! That's the ... thing of it, eh? It's the way things just work, the fates love to be tricky to give, give you that which you do not expect. Even now, I don't ... dare to believe that she *loves* me, not yet, only that perhaps she ... likes me – I have made some contribution to my field, after all – you're – you're not given a standing ovation for nothing, are you and ... I'll tell you a moment in time like this makes me feel that there really is some spirit of good about ... cornball, eh? The one other time I have felt this ... spirit ... is when my son, my son was young and I watched him eat. I used to ... love ... to see him eat. (jumps back into the here and now) Oh! Oh oh!

(GLIDDEN sees his forks, places them, and rushes back to the kitchen. PONY and CAPE step out of the bedroom. They have made love. They kiss)

Cape
I've never even liked a woman till I met you, you know.

Pony
No. How come?

Cape
I'm – ashamed of this but – women to me were just sort of cysts – dermoid cysts? I read about them, they're female hormones, just hair and oil and teeth, all in a – cyst – hah. That's all women were to – me.

Pony
Jeeps. You musta had a bad experience playin' doctor or somethin'.

276

Cape

Or maybe they were that way. Not you though you are so – good! I want to be like you, you're perfect.

Pony

No I'm not.

Cape

Yes! Hydra thighs and all! (slaps her bottom) Shit. No, really, you are, you're perfect. Per–

Pony

I have bad qualities.

Cape

What?

Pony

I don't like Jews. There was this family in Kirkland, the Wibbys? They lived out by the shoe factory, eh? So once me and Sherry got this can of rust proofer from her brother and we painted all over their windows with it. Then we grabbed their eleven year old Darlene? She was already havin' her period and we didn't yet, so we wanted to see what she was like, eh, so we took her to Sherry's parents' master bedroom. Everything was blue velvet, and we made her strip. Then we cut off all her hair because it was so blonde and we stuck it to their windows.

(CAPE laughs through his nose. PONY laughs shyly in turn. He laughs harder, so does she. He caresses her and they start necking)

Pony

Oh. Oh. (pulls him down to floor, is very passionate, then quickly jumps away) Oh no – Gol ... oh *no*!

Cape

What's the matter?

Pony

I was right! Like last night – in ... the middle ... it was so ... beautiful ... I was scared. I was scared 'cause I knew I'd do anything ... ANYTHING AT ALL ... for that ... feeling again ... not just sex. It's the thing with you – didn't matter that you're married. It was like we were upside down in one of them big *Nova Scotia vaves* – I was scared 'cause I thought I'd do ... real ... bad for that feeling ... ANYTHING, then I thought things'd look different in the morning and they did I thought they did but then just now when you were rubbing me down I got that again, I got that big wash and I know. I know now that I would. That somethin' has hatched and – I would ... do ANYTHING ... for ... to get that feelin' again. That I got with you. So ... I'm no different than when we did that to Darlene, no different at all, see?

277

Cape

(grabs her wrists tightly) What we did, it wasn't bad, Pony. It was beautiful like you said. It was *ecstasy*.

Pony

It's ... it's probably a sin to like me the way I am now, you know, a sex fiend, a home wrecker, it's probably ... (shaking, teeth chattering)

Cape

PONY. Get a grip on yourself. Like you told me– get a

Pony

You want me to? You want me to? For you, I will. I will even though knowing what I know about myself hurts worse than sharp sticks shoved up under all my nails, I'm gonna get a grip. Cape. 'Cause I love you. I love you more than anything else on this earth. (GLIDDEN, bringing in a cake, sings Herb Alpert)

Glidden

You say this guy, this guy's in love with you youuuuu – this guy's in looooove ... who looks at you the wayyy I do, tell me now ...

Cape

(gasps loudly) Oh no he thinks that Mum is gonna – Dad!! He-he – good morning!

Glidden

How-how does it look?

Cape

Ace, ace. Is this for–

Glidden

I thought a-a – sense of occasion would be nice.

Cape

Dad – remember Pony?

Glidden

Yes, yes. You must be starved! Will ya – stay to lunch? (goes to get another chair)

Cape

You look so, so well!

Glidden

I feel – like a young Sequoia– and – your mum always loved me in a tux, so I thought – why the heck not. What've I got to lose? (whispers) She's –

probably breaking it off with that fellow now – he'll be okay. Your mother always was good with human feelings–

(LOMIA and PASCAL open the bedroom door. The others hear LOMIA and PASCAL about to come out. CAPE looks desperately at PONY)

Pony
Oh-uh – pardon my nose sir but as a previous paramedic I don't think you should eat a thing. I think you should go to bed.

Glidden
Pardon? Oh no I feel better than I've felt in twenty years.

(LOMIA enters with PASCAL. Wearing an old private school sweater of CAPE's, she stretches)

Lomia
GOOD morning everybody. Ewww I feel all cakey. GLID! You're up and about! What are you ...

Glidden
Your presence, milady, has had a PANACEAN effect.

Lomia
What a charming thing to say. You look so elegant ... what a WONDERFUL set-up what's it–

Glidden
In honor-honor of you–

Cape
Ready baby? Watch me die.

Pony
Use your brain – make it right.

Cape
Why? I go down she goes with me.

Glidden
I – thought what the heck let's go to town after all these things only happen once ... Good morning, Pascal. Did you sleep well?

Pascal
What? Oh – my – eyes are kind of – filmy – um, scratchy, you know, but I can ... see–

Glidden
I'm glad of that. Did you sleep well? No, I already said that. I mean are you – ah ... no hard feelings, eh?

Pascal

No hard ... oh, about the *mould*? No – no I'm hon-honored to be here and – and I just ... want to tell you – that um – you – you look just like my old home form teacher and – we really – liked him ... He was a good – human.

Glidden

Good! That's good, would you like to stay to lunch? That is if it's not too painful for you?

Pascal

Painful? OH! Oh she's told you oh no, my ulcers – shrunk now – I can eat even ... pizza so lunch'll be ...

Glidden

La? Wouldn't we like Pascal to stay to lunch?

(LOMIA has been arranging things, looking in the kitchen)

Lomia

Of course! As long as he promises not to drool!

Glidden

THAT is a jab at ME, I'm afraid ... I always had my elbows on the table.

Lomia

Pony! Did you have a deep sleep?

Pony

Well, not very, really.

Lomia

I'm sorry, you must be ... tired ...

Glidden

(claps hands, puts on party hat) WELL. As master of cere-mony, I would like you all to ... get the heck in your seats!! Last one there's a dirty rotten so and so!

(CAPE and LOMIA run to the table. CAPE puts on a party hat)

Lomia

Yes sirreeeee sir!

Pascal

Oh my stomach is contracting like a snail? When you ... touch it ...?

Pony

You're not whispering today.

Pascal
No. No. It wasn't right. I'm re-thinking it.

Lomia
He's searching, right foof? Gliddie this is CHAMPAGNE!!

Glidden
I trust there are no teetotallers here?

Lomia
Eeeee. I always feel champagne in my ankles first.

Cape
So did Janis. My ex-wife.

Lomia
Janis didn't have ankles, just one long calf! Sorry, that was mean.

Pony
In Hawaii, thick ankles are a sign of great beauty.

Glidden
Well may I be so BOLD as to propose a toast?

Lomia
Carumba!

Glidden
Lomia!

Cape
To us!

Pony
Each of us!

Pascal
Yippyoooooooooo! (trying to show he can have a good time) Yip – yip (building) yip yip– Yippyooooo!

Cape
Pascal you're the life of the party! Well I'm gonna hork back some of that cake. (takes some)

Pascal
The icing is so white; like the great shark – um – almost mean – um. I mean ... in my ... personally.

Glidden
Thank you Pascal what a nice head of hair you have. (to others) Guess who made it?

Lomia
YOU?

Glidden
Mrs. Ainsley!!

Lomia
She still comes? OH I couldn't be in the same room when she was cleaning, what was her perfume? Fer-mented armpit mixed with SPIC and SPAN?

Glidden
We called her Atom Bomb!!

Lomia
Oh YES!! And remember her favorite snack was cold chicken fat, right from the pan?! She would–

Cape
I thought she was cool.

Lomia
She liked you very much. (pause)

Pascal
Being-being a cleaning lady must be very ... hard on the ... skin of your knees, I would think.

Glidden
Yes. (serves himself cake) Well, since speeches would bore us all to sleep, I'm going to share a little joke.

Lomia
Joke! I don't believe I've ever heard you tell a joke!

Glidden
(cuffs her playfully) Okay, which's it gonna be, wide-mouthed frog, or horses and coal? (pause)

Pony
Ah – horses and coal sounds good!

Glidden
Then horses and coal it is. Well. There was a horse and his – no – that's not it – there was a – hold on, hold on a second – Hang on a moment, I'll have her in a minute – (paces)

Cape
Mother you sound like a pig in a slop-trough.

(LOMIA looks up with horror, puts more cake in her mouth, chews it carefully and swallows)

Lomia
Do I? (pause; leaves table, goes to window)

Glidden
I've got it! Heh! Look at your mother. I bet she's hoping to see a red cardinal!! Heh Heh! SO – there were these two magnificent white palominos, and there they were, both fillies, down in the basement of a beautiful castle counting an enormous pile of coal. One, two– (blanks; rises) I wonder if you'd excuse me for a moment–

Pony
(walks over to LOMIA) I – ah – nothing – ah – personal but – ah – may I inquire as to how much you might weigh?

Lomia
Pardon?

Pony
I – didn't mean that I mean – jeesh what's wrong with me I mean – I want to know what it is you have when you walk into a room you – make me feel as though I'm flying in my sleep, you know? Do you – know what that is? Maybe ...

Lomia
It's because I – *love* being inside of my six layers of skin; it's de-licious in here – every time I breathe I sort of – breathe out *seeds, seeds*. I feel – I inside I feel like ... (honest) ... like ... sewage.

(GLIDDEN re-enters, and immediately speaks)

Glidden
And a thousand more to go! Well suddenly, just like that, two eggs went flying overhead in the sky, and these prize horses they looked at each other ...

Lomia
(to PONY) It's true.

Glidden
... and what in the hell do you think they said? They said, "tsk, tsk, tsk."
(pause)

Pascal

(clapping) Beautiful!! Soooo – *layered* – and – um –

Cape

I've never understood it.

Glidden

Neither have I!

Lomia

(lighting up) From over here it sounded wonderful! (kisses him) I'm so happy we're friends again, pooch. This is really fun. (kisses his cheek; puts on party hat)

Glidden

(pulls her onto his knee; in funny voice) Get in your place *woman*!! That always gets a rise out of her! Well darl, I guess we might as well tell them now, eh?

Lomia

Sure! What?

Glidden

She's playing innocent – WICKED woman– (whispers to LOMIA) Don't worry, I'll do it I – seeing as my wife is too shy, I would like to make a little announcement – concerning the both of us concerning our– Mr. and Mrs.-ness –we ... are ... going to be ... living together again ... as man and wife and it has made us both ... very happy. Hey a real Lucille Ball this one, you know what she told me? She promised, cross her heart and hope to die, that she will never take another book of mine into the bath and get all the pages wet. Now if you have ever seen my wife reading in the bath, and I trust that you haven't, you know that that promise is well let's just say–

Lomia

No Glidden. (takes his hand away)

(GLIDDEN makes a funny face as if he is about to be hit, then points to LOMIA)

Glidden

She doesn't like to be teased.

Lomia

NO GLIDDEN.

Glidden

(looks at her in a very "couple" way) My– (points to his hair, to where dandruff would fall and brushes off a bit)– no?? posture, oh am I – uh oh, by your faces, I've committed quite the stumblebum. I – oh no. Oh NO oh darn I – this is very embarrassing. Mr. Pascal? Will you accept my apologies – I just presumed that my wife had – told you I – I don't know what to say I – if there's any way we can make it up to you – I – please feel free to come to our home as often as you– Hey' What are you doing for Christmas next year I– Lommy makes a very good hard sauce, it's her specialty, isn't that so, Lom, now what's in it brandy, icing sugar –

Lomia
... Glidden ...

Glidden
Yes.

Lomia
What – what gave you the – idea that I was ... coming back to you?

(Pause. GLIDDEN, in total shock and humiliation, gets up slowly to leave the room. After about three steps, he stops, cocks his head, and shuffles to the window)

Glidden
Goddamn it the dingoes are out best get those sheep in! (goes towards front door)

Lomia
What's happening?

Glidden
Allllright, darl, you can go after them, but for goodness sake if you see an Abbo on walkabout don't run, they're faster than cheetahs, but give him a dollop of cooking fat and he'll be your friend for life. Oh yes, they're big on fat. They ... put it on their heads as ... decoration. Fat hats! Heh. They're a happy people as a whole, the colored people, happy ... and content ... (pause, a bit woozy) So. I guess the two of you will want to hop off and see what you can sal-salvage from the blaze! Here, let me give you that cheque now in case you need to buy some new "threads" – ya – can't go around in our honeymoon nightie forever!! Heh. I – trust you'll stay until you find another place?

Lomia
Oh ... Well. We – we would be very – grateful – are you – sure you don't mind?

Glidden
Mind? Why should I mind? If you can't be good friends with your estranged wife who can you be good friends with?

(GLIDDEN exits. CAPE starts to go out to bridge. Pause)

285

Lomia
Sonny, speaking of – dingoes, are the kids still in the freezer?

(CAPE stops, decides to try one other thing to get his mother back, turns, and puts up his hand as if taking an oath)

Cape
This spring, I promise, I will bury them this spring. (stays at door, facing into room)

Lomia
It has been three years!

Pony
Who are the kids?

Lomia
Our dachshunds! Erica, Gretchen and Hans – we had them for twelve years and they were all three murdered by a man in a what-do-you-call-it – topless car. The poor things were bacchic, gobbling up each others' viscera, dying all over the road and all – oh GOD all that that man could do was to say "Sorry." Ooooh.

(GLIDDEN returns with a cheque, and puts it on table)

Pascal
Dogs scare me.

Pony
Oooh they can probably smell it on you you know, they smell fear; it's a proven fact. They also smell softness and that's exactly what they smell on me. I'd do anything for a dog.

Glidden
(in pain) La! Give us a funny from your Ladies Home Business.

Lomia
No, Glid, you know I can't tell jokes – anyway I think it's time we– (knocks over glass)

(Still at the door, CAPE is desperate to rock the boat)

Cape
Excuse me Mother I wonder if you should consider while searching for apartments what your "roommate" has been – spreading – behind your back?

Pascal

(stands up, begins small giggle) You ... you, you people have a very complicated sense of humor don't you? And I'm beginning to catch on. Oh yeah, oh yeah, you're not leaving me behind 'cause I get it ... I get it, see, I –

Cape

Who's talking humor Pascal? I'm talking ... filth.

Lomia

Lay off him – chit!

Pascal

(to himself) Who's talking humor Pascal I'm talking ... filth. (quieter) Who's talking humour Pascal I'm– Oh yeah, *filth*, right! I know what you mean, you mean what I'm telling everybody in town, what I've been spreading around. Yeah I get it you mean about her being the the the the the WHORE OF BABYLON!! Yeah, *yeah*, like *my* crowd is all been wondering who it is, eh, and what do you know? It's the lady that lives with *me*, me ...

Glidden

This is worse than horses and coal.

Cape

Mum, I suggest you discuss this with the young man yourself, this is no–

Pascal

And you guys should have seen the fridge, it was crammed with these jam jars full of blood? Got to be the blood of saints right? And who keeps the blood of saints? –the WHORE OF BABYLON!! GO FOR IT!! St. Sebastian, St. Albans, St. Jude, St. Martin, St. Simeon, St. – I mean there's no room for milk, what's a boy supposed to think?

Glidden

What the hell kind of humor is ...

Lomia

It's the new humor I guess.

Cape

Except it's no joke is it Pascal? Anyway, chief, don't fret, that's not saints' blood, that's just nosebleeds. Our fridge used to be full of them too except we used to drink them.

Lomia

Nosebleeds? Beef juice! It's supposed to be very good for you, it said so in the ...

Pascal

So so hey! Is my humor on? Do I get to join the *club* – do I ...

Cape

Mother I know my allegation to be fact.

Pascal

WHAT, what? That she's the WHORE OF BABYLON?

Lomia

Well. We will decide whether or not I'm the Whore of Babylon at dinner. Right now, if we want to find an apartment, we have to get started. (picks up coat) And Cape, beef juice IS VERY good for you. (leaving) They did a study.

Glidden

At least come and have a look at the tiger lilies.

Lomia

Tiger lilies? I didn't know you'd grown tiger lilies, pooch, I *love* tiger lilies, they always make me sort of want to ... sit on them, you know? Come on foofy!! It's okay!

Pascal

See, I can do the humor too ... I can ...

(Before exiting, PASCAL turns back and takes a step towards CAPE. He is shaking)

I just ... you ... how did ... do ... do ... you want me to bring you back something? Choc ... chocolate? (takes a deep breath; smiles) I'm perspiring.

(PASCAL exits, leaving CAPE staring after him)

Pony

What is going on, Cape?

Cape

I ... I'm not ... sure.

Pony

Why ... why am I so ready to lie with ya and trick and cause trouble between two nice couples and humiliate a good man? Why ... what's happened in me that I even *like* doing it?? I get *off* on it, I ... (starts to leave)

Cape
You DON'T get off on it! (grabs her) Listen. Do you have a worst nightmare? Tell me your worst nightmare!

Pony
Why?

Cape
Tell me!

Pony
Why?

Cape
Tell me.

Pony
(eyes closed) Well, I go home, right? And there's these guys there, these tough guys drinking Lemon-Lime on the porch, and one of 'em's holding a carp, a great big brown carp, and I look down the mouth, and there are my folks! My parents, movin' ... their lips for help, all squished in a carp fish. And the guys are *laughin'*.

Cape
Yes. Well imagine that nightmare, never ending. Not when you wake up, not when you go to the bank, or ride your bike, the intensity never lets up. How long could you stand it?

Pony
Not ... very long.

Cape
Well neither can I. So help me end it. PONY. I want to love you ...

Pony
I believe you do, Cape.

Cape
Okay. There is one move we have left.

Pony
To ... ki-kill Pascal?

Cape
You wouldn't kill Pascal for me, Pony, and DON'T think you WOULD.

Pony
I –

(LOMIA and PASCAL can be heard, leaving)

Lomia
(off) 'Bye 'bye, pooch. I'll pick up some broccoli.

Pony
Do you ... want me to go into my fit? Then?

Cape
(kisses her hard) Yes. And remember, Queenie is on your *side*!

Pony
(whistles dog whistle to Queenie) If she hears anything she'll hear that.
Okay.

(PONY bends three times; her breathing becomes faster, she squeezes her
eyes shut, and says "mmmmmmmmmmmmmm")

Cape
Choke choke choke choke choke choke choke.

Pony
(has a coughing fit) I – I – I got some cake stuck.

Cape
(pats her hard on back) It's only wishing Pony – wishing very very hard.
Haven't you ever ... wished ... hard ... before?

Pony
It's not just the wishing Cape.

Cape
Wouldn't you do anything at all to save your father's life? Eh? (shakes her)
Imagine your father, rotting to death, DECAYING and –

Pony
(screams) YESS! Yes, yes I *would*! I would do anything, anything, to – to to
just have him spit, to have him spit on his hanky and clean off my face,
have him spit and wipe and I could smell it so strongly and ...

(PONY faints and CAPE hugs her, hard. She is dreaming that her dad is
wiping his spit all over her face)

Pony
Ha ha ha Dad! Daddy the spit's on my face, it's on my ... (wakes) Oh. I
guess I fainted.

Cape
Are you ... all right? (guilty, concerned) Are you –

Pony

No. No I'm not okay I don't think I'm okay in the least I think I blew a fuse, you know? I blew a fuse on account of I'm scared! I'm scared 'cause the old me is getting killed off by the new me, that hatched after we – This new me – I'm scared – I'm scared that when I say I'd do anything for you that maybe I mean – maybe I'd even – cut my mum and dad! (crying) My mum and dad, my – see – I've never felt two thoughts at once before.

Cape

(holds her tight) Pony. Why don't you go back to Kirkland Lake?

Pony

Do-do-do – you want me to?

Cape

No.

Pony

No. So I'm gonna help ya do what ya hafta do, 'cause you're right, I love you. I love you and – (takes his hand) Is this okay? I marry you ...

Cape

There's Dad coming back in. Why don't you go for a walk, eh? (kisses her) Everything should be all over by tonight ... and then we can go to Cape Race ... Eh?

(PONY, very moved, smiles. She exits. GLIDDEN comes in through the front door)

NOTEPAGES AND PAINTINGS

Dennis Burton

PROBLEMS INVOLVING BOTH P's and C's (NOT P's and Q's)

EG. HOW MANY WORDS, EACH CONSISTING OF <u>TWO VOWELS</u> AND <u>TWO</u> CONSONANTS ARRANGED <u>IN ANY ORDER</u>, CAN BE FORMED FROM THE LETTERS OF THE WORD "HALIBURTON"?

SINCE THERE ARE 6 CONSONANTS, 2 CONS. CAN BE SELECTED IN $6C_2$ WAYS AND FOR EACH OF THESE WAYS, THE 2 VOWELS, OUT OF THE 4 IN $4C_2$ WAYS

∴ THE NO. OF SELECTIONS $= 6C_2 \times 4C_2$

THE 4 LETTERS IN EACH COMBINATION CAN BE ARRANGED HENCE IN $\lfloor 4$ WAYS. ($4 \times 3 \times 2 \times 1$)

∴ THE NUMBER OF WORDS WILL BE: (a)$6C_2 \times$ (b)$4C_2 \times$ (c)$\lfloor 4$ ↘

(17)

(13) COMBINATIONS AND PERMUTATIONS OF n THINGS, r AT A TIME WHEN SOME ARE ALIKE.

EG. SINCE SOME LETTERS ARE ALIKE IT IS NECESSARY TO LIST ALL THE POSSIBLE SELECTIONS THAT CAN BE MADE, AND ARRANGE EACH SELECTION, SO A <u>TABLE</u> IS MADE

LETTERS OF THE WORD ANTENNA	CASES	COMB-INATIONS	PERMUT-ATIONS
N N N A A T E	3 ALIKE AND 1 DIFFERENT 3 N's AND 1 OF A,T,E	$1 \times 3C_1 = 3$	$3 \times \frac{\lfloor 4}{\lfloor 3} = 12$
	2 ALIKE AND 2 ALIKE 2 N's & 2 A's	$1 \times 1 = 1$	$1 \times \frac{\lfloor 4}{\lfloor 2 \lfloor 2} = 6$
	2 ALIKE & 2 DIFFERENT 2 N's OR 2 OF A,T,E 2 A's AND 2 OF N,T,E	$1 \times 3C_2 = 3$ $1 \times 3C_2 = 3$	$6 \times \frac{\lfloor 4}{\lfloor 2} = 72$
	4 DIFFERENT 4 OF N,A,T,E	1	$1 \times \lfloor 4 = 24$

SINCE EACH OF THE ABOVE SELECTIONS IS INDEPENDENT OF THE OTHERS OR ANY OTHER

∴ No OF COMB's $= 3 + 1 + 3 + 1 = 11$.

and No OF PERMS $= 12 + 6 + 72 + 24 = 114$.

PERMUTATION COMBINATION PISTOL

SELECTION IS A 'GROUP' A SYNONYM FOR COMBINATION

'ARRANGEMENT' IS AN ORDER OF ELEMENTS

$\lfloor 4 = 4 \times 3 \times 2 \times 1$

(a) $= 6P_2 = 6C_2 \times \lfloor 2$

$6C_2 \times \lfloor 2$ $\frac{6C_2 \times \lfloor 2}{\lfloor 2}$

$= 6P_2$ $= 6C_2 = \frac{6P_2}{\lfloor 2}$

$\frac{6P_2}{\lfloor 2}$

$= \frac{6 \times 5}{\lfloor 2} = \frac{30}{2} = 15$

(b): $4C_2 \times \lfloor 2$

$4C_2 \times \lfloor 2 = 4P_2$

$4C_2 = \frac{4P_2}{\lfloor 2}$

$= \frac{4 \times 3}{\lfloor 2} = \frac{12}{2} = 6$

$15 \times 6 = 90$

(c) $(90 \times 4 \times 3 \times 2 \times 1)$

$= 90 \times 24$

∴ $= 2160$ WORDS.

THE **FUNDAMENTAL** THEOREM

FIND ALWAYS, FIRST: THE SELECTION OF GROUPS, FOLLOWED BY THE ARRANGEMENT OF THE THINGS IN EACH GROUP, FROM THE GIVEN.

EG. PROBLEM: ① FIND GROUPS (OR PAIRS) OF DIFFERENT LETTERS, 2 AT A TIME FROM A WORD OF 4 LETTERS: A,B,C,D

FIND ALL FIRST ② THEN FOR EACH OF THESE 2-LETTER GROUPS, FIND THE NUMBER OF OF THEM

① FIND ALL THE WAYS 4 LETTERS CAN OCCUPY A SPACE. ANS. 4 WAYS. (A,B,C or D)

② FOR EACH OF THESE WAYS (4 WAYS) A SECOND SPACE CAN THUS BE FILLED IN ONLY 3 WAYS, BECAUSE ONE LETTER WILL ALWAYS BE IN SPACE 1.

(1) [A] OR [B] OR [C] OR [D]

SPACE (1) CAN BE FILLED IN 4 WAYS FIRST FOR EACH OF THESE WAYS (1) CAN BE OCCUPIED SPACE (2) CAN BE OCCUPIED ONLY BY THE 3 LEFT

[A][B] [A][C] [A][D] OR [B][A] [B][C] [B][D]

(1)(2) (1)(2) (1)(2) (1)(2) (1)(2) (1)(2)

COULD
COULD
COULD
COULD AN EXPLANATION OF THE DISTORTIONS OF 20TH CENTURY ART OR EVEN PREHISTORIC AND PRIMITIVE ART BE THAT THE MIND KNOWS THAT THE HUMAN FIGURE WAS AS BELOW!

3·26·71

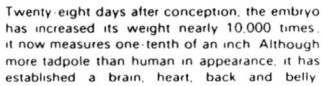

Length 3 4 mm

Twenty-eight days after conception, the embryo has increased its weight nearly 10,000 times. It now measures one-tenth of an inch Although more tadpole than human in appearance, it has established a brain, heart, back and belly

5 mm

At 32 days, the embryo has curled up Arms and legs begin to bud As if sketching the story of evolution, the embryo develops four clefts, comparable to fish gills Almost all the human organs are now being formed

10 5 mm

At 37 days, just over a quarter-inch long The arms are no longer paddles, but show forearm and hand regions The head begins to outrace other parts of the body in building weight but a well-formed tail develops too

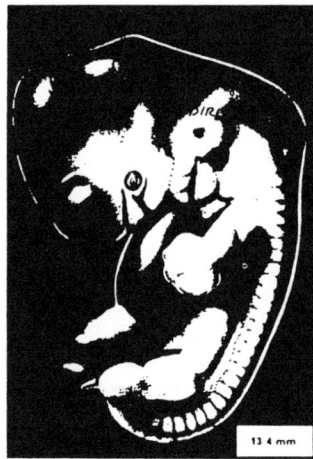

13 4 mm

Like a bird, the embryo at 40 days has one eye on each side of its head Cleft to the right of the eye marks the developing ear Transparent cartilage, later replaced by bone, makes it possible to see the embryo's beating heart

17 mm

Towards the end of the second month both male and female embryos develop the same sex organs even milk glands Later, each sex concentrates on developing the organs it needs At 46 days, the embryo is three-quarters of an inch long

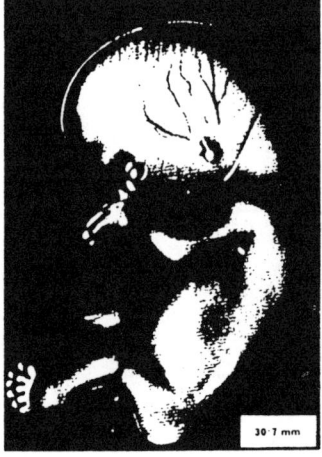

30 7 mm

Recognizably human, the embryo of 60 days is an inch and a half long and able to flutter its limbs The tail is less apparent and the eyes are moving to the front of the face In this week the eyelids form, soon to close until birth.

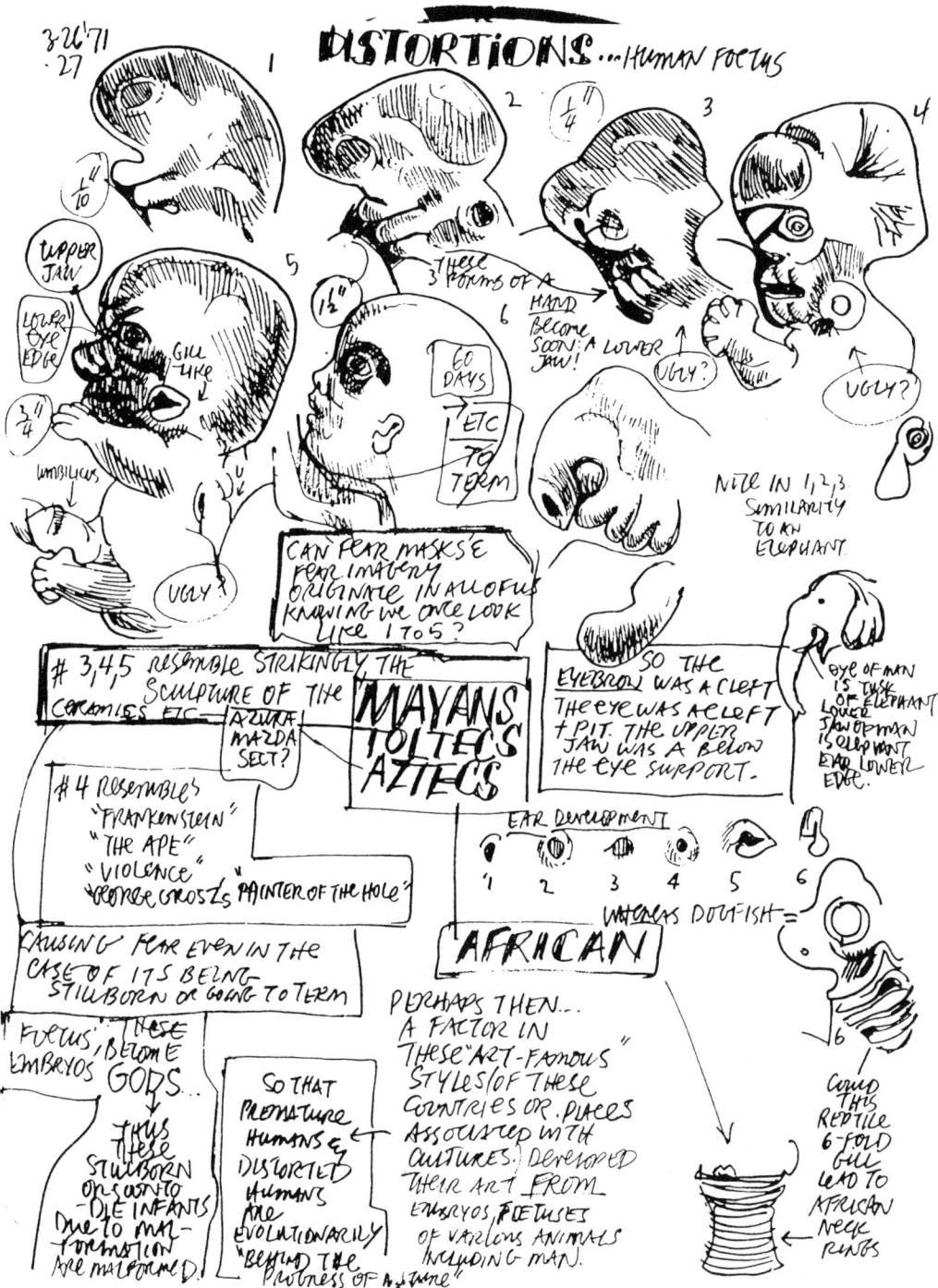

DISTORTIONS...HUMAN FOETUS

3·26'71
·27

1

2   1/4"

3

4

1"/10

UPPER JAW

LOWER EYE EDGE

5

GILL LIKE

3/4"

THESE 3 FORMS OF A HAND BECOME SOON A LOWER JAW!

UGLY?

UGLY?

1 1/2"

6

60 DAYS

ETC TO TERM

UMBILICUS

UGLY

NOTE IN 1,2,3, SIMILARITY TO AN ELEPHANT.

CAN FEAR MASKS & FEAR IMAGERY ORIGINATE IN ALL OF US KNOWING WE ONCE LOOK LIKE 1 TO 5?

3,4,5 RESEMBLE STRIKINGLY THE SCULPTURE OF THE CEREMONIES ETC.

AZURA MAZDA SECT?

MAYANS TOLTECS AZTECS

SO THE EYEBROW WAS A CLEFT THE EYE WAS A CLEFT + PIT. THE UPPER JAW WAS A BELOW THE EYE SUPPORT.

EYE OF MAN IS TUSK OF ELEPHANT LOWER JAW OF MAN IS ELEPHANT EAR LOWER EDGE.

4 RESEMBLES "FRANKENSTEIN" "THE APE" "VIOLENCE" GEORGE GROSZ'S PAINTER OF THE HOLE"

EAR DEVELOPMENT
1 2 3 4 5 6

CAUSING FEAR EVEN IN THE CASE OF ITS BEING STILLBORN OR GOING TO TERM

AFRICAN

WHEREAS DOGFISH =

6

FOETUS, THESE BECOME EMBRYOS GODS...

THUS THESE STILLBORN OR CAST TO DIE INFANTS DUE TO MALFORMATION ARE MALFORMED.

SO THAT PREMATURE HUMANS & DISTORTED HUMANS ARE EVOLUTIONARILY "BEYOND THE PRIMNESS OF A TIME"

PERHAPS THEN... A FACTOR IN THESE "ART-FAMOUS" STYLES (OF THESE COUNTRIES OR PLACES ASSOCIATED WITH CULTURES) DEVELOPED THEIR ART FROM EMBRYOS, FOETUSES OF VARIOUS ANIMALS INCLUDING MAN.

COULD THIS REPTILE 6-FOLD GILL LEAD TO AFRICAN NECK RINGS

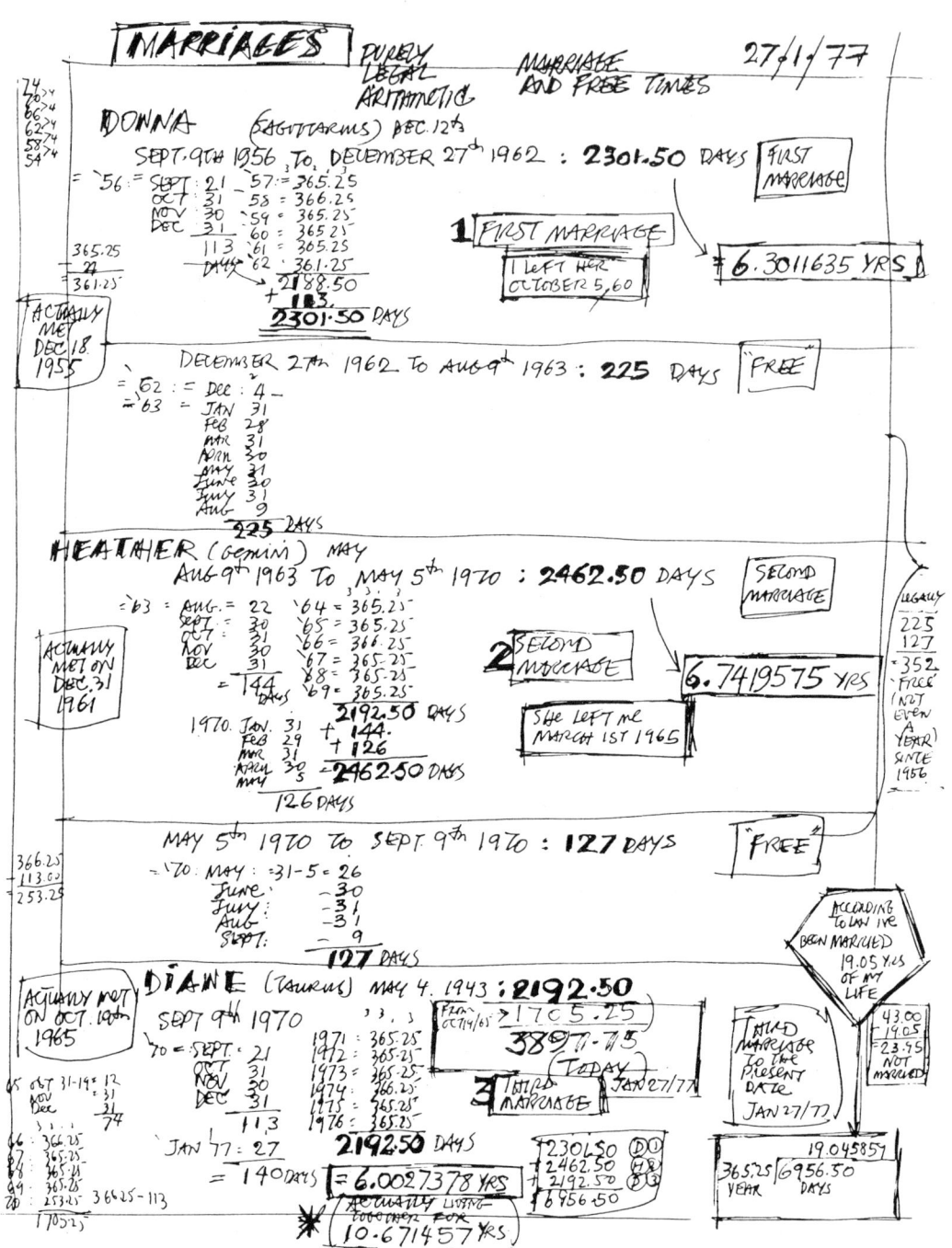

| MARRIAGES | PURELY LEGAL ARITHMETIC | MARRIAGE AND FREE TIMES | 27/1/77 |

DONNA (SAGITTARIUS) DEC. 12th

SEPT. 9th 1956 TO DECEMBER 27th 1962 : **2301·50 DAYS**   FIRST MARRIAGE

= '56 = SEPT. 21   '57 = 365.25
         OCT. 31   '58 = 366.25
         NOV. 30   '59 = 365.25
         DEC. 31   '60 = 365.25
             113   '61 = 365.25
         DAYS '62 = 361.25
                    + 2188.50
                    + 113.
                  2301·50 DAYS

1 FIRST MARRIAGE
I LEFT HER OCTOBER 5, 60

≠ 6.3011635 YRS

ACTUALLY MET DEC 18 1955

DECEMBER 27th 1962 TO AUG 9th 1963 : **225 DAYS**   FREE

= '62 = DEC : 4
= '63 = JAN 31
         FEB 28
         MAR 31
         APRIL 30
         MAY 31
         JUNE 30
         JULY 31
         AUG 9
         225 DAYS

HEATHER (GEMINI) MAY

AUG 9th 1963 TO MAY 5th 1970 : **2462.50 DAYS**   SECOND MARRIAGE

= '63 = AUG. = 22   '64 = 365.25
         SEPT. = 30   '65 = 365.25
         OCT = 31   '66 = 366.25
         NOV = 30   '67 = 365.25
         DEC = 31   '68 = 365.25
              = 144   '69 = 365.25
              DAYS
                       2192.50 DAYS
1970. JAN. 31   + 144.
      FEB 29   + 126
      MAR 31   = **2462.50 DAYS**
      APRIL 30
      MAY 5
      126 DAYS

2 SECOND MARRIAGE

6.7419575 YRS

SHE LEFT ME MARCH 1ST 1965

LEGALLY
225
127
352
FREE (NOT EVEN A YEAR) SINCE 1956

MAY 5th 1970 TO SEPT. 9th 1970 : **127 DAYS**   FREE

= '70. MAY : 31-5 = 26
       JUNE : 30
       JULY : 31
       AUG : 31
       SEPT : 9
       127 DAYS

366.25
-113.00
253.25

ACCORDING TO LAW I'VE BEEN MARRIED 19.05 YRS OF MY LIFE

DIANE (TAURUS) MAY 4. 1943 : **2192.50**

ACTUALLY MET ON OCT. 19th 1965

SEPT 9th 1970
'70 = SEPT. 21   1971 : 365.25
      OCT 31   1972 : 365.25
      NOV 30   1973 : 365.25
      DEC 31   1974 : 366.25
          113   1975 : 365.25
                 1976 : 365.25
JAN '77 : 27   **2192.50 DAYS**
= 140 DAYS   = **6.0027378 YRS**

FROM OCT 19/65 ≥ 1705.25
              3897.75
              (TODAY)
              JAN 27/77

3 THIRD MARRIAGE

43.00
-19.05
23.95 NOT MARRIED

THIRD MARRIAGE TO THE PRESENT DATE
JAN 27/77

19.045851

2301.50	Ⓓ
2462.50	Ⓗ
2192.50	Ⓓ
6956.50	

365.25 | 6956.50
YEAR | DAYS

✳ ACTUALLY LIVING TOGETHER FOR
10·671457 YRS

65 OCT 31-19= 12
   NOV   31
   DEC   31
            74
66 : 366.25
67 : 365.25
68 : 365.25
69 : 365.25
70 : 253.25   366.25-113
   1705.25

SHE SPEAKS

André Frénaud

1: Reckless
I don't spread out to please
despite what I pretend.
It's to give myself ease,
escaping from the beasts
by surrendering myself.

It matters little with whom.
It's for myself I lie down,
to keep out the night
by drawing it in.

It's to race breathless.
To find a nest
and lose myself.

The death which never tells,
the constant death which fills
me, so far miscarrying,
soon will have its place.

2: Without Pity
To learn about the world,
to discover the one I was deprived of,
I opened my legs.

Large enough not to miss him,
smaller than an eye on a peacock's tail.

Beauty wavers with me,
always defeated huntress.

I am ready, if you please me,
paying in kind, I lose myself.
Instead of passion, curiosity.
Shrewd, I keep my heart in reserve.

And it's always the same dismay.
A hundred bodies, a hundred too many
reveal the weakness of my hope.

All my branches are lopped.
Have I any regrets left?
After so many false caresses
my handsome thighs are dead wood.

3: If I Give Myself
Little pleasure, lasting guilt.
I will try all those irrelevant bodies.
If remorse could feed me
I would grow plump.

I no longer know what hurts,
or if I have fear, or hope
to flee their coarse dreams,
flung at me, like beasts.
I tremble when I am brave.
I am sly when I tell the truth.
I sparkle without pleasure.
I am secretive without a secret.
I'm arid as a desert.

I yield, therefore I am.
I care little for their needs.
For a second I free myself,
I exist in spite of all.
I am so proud in the bed,
Radiating, spreadeagled.

My outflung arms shall avenge me,
against my father, against a world
where the sun does not light,
against the rocking moon,
against all the cold that comes.

Translated by John Montague

TURAS

Seamus Heaney

These pieces were begun in California in 1970/71 although the greater part of them came to a head in May and June, 1974. When I returned to Belfast there seemed to be a block in the air: those first pieces had been attempts to touch what Wordsworth called "spots of time", moments at the very edge of consciousness which had lain for years in the unconscious — or half-conscious — as active lodes or nodes; yet, coming back to Ireland a month after the introduction of internment my introspection was not confident enough to pursue its direction. The sirens in the air, perhaps quite rightly, jammed those other tentative though insistent signals. So it was again at a remove, in the "hedge-school" of Glanmore, in Wicklow, that the work was returned to.

I think of the things now as points on a psychic turas, stations I have often made unthinkingly in my head. I wrote each of them down with the excitement of coming for the first time to a place I had always known completely.

S.H.

Cauled

They thought he was lost. For years they talked about it until he found himself at the root of their kindly tongues, sitting like a giant fieldmouse in the middle of the rig. Their voices were far off now, searching something.

Green air crept over his arms and legs, the pods and stalks wore a fuzz of light. He caught a rod in each hand and jerked the whole tangle into life. Little tendrils unsprung, new veins lit in the shifting leaves, a caul of shadows stretched and settled round his head again. He sat listening, grateful as the calls encroached.

They had found him at the first onset of sobbing.

Hedge-school
The tan clay between the stones in the foot of the hedge was cool and moist. Nettles, docken and ivy flourished on the ditchback. The whitethorn was green as the blackthorn.

Their skirts brushed away over the headrim, their voices humble and familiar as pads across grazing. How the big air of the evening was saddened by them, as if it lay over utensils on a back window-sill, as if it might begin to whisper, "Pray for us, pray for us, pray for us ..."

Primroses grew in a damp single bunch out of the clay bank, little moonlit whirlpools, imploding pallors, star plasm, nebula of May. He stared himself into an absence, until "Pull them for the May Altar and hurry up."

He knelt and reached the stems. "Hurry up." Pods-ridges, legs of nestlings.

Patiently, deliberately, they retraced their steps. "What are you crying about now, son? Come on, come on, we have to go. There's a good boy." He walked behind them, homesick, going home.

Nesting ground

The sandmartins' nests were loopholes of darkness in the riverbank. He could imagine his arm going in to the armpit, sleeved and straightened, but because he once felt the cold dab of a dead robin's claw and the surprising density of its tiny beak, he only gazed.

He heard cheeping far in but because the men had once shown him a rat's nest in the butt of a stack where chaff and powdered cornstalks adhered to the moist pink necks and backs, he only listened.

As he stood sentry, gazing, waiting, he thought of putting his ear to one of the abandoned holes and listening for the silence under the ground.

Sinking the shaft

He once woke late, the sun already warm on the linoleum, strange voices in the yard, and insistently, as if prolonged from underneath his sleep, a contralto metal note, the flinty bite of spades at gravel. The men had come to sink the pump.

It was a big wound in front of the back door. Backs and elbows skylined at ground level but by the afternoon, from the mouth of the hole, nothing but a light spray of sand that dribbled gold and capped the dark heap at the rim. Some of it fell back in as he climbed and looked over.

"Are you not for coming down, young Heaney?" A stirabout, a gleam, a wet bronze puddled by their wellingtons. "We're not a mile off it. Would you not come down?"

Snouted, helmeted, the plunger like an active gizard, the handle dressed to a clean sweep, set on a pediment inscribed by the points of their trowels, I suppose they thought it never could be toppled.

Water babies

We were busy in the fetid corner we christened Botany Bay where the ducks garbled and the wagtails flew with desultory urgency. You pumped, I dammed. We opened sluice-gates, flooded mucky runnels and set sails by our black marina, penning white feathers into old potatoes. Sometimes a bomber warbled high above us, sometimes a train ran brangling through the fields and small ripples shimmered quietly across our delta.

Perversely I once fouled a gift there and sank my new kaleidoscope in the puddle. It had arrived from far away, causing a great éclat among the elders. Its bright prisms that offered incomprehensible satisfactions were messed and silted: instead of a marvellous light-ship, I salvaged a dirty hulk.

Patrick and Oisin

It was fern and ivy talk, meshed and tenebrous. In the stove-warmed kitchen their tongues uncurled and seeded, the names of neighbors flowered like hothouse weeds, a local undergrowth mantled the hard stones of "calumny and detraction". And there he sat, pondering his catechism with its woodcut mysteries, its polysyllabic runs, its "clandestine solemnizations", its "consanguinity and affinity".

Father Hughes had clapped the frost out of his gloves and clappered the silenced room. "Hands up who said their morning prayers this morning?" His hand was a tendril stretching with the others. "Who'll say their catechism?"

The night wore on. The phrases that had sapped his concentration atrophied, incised tablets mossed and camouflaged by parasites and creeping greenery.

England's difficulty

I moved like a double agent among the big concepts. The word "enemy" had a toothed efficiency, a mechanical and distant noise beyond that opaque security, the autonomous ignorance.

"When the Germans bombed Belfast, it was the bitter Orange parts were hit the worst."

He was on somebody's shoulder, conveyed through the dark yard to see the sky glowing over Anahorish. Grown-ups lowered their voices and resettled in the kitchen as if tired out after an excursion.

Behind the blackout Germany called the lamplit kitchen through fretted baize, dry battery, wet battery, capillary wires and domed valves that squeaked and burbled as the dial hand absolved Stuttgart and Leipzig.

"He's a playboy, this Haw Haw. By God, he's the boy can leave it into them!"

I lodged with the "enemies of Ulster", the traitors within the gates. Squires of the cockpit, barkers of auction notices, arbitrators of the burial grounds. Adept at banter and disguise, I crossed lines with elocuted passwords, manned every speech with checkpoints and reported back to nobody.

A visitant

It kept treading air, as if it were a ghost with claims on us, precipitating in the heat tremor. Then, released from its distorting mirror, up the fields there comes this awkwardly smiling foreigner, awkwardly received, who gentled the long Sunday afternoon just by sitting with us?

Where are you now, real visitant, who vivified "parole" and "POW"? Where are the rings garnetted with toothbrush, the ships in bottles, the Tyrol landscapes globed in electric bulbs?

"They've hands for anything, these Germans."

He walked back into the refining lick of the grass, on past the particular judgements of captor and harborer. As he walks yet, feeling our eyes on his back, treading the air of the image he achieved, released to his fatigues.

The wanderer

In a semi-circle we toed the line chalked round the master's desk and on a day when the sun was incubating milktops and warming the side of the jamjar where the bean had split its stitches, he called me forward and crossed my palm with silver.

"At the end of the holidays this man is going away to board in Derry, so here's a florin for him because he won the scholarship. And we all wish him good luck. Now, back to your places."

I have wandered far from that ring-giver and would not renege on this migrant solitude. I have seen halls in flames, hearts in cinders, the benches filled and emptied, the circles of companions called and broken. That day I was a rich young man, who could tell you now of flittings, night-vigils, women's cried-out eyes.

Cloistered

Light was calloused in the leaded panes of the college chapel and shafted into the terrazo rink of the sanctuary. The duty priest tested his diction against pillar and plaster, we tested our elbows on the hard bevel of the benches or split the gold-barred thickness of our missals.
I could make a book of hours of those six years, a Flemish calendar or rite and pastime set on a walled hill. Look: There is a hillside cemetery behind us and across the river the plough going in a field and in between, the gated town. Here, an obedient clerk kissing a bishop's ring, here a frieze of seasonal games, and here the assiduous illuminator himself bowed to his desk in a corner.

In the study hall my hand was cold as a scribe's in winter. The supervisor rustled past, sibilant, vaporing into his brieviary, his welted brogues unexpectedly secular under the soutane. Now I bisected the line AB, now found my foothold in a main verb in Livy. From the dormer after lights-out I revised the constellations and in the morning broke the ice on an enamelled water-jug with exhilarated self-regard.

I was champion of the examination halls, scalding with lust inside my daunting visor.

Turas

On my first night in the Gaeltacht the old woman spoke to me in English: "You will be all right." I sat on a twilit bedside listening through the wall to fluent Irish, homesick for a speech I was to extirpate.

I had come west to inhale the absolute weather. The visionaries breathed on my face a smell of soup-kitchens, they mixed the dust of croppies' graves with the fasting spittle of our creed and anointed my lips. *Ephete*, they urged. I blushed but only managed a few words.

Neither did any gift of tongues descend in my days in that upper room when all around me seemed to prophesy. But still I would recall the stations of the west, white sand, hard rock, light ascending like its definition over Rannafast and Errigal, Annaghry and Kincassalgh: names portable as altar stones, unleavened elements.

Ballad

Blood ran a jewelled delta down the back of the lorry, the ascetic boy screamed for relief, the riddled lorry hammered on for the border. And with the constabulary closing on them, they left him dying there on the cold floor of a barn.

When exhaustion had been nominated peace, I went to ceilidhes where his name was a host on the singer's tongue, his tale an insubstantial wound we dipped in beyond question and doubting.

We sat on benches round the hall that was dark and close as a grave-watcher's hut. The band was backstage at their tea, the dancefloor an area cleared before his honored tomb. It was there, when the song and anthem of applause had sowed us all with quiet, I grew to love the manifold griefs of chanters and assuaging bows.

Alias

I went disguised in it, pronouncing it with a soft church-latin *c*, tagging it under my efforts like a damp fuse. *Incertus.* Uncertain, a shy soul fretting, and all that. Expert obeisance.

Oh yes, I crept before I walked. The old pseudonym lies there like a mouldering tegument.

OBASAN

Joy Kogawa

Chapter Fifteen

I AM SOMETIMES NOT CERTAIN WHETHER IT IS A CLUTTERED ATTIC in which I sit, a waiting room, a tunnel, a train. There is no beginning and no end to the forest, or the dust storm, no edge from which to know where the clearing begins. Here, in this familiar density, beneath this cloak, within this carapace, is the longing within the darkness.

1942.

We are leave the B.C. coast – rain, cloud, mist – an air overladen with weeping. Behind us lies a salty sea within which swim our drowning specks of memory – our small waterlogged eulogies. We are going down to the middle of the earth with pick-axe eyes, tunnelling by train to the Interior, carried along by the momentum of the expulsion into the waiting wilderness.

We are hammers and chisels in the hands of would-be sculptors, battering the spirit of the sleeping mountain. We are the chips and sand, the fragments of fragments that fly like arrows from the heart of the rock. We are the silences that speak from stone. We are the despised rendered voiceless, stripped of car, radio, camera and every means of communication, a trainload of eyes covered with mud and spittle. We are the man in the Gospel of John, born into the world for the sake of the light. We are sent to Siloam, the pool called "Sent." We are sent to the sending, that we may bring sight. We are the scholarly and the illiterate, the envied and the ugly, the fierce and the docile. We are those pioneers who cleared the bush and the forest with our hands, the gardeners tending and attending the soil with our tenderness, the fishermen who are flung from the sea to flounder in the dust of the prairies.

We are the Issei and the Nisei and the Sansei, the Japanese Canadians. We disappear into the future undemanding as dew.

The memories are dream images. A pile of luggage in a large hall. Missionaries at the railway station handing out packages of toys. Stephen being carried on board the train, a white cast up to his thigh.

It is three decades ago and I am a small child resting my head in Obasan's lap. I am wearing a wine-colored dirndl skirt with straps that criss-cross at the back. My white silk blouse has a Peter Pan collar dotted with tiny red flowers. I have a wine-colored sweater with ivory duck buttons.

Stephen sits sideways on a seat by himself opposite us, his huge white leg like a cocoon.

The train is full of strangers. But even strangers are addressed as "ojisan" or "obasan," meaning uncle or aunt. Not one uncle or aunt, grandfather or

307

grandmother, brother or sister, not one of us on this journey returns home again.

The train smells of oil and soot and orange peels and lurches groggily as we rock our way inland. Along the window ledge, the black soot leaps and settles like insects. Underfoot and in the aisles and beside us on the seats we are surrounded by odd bits of luggage – bags, lunch baskets, blankets, pillows. My red umbrella with its knobby clear red handle sticks out of a box like the head of an exotic bird. In the seat behind us is a boy in short grey pants and jacket carrying a wooden slatted box with a tabby kitten inside. He is trying to distract the kitten with his finger but the kitten mews and mews, its mouth opening and closing. I can barely hear its high steady cry in the clackity-clack and steamy hiss of the train.

A few seats in front, one young woman is sitting with her narrow shoulders hunched over a tiny red-faced baby. Her short black hair falls into her bird-like face. She is so young, I would call her "o-nesan," older sister.

The woman in the aisle seat opposite us leans over and whispers to Obasan with a solemn nodding of her head and a flicker of her eyes indicating the young woman.

Obasan moves her head slowly and gravely in a nod as she listens. "Kawaiso," she says under her breath. The word is used whenever there is hurt and a need for tenderness.

The young mother, Kuniko-san, came from Saltspring Island, the woman says. Kuniko-san was rushed onto the train from Hastings Park, a few days after giving birth prematurely to her baby.

"She has nothing," the woman whispers. "Not even diapers."

Aya Obasan does not respond as she looks steadily at the dirt-covered floor. I lean out into the aisle and I can see the baby's tiny fist curled tight against its wrinkled face. Its eyes are closed and its mouth is squinched small as a button. Kuniko-san does not lift her eyes at all.

"Kawai," I whisper to Obasan, meaning that the baby is cute.

Obasan hands me an orange from a wicker basket and gestures towards Kuniko-san, indicating that I should take her the gift. But I pull back.

"For the baby," Obasan says urging me.

I withdraw farther into my seat. She shakes open a furoshiki – a square cloth that is used to carry things by tying the corners together – and places a towel and some apples and oranges in it. I watch her lurching from side to side as she walks towards Kuniko-san.

Clutching the top of Kuniko-san's seat with one hand, Obasan bows and holds the furoshiki out to her. Kuniko-san clutches the baby against her breast and bows forward twice while accepting Obasan's gift without looking up.

As Obasan returns towards us, the old woman in the seat diagonal to ours beckons to me, nodding her head, urging me to come to her, her hand gesturing downwards in a digging waving motion. I lean towards her.

"A baby was born," the old woman says. "Is this not so?"

I nod.

The old woman bumps herself forward and off the seat. Her back is round as a church bell. She is so short that when she is standing, she is lower than when she was sitting. She braces herself against the seat and bends forward.

"There is nothing to offer," she says as Obasan reaches her. She lifts her skirt and begins to remove a white flannel underskirt, her hand gathering the undergarment in pleats.

"Ah, no no Grandmother," Obasan says.

"Last night it was washed. It is nothing, but it is clean."

Obasan supports her in the rock rock of the train and they sway together back and forth. The old woman steps out of the garment, being careful not to let it touch the floor.

"Please – if it is acceptable. For a diaper. There is nothing to offer," the old woman says as she hoists herself onto the seat again. She folds the undergarment into a neat square, the fingers of her hand stiff and curled as driftwood. Obasan bows, accepting the cloth, and returns to Kuniko-san and her baby, placing the piece of flannel on Kuniko-san's lap. Both their heads are bobbing like birds as they talk. Sometimes Kuniko-san bows so deeply, her baby touches her lap.

Leaning out into the aisle I can see better, and the old grandmother nods, urging me to go to them. Kuniko-san is wiping her eyes in the baby's blanket, revealing the baby's damp black hair.

The baby doll I have brought has a hard lumpy brown wave for hair on the top of its hard head. I hold it on the train's window ledge on its buttocks and short bow legs in its pyjamas and blue wool hat.

Another doll I have brought is a Japanese child doll my mother gave me before she went to Japan. It was meant to be mostly ornamental and has an ageless elegant face – tiny red bow lips open slightly in a two-toothed smile, clear exact eyes with black pupils in the centre of the dark brown irises, tiny pinprick nostrils. Its hair, like mine, is a stiff black frame, the bangs a straight brush across the forehead. The right hand is a round fist with a hole in the middle. She carries a stick with a colorful box at the end and two threads with beads. Sometimes I replace the stick with a curved green wire branch on which are clustered tiny hard red lacquered dots for cherries and delicate five-petalled paper flowers. The red flowered ki-mono, which is not for removal, has been removed and the doll is no longer pristine and decorative. The legs, though wired in place, are dislo-cated and she cannot stand on her own. The fingers of her left hand are broken. Obasan suggested I take another but she is my favorite doll. She wears an over-sized orange print dress from one of the other dolls in the kitchen bin, plus a coat. I stand her up to look out of the window at the passing scenery. Her feet clack against the pane.

"See," I whisper to her.

The doll does not respond. If she understands, she nods or she bows full tilt, but if she is unsure, her feet clack irritably.

Stephen is scowling as Obasan returns and offers him a rice ball. "Not that kind of food," he says, Stephen, half in and half out of his shell, is Humpty Dumpty – cracked and surly and unable to move.

I have seen Obasan at home sometimes take a single grain of cooked rice and squash it on paper, using it for paste to seal parcels or envelopes. If I could take all the cooked rice in all the rice pots in the world, dump them into a heap and tromp all the bits to glue with my feet, there would be enough to stick anything, even Humpty Dumpty, together again.

Unlike Stephen, the doll is quite happy and secretly excited about the train trip.

"Want that?" she asks Stephen, looking at home with her bright almond eyes and pointing to a sandwich.

Stephen ignores her and stares at the tree tops zipping past the window.

"Humpty Dumpty sat on a wall," she says to herself.

"Humpty Dumpty had a great fall ..."

Getting no response from Stephen I turn to my other toys – the red, white and blue ball, the Mickey Mouse with movable legs which can rock and walk by itself down an incline, the two chicks from the sewing-machine cabinet, a metal cicada which can be squeezed making a "click click" sound.

Stephen ignores everything and stares out the window at the changing shapes of sky. In a fit of generosity I take my ball and give it to Stephen. "You can keep it," I say solemnly. "It's yours." I put it in his jacket pocket where it forms a fist-size lump.

The train moves in and out of tunnels, along narrow ridges that edge the canyon walls, through a toothpick forest of trees. Eventually the doll grows sleepy and falls asleep in the blanket that Obasan has arranged on her lap. Obasan's hand taps my back rhythmically and her smooth oval face is calm.

Chapter Sixteen

Twenty years later, in 1962, Aunt Emily wanted to take a trip through the interior of British Columbia. Off we went – Uncle, Aunt Emily, Obasan, and I – through Banff, down the Rogers Pass, through Golden, and Revelstoke, Uncle pointing out a small side road which he said was the place his work camp had been. I drove through what was left of some of the ghost towns, filled and emptied once by prospectors, filled and emptied a second time by the Japanese Canadians. The first ghosts were still there, the miners, people of the woods, their white bones deep beneath the pine-needle floor, their flesh turned to earth, turned to air. Their buildings – hotels, abandoned mines, log cabins – still stood marking their stay. But what of the second wave? What remains of our time there?

We looked for the evidence of our having been in Bayfarm, in Lemon Creek, in Popoff. Bayfarm and Popoff were farmlands in Slocan before the tar-paper huts sprang up. Lemon Creek was a camp seven miles away carved out of the wilderness. Tashme – formed from the names of Taylor, Shirras, and Mead, men on the B.C. Security Commission – also rose overnight, fourteen miles from Hope, and as quickly disappeared. Where on the map or on the road was there any sign? Not a mark was left. All our huts had been removed long before and the forest had returned to take over the clearings. What remained the same was the smell of pine and cedar. The mountains too were unchanged except for the evidence of new roads and a larger logging industry. While we stood there in Slocan, we could hear the wavering hoot of a train whistle as we used to years before.

But the Slocan that we knew in the forties was no longer there, except for the small white community which had existed before we arrived and which watched us come with a mixture of curiosity and fear. Now, down on the shore of the Slocan lake, on the most beautiful part of the sandy beach, where we used to swim, there was a large new sawmill owned by someone who lived in New York.

We left Slocan and drove towards Sandon. The steep one-vehicle road dropped at such a perilous and tortuous slope, I turned around the first chance I could get. What a hole!

"It was an evacuation all right," Aunt Emily said. "Just plopped here in the wilderness. Flushed out of Vancouver. Like dung drops. Maggot bait."

None of us, she said, escaped the naming. We were defined and identified by the way we were seen. A newspaper in B.C. headlined, "They are a stench in the nostrils of the people of Canada." We were therefore relegated to the cesspools. In Sandon, Tashme, Kaslo, Greenwood, Slocan, Bayfarm, Popoff, Lemon Creek, New Denver, we lived in tents, in bunks, in skating rinks, in abandoned hotels. Most of us lived in row upon row of two-family, three-room huts, controlled and orderly as wooden blocks. There was a tidy mind somewhere.

Some families who had gone ahead or independently had been able to find empty farmhouses to rent. In Slocan, several families lived in an abandoned bunkhouse at an old silver mine. Our own house was just a two-roomed log hut at the base of the mountain. It was shabby and sagging and overgrown with weeds when we first saw it on that spring day in 1942.

"Thank you, thank you," Obasan says to a man, an ojisan in a grey cap who reaches up and puts an arm around Stephen hesitating at the top of the train steps. I pick up Stephen's crutches and follow him as he is carried through the slow crowd of boxes and bodies. People are bustling about on the wooden platform in groups, carrying luggage here and there. Even in all this crowd, there is a stillness here. The sudden fresh air, touched with the familiar smell of sawdust, is crisp and private. Yet there is a feeling of open space. Through a break in the crowd, I can see a lake with a sandy beach and drift logs. All around its edge are mountains covered in trees, climbing skyward. The highest farthest mountains are blue and purple and topped with white snow.

I am holding Obasan's hand and looking around when I hear Stephen say "Hello, Sensei." Sensei is the word for teacher. I look up and recognize Nakayama-sensei, the round-faced minister with round eyes and round glasses from the Anglican church in Vancouver. He is talking to Obasan and to the man who helped Stephen. The boy carrying the kitten is holding the hand of a woman in a blue dress who is waiting to speak to Nakayama-sensei.

"It is not so far," Sensei says to Obasan. "I will show you the way." He turns to the woman in blue and nods gravely, says a few words to the ojisan and to a missionary, then disappears into the crowd.

Except for Stephen on his crutches, we all carry bags, furoshiki, suitcases, boxes and follow Ojisan down the middle of the road, past the gaunt hotels

311

swarming with people, like ants in an overturned ant-hill. Ojisan puts down his heavy box and we wait till he returns with a home-made wheelbarrow.

"Ah, joto, joto," Nakayma-sensei says rejoining us, "excellent, excellent."

We arrange our luggage and follow Nakayma-sensei and Ojisan down the street again, turning to the left past a building with the sign "Graham's General Store," and we walk up the flat gravel road through the valley to the mountain's foot. There are no streetcars here, no sidewalks or large buildings. On either side of the road are a few houses, smaller than the ones in Vancouver.

As we pass a wooden bridge over a creek, I think of the curved bridge over the goldfish pond at Obasan's house, and the bridges Stephen and I made in the sand to the desolate sound of the sea, and the huge Lions' Gate Bridge in Stanley Park, and the terrifying Capilano swinging bridge that trembled as we crossed it high up in the dangerous air.

Perhaps it is because I first missed my doll while standing on this bridge that often in the evenings, when I cross it, I feel a certain sadness.

Obasan, carrying a large furoshiki, waits for me as I linger looking down at the water burbling over the stones and a crow hopping on the bank.

"Where is my doll?" I ask, calling to her. I am not carrying anything since putting the bag of food and the furoshiki I was given onto Ojisan's pile.

Obasan looks startled and utters that short sharp word of alarm.

"Ara!"

She puts down her furoshiki and opens it, then calls to Ojisan.

He and Obasan examine the boxes on the wheelbarrow, lifting them off one by one.

"Objisan will find your doll," he says heartily as I reach them. He squats down and faces me.

"The others are in the bin in the kitchen," I tell him.

His round face, crinkly with laugh lines, bounces like a ball. I do not doubt that he will bring them all. He slaps his knees as if the deed is already accomplished.

Stephen, on his crutches, has disappeared ahead of the rest of us. The mountain, immediate and immense as night, swallows us as we turn onto a path into a clump of trees.

"Stephen! Wait!" I call, running to catch up with him.

I find him and Sensei peering into the woods. There is nothing to be seen except trees, trees and trees. The ground under our feet is soft and bumpy with needles, moss, pine cones, and small acorn hats. On either side of the path, green fronds of ferns are everywhere, open and extravagant as peacocks.

"See that, Nomi?" Stephen says, pointing. I can see nothing and everything, a forest of shadows and green shapes. "Over there," he says impatiently.

We walk a few steps farther down the path and there, almost hidden from sight off the path, is a small grey hut with a broken porch camouflaged by shrubbery and trees. The color of the house is that of sand and earth. It seems more like a giant toadstool than a building. The mortar between the logs is crumbling and the porch roof dives down in the middle. A "V" for victory. From the road, the house is invisible, and the path to it is overgrown with weeds.

"That's our house," Stephen says. "Sensi told me."

We wade through the weeds to the few grey fenceposts still standing beside a gate flat on the ground, anchored to the earth by a web of vines. Behind the house, the mountain lurches skyward above a vertical rock wall. When I look up the side of the mountain, above the grey rock, to the left, there is a thin stream of water falling straight down a grey rock wall.

Stephen clumps up the porch steps and pushes his way in the front door. It scrapes along the floor. I stand at the broken gate waiting, then follow him, crossing the rickety porch step. The pine-green outside air changes suddenly to the odor of attic grey. Everything is grey – the newspapered walls, the raw grey planks on the floors, the two windows meshed by twigs and stems and stalks of tall grasses seeking a way in. A rough plank bed is in the middle of the room. Greyness seeps through the walls and surrounds us. "See that?" Stephen says, pointing to the ceiling which is an uneven matted mass of fibres. "That's grass and manure up there."

"What?"

"Sure. Cow manure."

"Says who?"

He shrugs his shoulders.

The ceiling is so low it reminds me of the house of the seven dwarfs. The newspapers lining the walls bend and curl showing rough wood beneath. Rusted nails protrude from the walls. A hornet crawls along the ledge of a window. Although it is not dark or cool, it feels underground.

There is no expression on Obasan's face as she comes in following Nakayama-sensei and Ojisan. The room is crowded with the three adults, the suitcases, boxes, Stephen, and me. Obasan takes a handkerchief from her sleeve and offers it to Ojisan. "Such heavy things," she says. "You must be weary."

"Ah," Ojisan says, "when one is almost fifty."

"Chairs just to fit," Sensei says pulling up the wooden boxes. "A small house for small people."

Ojisan reaches up to touch the ceiling. "Short people lived here, the same as we are."

"So it seems," Sensei sighs.

Obasan sits beside me on the edge of the bed.

"Together," Sensei says, "by helping each other ..." It sounds half like a rallying call, half like an apology as if he is somehow responsible.

"As long as we have life and breath," Ojisan says.

"That is indeed so," Sensei repeats, "while we breathe, we have gratitude." It is comforting to hear them talking calmly.

"For our life and that we are together again, thank you. For protection thus far, thank you ... " Nakayama-sensei is praying with his eyes open.

I follow Stephen into the other room. A rusty wood stove is against one wall. Stephen is poking at a bolt on the back door and pushes it back finally with the edge of his crutch. The rusty screen door opens with a scrape and shuts with a dusty clap as Stephen and I go outside.

Ah! The green air once more.

313

As we stand here looking over an overgrown tangle of weeds and vines, the air is suddenly swarming with butterflies. Up and down like drunken dancers, the gold and brown winged things come down the side of the mountain fluttering awkwardly. There are dozens of them. Some park like tiny helicopters on grass stalks, flexing their wings as if for take-off. Others hover near the ground before spilling back up into the air, ungainly as baby ballerinas. They are all dressed in the same velvet brown.

Stephen whacks his crutch into the grasses, scattering the butterflies. Each wing bears two round circles of gold and when the pairs are spread, they are infant eyes, staring up at us bodiless and unblinking. I stare back as Stephen tramples and slashes, hopping deeper and deeper into the tall grasses, swinging his crutch like a scythe. Within moments, the ground and grasses are quivering with maimed and dismembered butterflies. The ones that are safe are airborne and a few have reached the heights of trees.

"They're bad," Stephen says as he wades through the weeds. "They eat holes in your clothes."

His crutch clears a wide path through the middle of the backyard as he continues his crusade. When he reaches the end of the yard, he turns around. Some brambles and vines are clinging to his pant leg and one butterfly he cannot see is hovering above his head.

"UNTITLED"

John Meredith

TRAVELS

Yehuda Amichai

You came via Haifa. The harbor was new. The child was new.
You lay on your belly, not to kiss the Holy Land
but because of the riots of 1936.
British soldiers, wearing the cork helmets of a crumbling empire
threw open to you your life's new kingdom. What's your name?
Threw open to you with their tattoed arms: dragons,
women's breasts, thighs; a dagger, the coiled serpent, a rose,
girls' buttocks. Since then this view has sunk deep within you
not to be seen from outside; painfully engraved and as deep
as your soul, itself an inscribed parchment, a mezuzah
lying aslant the length of your inner body.
You became a collector of pain in the tradition of this country.
My God, my God, why? Have you forsaken me?
My God, my God. Even then you had to call him twice.
The second time already a question, a first doubt: my God?

I am sitting here now with my father's eyes,
and with my mother's greying hair on my head,
in a house that belonged to an Arab
who bought it from an Englishman
who took it from a German
Who hewed it from the stones
of Jerusalem, my city:
I look upon God's world of others
who received it from others.
I am composed of many things
I have been collected many times
I am constructed of spare parts
of decomposing materials
of disintegrating words. And already
in the middle of my life, I begin,
gradually, to return them,
for I wish to be a decent and orderly person
when I'm asked at the border, "Have you anything to declare?"
so that there won't be too much pressure at the end
so that I won't arrive sweating and breathless and confused
so that I won't have anything left to declare.
The red stars are my heart, the Milky Way
its blood, my blood. The hot khamsin
breathes in huge lungs, my life
pulses close to a huge heart, always within.

In the rising mists from below, in the blueish holy light
in his great hollow dome, I saw
the Lord of the world in all his sadness,
a radar God, lonely, circling round and round
with his huge wings, with sad movements
of primordial doubt.
Yes yes and no no, with the sadness of a God who knows
that there is no reply and no decision: only turning.
What he sees makes him sad. And what
he doesn't see makes him sad. What he records
is the code of sadness for humans to decipher.
I like the blueish light and the white of his eyes
which are blind, white screens
in which men read what will happen to them.
Again Massada. Again Massada. Not again.

I am a solitary man, not a democracy.
The executive, the loving and the legislative power
in one body.
The hating power and the hurting power
the blind power and the dumb power.
I wasn't elected. I am a demonstration, I raise
my face like a poster. Everything is written there. Everything.
Please, there's no need to use tear gas,
I'm weeping already. There's no need to disperse me.
I'm dispersed.
The dead are also a demonstration.
When I visit my father's grave. I see
the tombstones raised by hands of dust below:
they're a mass demonstration.

Translated by Ruth Nevo

THE EMPTY BED

Yehia Hakki

When you walk down Rayhan Street coming from Imamayn Square there is a small shop on the left hand side. It is like the other shops: poor, close-set along the naked, narrow side-walk, hidden in darkness. A veil of stifling air has been woven by a spider who died long ago. Nothing remains but petty fortune, sleep and paralyzed time; the rusty springs of motionless dolls grown old. Eyelids, as if pulled by cords, drop like heavy door-latches.

But lift your eyes a little as you walk by this shop and you will see a sign above the door. For a moment your heart will stop. You will look aside and hurry away. Perhaps you will stumble and ask yourself: Why is this damnable trade crowded in with other stores? Why here, flush against those shops praised in the Holy Book, among owners with whom you would gladly shake hands or sit for a cup of tea? There is something wrong in this neighbourhood: a leper in the harem of an eastern prince, drunk on milk, sips from the hands of an illustrious pimp.

To the right of the store lives a grocer. The rugged dusty boards near the entrance of the store are covered with soured eggplants, each vomiting ripe seeds from its belly, each so rotten it makes the mouths of vulturous customers water with desire.

To the left lives a leather-craftsman. He works the butcher's remnants. See the back of that suitcase? Crafted from a cow's flank. And that one? From a goat's belly. All are for separation and immigration, and you will see them cast about in depots, thrown on to luggage racks, roaming the world like spirits.

Then you catch the odour of a passing donkey-cart, a chicken coop-like cart with no roof or walls, crowded with brooding women in black, each upon her egg. Woe to her who does not hatch, for they are strictly supervised by a hawk, forever greedy, waiting to swoop down upon the chicks. The donkey who draws the cart is skinny, and the driver, though breathless, seems hungry.

Look back one last time at the sign over the shop: it is the essence of modesty; it covers the whole earth with its shadow; it seems to be falling down, yet it is eternal. See the elaborately written white letters cracked like the shell of a tortoise: Public Undertaker, Imamayn District.

A young apprentice passes through the entrance of the dark cave-like store and descends into its depths. He comes out carrying a new coffin and wrapping cloth which he hangs on a nail at the side of the shop. Then he sits down and hones his fingernails on his striped robe.

A small family lives on the opposite side of the street; father, mother and son (the first apple on the tree had also been the last). Nobody knows

318

much about them. Neighbours believe the family wants to live alone. They claim the three wish to conceal either great happiness or great misery. Those who believe that happiness lurks behind the veil of privacy cite those feast days when festive streams of light pour out through the windows of this home, and joyous laughter can be heard. There is nothing like this light of happiness in the whole district. But those who maintain that misery is the cause of such seclusion point to an event which recurs once or twice each month. An old car stops in front of this house – a car physically and spiritually exhausted like a pregnant woman with a smothered baby in her womb, a mother who gives birth to death. A giant chauffeur steps from the car and opens the door for a tall thin sallow man, furtive, with dishevelled hair. He grips the car door, then the door of the house, looking around slyly, shrewdly, waiting for the moment when he can run away and regain his freedom to pursue the wicked enemy who robbed him of his soul and spirit, his reason and logic. But he doesn't know who his enemy is. The chauffeur pushes him forward; he holds the slim man's face between his huge hands, so that he cannot twist his neck and insult passers-by, like you, with bullet-like looks and language that would disgrace a brothel.

When this filthy noise begins, all the windows of the house slam shut at once, as if locked automatically, untouched by human hands. Within an hour or two, the chauffeur reappears, still chewing his meal busily and wiping his moustache. The tall, soft, emaciated boy is holding the big man's hand, but when he sits in the car, he begins to groan and moan like a traveller returning from a long journey on a lame mule, knowing that soon he will be in his bed.

Often, after the car is gone, the boy from the cafe next door appears with a bucket full of water. Standing on the sidewalk, he takes a healthy swing and empties his bucket with a powerful sweep. You feel the earth quiver with delight as the water splashes over its skin, and the aroma of nicotine spreads, like an opiate soothing the nerves of the passers-by, men, horses, mules, and donkeys.

But the truth is much simpler than theories. The curtain of privacy is drawn to hide neither happiness nor misery. There is another reason, which lies closer to human nature. After all, superstition and self-deception are of the imagination, not of reality; both shine only to dim the truth. You see, the family has broken with the world. They believe life is a hornet's nest, a time bomb, a wineskin which, when the seal is broken, will ruin one's reason. For them, life is no progression in which the new perpetually outgrows the old, and the horizon widens the higher you climb. No, their life is a horizontal line, faint and straight, made of millions of colorless spots. Their food is chewed in advance by pestles and meat-grinders: their vegetables and meat are mashed together into a stale pap. They relish the loss of flavor.

The family had withdrawn from life, fearful of an aridity in which they might drown, a flood which might suck them dry. And so, they were sure to be free from suffering, free from regrets, from the abominable faithlessness of friends, free from grief over the meanness of their own souls. They ceased to name the days. They told time by the movement of shadows or the cries of migrant birds. He who shuns men approaches nature. The days became confused, so did their ages: the husband called his wife "Mother", she called him "Father", and both called their only son "Brother". He called his mother, "My Bride". The son seemed to have forgotten his father's name. He never spoke to him, and if the father was absent he simply said "he", or "him". Often, standing back to back, father and son turned to find themselves staring at one another. The son felt his father was spying on him with his piercing, flickering eyes; the father felt his son's eyes carried the look of a man holding a sharp scalpel hidden in his palm. Quickly, they gave each other embarrassed, apologetic smiles, like children caught cheating at a game, and the smiles turned into looks which spoke of love, understanding and mutual esteem. All this, in the twinkling of an eye. It proved that the family was close together, sharing an unusual distinction: their hands were all soft, smooth and tender; they had stopped extending them to each other.

Their lives lacked any direction The parents showed neither surprise, nor objection, nor regret when their son quit Business School. He had neither grief nor worries, but a year of studying made him positively ill. He detested money, accounting and statistics, and when he cursed he spat out a number. It was the same with literature; after another wasted year his mind and tongue went out of control and he found himself speaking nonsensical rubbish. He quit and his parents said nothing. For the next year, he was idle at home. But then his life changed completely. He went to Law School, and it was there that he finally anchored his boat. He was not a brilliant student; he passed, though at the bottom of his class, until the last year before graduation. He was at rest in his studies. What he liked about the law was its complete removal from the revelation of nature, from nature's complications and contradictions, from its claim that injustice sometimes is disguised as justice. Nature makes no final judgment, at least, not until the destruction of the universe. But in the Law, there was always judgement, because it created its own independent system of logic, a beautiful construction on paper, which was nicely and coherently divided into cause, effect and speedy execution. The study of law meant the destruction of life's own organic structure, so that logically numbered categories were constructed from life's ruins. The judge does not judge from his experience, never, but always from his books. Paper is clearer than truth. Honest candour and lying are both rejected unless supported by irrefutable evidence. Vice is well-defined and concrete; virtue is vague and faltering and of no account. A judge will punish the man who betrays his wife, but will never reward the husband who remains faithful beyond the honeymoon. And so, the virtue of the law is that it saves humanity by converting the world of the spirit into logical argumentation; differences between the learned and the ignorant, the volunteer and the conscript, disappear. So too, the word "Fate" is erased from the dictionary and the word "Pity" is eliminated as well. This is sanctioned by the precise logic of the Law. No matter how many injustices are created, logical, sequential argumentation is preferable to a just law based on incomprehensible logic. Legal logic is so far removed from the revelation of nature that the young man gradually lost all sense of the distinction between vice and virtue. He became like the beggar who receives and never gives, who avoids crowds and the vivacity of life, and who lies down and sleeps on the sidewalk in front of a mosque: he is bare-chested and prey to the rays of the sun and the hordes of lice. When he feels the two flowing together over his body he is seized by a thrill which is at once both pleasure and pain.

However, before entering the Law School, the young man had spent that idle year at home, and with nothing to do, it was only natural that one particular profession appealed to him as the cure for all his maladies, a profession which appeared to be the simplest, the noblest, the truest and the most sensible – that of the husband. He was a virgin, yet he insisted that he should marry either a widow or a divorcee. And so, without interference from his parents, he chose the factory in which to practise his new profession. He refused to review the lists of relatives, neighbours and acquaintances; instead, one fine day while sitting in his house, he simply stretched out his hand, like a Bishop blessing an Emperor, and laid it on the head of a poor girl. He said only one word: This one! – exactly like a child in a toy store. His soul was overwhelmed with joy. He felt he had finally returned to Nature, and was proud that he had crushed underfoot all the traditions invented by men for the winning of a wife: the pursuit and chase, the prize, the negotiation of the contract, the combat, the courting and the sighing. He secretly laughed to himself. By chance he had discovered that the secret of a woman's misery in our time lies in the traditions and values which she has inherited from all the grandmothers and great-grandmothers. She expects her suitor to employ all these techniques, and yet she claims, because she is civilized, that only courting is really necessary. Why should the young man bother himself with such headaches?

The chosen penniless girl came with her parents to visit. Her father was a tenant who lived on land belonging to the young man's family, and he came to town twice a year, during summer and winter, to pay his rent. The daughter wore a simple dress of old-fashioned dyed silk, no shoes but slippers, and her veil revealed virtually nothing of her face. She was extremely shy, and if spoken to, she would have buried herself in the ground. The young man assessed her pinkish heels and the visible fragments of her face and concluded that she would be good for him. A naive, raw girl, with downcast eyes that did not dare to stare; a forehead incapable of thought; a body in which the beauty of its individual parts was lost to the beauty of the whole; heavy curly hair which, when washed and braided and hanging down upon her cheeks and forehead, would be beautiful. He would love to wash it himself, and his tongue would find the soap as delicious as sweet wine.

He knew that the girl had been married to her cousin in the village. Her husband feuded with another man, and this evil and vengeful man had waited for the bridegroom to return from the fields and had riddled him with bullets from his homemade rifle. Then he had carried the mangled corpse home to the bride. She had wiped her husband's wounds with a handkerchief, thus bloodstained twice within the week. In her, the young man had found his ideal. She met all his requirements; she was easily

321

accessible and somebody had already laboured over her and undone her knot. He thought of her as he would a new pan for frying: he would rather that somebody else dirtied his nails and scraped his knuckles seasoning it for the cooking; indeed, the young woman was a better deal than a frying pan; already, she had been greased and seasoned with her own blood and the blood of her murdered husband.

To complete his happiness, the young man furnished his room in the peasant style of his wife's class: a mat by which the wooden clogs could be left, an iron bed with wooden planks, a pink silk mosquito net, red and green trunks to store clothes, and a basin for washing. But when the trousseau was finally ready he was surprised to see the bride draw to her mother's ear and whisper, and then turn her head towards the wall from sheer shyness; at the same time she was squeezing her mother's hands to keep her from speaking. When the young man was alone with his mother-in-law she said that her daughter would have preferred a spring mattress instead of those wooden planks. After all, she was marrying a man from Cairo.

On that mattress the young man received the greatest shock of his life. His whole being was shaken. His dreams were cast to the wind. He was naked in the midst of the ruins, nursing the wounds of his confusion. On the wedding night, the raw and simple girl had become a wild beast. Her down-cast eyes glistened like a hawk's, flickered like a flaming sword or like a midnight pyre, and all the waters of the holy rivers would not have put out that fire. Her look rasped his body like a file. Her forehead, which had never betrayed the wrinkle of a single thought, now was engraved with a court order; there could be neither delay nor appeal. The tight thin lips opened and closed, swollen, quivering and panting, at one moment the round cone of a volcano, then a whirlpool, then a sharp line like the edge of a knife, contracting, opening, as if there were a hook in her gullet being yanked by a merciless hand. Her teeth gleamed with a hunger which frightened away the darkness. The parts of her body, which had been subsumed by the charm of the whole, claimed their rights and proclaimed, violently, their individual beauty. Even her big toe stretched to carry its head high. She was voracious, yet contradictory: the palms of her hands remained relaxed and generous, her arms tender, her saliva like honey, and her breathing that of an innocent child.

What should he do? He had wanted only pleasure for himself, not to be overwhelmed by liabilities. He refused to accept obligations forced upon him, neither poll tax nor any other invasion beyond the wall of his privacy, his cultivated dignity. Content with his safely secluded self-esteem, he would allow no-one to examine his nakedness; the hand that sought to scrutinize and weigh him in the scales, that hand ought to be cut off.

Despite his convictions, he came to no conclusion. But the raw simple girl did. She was patient through the second night, but on the third she kicked him with her foot and said: "We women from Upper Egypt were made for men from Upper Egypt. I piss on your money, elegance and beautiful words." And as if the voice of fate possessed her, she added: "Find yourself a mummy daubed with red and white and black. Your town is full of them."

322

She got up and gathered her clothes. For the first time the perplexed young man saw her fine beautiful nose, her long slender neck, and her firm strong legs which the noblest of Arab horses would have envied.

The next morning, she went away with her mother, as if fleeing a sleeping captor who might awake any moment. Her black dyed silk dress hung forward, as if she were ready to run. And so, her second marriage had also lasted less than a week. When the mother thought she saw tears in her daughter's eyes, she consoled her. She told her not to be sad; this was her *kismet*, and the raw and simple girl answered quietly to herself: "How good and stupid you are, mother. If I were to cry, I would cry in memory of my first marriage."

Left alone, the young man sought out prostitutes who would satisfy his desires. They had no rights over him, nor were there obligations. He paid cash and refused to barter, for bartering was primitive, a process to be replaced by progress. At first, he made no distinction between the women. But soon he became more selective. He wanted only those whores who attracted customers like sugar a swarm of flies. He was pleased when he found himself lost in the huge crowd: his face had become a mask, yet his paradise eluded him. Even the busiest and most popular would occasionally turn her head, or her mouth would quiver, or a sudden movement of her arm would upset his confidence. All he wanted was to find a woman whose face would be completely immobile and frozen; a face of wax; lips like wooden molds; arms paralyzed; a body as cold as white snow.

It is hard to know what would have happened to him if he had not caught a mysterious disease. He was in bed for a long time. The doctors said it was only a harmless microbe found in the body of any healthy man. Usually, it was destroyed by the red corpuscles without complications or medicinal aid. However, the young man's body failed to resist, not because of any organic malfunction, but because of his total lack of will. He was a pendulum swinging between the sweet fragrance of life and the stinking putrefaction of corruption. No living spirit, but only a mechanical spring moved this body. Gangrene had eaten away the flesh from under his skin and his eyes glimmered in their deep sockets. He was a barely breathing creature. The doctors told his father to consult a psychiatrist.

This stung the young man. As soon as the doctors departed, he got up and went to the bathroom to exorcise and cure himself. He said farewell to his past, and washed and cleansed his body. When he returned, there was a gentle, contented look in his eye, and he moved easily and harmoniously (consequently, he was later considered dull and apathetic). He took meticulous care of his fingernails, carefully selected his neckties, and saw that his clothes matched in perfect elegance. He moved with the languorous coquettishness of the effeminate, speaking in a low, melodious voice. In his eyes there was a mellow lustre, as if painted with honey; his tall figure was bent slightly forward, seemingly deferential to all around him. All this did not hurt him. It made him appear more respectable, and more intelligent than he really was. Some said that his stoop had given his eyes a cunning and inquisitive look, but God knows he was innocent of that.

323

This period in the young man's life came to an end when he entered Law School. His fellow students immediately noticed his elegance and noble dignity. They surrounded him without being aware of why they were attracted to him. Was it his fingernails, his tender hands, the honey flowing from his eyes, or the melody of his speech? But no one became his real friend. And yet, he was not lonely. He was comfortable and always a sweet smile accompanied the honey of his looks. The other students said he was the model of kindness and good behaviour, and added: "This is how a son of high society behaves."

It was the fall of the year before his licentiate examination. The Nile had receded following the summer floods, and through his window the young man watched the dark-brown muddy waters flowing down from the distant mountains, with innumerable waves like the scales of a fish. The river was done with the generation of the earth and was disappearing into its cave to hibernate. It had lost its virility; everything seemed cold and dark and overpoweringly grim. Only the fields, which had forgotten the time of their naked sterility, put on a shawl of buds and blossoms – they offered the gift of themselves to the bees and animals. Through his window the young man watched the blue sky where cool breezes suppressed all malice, and with his eyes he followed the flight of a cluster of freshly combed virgin clouds, which seemed to joke with the people of the earth by mimicking their familiar pastimes. It was a if a hidden hand had suddenly poured joy and happiness over the world. A plover with large black wings cried while bathing in the sunlight. "A good omen," his mother used to say. The bird's cry lasted only a second, that second in which man shakes off his chains and slavery, his fears and doubts, his fancy and filth, that second in which man turns innocent, a pure being endowed with perfect freedom, equal only to that of an angel or a devil. This new freedom filled the young man's heart and shook him. He could not understand why this freedom was not fully clear and comprehensible to the midget that he was, halfway between angel and devil. And so he rejected it and turned his head slowly towards the wall. Boredom overcame him, and he felt a bitter poison in his throat, a poison which replaced his blood, flowed in his veins, deposited dirt between his toes, a poison which had to be sweated out of his body.

It was unusually late for him that day when he went out. As he stepped onto the street he noticed the small shop opposite his house. It had been closed for some time, but now it was open again, and he saw a man on a ladder hanging up a sign: "Public Undertaker, Imamayn District." He felt a sting in his heart. Was it mere coincidence that time, on one single morning, had embraced both his weariness and the arrival of the messenger of death? Was this the traveller whom the bird had predicted? Or were these events preordained? Were they serving some secret purpose?

He saw the undertaker's apprentice – who told the man on the ladder to hurry. When the workman was down the ladder, the apprentice brought out a coffin and hung it up by the side of the door. Then the apprentice turned, as though he knew that somebody was watching him. Their eyes met, and the young man saw the apprentice as if his image were etched in isolation apart from the world around. He saw a boy who had a body like a cotton sack, short with overly large arms and hands, a low heavy forehead and narrow eyes. His eyes flashed with the gleam of silver spangles, and the whites told of cunning, a disturbed and evil mind with the hunger of an animal: in short, a beast ready to kill. The young man was sure that he had seen the boy before … And his look was familiar; it was his father's, just before he took a pipe of opium or a shot of cocaine.

As he turned to leave, the apprentice raised his hand to his forehead and greeted him with a friendly smile. The young man walked away, knowing he would be back.

The two men became friends. The young man spent his evenings with the apprentice, and they sat together in front of the store. At first he came down dressed in his suit and shoes, but soon he saw no reason why he should not wear his slippers and *jallabyia.*

The apprentice talked about his job: its seasonal ups and downs, its past glory, its rituals, and its tricks and crafts. Then one day he said to his friend: "Since you listen to me with such curiosity and ask me about everything with great interest, why don't you come with me next time I have a customer? I'll say you're one of us, and no-one will ever find out." In his boredom the young man accepted the offer. Then he left.

He had never seen a corpse before. But now he and his friend entered a narrow, muddy lane. When they approached the dead man's house, the mourners recognized the boys and began screaming, wailing, striking their cheeks and beating their breasts. The two friends heard the sound of heavy pounding footsteps on top of the roof. It was like a sick woman at an exorcism who hears the drums begin to play. The young man felt his heart beat. He put his hands over his ears. Then he was on his way, following his friend, through a crowd of young boys who celebrated the funeral. This contradiction between the drumming and the boys' faces calmed him. They went up a narrow staircase which the apprentice quickly measured with his eyes; it was big enough for the coffin. As they entered the apartment, the wailing and screaming broke out again. Despite the tumult, the young man heard the hissing of a gas-stove, and he knew the relatives of the dead had not forgotten to boil water. Wet-eyed women dressed in black surrounded him, but he thought they were receiving him like they would a first-aid man. One old woman patted him on the shoulder and said: "See to your job now, my son, God will help you." Only now did he understand how undertakers could be content and happy with their work and proud of themselves. The apprentice led him into an adjacent room where the corpse lay upon a mattress on the floor. He asked him to help carry the corpse into the bathroom where a table had been prepared. Everything was there: the gas-stove with a huge pot of water boiling over it, the mug and the bowl, the cloth and the soap. Some of the family, however, did not allow the body to be touched by strangers unless it was absolutely necessary, and therefore they carried the corpse to the table themselves. The apprentice then asked them to leave, and only one old man, a sheik, remained to read verses of the *Koran.*

Like a cook baking bread and tossing dough, the undertaker's apprentice threw off the white sheet which covered the corpse. His friend thought of the wings of a mythological bird, hovering around and around, trying to touch him. But then the shroud was gone, and for the first time in his life the young man stood before a dead person. He was faced with the division of things into two kingdoms: corpses and non-corpses. Something stiff and yet made of tender flesh; something shaped like a man, and yet not a man, neither animal nor stone. But what touched the young man most was that when he looked at the corpse, he did not know whether he was confronted with resignation which had reached the point of torment, or torment at the point of resignation. Was the corpse a suppressed cry of pain, or was it the echo of a song of praise? Was it an exclamation of joy: "I am your servant, my love"; or was it a dumb moaning: "It is enough, my Lord?" It was neither one nor the other; it was nothing at all. The thing was nothing, only the picture of a man, a picture that does not turn its head, that does not twist its mouth, and whose arms do not thrust forward.

The young man's fear left him and he started to wash the corpse, gently and cautiously, so that the apprentice became impatient and shouted: "Hurry up – before they hide the quilt."

The young man began visiting the shop every day in his *jallabyia* and slippers. He insisted on accompanying the apprentice on every mission, and he would even rush to answer a call before his friend. To him a day without a corpse became a dull day. He worked with the passionate enthusiasm of an amateur who loves his craft, and his fingers trembled with the desire to examine the merchandise thoroughly. Corpses look alike at first sight, but to the contemplative lover they are different indeed: Are the hands stretched out or clenched? Are the legs straight or are the knees bent and raised to the chest like a new-born child, so that the apprentice has to push them down with all his weight to close the coffin (at time he wishes he had a saw or a hammer)? This one is a midget, heavy as lead; this one is a giant light as a feather; that corpse is only decaying flesh on rotten bones; that one is an inflated balloon; here is a face cramped together in fear, and there is a tranquil face enjoying a peaceful sleep.

The apprentice realized that the young man was unable to leave him. He saw how his smile had become even gentler and meeker, his eyes even sweeter and his body softer. And so the apprentice moved closer toward his friend, and whenever they sat together in front of the shop, he would put his arm around his shoulder and down to his waist. Whenever he spoke to him, he would hold his mouth close to his ear. And in this manner, he one day whispered: "If you don't know what to do with yourself, just give yourself to me. Don't be coquettish. And don't be afraid. Just follow me. It is quite dark inside the shop, and there's a coffin that's big enough for both of us." The young man renounced the snake and the incense; but he never complained nor became angry. His mind was far away, wandering in the world of the grave.

The apprentice resorted to a trick. He appeared to avoid the young man, as if having given up hope, or as if he had regained his senses. He began cursing the times and speaking regretfully of the old days. When he had lulled and numbed his friend with words he suddenly announced that he had extraordinary news.

"Did you hear? Our boss' wife says she has had the best job of her life. This blessed morning she was called to the bed of a dead bride-to-be, and from a very rich family. The girl was to be married the day after her death. The white dress was ready, the maid had taken her to the bathroom. The maid had barely finished washing and rubbing her body with perfume when the rich girl held her hand over her heart, sighed and died. The funeral was grand: music accompanied the procession and people scattered henna all over the grave. The family insisted that the bride be buried in her wedding-gown and that a bouquet of jasmine be laid in the coffin."

A bride in the blossom of youth, washed twice, in her wedding gown and covered with jasmine.

"Is she fair or dark?" the young man asked, his voice trembling.

"Dark. Probably from Upper Egypt," the boy whispered. The young man jumped to his feet and seized the apprentice by his collar.

"Take me to her grave!" he commanded.

"On condition that you let me. Only on condition that you let me."

Two shadows stole away into the darkness: one a ravenous beast about to devour naked flesh, and a broken, putrid soul who had lost the mercy of the Lord.

One morning, the message is brought to his family from the hospital: their star has fallen during the night. His bed is empty, waiting for another.

Translated from Arabic by Samar Attar

THE GOOD LIFE

Claude Gauvreau

[The interior of a house, at once slightly austere and slightly weird in its proportions. To the left, almost in the center, a closed door that leads to another room of the house. A man and a woman enter, both wearing wedding clothes. The man wears black gloves.]

The Man: Hands in the abyss making leaves. That's a wedding.

The cup running over with love like seaweed on the porch.

A stream of clouds dives into the hearts: king-fisher.

Wreaths in cheeks, peace sculpted in the worried profiles of existence.

Sugar woman. Hebrew.

Hebraic joy in the procession of the symbolic orange.

Spread wings in the conjugated marbles.

I see the furrows, I notice the wound of the roots. The poet who came into our souls by the keyhole.

The buds make faces in the sour lake, but the chattering of the turkish tooth floats up in the shady catacombs. Superior life! Acid delirium! the parallel cones set on the spheric circle and moss of foam like mercury, the amber-coloured sponge.

Apollo's desire. Spontaneous springs.

Keys to bliss. Keys to blisses.

Reflection smiling on my beloved's steel breasts.

I feel the clenched repentance of solitude. Clear voices, mauve-scented soup-tureens. Ideal! Idea. Ideal: Pure zeal.

The Woman: My belly, cradle of life and consecrated urn. Spheres affiliated in the arch of aged autumn. Powder of kisses in the damp ditches of white gardens. Versicoloured hysteria.

The sublime fraction of golden Armenian curls.

Entrance and procession of children.

Arbitrary farandole in the yellow brick paths.

[The man and woman sit on a sofa, kissing tenderly. The lights go out. After a moment, only a beam of whitish light reappears, not enough to show the background; this would give the impression of being suspended in mid-air. The man, dressed only in white tights and his black gloves, is standing up, and at his feet is a conical ball of white string.]

The Man: I am dreaming.

[A piano is heard, languidly playing a five-note theme. The man, who now moves with jerky motions, bends to pick up the ball of string. But each time he is about to grasp it, another note of the theme is heard and the ball of string jumps out of his reach. This occurs with all five notes. Then, the beam of whitish light disappears and the stage is dark. The five notes of the theme are heard once again in the

darkness, then the lighting returns to normal. The man, dressed normally, is sitting alone on a sofa and he rubs his eyes with his gloved hands.]

The Man: I dreamt.

[The lights go out. In the darkness, the five notes of the theme are heard. The lights come on again. The man, standing on a chair, hangs a picture on the wall. The woman, in a dressing gown, is sitting on a sofa.]

The Man: The lights like malevolent dreams. The backs of shadows forever lost to the ashes of humanity.

I see the ropes that encircle mankind. I see the bodies mutilated by remorse.

I understand the ropes pinned in memory.

Woman with chocolate nails, with eyelashes of armistice, you are mine.

I am the seal that has plunged into the streams of syrup. Beaten unfeeling chopped like the notes of a flute.

The walls like grey deserts levelling their faces long as anticipations.

The beloved raspberry in the secret valley and the accessory silence.

The bronzed butterfly wings.

Obsession. Love.

I rock myself in my arms and harmony comes out my ears; decayed tooth in the spiral.

[From the next room the five-note theme is heard, played on the piano.]

The Woman: My sister. My twin sister is playing the piano. She is there.

The Man: Your twin sister?

The Woman: Fingers at the door of dimensions sucking white arms which wave against a black background and compete in speed.

[The lights go out. In the dark, the five notes of the theme are heard. The lights come on. The man and woman, wearing tennis togs, stand kissing.]

The Man: Peace, silken-eared snake in the damp laundry of noon.

I screwed your body in space suspended between two facing mirrors; and your image forever climbs the rungs of the infinity of numbers.

Woman's ear and skin of a pink pig.

Ah! I'm having fun.

Man's skin like an ox horn in the influence of the icy rose-window skies.

Autumn is hatching summer.

Tonight I shall lie on your body in the black redemption that slips from stones dreamed nonetheless.

[From the next room, the five-note theme is heard on the piano. The man listens, dreaming.]

The Woman: Dressed in white in the hesitant foot-bridges we are the soap bubbles.

Throats of madness in basins full of perspiration.

Ahoy! Clowns of beggary, shout yourselves hoarse in centenarian cassocks!

Shell the seeds make the sculptures urinate! Death to tapestry! I've got my man.

The sipping whispers in the aerial grass.

School is out! Breast-plates are nailed!

The Man: I believe it.

[The lights go out. The five notes of the theme are heard in the dark. The theme lingers on and is still heard when the lights come on. The man, in ordinary clothes, wearing his black gloves, stands next to the door, musing. The theme is still heard. The man walks towards the door, bends down and looks through the keyhole, but he immediately jerks back, covering his eye with both hands.]

The Man: The pain in my eye!

Nothing! There is nothing to see! Frothy peaks of green vapour thicker than bearskins!

My lowly eye. My diminished eye. My wounded eye. The pain in my eye! Light that blinds!

[The lights go out. The five notes of the theme are heard in the dark. The lights come on. The man and woman, wearing ordinary clothes, stand facing one another. The man is holding a newspaper in his right hand.]

The Man: The quilted captainries have absurdly abased themselves.

Let's be serious.

If I found a reed with its root in a nickel cupboard, I would run to wash myself and I would listen, anxious.

The throbbing parade in an olive capital which is made of plums.

Let's discuss that!

Judases come to scratch the dirt of our lawns, penis in the air.

Absurdity truer than the bearded mounds.

Critical swelling. I discuss it canonically. Voices of brewed nuggets in the woodcutter Russian hands.

You have your ladies, all is well, do not go fishing for the crescent moon.

The death of captives in the pools of tomato juice. Perplexed. So in that way cancers progress like oysters on the inside of a jar.

Juice of palisades. Effort hernia completion.

We are not the sort who labour in flashes of mud.

Parasol against the half-breed insinuations.

Serbian misconduct and medieval remonstrance. Think of the children covered with green vines.

Day bathes in gloom laid flat by the scythe.

Proud panoply.

[The first four notes of the theme are heard from the next room. The man listens. The fifth note does not come. The man, frozen in expectation of the fifth note, is as unfeeling as a lead statute. Nothing happens. The woman totters many times and then finally sinks down, turning on herself as in a whirlpool. The man does not budge. Then, the fifth note is heard very faintly, and then the man rushes to the woman. He bends over her.]

The Man: She is dead.

[He draws himself up mechanically and turns to the door which he stares at, dreamily. He waits, he does not move. Then he takes off his black gloves and walks towards the door. He stops, then opens the door. Nothing comes from the room but a thick, clammy, inexhaustible green light. It seems that there is nothing in the next room but that light, covering everything. The green light strikes the man's face and he hastily retreats, covering his eyes with his hand.]

The Man: Ah! My eyes! It gnaws my eyes!

[He quickly pulls himself together and enters the room. We can no longer see him. He comes back after a moment, his eyelids tightly clenched with pain. He has put on the black gloves again. The door closes.]

The Man: She died beside her piano.

I see the windowless cellars in the light of the sun.

Drunkenness intoxicates and falls like sick leaves.

Nothing. Nothing. The desert. The sign in the filthy weights.

At last, the soul has hushed its dawn.

The black snakes scatter in the dusty hay fields.

Adamic treachery. The dead in the bloods of the oxen.

Reddened slate. Headless poplar.

The mimes catch fire.

Cut-off. Leprous mug more unsettled than acid contritions. Barrier. Scarf of the innate veins.

The fox-terriers plunged in orthodox marriage contracts.

Cossack boot in the devastated plains. Conclusion. Initiation.

I see the cellars, the cellars, the cellars.

[Then the five notes of the theme are heard from the next room. The man turns towards the door and stares at it, perplexed and frightened. The lights go down and out. In the darkness we hear the five notes of the theme trailing after each other while the light returns, and they continue once the light is back to normal. The man is still in the same position with the same expression on his face, but he has wrinkles on his forehead and grey hair at his temples. The woman is gone. The theme finally stops.]

The Man: Smoking pies. I boil more than the intelligence of a calamitous man.

I live the universe of landings without stairs.

The makers of umbrellas for sheep laugh in my face

because we are brothers. We are from the same plague.

[The five notes of the theme are heard. The man opens the door with a sharp blow. Instinctively, the man lifts his hands to his eyes, but he controls himself and forces himself to look at the green light.]

The Man: Nobody there.

[The door closes. The theme is heard again, repeated many times. The man approaches the door without making a sound, bends over furtively and looks through the key hole.]

The Man: Nobody there. Nobody there. And my eyes hurt.

Ah! the assorted turds that vegetate in your patiences!

The mature man is as flexible as a reed.

[The underlined part is sung to the five notes of the theme, without accompaniment.]

I see the cellars *The cellars cellars*

I see the cellars *The cellars cellars*

Homeland with a hundred faces cut up into abscissae. Who will read the depth of the common sense truths?

[The theme is heard.]

Clubs in hand. Shameful peasants. Panting Atlas. Minute proceedings. It's the exegesis of Spring.

How many winds?

Fathers! The saxophone clans in the villages.

Requisitioner of clumsy deaths.

I want to kiss maiden's legs.

Ah!

My hands! My hands! It's my hands! My hands that are playing!

[He takes off his black gloves with his teeth. There are no longer any hands under the gloves, the cuffs are empty. The man looks at his cuffs close up, because his eyes are feeble. He drops his gloves on the floor. With a kick, he opens the door.]

The Man: Completely useless! My hands! On the piano, my hands! Those are my hands playing! I can see my hands playing the piano!

[He has fully entered the room and can no longer be seen. Suddenly, he is heard howling. Finally, he reappears. The door closes.]

The Man: I am blind.

The stations in the distance, the stations forever in the distance.

[Someone knocks at another door. Common men come in, both wearing overalls.]

First Common Man: We are the movers.

The Man: Ah!

Second Common Man: We've come to move the piano.

The Man: *[as in a dream]* Ah! Just a minute.

[He picks up the gloves with his teeth and goes into the room. He comes out again without the gloves. The movers, without hesitating, go into the next room and come out with the piano. The door closes. On the piano are the two hands, gloved. The movers disappear with the piano.]

The Man: Butterfly, get up.

Valves crystallized in the seas of iodine. The Huns with bony canes walk in the middle of lukewarm paths, they are caravans of camels in the Sahara.

Embossed in the leaves too slow for life like the Dead Sea.

Who walks like puppets in the raw autumn like the sun in centuries gone.

Explosive powder under the soles of centenarian feet.

The stroke faintly twisting in the mists of autumn.

Pains like the beads of a rosary.

Slow death slowly bent like the statue's head by time.

I had ten coins. In the dictatorial flame of white suns.

The yellow one fell in the nostalgic forests of the mornings.

Nostalgia in the buttoned bellies, under the golden chains of almonds.

The chevaliers of Auvergne keep me company in the obedient spring.

Caressing obsession. Chain of lugubrious pier in the more vivacious smiles.

Lessons of tenderness in the blond evening.

Silver-plated mechanisms sink in the supernatural stages.

The old brothers are flowing, flowing.

Adamic silk. I need tenderness in the palms of my anxiety.

Anxious benediction you who give up in the broadside of timid and reckless clouds.

Bend your forelocks, sincere ones, in wheedling bumpkinries.

Industrious cracks in the time of human lives, it's the canal with black boats that forget themselves in their fantasies.

We are weary. Our legs bleed. Our livers fester.

It's the Algonquin chief who does not forget the banks of creamy sands.

Noisy dogs adorn our solitary thoughts. The nun's veil gets lost in our stately breasts. Sad Frederick in the spiritual oils. It's the defections of uncles who die, skeletons, in the swans' mirages.

Decked-out sweetness. Abnormal boredom in human sorrows! O, the lullaby thoughts.

It's a man who strolls in the lone house.

I am afraid in inhuman comforts.

O fiscal torment. Brutal profligacies offer themselves masked in the countries of black wings.

I am a generation of old youth. You paid dearly for your passports, awfully dearly.

You are the young who dreamed of chimneys with blinding metal.

We are leaving in the thorns of sparks.

Smiling hope that falls in the cutting toenails.

Ah! the foggy cousinhoods.

I signal with my arms at the haughty future like a sailor covered in cankers of boredom.

[At that moment, the five notes of the theme are heard from the next room, played on the piano. The man shudders. He turns heavily towards the door, almost with despair. He looks at it, and then, deliberately, he goes towards the next room and walks in. The door closes after him. Silence. We hear noises like chairs being moved around, like hammering on the wall, like the uproar of an angry man, a general confusion. Then the five notes of the theme are heard in a very high, thin piano sound. Then the theme is played on lower notes. And then everything rushes headlong. The theme is heard played louder and louder by an orchestra. The five-note theme is played by the orchestra in a crescendo that amplifies infinitely.]

CURTAIN

Translated by Ray Ellenwood

KÉBÉKANTO OF LOVE

Gérald Godin

We'll take off minus bullets and baggage
my tit-propelled tugboat
O migration O tourism
my wives will be left with
only the parings of my heart
from my whittled loves

I'll wheel around on you one night unannounced
I'll be decked out in the door like a suit of armor
breathless I'll hike up your skirts so my hands can see you
you'll cry like the month of never
your heart bouncing off the table
we'll do the iceberg float in mulberry redcurrant wine
dead drunk as a skunk
in the OK affairs of the heart and bread

when death comes between two breast-strokes of the heart
at the crucial moment
we'll pretend we're stone deaf
the last card you'll lay on me like a love-nip
on the neck will be the queen of spades
and torn apart by a thousand fan-tailed curses
I'll take off after my mothers and fathers
on the eternal
search for chokecherries

when I go ass over teakettle
one autumn evening or wherever
I'll cover your neck at choker-time
with a basket of little white lamb kisses
and when I settle like stale milk

to the left of the wood-stoking stove
when the call to Mass has cleared the house
come what may in my cherrywood rocker
you'll be the only reason my little sweetie
that my rocker croaks on
like a heart
once I'm off in the by and by of my mothers and fathers
on the eternal
search for chokecherries

my basket of lambs will run down your neck like scales
every evening after supper
at the hour when I usually
pop up at your place
like a jealous lover

buzz off buzz off death will tell me
I've cocked an eye on your life for one last time
like a snared bird my insane eyes swoop from sink to stove
intrepid traveler I'll snap you up everywhere
by the fistful
and torn apart by a thousand fan-tailed curses I'll take off
too little too late
but pleased as the blue pea-souper
under the midnight sun

you'll find me again between the pages
of my *phrases joualesques* a pressed black flower
we'll sup together again
on mulberry redcurrant wine
between two baskets of kisses soft as our shawl
on official nooky nights

Translated by Barry Callaghan

SEVEN DRAWINGS

Tomi Ungerer

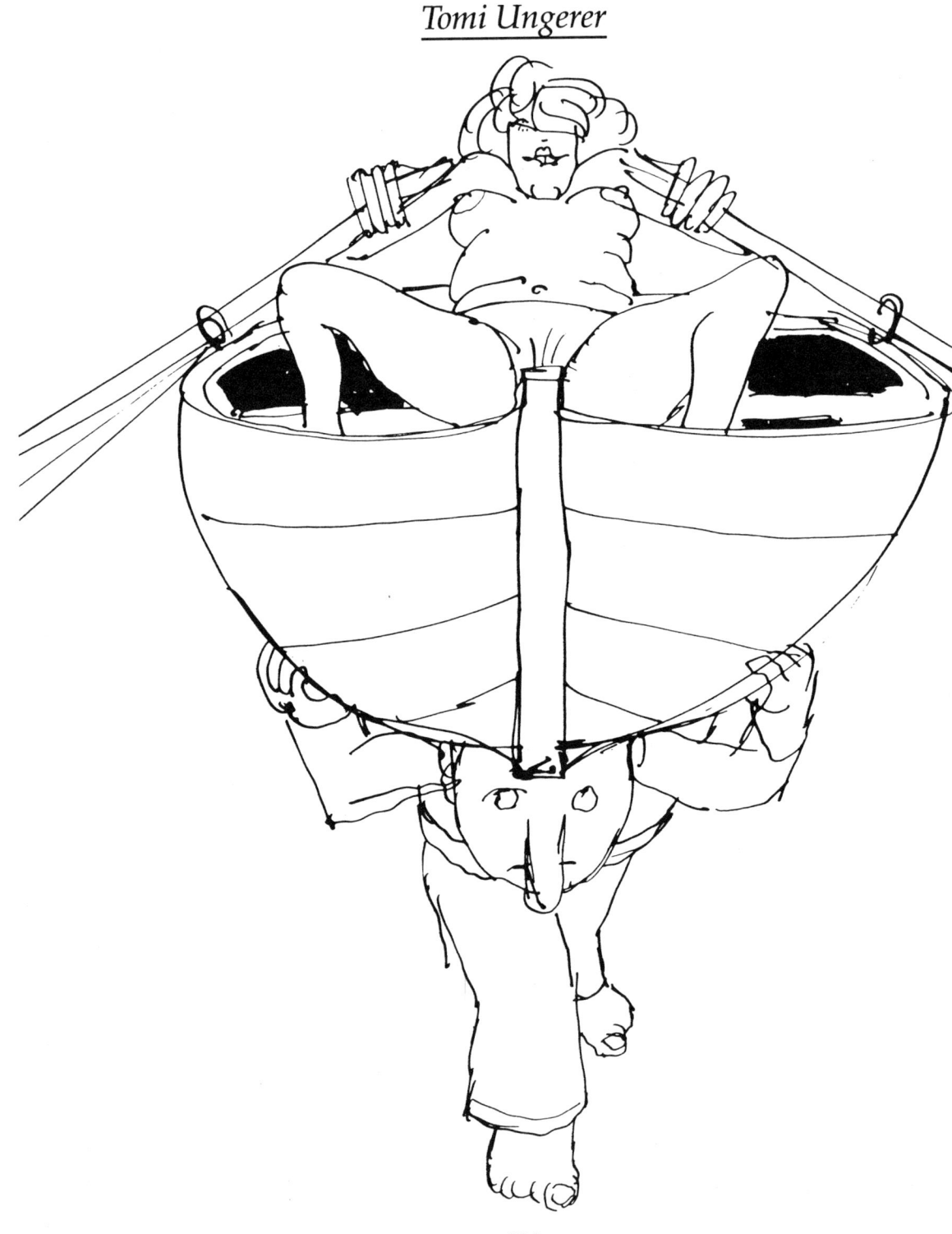

memories

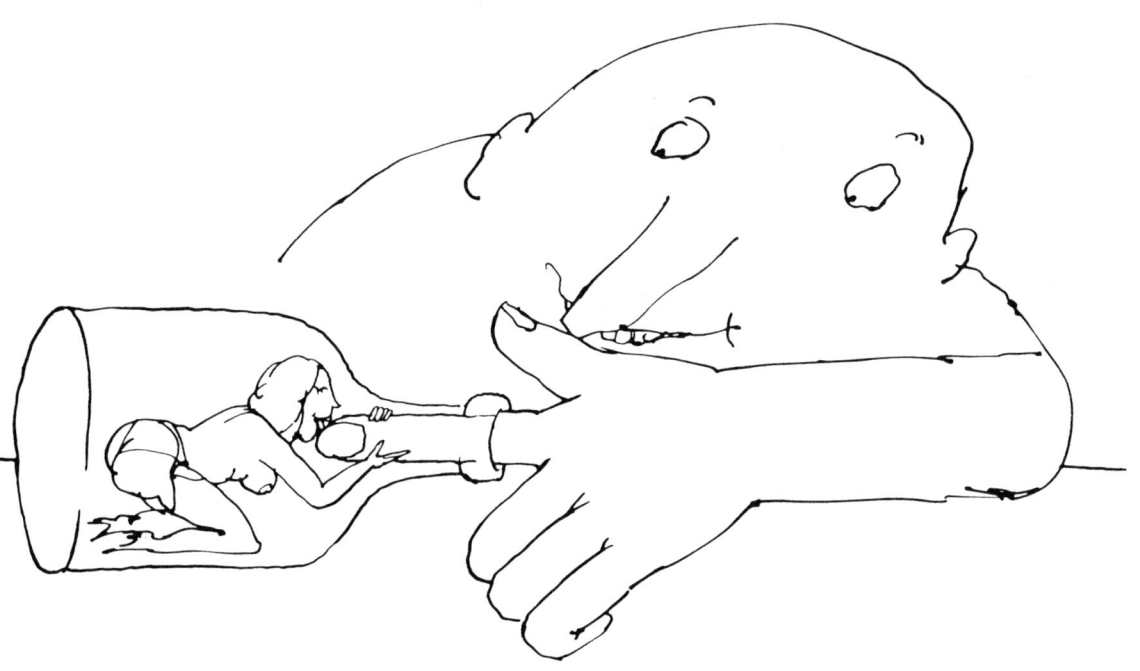

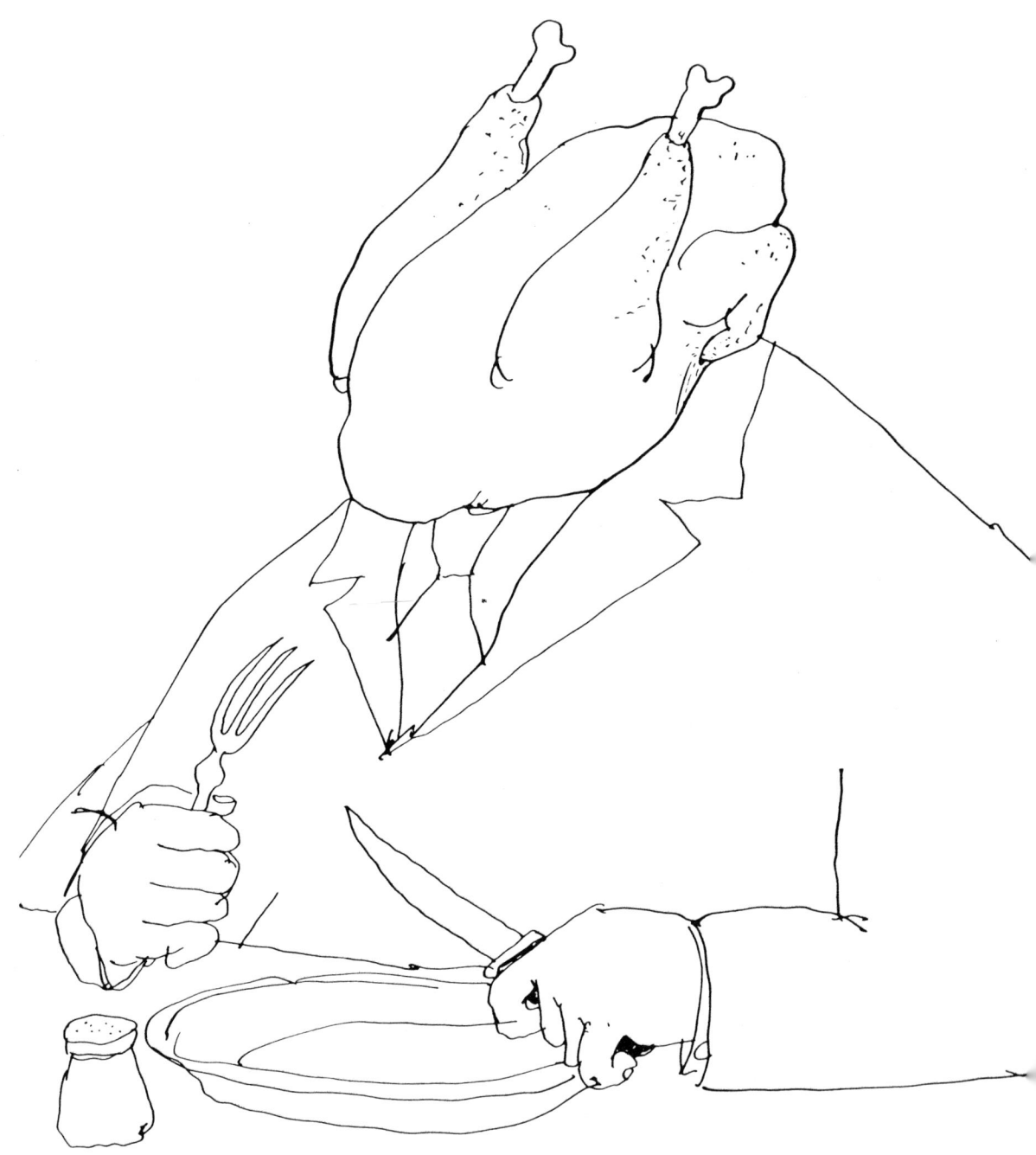

TWO POEMS

Margaret Avison

Light I

The stuff of flesh and bone
is given — datum. Down
the stickmen, plasticine people,
clay-lump children, are lain, strewn,
each casting shadow in the eye of day ...
Then, listen. I see
breath of delighting rise from
those stones the sun touches
and snarling breath
as a mouth sucks dank air
They stir and turn and move, and power
to build, to mine, are ours.

The stuff, the breath, the power to move our bodies
and with them things: data. What is
the harpsweep on the heart for?
What does the constructed power of
speculation reach for?
Each of us casts a shadow
in the bewildering day,
an own-shaped shadow only

The light has looked on light.
He speaks from elsewhere
breathing impasse-torn hope
in us,
that near.

Light II
That picture, taken from the
wing window, shows a shadow.

High up, between
the last clouds and the airless
light/dark, any shadow is
— apart from facing sunlessness —
self, upon
self.

Nights have flowed;
tree shadows gather: the sun dial
of a horizoning hill in Lethbridge measures the
long grassy afternoon.

Still, freed from swallowing downtown blocks of shadow,
I note self shadow, on
stone, cement, brick,
relieved, and look to the sun blue.

So, now.

RODIN'S HAND

Michel Lambeth

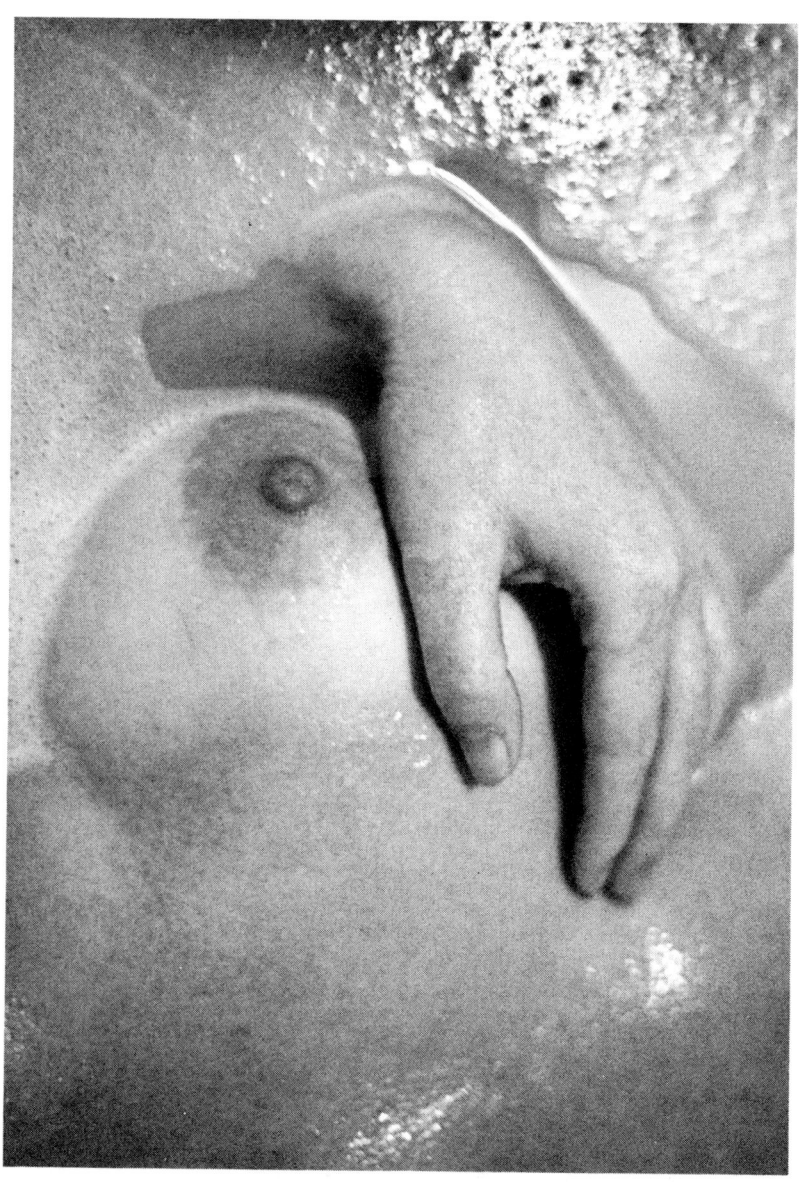

KYRIE

Harry Somers

Soloists – Soprano   Mixed Chorus   Orchestra – flute
           Alto   oboe
           Tenor   clarinet
           Bass   cello

                                                               3 trumpets
                                                               piano

                                                               4 percussion men.
                                                               (possibly 5)

It is my conviction that in certain words of ancient origin the inner meaning is revealed, not in semantics, but in their sounds, and not necessarily in the order in which they have been handed down from generation to generation.

Kyrie – explanatory notes

Phonetics –

The three basic vowels of 'kyrie eleison' and 'Christe eleison' are represented by the simplified phonetic symbols i e o (kirie eleison kriste) The open 'a' (pronounced 'ah') is also used.

The six consonants – k r l s n t – are represented as written, the 'Ch' of 'Christe' represented by 'k'. Permutations & combinations of these basic elements make up the 'text'.

N.B. The consonantal sound is to be sustained if –

1) it is clearly given duration, as opening solo 'mm', and page 5 tenor ♩, ♩. etc.

2) where it is preceded by a vowel and <u>underlined</u> – as page 12, 3rd tenor o. at end of page. (This occurs more frequently from page 36 on.) If consonant is not underlined when combined with a vowel, then it is the vowel which is sustained.

N.B. The cross, ✕, denotes a gradual transition from one sound to another for the duration of the sign. e.g. the open vowel 'o' to the closed 'mm' on page 1, ' o ✕ mm'.

Colour tone –

    Normal – no sign
    Glottal – ▨▨▨▨▨
    Nasal – ⋈⋈⋈⋈

The three are clearly illustrated on pages 1, 27, and 28.

Pitch –

1) Pitch is indicated at the beginning of a line by clef and note. Until otherwise indicated, that is the pitch to be used. (Solo, page 1 on. Male voices #4 on. etc.) Orthodox pitch indications are clear. e.g. Soprano in #4, and chorus at page 36.

2) Glissandi are used frequently and in diverse ways. They are continuous and gradual from the point indicated to begin to the point indicated to conclude. The varied and longer ones are indicated by straight diagonals either ascending ⎯, descending ⎯, combined ⌒⌄, (As page 1 of soprano solo.), and by arcs ascending ⌒, descending ⌄, interrupted ⌄ ⎯. (In basic terminology these are glissandi either accelerating or slowing as they rise or fall.)

    The same principle is applied to notes of specific duration as #1, cue 3 of soprano ⎯ ♩♩♩♩. Here the single line represents the gliss, and the two parallel lines a tie to the to the point where the gliss starts and ends, there being no 'break' in sound.

3) 'Oscillations' 〰〰 These are simply faster glissandi moving in repeated sequences between two fixed points. They vary from slow to very fast. The very fast are vibrati.

    A slow oscillation to fast is shown in the soprano solo in #2.

N.B. Special attention must be paid to controlled oscillations of specific numbers as indicated in the score.

    e.g. Soprano solo page 19 ⌄〰⌄' The short vertical strokes indicate beats, the curves indicate two 'oscillations' per beat.

Duration —

1) Specific

[A] Indicated by traditional symbols such as whole notes, half notes, quarter notes etc.

[B] By small equadistant vertical strokes · · · · to indicate beat units of equal length, as from page 19 on.

[C] Square note ☐ is held for long duration at discretion of performer.

[D] Square notes with numbers [8] (Sop. page 18) number indicates number of quarter notes or beat units as total duration of that particular note.

2) Non specific as indicated by relative lengths of pitch lines, as in soprano solo at opening. (Up to 20 sec.)

Seven pause signs are used ranging from long to short : ⌒ 10 sec. circa , ⌒ 8 sec., ⌒ 6 sec., ⌐ 4 sec., ⌃ 2 sec., ⌃ 1 sec., 9 ½ sec. These are all subject to individual interpretation.

Tempi — multi simultaneous tempi page 5 on and page 36 on.

1) There are 13 different tempi.
2) Each tempo is indicated by a number. Numbers range from 1 to 13.
3) The fastest tempo is tempo 1. The quarter note is the basic unit.
4) All other tempi are compounds of tempo 1. E.G. Tempo 2 is twice as slow as tempo 1. The quarter note (♩) of 2 equals a half note (♪) of tempo 1. Tempo 3 is three times as slow as tempo 1. The quarter note (♩) of 3 equals the dotted half (♩.) of tempo 1. Etc.
5) Therefore tempo 13 is the slowest of all, it's quarter note equals 13 quarter notes of tempo 1.
6) Therefore each tempo is created relative to tempo 1
7) On the score the quarter note of tempo 1 equals ¼ inch, a half note ½ inch, and so on. The other tempi relate accordingly. i.e. The quarter note of tempo 2 equals ½ inch, the half equals 1 inch etc.

N.B. 8) Entries occur assymetrically starting at points indicated on the score. There <u>starting</u> points therefore, are <u>not</u> necessarily in direct simple relation to the other tempi.

9) Because of the great difficulties involved in maintaining pitch and multiple tempi, I would suggest that the male chorus be pre-taped for sections #4 and #6. Using a multi track tape recorder, a few singers taking a number of parts, could tape each voice individually, thus keeping control of pitch and durations. Then the tracks could be mixed for mono, stereo, quadrophonic, or more, speaker systems. The 'cut off' just before #7 could be controlled by the operator of the play back. From section #7 the male chorus would join the rest 'live'.

Intensity (Dynamics) —

For the most part standard symbols are used.

The ◀︎▥▥▥ sign used in the percussion in the opening section indicates a crescendo from pp to whatever degree of f is felt to be right, then a sudden release, or "spin-off" of the scraper leaving the gong to vibrate.

347

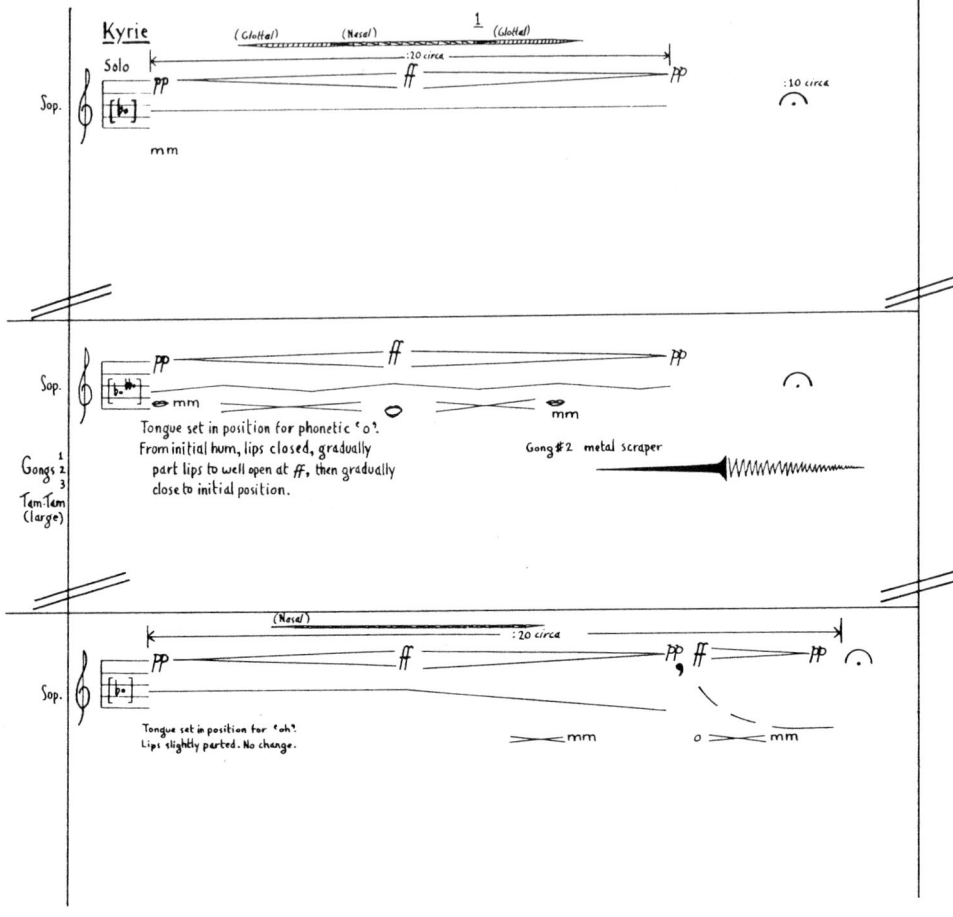

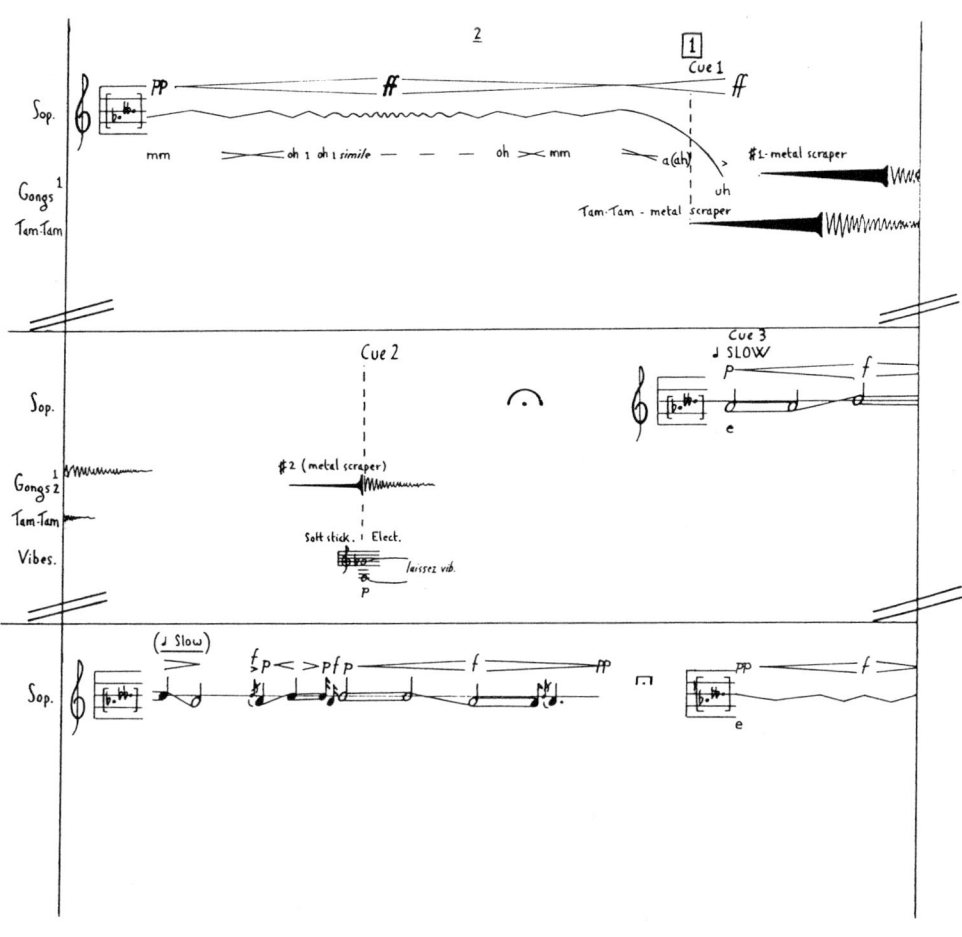

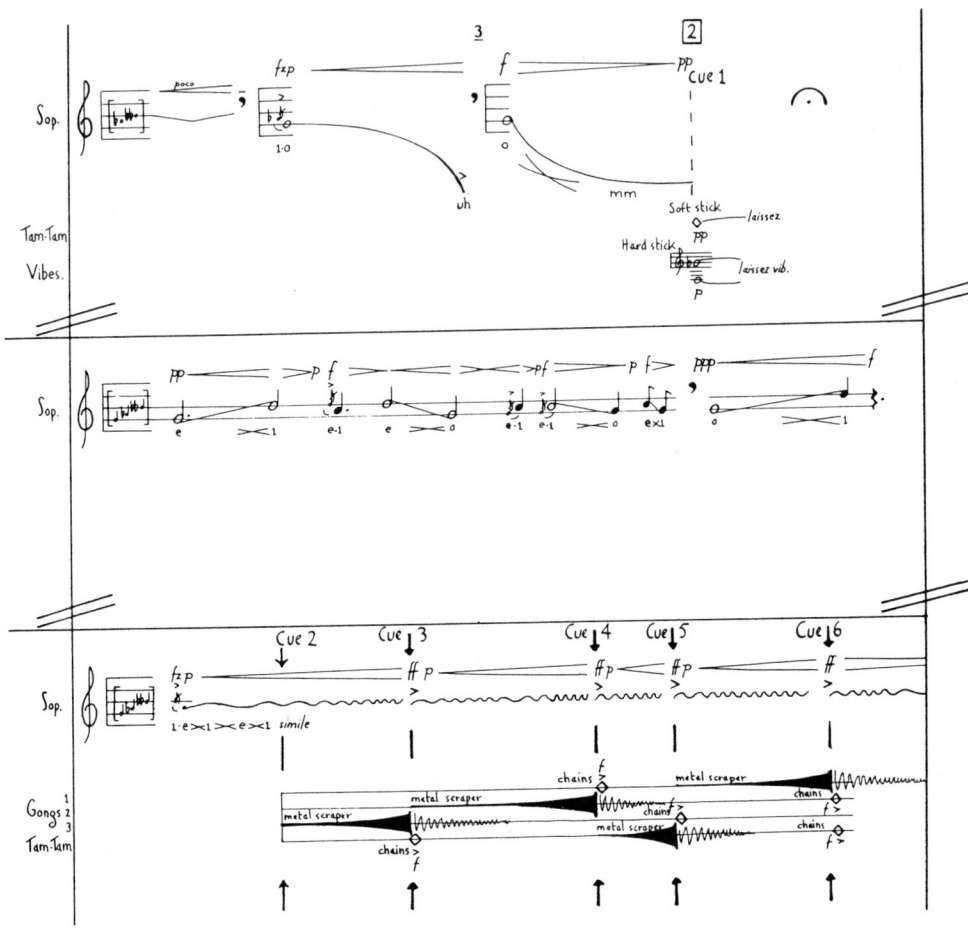

350

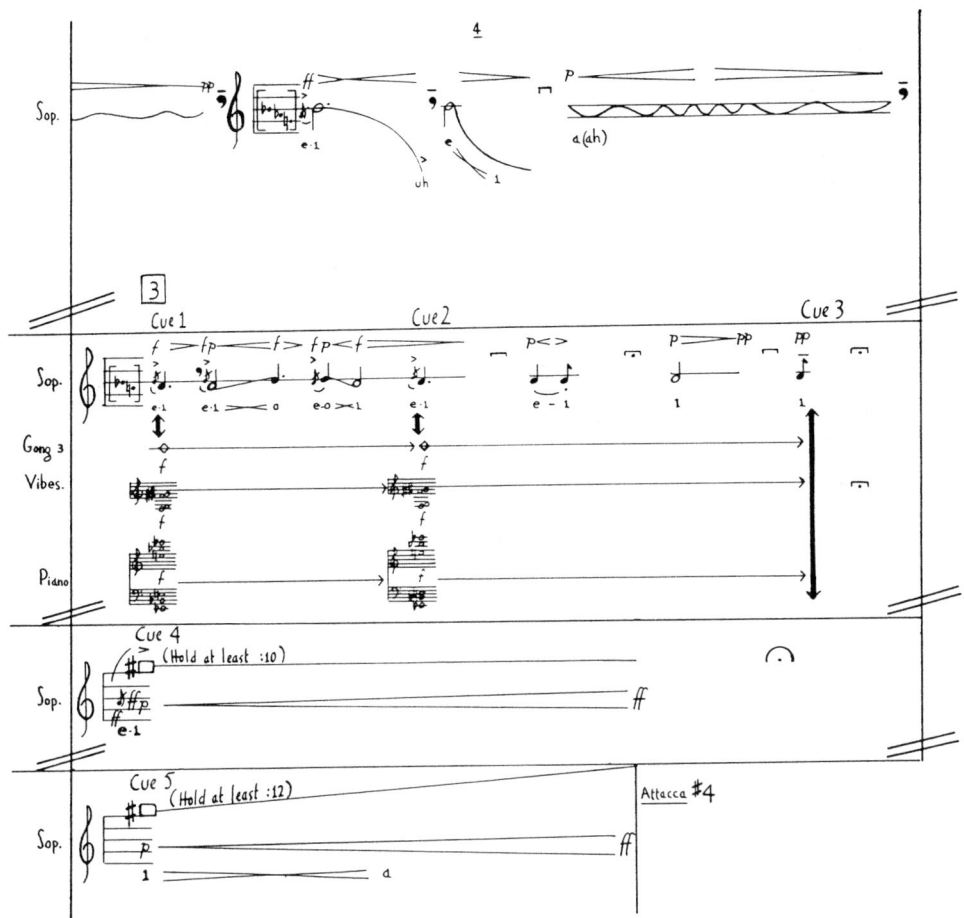

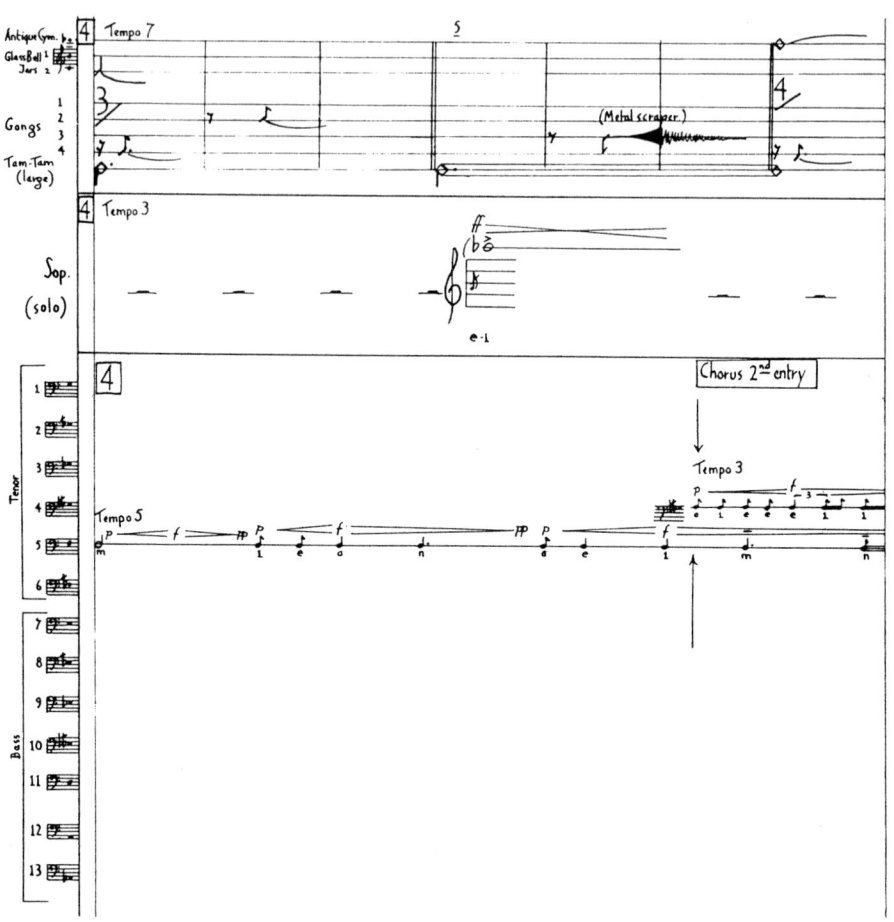

CATACOMBE DEI CAPPUCINI

Irving Layton

They supplicate, they pray, their deathlike silence
harangues; but chiefly they mock our presence
with their own and mock with such diverse nuance
of malice horror disdain that the prayed-to God
who made and put them here to stand stuffed with straw
withering against the walls or to crouch in glass tombs
is surely abashed, and drowns out with laughter
of his own the savage laughter in these corridors

Look, my friend, at those niches; there you will find
clearly defined what the anthropoid's uniqueness
comes down to: it is to wear grinning at the end
when the years have thwacked and squeezed out all offense
just such a subtle look of meekness and contempt
on your petrified skull. O peerlessly human
is the malediction on those lipless jaws
giving final judgment on our journey here

They mock themselves, they mock their past lives
what they were and what they did: senator
priest physician lawyer and grand lady born
white-gloved and bonneted for the season's ball:
you could say featured here for all to see
is the Christian's venom against the valour
and pride of life and that some rancorous monk
lined up this masque of smirks to mime his fury

Only the children cuddle like faded dolls
left on shelf or wall after the Xmas sales
they alone lack the look of spiteful mimicry
and present a sad mien, an animal dumbness:
to the women death, it seems, was a trespass
or indignity, perhaps an irksome shift
from a good gossip, a winning game of cards
but the tots, alas, died before they got the drift

All these sad corpses, each one decomposing
in the slow fire of time; on the straw-filled scarecrows
faded cards giving the name and date of expiry
which translates into: 'Lord, we have seen the glory!'
Did life pummel them into these grimaces?

Doubtless. My mind caresses each fleering chalky skull
even as it consigns with matching derision
this grisly harlequinade to a blazing furnace

Palermo,
July 1976

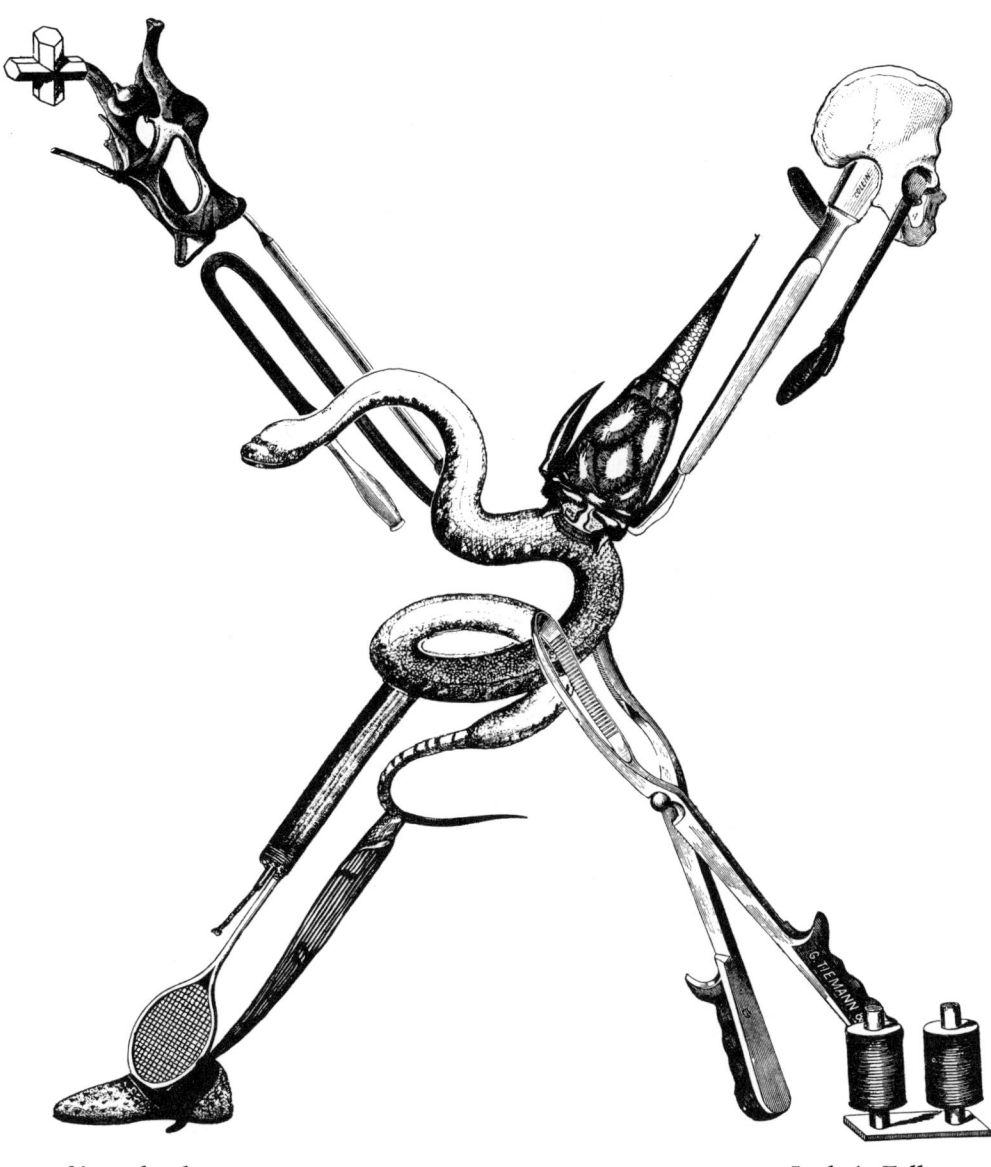

X marks the spot   *Ludwig Zeller*

THREE POEMS

Paul Celan

Time's Eye

This is time's eye:
it squints out
from under a seven-hued eyebrow.
Its lid is washed clean by fires,
its tear is hot steam.

Towards it the blind star flies
and melts at the eyelash that's hotter:
it's growing warm in the world
and the dead burgeon and flower.

With Letter And Clock

Wax
to seal the unwritten
that guessed
your name,
that enciphers
your name.

Swimming light, will you come now?

Fingers, waxen too,
drawn
through strange, painful rings
The tips melted away

Swimming light, will you come?

Empty of time the honeycomb cells of the clock,
bridal the thousand of bees,
ready to leave.

Swimming light, come.

Mandoria

In the almond — what dwells in the almond?
Nothing.
What dwells in the almond is Nothing.
There it dwells and dwells.

In Nothing — what dwells there? The King.
There the King dwells, the King
There he dwells and dwells.

Jew's curl, you'll not turn grey.

And your eye — on what does your eye dwell?
On the almond your eye dwells.
Your eye, on Nothing it dwells.
Dwells on the King, to him remains loyal, true.
So it dwells and dwells.

Human curl, you'll not turn grey.
Empty almond, royal-blue

Translated by Michael Hamburger

WHERE THE SUN
DON'T SHINE

Hugh Graham

Excerpted and adapted from the radio play.

Narrator
On a day in 1904, Latimer Davenport stepped down from the train on the road leading into Maskinonge Township,

A train fades to the sound of crickets and footsteps on a country road.

dressed in white duck trousers, a straw boater, blazer, and bow tie.

The crickets fade to the sound of crows cawing.

Narrator
It was another day before he was in Maskinonge.

Footsteps up onto wooden porch, followed by a knock at the door. The door is opened.

Woman
(Unpleasant) What do you want?

Latimer
Good day, Ma'am, can you tell me where the Eben Rawlinson place is?

Woman
Right over there where it's raining ... See that bolt of lightning?

Latimer
Where?

A distant roll of thunder.

Woman
It's gone now. *(Pause)* There it is again.

Latimer
Ah ...

A closer roll of thunder.

Woman
Head for there.

Latimer
Thankyou.

Rain begins suddenly as footsteps resume on the road.

Narrator
The Rawlinson place lay spread out upon the ridge of a worn-out cow pasture. The rambling unpainted house—

The rain fades to:
Music: the ominous opening of Beethoven's Fourth Symphony.

—stood starkly on the crest with sagging gallery porches and half-drawn blinds. Beyond were the hulks of once prosperous barns, the whole place reeking of arrested time, as if this ruined fiefdom were itself a testament to human mortality ...

The music is held, then fades to:
A downpour of rain, and footsteps up onto wooden porch followed by a knock on the door. After a pause, the door is opened.

Latimer
Good day, is this Rawlinsons'?

Isaac
Yeah.

Latimer
I'm Latimer Davenport. *(Pause)* The hired hand ...

Pause. There is no response.

This ... *is* Rawlinsons', isn't it?

Isaac
Yeah.

Latimer
(Pause) You advertised for a hired hand? *(Pause)* Well I'm the hired hand ... and I'm here. *(Pause)* Well? ... Shall I ah ... *(Pause)* I'm all ready to begin. *(Pause)* So what do I do? ... Do I just come in or do I just ... Do I ...? What do I do?

Elmira
(Calls from inside) Isaac, who's that?

Isaac
Never seen him before.

Elmira's footsteps approach from within.

Elmira
It's the hired hand from Toronto. Let him in.

Latimer's footsteps across the threshold.

Latimer
Ah. Thankyou.

The door is closed. The house is in silence.

Latimer Davenport, how do you do?

Elmira
I'm Elmira Rawlinson, how do you do? This is my brother Isaac.
Isaac's footsteps recede down toward the back as he murmurs:

Isaac
We don't need no hired help.

Elmira
Don't mind him. Come on in, you're just in time for dinner.

Elmira's and Latimer's footsteps from the front hall into the kitchen, where we hear the sounds of the Rawlinson family eating dinner in silence.

Elmira
There's a place for you.

The sound of two chairs pulled out.

This here is the new hired hand. This is my mother and father, this here is Elmer, you've met Isaac, and this here is Matthew.

Latimer
Latimer Davenport, how do you do?

The Rawlinsons continue to eat their dinner in silence.

(*Nervously, at length*) Have you ... ah, have you been having good weather here?

Frank
(*After a pause, mumbles to Elmer*) Ever a fella to natch nary a pole in yonder.

362

Latimer
I beg your pardon?

Elmer
(*Mumbles in answer*) Yeah ...

Isaac
(*Murmurs*) Flatten tightly by the round, he'll give you a din by Tuesday melkin'.

Matt
(*Mumbles*) Yeah ... Ever for nigh on a titch in hell ...

Ellen
(*Mumbles*) Tarry in four, he'll tether for a mark in two.

Frank
(*Mumbles*) Yeah ...

Matt
(*Mumbles*) Yeah ...

Frank
(*To Latimer, loudly*) Eh?

Latimer
Yes?

Frank
(*Mumbles*) You ever tray in a dell down to nether bottom for nigh on a titch in hell?

Latimer
Beg your pardon?

Frank
(*Distinctly*) I asked you, you ever tray in a dell down to nether bottom for nigh on a titch in hell? Speak English?

Elmira
It's an archaic rural dialect.

Latimer
Ah ... I'm sorry, I—

Frank
Well, spring is nigh upon us, we've labor to commence!

363

Matt
You already said that. It's summer now.

Ellen
He just likes the sound of the expression.

Frank
All together now!

All
(*Except Latimer; in unison*) Spring is nigh upon us! We've labor to commence.

Frank
(*Hollers*) Elmer!... Elmer!!

Elmer
I'm here! I'm settin' here.

Frank
Why didn't you say so the first time?

Elmer
You never asked.

Ellen
The boy's hard of hearing!

Frank
(*Loud*) Why'd you take so long bringing Granpa down yesterday?

Elmer
It's out in the barn.

Ellen
Not so loud, I said, he's hard of hearing.

Frank
(*Normal tone*) Why'd you take so long to bring Granpa down yesterday?

Matt
Why? You wondering about his will?

A shocked silence.

Ellen
Matthew!

Frank
What's that to do with anything?

Matt
What with great-uncle Jim being sent off to the asylum and all ...
Frank crashes his fist on the dinner table.

Frank
How dare you talk that way on the demise of your grandfather! Never again, you hear me, you sonofabitch?

Silence. The dinner sounds fade to:
Music. The opening of Beethoven's Fourth Symphony.

Narrator
That afternoon it was too wet to work, so Isaac took Latimer around the property.

The music fades to:
Heavy rain in a field and two pairs of footsteps on wet ground.

Isaac
That's one of the cows ... *(Pause)* That there's the barn ... *(Pause)* And that's fields beyond.

The rain and footsteps fade to:

Narrator
It was 1904, but the Rawlinsons still seemed to live in the nineteenth century. By evening it had cleared and Elmira showed Latimer to his room.

A match is struck.

Elmira
You'll have to excuse this lamp. A lot of the rooms are closed off and there ain't a lot of light up there.

Elmira and Latimer climbing wooden stairs. Downstairs we hear the receding noises of arguing and shouting.

Latimer
I must say, it's a very big house.

Elmira
We had a family reunion here years ago and it stayed, so we had to build.

They reach the top of the stairs and their footsteps proceed down the upstairs hall.

That there is Isabelle's room, closed off in '81.

The terrible coughing of an ancient woman behind a door.

The family reunion that stayed: Granpa at centre; Elmer behind and to his right.

And that there is Isabelle. Second cousin twice removed, first from the downstairs bedroom, then from the upstairs. *(Pause, they continue)* This here is Cousin Bob's room. He died in a threshing accident in '78 *(Pause)* This here is Uncle Will's and he's been—or rather Robert's, sorry, Robert's alive, it was Will was killed and it was a mill accident, so that's closed off too.

Robert or rather Will who was killed in a threshing accident; no, it was a mill accident.

From behind another door, moaning with the rattle of chains.

Elmira
Don't take no notice of that.

They stop at the end of the hall.

And here's your room.

Plaster falls as she rattles the door knob.

We never did get round to replastering there. *(She groans, pushing against the door)*

The door is forced open, the hinges creak, their footsteps enter the room.

This here was Granpa's room.

Latimer
Didn't you say he's just—?

Elmira
I came up and he had passed on. Funeral's tomorrow.

Latimer
Ah ...

Elmira
Gol, the air is stale.

Elmira's footsteps cross the room to where the window is opened on the other side, admitting the myriad sound of crickets from the fields.

Elmira
Don't mind about the bed, I'll get you clean sheets. Just set down your bags.

Latimer
(Pause) By the way, how far is the nearest main town, you mind my asking?

Elmira
'Bout ten mile. Town of Maskinonge.

Latimer
Do you go there much?

Elmira
Twice a year.

Latimer
Just for provisions, or—?

Elmira
Sightseeing.

Two distant blasts of a mournful train whistle followed by the sound of a train passing

Must be ten past five. Maskinonge Central's back on the rails ... You know they had the wreck Thursday.

Latimer
Yes, I heard.

Elmira
We call this here the room with a view 'cause you can see the drowned land yonder where the railway runs through ... Biggest windfall Granpa ever had, bless his soul, took the railroad for a right bundle.

Music: The ill and sinister 'Prelude and Death of Kane,' (Music from 'Citizen Kane').

He got them to come seven mile out of their way to build on that there swampy land, sold the whole right of way to 'em and several times the tracks have sunk down in the mire and caused wrecks.

The music diminishes slowly.

(Pause) There's many a hired man tried to leave here on that train ... but it was going too fast.

The passing train fades.

Latimer
(Pause) Well, I suppose I'll turn in now. *(Pause)* Get out of these clothes, they're a bit damp. *(Pause)* If you don't mind.

Elmira
No, go right ahead.

Latimer
Perhaps we'll see you in the morning.

Elmira
(Pause, distantly) You know, you're the spitting image of Bill Bradshaw ...

Latimer
Yes, well I—

Elmira

He was a salesman come round here once ... Right fine-looking man ... He stayed a while and then one night he disappeared ... supposed to've had some kind of mishap, an accident ...

Latimer

Ah ...

Elmira

He was like you, he'd nice Sunday clothes ... And manners ... He wasn't one to get drunk and grab a stick of firewood and hit someone, he wasn't like that ... He was a gentleman ... he was the only ray of sunshine in Maskinonge ... And then he was gone ...

Latimer

I see.

Elmira

I been trying to leave here myself for over seventeen years now.

Latimer

Funny, you don't look a day over twenty-five ...

Elmira

I'm seventeen.

Frank

(Shouts from downstairs) Elmira!

Latimer

Someone's calling you.

Elmira's footsteps hurry across the room. The door is slammed shut.

Why did you close the door?

Frank

(Hollers louder from downstairs) Elmira!!

Elmira

Excuse me, but you have to help me. Afore Granpa died, I was the only one didn't wait on his death, you understand? The others wanted the estate, but not me, and he knew it and he hated them for it ... Well, he told them it was under the floor, but he took me aside last year, and he give me a note about the real location of the deed and fortune.

Frank

(Hollers again from downstairs) Elmira!!

369

Elmira

Look. See them dead elms? In the north field? Meet me there afore dark tomorrow.

Her footsteps hurrying to the door; the door opened.

Frank

(Downstairs, his voice louder through the open door) What you doing up there!?

The door is slammed shut.
Music: piano; the haunting return of the theme at the end of Mussorgsky's 'Pictures at an Exhibition' for piano.

Narrator

In the closet, Latimer noticed that two floorboards already seemed to have been pried up. He went to bed, but couldn't sleep. Perhaps it was the twilight in the dusty window, the smell of mildew. Then again, it could have been the buzzing flies and empty patent medicine bottles, or even the meathook in the middle of the ceiling with a fragment of frayed rope above an overturned chair ... and yet he determined to stay ... because in spite of everything ... the girl was good-looking.

The music dimishes to:
A field of crickets and scythes cutting hay.

The following day, they put Latimer to work. Never having used a scythe, he stayed as far from the others as he could, fecklessly flailing the blade and bending and flattening the grass. When he got tired, he would simply drop the scythe, turn his back, and wave his arms about to give the impression that he was working.

The crickets and scythes fade to:
Music: the eerily romantic sequence 'Kane and Susan' from 'Music from Citizen Kane.'

That night, after supper, Latimer went for a walk. He sensed it was unwise to keep the rendezvous, but he already found Elmira irresistible. Even among the sodden pastures and wind-blasted wastes, she was more beautiful than he remembered; even the fields were transformed by a rare clearing of the sky at twilight.

The music fades to:
Crickets and Latimer's and Elmira's footsteps in long grass.

Elmira

I should explain something to you about my brothers. They're ... well, they're a bit on the surly side, but don't get the wrong impression. They're far worse than they appear to be.

Latimer
(Pause) Yes, well, I was going to say, if you should ever happen to come down to the city some time—

Elmira
Listen to me afore you do anything foolish. Them floorboards were tore up in your room yesterday.

Latimer
Yes, I noticed.

Elmira
So somebody noticed that title deed and fortune ain't where Granpa said. Well this here is the note he give me.

A document is unfolded.
Music: 'Citizen Kane': 'Prelude to the Death of Kane.'

Elmira
(Reads) "My estate, the title deed to lot 17, concession 9 of Maskinonge Township, and the $75,000 I swindled from the railway—

In the distance we hear two blasts of the train whistle.

—is buried on the property at the furthest extent of the shadow cast by the second dead elm east from the creek in the north pasture on November 22 at 3:18 P.M."

The music fades to:
Blowing wind and dead leaves.

When autumn came, Latimer knew it was only a matter of weeks before the elm would cast its shadow, and now the family spent their evenings increasingly in the kitchen while Elmira played the organ in the parlor.

The blowing wind and dead leaves fade to:
Music: the massive organ playing behind the parlor door: Widor's turbulent and surreal Symphony No. 9 for organ. Clock ticking and rocking chair rocking.

Frank
(Pause) Open the window.

The window is opened.

Pass me the shotgun.

The shotgun is knocked against the table, followed by a blast.

371

Ellen
Groundhog?

Frank
Nope, travelling salesman. *(Silence)* Gimme the newspaper.

The newspaper is passed, a page opened.

Ellen
Who's dead?

Frank
Look for yourself.

Ellen
I can't read.

Frank
Neither can I. *(Hollers)* Elmira!

Elmira
(Shouts from behind parlor door) What!

Frank
(Shouts) Come and read the newspaper!
The organ stops abruptly.
The parlor door opens, followed by footsteps approaching into the kitchen.

Here.

The newspaper is passed.

(Long pause) Well, read it!

Elmira
I am reading it.

Frank
Aloud, read it aloud!

Elmira
(Reads) The Maskinonge Daily Mourner. Canada, October 27, around the turn of the century. Weather: grey skies over an oppressive landscape, the same next month, chance of sun in the spring ... Wave of Marauding Tramps Threatens County. A Farmer Hangs Himself in his Barn. Epidemic of Insanity in Port Simcoe. Maryville: A Travelling Salesman Discovers a Farmer Hanged in His Barn By Insane Marauding Tramps. McPhail's barn burned.

Frank
Who's arson was that? Was that ours?

Isaac
Yeah.

Frank
Who did it?

Isaac
I did.

Elmira
'Editorial: Strychnine is the best way out of difficult mortgage payments.'

Frank
Read that one.

Elmira
That's all it says.

Ellen
How 'bout International News?

Elmira
Which county?

Ellen
Perth.

Elmira
Overrun with tramps.

Isaac
World News?

A page is turned.

Elmira
A Horse Dies in the United States. A Man Falls off a Ladder in Kentucky.
A Woman has Hysterics in New York. A Farmer hangs himself in France.

Frank
What was his name?

Elmira
(With difficulty) Jean-Pierre Charette.

Frank
Don't know him.

Ellen
We don't know nobody in France.

Elmira
Here's a headline with a story to it. An old farmer dies mysteriously at 112. A neighbor's barn burns the same night. Travelling salesman missing on property suspected of murder to help obtain the inheritance. A relative believed to be named in the will committed to the asylum. Long tale of arson and murder.

Ellen
Could have happened to anyone.

Frank
Sounds like Craigs or Prewitts.

Craigs or Prewitts.

Ellen
It's not specific enough. Who's the old man that died?

Elmira
Says Eben Rawlinson.

Music: ominous opening of Beethoven's Fourth.

Frank
Sounds like us.

Ellen
Yeah, last year.

Frank
Read on.

Elmira
Railroad fortune missing on property. Family member believed to withhold secret of location.

Frank
(Angry) That's us! That's us!

Music: fade.

It *is* us!

The rocking chair rocking and the clock ticking for a moment in silence, and then fade to:
Music: music from Citizen Kane: the 'Xanadu Theme.'

Narrator
Having read about themselves in the paper, the Rawlinsons watched each other more carefully then ever. By November, a silence had fallen over the house.

Music: fade to:
Footsteps crossing a room.

People seemed to go in and out of rooms without apparent motive.

A door slams, followed by muffled hollering and curses in another room.

And Frank Rawlinson would be heard delivering a stream of abuse, only to be discovered alone in the kitchen with a bottle of whisky.

Music: Citizen Kane: 'Kane and Susan.'

Narrator
But November 22, the day of deliverance was approaching, and Latimer could hardly sleep; he was worried because the ground was hardening with frost and they might not be able to dig. Finally, it was only a matter of hours before the tree would cast its shadow and he and Elmira would realize their dreams; they would move back to the city, buy a house, and he would reapply to become a bank clerk with the possibility of promotion into the loans department.

Music: fade.

Five Poems

Joe Rosenblatt

Narrowly He Nipped Thru The Slender Trees

narrowly he nipped thru the slender trees
slendered his naptha burning skin
thru the blades of terror, slipped quietly
into the word-drowning pool...

serpents love the pressure of water around their middle
he was a virile snake, his eyelashes flickered
the air turned crisp as a paper infant
subway ants creeped over the big bellied leaves
& pregnant cat fish coughed in the waters

narrowly he nipped thru the tenders
& around the contours, stretched his suit
in that naptha burning air.
near the gurgling pool
tom the snake-napper smiled wistfully
for the reptile had tufts of clean ivory
& it was a large & unusual elephant snake

(a deep hole followed tom thru the wheezing forest
it had very soft brown eyes & was very clever
to hide in the corners of the shadows)

the snake hunter loved his snake
but he loved the oils, & the wee ivory more:
somewhere, other ripened elephant snakes
closed their wet eyelids
in the camphored heat of the late afternoon.

It was late in the afternoon

all day the rain sang
& the piglet silence drowned in the mud
it was late in the afternoon
when a small boa put on a smart necktie
to amuse the midget hogs grunting.

drops formed into tadpoles with blue eyes
to witness the spawn of Creation blooming
like fat glow-worms after a sunset.
the boa turned away from his reflection
loosening his necktie, he was all sex
stuffing a slippery mind into a circuitous vision —
The day was hot, he would wear trousers cut low.

it was late in the afternoon
& the virulent tadpoles were tired
from mesmerizing cats in the angora sky
who drifted away purring their strength
to a forest radiating green scripture.

Harbor lights from heaven burn
in the brittle eyes of reptiles after a rainfall
when valves open in the black earth...absorbing...absorbing...
when the warm tendrils caress the moment
curling in its shell to sleep the escargot of sleep.

Sleeping Lady Sonnet: II

More serpent than serpent in weaving motion
she absorbs waves under flowing skin,
tiny complexes trapped in circuitous sin:
— feline stirrings in transformation —
shimmering dance, O she's Mystification
thru our looking-glass — she raises her grin
above the Evening's sleeping mannequin
& dreams darkness in with its sick plutonium.

Lightly she glides into the soul's low bedroom,
voices bubbling: "you've been here before
swimming in silence mooned in a white tomb
where teardrops vibrate on the warped floor,
Sweet Lady, you'd have made a lovely goldfish against the
Gloom
dazzling a lunatic fumbling at the round door."

Sleeping Lady Sonnet: III

Welcome to my parlour, diaphanous lady
we've met before in another room
where silence nudged each corner cool & shady
& both our moons suffused as in a marbled tomb.

Juicier than eels, out of vapid air she eased
her feverish tongue . . . turned its pointed love —
Like some pampered nymph, ripe & very pleased,
she lifted pure torso to her Maker . . .

who dimmed her in a space between His eyes
where voices cried from deep inside: "my paramour,
lie down in the parlour, a bride supine,
we'll soon be stars . . . part of the slime."

Sleeping Lady Sonnet: XVI

in cesspools of love where trouble is deep
i get snakes in my head, got snakes in my skin,
woe so much pain from each spittin' flame,
into slimy waters these eels slip away

o ye that are born of lightning & methane
again & again your design blooms in my brain
attached to a navel, stuck deep in a drain
— hello Solar Glow, let's float on th' surface —

down in her Chamber I found myself drownin',
meandering shakers appeared with poison —
shimmying, they played out their misery
& they were familiar, & cruel, my own

: I had worn them to bed, weddings, & undulant memory
but they were faces lost at th' bottom.

DRAWINGS FOR THREE NOVELS BY MARIE-CLAIRE BLAIS

Mary Meigs

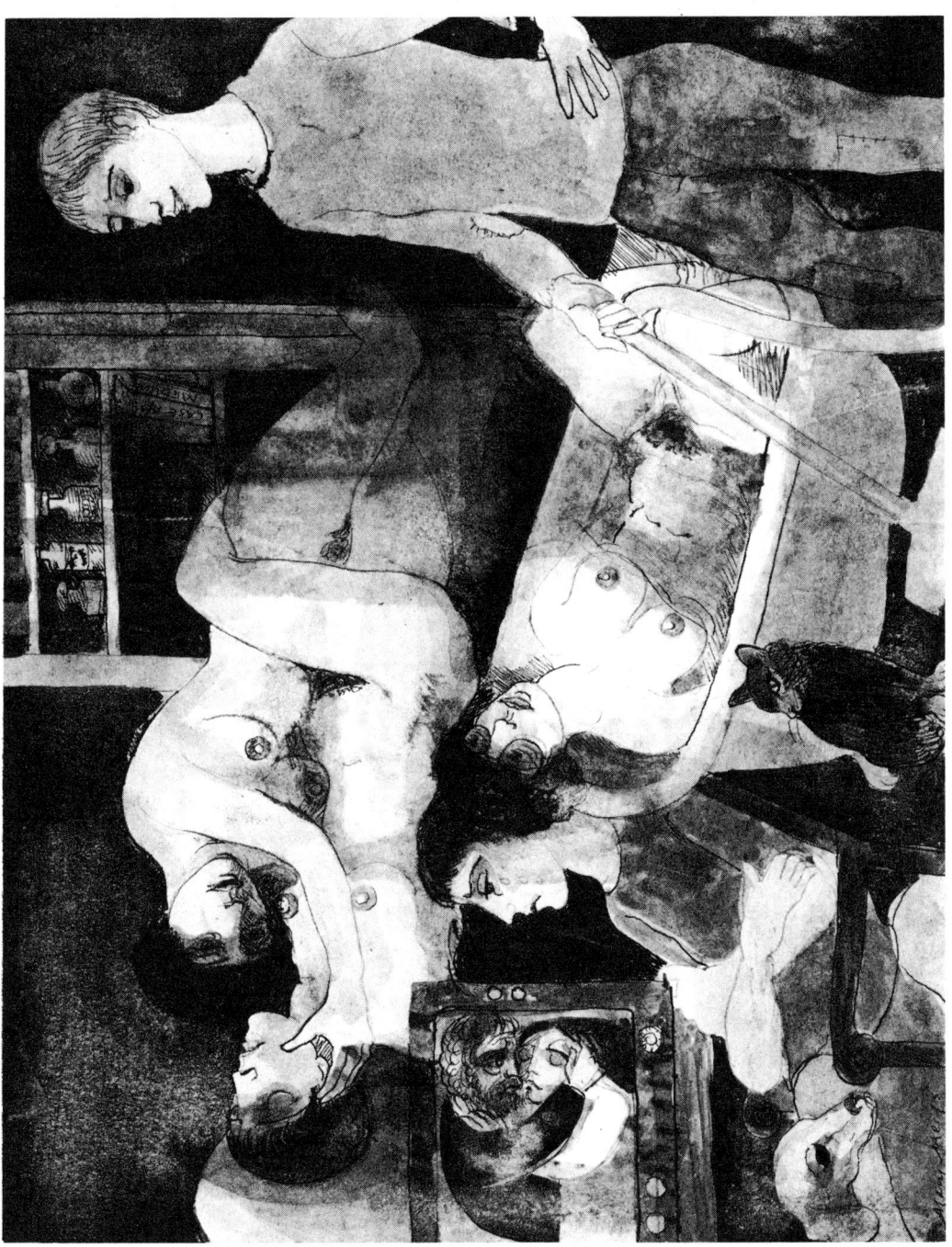

380

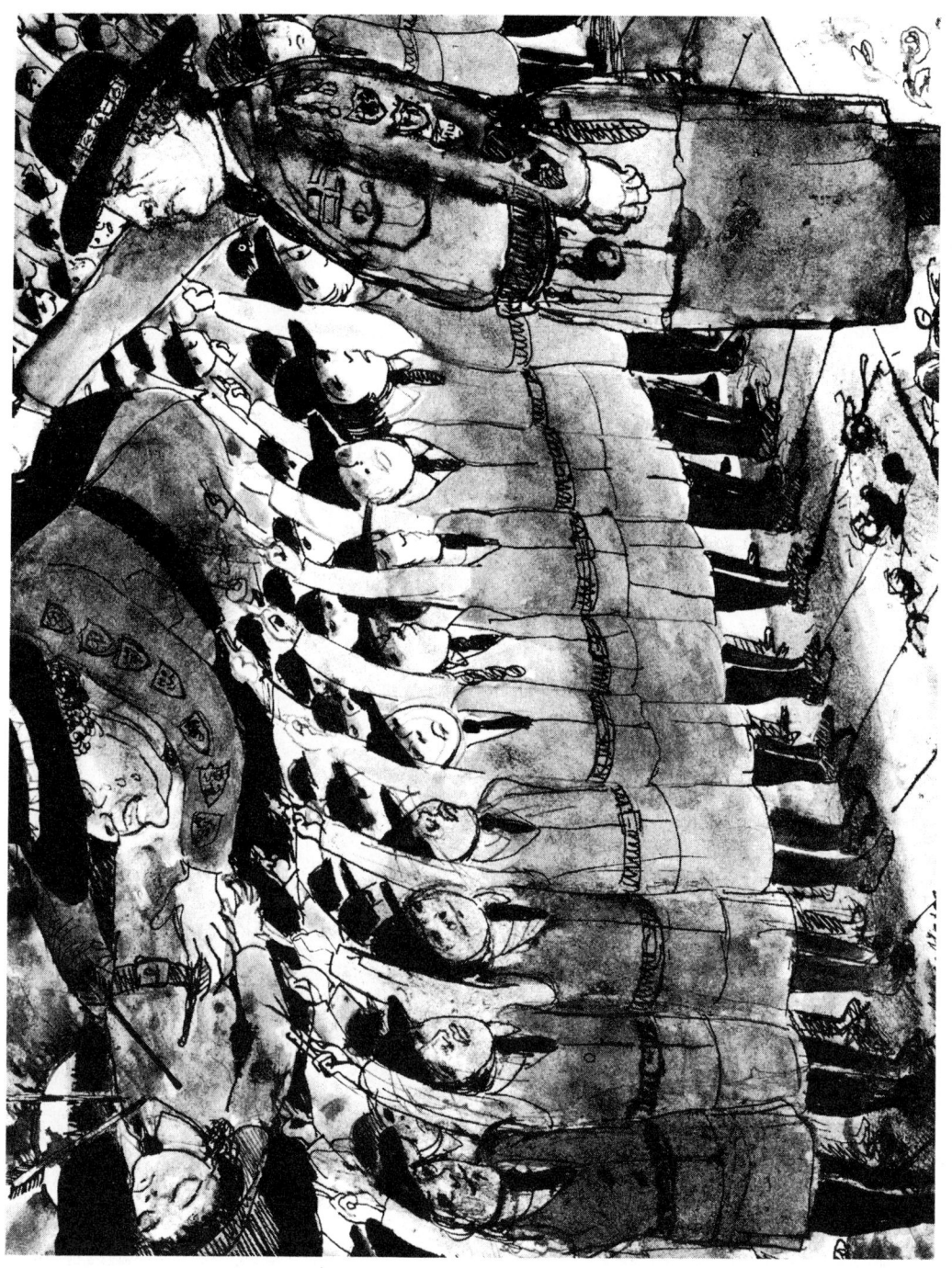

382

383

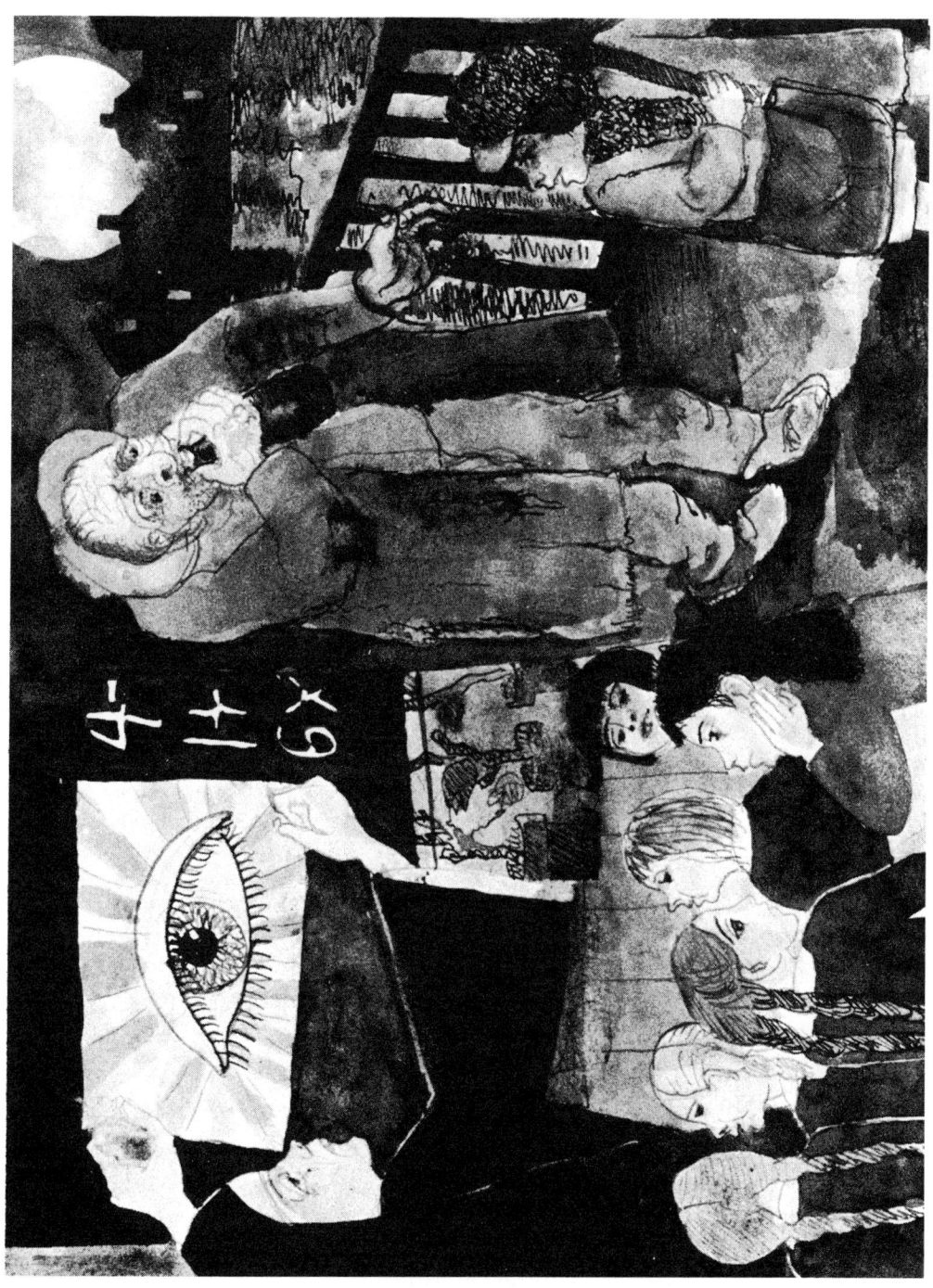

A TECHNICAL SUPPLEMENT

Thomas Kinsella

1

Blessed William Skullbullet
glaring from the furnace of your hair
thou whose definitions – whose insane nets –
plunge and convulse to hold thy furious catch
let our gaze blaze, we pray,
let us see how the whole thing
works

2

You will note firstly there is no containing skin
as we understand it, but 'contained' muscles
– separate entities, inter wound and overlaid,
firm, as if made of fish-meat or some
stretched blend of fibre and fat.
This one, for example, containing – functioning *as* –
a shoulderblade; or this one like a strap
reaching underneath it, its tail
melting into a lower rib; or this one
nuzzling into the crease of the groin;
or this, on the upper arm, like a big leech;
even the eyes – dry staring buttons of muscle.
It would seem possible to peel the body asunder,
to pick off the muscles and let them
drop away one by one writhing
until you had laid bare
four or five simple bones at most.
Except that at the first violation
the body would rip into pieces and fly apart
with terrible spasms.

4

The point, greatly enlarged,
pushed against the skin
depressing an area of tissue.
Rupture occurred: at first a separation
at the intensest place among the cells
then a deepening damage
with nerve-strings fraying

Fig. 1.

387

and snapping and writhing back.
Blood welled up to fill the wound,
bathing the point as it went deeper.

Persist.
Beyond a certain depth
it stands upright by itself
and quivers with borrowed life.

Persists.
And you may find
the buried well. And take on
the stillness of a root.

Quietus.

Or:

5
A blade licks out and acts
with one tongue.
Jets of blood respond
in diverse tongues.

And promptly.
A single sufficient cut
and the body drops at once.
No reserve. Inert.

If you would care to enter this grove of beasts:

6
A veteran smiled and let us pass through
the dripping groves in Swift's slaughterhouse,
hot confusion and the scream-rasp of the saw.
Huge horned fruit not quite dead
– chained, hooked by one hock, stunned
above a pool of steaming spiceblood.

Two elderly men in aprons waded back and forth
with long knives they sharpened slowly and
inserted, tapping cascades of black blood
that collapsed before their faces onto the concrete.
Another fallen beast landed, kicking,
and was hooked by the ankle and hoisted into its place.

They come in behind a plank barrier on an upper level
walking with erect tail to the stunning place ...
Later in the process they encounter
a man who loosens the skin around their tails
with deep cuts in unexpected directions;
the tail springs back; the hide pulls down to the jaws.

With the sheep it was even clearer
they were dangling alive, the blood trickling
over nostrils and teeth. A flock of them waited their turn
crowded into the furthest corner of the pen,
some looking back over their shoulders
at us, in our window.

Great bulks of pigs hung from dainty heels,
the full sow-throats cut open the wrong way.
Three negroes stood on a raised bench before them.
One knifed the belly open upward to the tail
until the knife and his hands disappeared
in the fleshy vulva and broke some bone.

The next opened it downward to the throat,
embraced the mass of entrails, lifted them out
and dropped them in a chute. And so to one
who excavated the skull through flaps of the face,
hooked it onto the carcass and pushed all forward
toward a frame of blue flames, the singeing machine.

At a certain point it is all merely meat,
sections hung or stacked in a certain order.
Downstairs a row of steel barrows
holds the liquid heaps of organs.
As each new piece drops, adding itself,
the contents tremble throughout their mass.

In a clean room a white-coated worker
positioned a ham, found a blood vessel with a forceps,
clipped it to a tube of red chemical
and pumped the piece full. It swelled immediately
and saturated: tiny crimson jets
poured from it everywhere. Transfused!

10
It is so peaceful at last:
sinking onward into a free reverie
– if you weren't continually nudged awake
by little scratching sounds
and brushing sounds outside the door

389

or muffled voices upstairs.
The idea was to be able to step out
into a clean brightness onto a landing
flooded with sun and blowing gauze
like a cool drunkenness, with every speck of dust
filtered out of the air!
To follow the graceful curve of handrail
and relish the new firmness underfoot,
the very joists giving off confidence.

What an expanse of neglect
stretched before us!
Strip to the singlet and prepare,
fix the work with a steady eye,
begin: scraping and scraping
down to the wood,
making it good, treating it …
Growing unmethodical after a while,
letting the thing stain and stay unfinished.

And we are going to have to do something
about the garden. All that sour soil
stuffed with mongrel growth
– hinges and bits of slate,
gaspipes plugged with dirt.
Disturb anything and there is
a scurrying of wireworms and ribbed woodlice
or a big worm palely deciding.

That door banging again.
If there is anything I can't stand …

We have to dig down;
sieve, scour and roughen;
make it all fertile and vigorous
– get the fresh rain down!

11
The shower is over.
And there's the sun out again
and the sound of water outside
trickling clean into the shore.
And the little washed bird-chirps and trills.

I have been opening my mind to some new poems
by a neglected 'colleague' of mine
– with some relief. One or two
of a certain quality.

Fig.2.

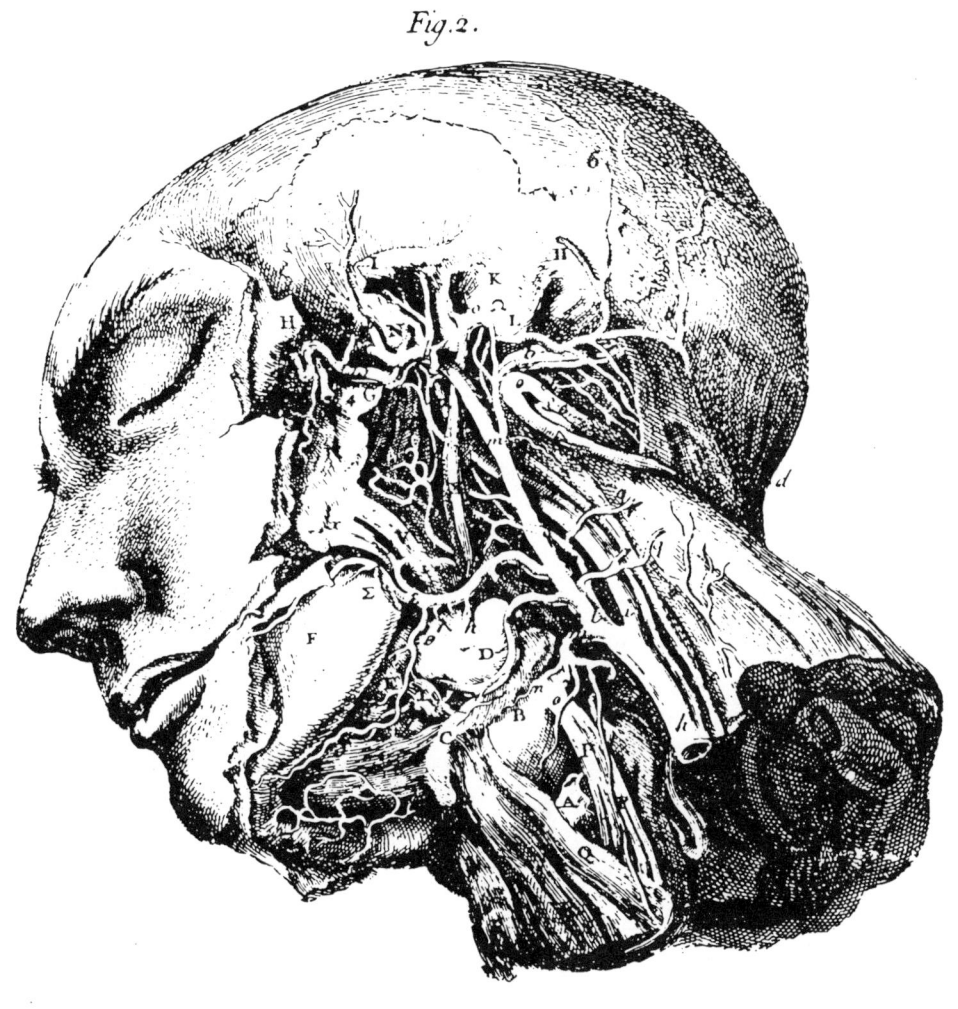

391

A watered peace. Drop. At the heart.
Drop. The unlikely heart.

A shadow an instant
on the window. A bird.
And the sun is gone in again.

(Good withdrawn, that other good may come.)

We have shaped and polished.
We have put a little darkness behind us,
we are out of that soup.
Into a little brightness.
That soup.

The mind flexes.
The heart encloses.

LAS FICAS CITY

Alexandre Amprimoz

Our village was called Strangolarane. It meant 'the place to strangle frogs.' The old folks knew an older name – Strangolagalli. Since Roman times they had enjoyed wringing the cockerel's neck, emblem of the French fighting spirit.

In 1215, as the English signed the Magna Carta, they burned another witch in Strangolagalli. She was my ancestor, Vita Vitale. The parish priest had found a French parchment in her house. The Inquisitor concluded: "This woman speaks perfect French, therefore she is the incarnation of Evil!" Since then, parchment has become a family tradition. I collect it myself, ivory colored sheets, a few black notes of medieval chant.

During the War, to prove he was a penultimate Fascist, our Mayor had all the Strangolarane houses painted black. He and his friends claimed the new regime would last two thousand years, so he stocked gallons of black paint to impress "the most handsome man in the world" – as Mussolini had his circle of friends call him. A German architect studying under Speer was dispatched to Strangolarane and, after months of planning, an underground tunnel was built to store the paint.

But Fascism is long gone. The local butcher, a Communist who lost his left eye arguing over a 2-to-1 bet at a cock-fight, promised to repaint all the village houses red if elected. Once in power, the new Mayor, who'd sworn he would not raise taxes, found himself in a predicament. The underground stock of black paint was too tempting to resist. His wife, once arrested in a village up in the hills for having sex with a Percheron, had an idea. The commitment to red could be kept: all the women in the municipality received a pair of red panties for Christmas. The black paint was held in reserve.

The nuns at the Orphanage of the Abandoned Apostle tried on the scarlet garments and wore them for their Sunday bicycle ride, and then rewrapped the handfuls of red rayon and wrote on the package: "Returned unopened." An angry objection to the panties was raised by our local hair stylist, Hanz Tranz (no French coiffeur for us, no sir! Strictly from Hamburg!). Hanz in a fit of pique said that offering red panties to women only was an act of crude discrimination. "I was so mad I saw red," he said. The Town Council agreed and re-allocated the nuns' little bundle to the Cut-N-Curl artist rather than send it back to Taiwan. Hanz, after all, was worth a dozen nuns: they would never vote Communist.

Apparently, other men saw red as well. By the following autumn, a startling number of babies bobbed up among the cabbage leaves. Storks were busier than ever and the orphanage had to order bunk baby beds. Even the widow Rosa Rossi had a baby. Every Sunday afternoon she took her folding deck chair and went to knit beside her husband's tomb. She

393

spoke aloud to the deceased. "I have been loyal to you to the grave," she said. "The child has your name Marcello my beloved."

It was a village in which nothing went to waste. Little kings lay nibbling among the cabbages and every spring the stone cottages and stores were painted black. This ritual, written up in a Munich Motorist Magazine and an Amsterdam journal devoted to sado-masochism, turned the village into a tourist attraction. Hundreds of people wearing either lederhausen or leather suddenly appeared in the streets. Once known for fig trees and a small casino, Strangolarane changed its name, the only Italian location with a foreign ring: *Las Ficas City*.

To amuse visitors, a village idiot always stood on duty beside the town fountain; town councillors took turns playing the fool with pride and enthusiasm. But Hanz was outstanding as the idiot, wearing his red panties over his hand-stitched black leather clown outfit. "Filthy pictures, Monsieur?" he asked the German tourists. "Better to burn in hell now that you're married." The ladies bought strangely shaped soaps and feather ticklers from him, particularly stout ladies rooted to the cobbles in their thick-soled walking shoes. "Mein Gott, mein Gott, warum hast Du mich verlassen?"

One day I heard the shrieks and sobs of children. I ran from our table at the outdoor café to see what was happening. Grandfather followed me. A lady I'd seen before, who ate long licorice sticks out of a small brown paper bag and often held aloft a dangling tendril of candy for her son to take with his little chicken teeth, was crying as loudly as Rosa Rossi had at her husband's funeral.

Three men, ignoring the gathering crowd, were dragging furniture out of a house, tumbling it into the street. Pots, pans, the clatter and chimes of an old cuckoo clock. The stunned bird bobbed at the end of his sprung coil. The police with their white gloves were there. They waved their arms, directing stars that would not be seen till nightfall. German tourists, believing a rustic play was part of their tour, applauded, showing that they understood everything. The three movers took a break, sharing a match as they had a smoke. "Three men on a match," one stern woman – a school teacher – said. "No good will come of this." They were indifferent to her as they were to the householder's suffering, or the boy who had a licorice length hanging from his mouth. A town councillor, unaware of what was going on, came by beating a child's tin drum with a pewter spoon. He had rouge on his cheeks and he'd forgotten to tie his floppy shoes. He was singing something from Puccini. The movers butted their cigarettes in a tea cup and the German tourists gave them a generous hand. The idiot councillor doffed his hat and tried to lead the visitors away from the house to the souvenir shops, but the audience grew larger, becoming a forest of feathered alpine hats.

"What's going on grandfather?" I asked.

"Don't you see, these poor people are evicted—thrown out of their home."

I refused to believe people could be thrown into the street. I reminded grandfather that we needed a new maid; after all, Anna had married a man with a five-speed bicycle and moved away. So grandfather stepped forward and hired the shrieking slender woman, who immediately agreed and said she'd bring along her licorice-eating boy.

The German tourists, seeing us step onto the stage, so to speak, broke into enthusiastic cheers. I asked grandfather for his black felt hat. I passed it around. To the idiot councillor's dismay, I had trouble keeping the liras and marks from falling out. When the shrieking woman accepted the money and leaned down and swept her son into her arms, burying his face in the hollow between her thighs, the crowd cheered.

Grandfather paid the notary. The three burly men shared another match and another cigarette and moved the furniture back into the house. The German tourists understood this was the end of the play. They applauded vigorously.

By evening, the incident had been reported to the Communist Mayor. The next day at noon, we heard the cries of the woman and sobbing children. The three movers were there, the notary and the police. The Mayor and his son stepped forward. The German tourists clapped:

"Bravo! Bravo! Bravo!"

The son was passing the hat: and this is how street plays became a tradition in our village. Soon, at the urging of our lone medieval scholar, there were other little scenes played out...The Great Flood, The Crucifixion (with Hanz in a false beard on the Cross), and the End of the World, in which all the nuns paraded in single file carrying a long chain. Grandfather was outraged. He had his house painted white. A few neighbors followed suit, and stood in their doorways, their arms crossed, their jaws set. But the glistening white houses seemed to disappear in the sunlight and no one noticed they were gone. The old alleys seemed empty, so full of light. Birds nested and sang in the eaves. But tourism declined and our troubles began. Las Ficas City turned against us. There were rumors that we'd painted our house white because we kept parchment. We were accused of hiding French books in our attic. One fine morning a truck-load of frogs was dumped on our front lawn.

That year, we ate pickled frog legs every day, except Sundays, when we ate Stracciatella – eggs in a broth – and watched Rosa Rossi go by our house, wheeling Marcello in his baby carriage on their way to the cemetery. Of course, we still went to mass, but on our way back – though no one put on the little plays anymore – we would still see the nuns carrying the long chain, and behind them, Hanz and his sloe-eyed mistress, a sixteen-year-old sailor, going down to the station. "We all go down to the sea in ships," he cried out giddily. The Mayor's wife passed the afternoon painting large horses on Ready-Stretched canvas in the municipal park. She had a huge sign: SALE. Still, the German tourists did not come back. Our neighbors who'd painted their houses white were feeling the financial pinch; they readily accepted several gallons of black paint. They painted their houses. "Why, there's Aldo's house," someone said. "I'd forgotten it was there." Some even painted their windows. The alleys became dark. The birds in the nests in the eaves never sang. One afternoon, when Grandfather took us all down to the cabbage patches to show us plants the size of brussel sprouts, the Las Ficas police – spellbound by the Watergate hearings with Italian subtitles on T.V., – didn't see the Mayor and his councillors break into our house.

All our parchments and all our books were loaded onto carts pulled by the idiots to the village square and set ablaze. We could see the smoke and hear the reveling as we returned to the heart of the village. The white column pushed through the blue sky like a tall flower. I wept for my favorite parchment: a fourteenth-century Russian translation of the Magna Carta.

Of all the people in the village, only Hanz Tranz objected to the auto-dafé, and he was leaving, saying good-by, for he had found true love by the seashore, on the docks. He introduced his sailor fiancée to me, a talented ventriloquist and transvestite named Vita Vitale, who picked me up in her arms and gave me a long kiss on the mouth. I felt a kind of dizziness, a mystical white light shedding all around me as she threw her voice across the room, her lips still pressed to mine. "Oh, you little devil you," the voice cried out of the white light. Hanz and Vita left Las Ficas City. The German tourists never came back, and after a few years, when all the black paint was used up, the houses began to look grey and dowdy. Grandfather died, I went away, and on the Sunday morning I took the train, only the nuns in single file, carrying their chain, came to see me off, blowing me a kiss "Good luck in this Dance of Death," the Mother Superior cried, standing in the cloud of steam coming from between the great flanged wheels of the engine.

THE MAGIC BOX:
THE ECCENTRIC GENIUS OF
HANNAH MAYNARD

Claire Weissman Wilks

While sifting through prints and glass plates in the archives in Victoria, British Columbia, I came across a half-dozen photographs unlike anything I'd seen anywhere. They were taken by a woman, Hannah Maynard. She was known locally, but I discovered that there was no special interest in her work. Upstairs in the archives, there were boxes of glass and celluloid negatives locked away, old images stored but never seen. It became clear, holding these to the light, that Hannah Maynard was an original, a woman of genius ably assisted by her enterprising husband, Richard.

They were born in Cornwall, England, and they'd come to Canada in 1852, still in their early twenties. He'd been a boot maker and a seaman, but he'd also had the gold lust, and so he first settled his wife in the small town of Bowmanville, Ontario, and then took a boat from Boston down to Panama, crossed the Isthmus, and sailed up the Pacific to Vancouver Island to the small but fashionable outpost town of Victoria. The boat blew up in the harbor. He was not hurt. He prospected for gold but found none, so he set up a boot store and sent for his wife.

She arrived with their two children, a huge box camera with extensible bellows, and opened a portrait studio beside the store. While he'd been panning for gold, she'd learned photography. Both businesses prospered and she taught Richard how to take pictures. They eventually closed the shoe store and opened a new portrait emporium on Pandora Street. They took pictures for sixty years and died a few years short of the First World War.

She was a woman of extraordinary character and talent, somehow in touch with every new photographic technique, pushing those techniques to their limits. With the discovery of how to construct montages on glass plates, she created her *Gems of British Columbia*, hundreds and sometimes thousands of children's faces arranged in greeting card designs. When hired by the city police to take the mug shots of criminals, she used mirrors for a full face and profile effect, which was not surprising because she seemed to see multiple images in all people and things around her. She seemed obsessed with faces – putting them in showers of water and leaves, picture frames within frames, and was compelled to photograph herself. She constructed self-portraits full of sardonic humor, isolating herself in fragmentary selves: looking at herself, unmocking, perplexed, a middle-class stern-faced woman always in the same black dress, experimenting with time, with space, surrealistically ahead of her time, in her own space.

398

GEMS OF BRITISH COLUMBIA

Sentence 6 months in each of four counts to run concurrently April 4. Arrested by Det Perdue charged with obtaining money by false pretences, by means of "Confedssats" notes.

This reproduction renders the effect of a bas-relief. Maynard built up the features of the face and body from behind, raising the shoulder puffs, without distortion, almost an eighth of an inch. It a was process in which blotting paper was attached to the back of the print and the portrait was embossed by tooling in a circling motion with a bone or ivory paper knife. A handbook in 1911, long after she'd completed this portrait, advised: "The work must be done very gently, as the blotting paper is damp, and the tool may go through and spoil it." Once the embossing was done, it was filled with plaster-of-Paris or papier-maché. Few such bas-reliefs exist in the world.

SINGING AT THE WHIRLPOOL

Miodrag Pavlović

Head

Our head
resembles the sun
shells
a runner among fish
is oval
is ovaleloquent
and hard as stone
when asleep
it hunts down
the dead, confronts fire
or counsels from the village mount

Lost in thought
the head
itself
is sunken treasure

Water

Water flows
Water flowswater carries
water seeps into
water seeps intothe bones
you can fall through water
you can fall through waterand be gone
bleaching water
will quench your thirst

you stay white
as the flesh of fish
as the flesh of fishand silent
while water
impales you

Body and Soul

A stone
seminates itself
surmounted
by its shadow

Dead

They like to joke
and snare you
shove you into the river
shriek near an owl
while we sleep
the dead worry about themselves
terribly lazy
they feed
on our pity
sometimes heal someone
when they're together
dreaming
they're alone in the world

Translated by Barry Callaghan

Mario Mascarelli

FROM THE MUD HUT

Jennifer Rankin

Layers of grey rain thrown by the wind
hard and fast against the walls of this room

This rain
drawn from the ancient ravine
pulled up from the shocked abyss
hurled now out of the vast plateau

This rain
that drives against bone
against skull
against these old protective walls

surely this is a new rain lashing the glass.

Once he sat at that table.

He was grey.

He licked his lip not like a stranger.
His lip was wet with sore.
His lip was broken into by hairs from under his skin.

He offered his lip to me.

He came out of the long hall and he offered his lip
he came out of the empty second bed
he came out of the scribbling and the screwed up paper
he came out of the black phone
he came out of the window seat where I sat watching the gate

he came out of the sudden question of the schoolyard
he came out of the orange peel thrown over my shoulder
and the pattern it made in the dirt

and the voice of the teacher and her strident no-nonsense
and my thin narrow bed and my mother awake
and the hymns at the church and my hours of reading

now he sits again at the table
and he licks and he licks at his weeping lip.

I am chasing the end of that shadow
drawn out now for the last days of summer
filtering down the needles of she-oak
into the gully and the laughing of my brother
who chases me around and around this paddock
smaller in day's light
spinning now
until I trip on that old gnarled stump
crash down into this crumbling earth
hot and sweating with my brother entangled
crying now digging in with my nails earth cold in my hands
clawing my way in my way out my way back
and the air is leaving my chest
hit hard in my back his fists thumping again and again
my voice lies in my lungs
I rasp at the air full of his laughter and the sun
and the smell of crushed and rotting grass
I know she is watching
knitting under the corrugated roof
I feel her steel needles nick sharp into my gasp.

There is a man on a world trip.

He carries a briefcase and a travel brochure
a wife in his neatly darned sock
a lover between the lids of his eyes

he is here to study the earth

I offer to take him back with me
into the open paddock
through the rattling door and into this room.

He raises a glass of wine to his lips
he toasts my house my country myself

I say, 'Then I will show you this house'

I walk away and he swills down his wine.
I go into the mud walls.

He crawls on his knees about the room.
He is searching, searching, searching

I watch from the old earth fault.
In the morning he will fly out.

411

Tonight I remember the openness.

Again I feel the ridge on her finger
again I see her hands hurled away

on my mouth is the flesh of my father
stuck from his seeping lip.

But tonight I take my body away from the sky.

Now I hold onto this old flesh
I dig myself into this earth
I shield my eyes from the stars
I dig in, I tether myself down.

Jane Eyre

Mary Meigs

THE ZONE OF HARDY DECIDUOUS FORESTS

Réjean Ducharme

We're destroyed. It's terrible to think how horrible it really is.

She's called, she's come, she's seen us again, we've let her down.

"Well, dear boy, what are we going to?"

"We're going to do like we've always done: we're going to tough it out till it goes away."

"This time it's too much; if you can't come up with something better than that I'll crack, pop, burst wide-open, die."

We've turned off the TV but that doesn't stop us from watching it. We're huddled up, burning it. But flesh doesn't burn, it melts. So we're melting, stuffed with charcoals, Nicole huddled in the arms of the easy chair, me on the floor huddled between her legs. The easy chair's covered with red leatherette; it's followed us around for ten years on its four small legs with their varnish worn off; it's good for watching TV; we bought it for $5 when we got stranded in Montreal and went to the Salvation Army to buy all our furniture.

Nicole's thighs open and close around my neck in a string of grievous orgasms in which the grief remains unrelieved. It takes all my strength just to hold my head on, to keep it from rolling onto the linoleum. Things are rough. From time to time a single curse word, carried like a bubble across the boiling spittle, breaks from our lips: "Fuck!"

Petit Pois explained it to us very well: yesterday was "out of sight" because she was "high"; tonight she was "down," she'd had a "bad trip." It's pure asphyxiation. Our arms are drowning in an impotence which is stretching their muscles as far as they'll go. Our hearts, swollen larger than our chests, are suffocating, sinking slowly downward. Bathing in acids, our insides are writhing, leaping, rising; our stomachs are emptying out through our mouths, our noses, our ears. Too much blood under too much pressure; if we weren't gripping our arteries with our fists they'd strike about like lashes. We had a *kind, warm, passionate* friend and we've lost her. Yesterday she spent the whole night giving us her heart; just now she spent the whole night pulling ours up by the roots.

What took place that was so major? Nothing. Nothing that was very dark and dire. Yesterday, ardent. Today, absent. Yesterday she needed to touch us. Today she didn't stop playing with the buttons on her blouse and asking herself, aloud or under her breath, how she could have cracked up on nothing but a little piece of hash.

"I had to go to Hôtel-Dieu to see my uncle who's got cancer. That kind of thing scares me. I smoked the little bit that was left in a pipe, a little nothing piece. I get to the hospital, open the door – crash: cold chills up and down my spine, my stomach's churning, I'm choking back screams, I can't go through with it ... I did an about-face, walked over here, and blew two and a half hours, the only girl with nineteen fat, loathsome Greeks. Talk, tickle me under the chin and say 'goo-goo,' make me laugh, do something."

"What're you having?" She'll finish her glass of Seven-Up, which has been sitting so long it's had time to turn yellow. "Like the place?" We chose the Thalassa Bar because it's the quietest in the Plateau. She says she doesn't find it very swinging, but we have a feeling she doesn't care one way or the other.

She had the resigned air of one who's fated – to be bored ... so much that even before we'd begun to speak we had nothing left to say. So we played the role of fans and interviewed her. She raised those antennae artists say they have and did her best to give us a few good "flashes."

"What do you think of friendship?"

"As far as I'm concerned, somebody who comes on with friendship is insulting me. I hate it. If you can't feel more than that for me then don't bother me!"

She kept looking at her Mickey Mouse watch (it isn't made to show the time but to show that it doesn't show the time and thus that you don't want to know anyhow, but she was looking at it for another reason). I finally gave up and understood, and I went to ask the bartender what time it was.

"Ten-fifteen." She yawned.

"Are you tired? Do you want to go to sleep?"

"Oh, I don't know. You two decide for me."

We went down the Thalassa Bar's steps without a word. We walked to Park Avenue without a word, speech gone forever. In the cold night, there before the smooth, naked mountain upon which the moonlight lay shimmering like a final fall of snow, we ran to hail a Diamond taxicab that was moving fast while the traffic signal still showed green. I opened the '69 Chevrolet Biscayne's grey metal door. She entered head first, stooping low. And I've never seen anything less sexy than those thin panties, which she revealed without meaning to, like all women when they're stepping into a car.

We watched the taxicab join a group of other cars and descend the hill, sinking out of sight as it went under the overpass.

All of a sudden we found ourselves sitting in the small shelter at the bus stop; we saw cars go into spins, slide, overturn and squirt blood of every color like cockroaches. The thousand-watt bulbs on the lamp posts were exploding like bombshells. Park Avenue was buckling, splitting, throwing its morselled asphalt in our faces.

She didn't even say goodbye. "Fuck!" We don't want to go to bed in this state, we're too afraid our hide-a-bed will close over us like a coffin. Our apocalyptic visions return. Nicole begins to cry. Her hand, which was smoothing my hair, grips it, yanks it, pulls it out.

"This has got to end. We've got to fight back. Let's get up, lady, and go have a real orgy, O.K.?"

Nicole turns on the Front Right burner of our electric stove. Nicole puts water in the pot: Nicole's going to make the coffee. I plug in the toaster, get out the butter, bread and cheese: I'm going to make the sandwiches. We're going to stuff ourselves. We'll eat till we bust! Fuck my waistline!

It hurts! Come on, is this any way to be? So we're suffering … is there anything more common, vulgar, vile, more fingered by every conceivable sort of sweaty, sticky hand, more tossed and turned in every conceivable sort of sodden bed? The city of Montreal is foul with every kind of squirming, twisted, writhing despair. It's swarming with despair, infested with it. Suddenly, it dawns on us: there are too many people like us, we find that disgusting. It's this very disgust over how many there are who're sick at heart that'll save us. Our contempt and our pride'll send us shooting like sparrows out of the sewers where, in the froth and stench, they lie wallowing. NOT US! The more of them there are the less we want to do with them! NOT US!

Before, it was hard: the Kraft cheese slices would stick together. It's better now: they come wrapped individually in cellophane. I'm busy gulping down my fifth sandwich like it was nothing. Nicole's giving it all she's got to finish her third. She can't make it. It won't go any farther than her Adam's apple. I ask her how things are. She answers that they're better, really better, she's not just saying it to make me feel good.

Got to hold on till tomorrow at any cost, till we've slept. Tomorrow will bring nothing since it won't bring *her*; but tomorrow we *won't care*. Tomorrow's – over there somewhere. Tomorrow, nothing, *nothing whatsoever*, which is precisely what'll please us most. We'll be so glad about tomorrow's nothing that in a fit of freedom we'll seek our revenge. We'll glue the thousand pieces of our monotony back together, then smash it yet again into a million on her photogenic, champagne-is-boring face. Even if it's cancer she's given us we'll find a cure and then see her sink to her knees beneath the burden of our health. Harpy! Leftist Intellectual! Slut! Fat-butt! Blimp! Tub! Queen of the Tubs!

This radiator's been around so long you'd think it's had a full life. Several coats of white paint, like a growth, have swollen its vermicular markings, rounded off its side-angles, absorbed its screws, turned its large nuts into huge warts. In the spaces between the pipes grows black moss in which moths, flies and cockroaches reproduce. We meditate on the kitchen radiator. There's another in our other room, the *salon double*. Which is how they term a bedroom which can be turned into a living room, that is, a living room whose sofa conceals a bed (hide-a-bed).

We live on the second storey on the north side of what was formerly an otorhinolaryngology clinic on Esplanade. Between Duluth and Mount Royal Streets, fifty beautifully old houses stand shoulder to shoulder, damming up the pool of nature flowing off the mountain; that's where we are. They've been bought up on the instalment plan by Greeks, Italians, Poles and Lithuanians, and now hive swarms of immigrants and bums. Our Lithuanian is a baker's helper at Arena Bakeries; he fixed up the basement; he lives there quietly with his wife, who speaks not a word of Bilingualism, his two children, college kids, the pipes and a tangle of electric wires. The tenants on the ground floor: haven't seen them, don't know them. Our neighbor is a little blonde German thing whose face seems frozen in a frown and who drives a mustard-yellow Ford Torino Fast-Back (she must be a bunny at the Playboy club: she's pasted a rabbit on one of her small side-windows). Everybody's down on us because we don't give much thought to housekeeping. When National Chemical Extermination comes to fumigate, they see it's us who're dirty; they tell the Lithuanian; the Lithuanian tells the other tenants; and everybody talks behind our backs … The way we see it, no roach could sting as hard as the little bitchy blond when we meet her in the hallway and it's little bitchy blonds National Chemical should rid us of.

Our reading lamp's not working at the moment. Last night, in the middle of the Introduction to Brother Marie-Victorin's *Flore laurentienne,* the bulb blew; out came a kodak flash; it had given up the ghost.

We don our windbreakers, we go downtown on foot, we go into Pascal Hardware's castle. We like to go there. We rummage through cases overflowing like treasure chests with nails, nuts, and bolts. We gather up fistfuls of shiny gold and silver screws as though they were ancient coins. They sell everything. Even telegraph poles. But you're now allowed to climb them to try them. (Bad joke.) You can't buy *one* hundred watt bulb; they come two to a package: you have to buy them both or do without.

Feeling the need to walk a bit more, we go down to the Forum with our two Sylvania bulbs. It's not far, but the trip there and back is enough to give you an appetite. Just past a Honda showroom we stop in a rather ordinary-looking restaurant. Eat a hot dog, eat some french fries, look around. The cashier isn't behind the cash register. She's sitting two stools down from us, eating a steak on a kind of bread board. The electric clock is directly in front of us; it has a large, black, neon-haloed face; between the 5 and 6 of the phosphorescent ring of numbers the big hand takes little leaps at regular intervals which will allow it to catch up with the small hand. Stuck under the clock is a white fish with grey fins, a plastic trophy of stupefying insignificance. Its ordinariness is so dense you have to look ten times before seeing the thing, so deep you turn away for fear of being swallowed up in it.

Thinking it polite, the waitress puts the bill face down on the counter. I turn it over quietly. $1.62! Fuck! On Saint Lawrence Boulevard we could have eaten a dozen hot dogs for $1.62! It takes all we've got to keep from losing our tempers and exploding and breaking everything. $0.45 for a hot dog! What cruelty! How low can you get! To calm ourselves, defuse our anger, to keep from waking up in jail, we tear a napkin along the creases and on the too-porous paper we write a letter.

We would make gentle every manner of thing, remake ourselves serene. So, let us set about loving all, henceforth forbearing to discriminate, accepting all, even assembly-line fishes, embracing all with an equable heart, even bills swollen with greed. Our horror and disgust only serve to aggravate our injuries and to heighten the pleasure of their agents. So, let us suffer such feelings no longer; let us feed our venom, our armor, our very clothes to the flames, and let us offer ourselves, tender ourselves, give ourselves to those who would fuck us.

The cashier's half-hour for lunch isn't up yet. The waitress is replacing her. At the moment the waitress doesn't have time to take our money: she's busy taking the orders of a table of four. The bastards want to rob you but only on the condition that you'll give them a chance to catch their breath. The waitress is the jittery, rushed, ever-in-a-hurry type. Like with all jittery, rushed, ever-in-a-hurry types, the mouths of the pockets of her wash-and-wear blouse are stained with ink splotches. The pressure of upsurging insults is growing, pushing, leaning heavy against my taut lips. Aware of it, Nicole whispers, "What did Charles Gill say?" (He said, "I'm a man without hope but I never give up.")

We leave the restaurant behind, but not the shameful exploitation of which we were victims – and now, along with everything else we'd like to vomit up and get out of our systems but can't, into our gullets come bits of dialogue from The Way She Is.

"Do you know Venice?" asks Eddie Constantie.

"No, no one has ever introduced me to it!" replies Françoise Brion.

We walk past a telephone booth. We have too great a need, need pure and simple, to be able to resist any longer. In common unspoken agreement we turn around, we run. Fate's against us: some bum or prick of a prankster shit in the booth; in my haste I step right in it. I'm a man without hope but I never give up; therefore we forget the shit and dial the number.

"If Roger answers we hang up, O.K.?"

"O.K. boss!"

Roger says hello. We hang up. Despite the hot dogs, the pile of shit, all that, it does us good to hang up in the face of a childhood friend who's getting ahead ... (People who get ahead get ahead for the sole purpose of making you feel like shit, buddy.)

It's eleven-thirty. Thirty minutes to go.

(In order not to spend our time waiting for her ring, we phoned her to ask her if she was planning to phone us.

"It's against my nature as an Aquarius to make plans. I never plan to phone you and I never plan not to phone you."

Short and sweet. Stiff and hard. We told ourselves, "Fine, well, that's it, somebody else who thinks we get attached too fast." Why does she call us her treasures, why does she kiss us on the mouth, why did she let us in on her most obscene secrets, if she scorns our attachment? People do everything to make you want them, then when you want them they're not pleased.

"Maybe I'll never phone you, but if I ever do I'll phone at *midnight* ... That O.K., man?")

A quarter to. *The Wolf of Malveneur*, an old horror movie which seems to be a bit of a horror itself, is showing on channel 2. Our eyes are too busy listening to the telephone to see what they're watching. When there's only a quarter of an hour left we lose our grip; we're helpless as need and fear, coupled, take us, sweep us away; till the final moment we fall at breakneck speed down a slope which becomes steeper and steeper to straighten finally into the sheer flank of nothingness.

Ten to, five to. Our ears become taut, they strain, quiver, begin to predict, to lie. In their atrocious impatience to hear the telephone ring, we've seen them leap forward in time to go listen in the seconds and minute ahead. We don't hear the water for the coffee boiling now: there must not be a

417

drop left in the pot. Who's going to turn off the burner? We're much too busy! From head to foot we begin to listen through every pore. It's not us any longer who're coming and going between the red easy chair and the hide-a-bed, it's four ears which have devoured us. We want so badly to hear the telephone ring that our fibres produced a kind of hypnotic pre-echo, and it works so well on the receiver that we see its black bakelite holding itself back, pulsating and ready to rear, it's going to burst like a bladder any moment now.

Afraid, we're afraid, Tub, so afraid you'll close yourself off, that you'll seal up the only door leading us out of our dark cell, our closet, our trash can, that your fancy will release us as abruptly as it seized us. Afraid, we're so afraid of those poets, stars, anchorites – visionaries, revolutionaries, extraordinaries everyone of them – who station themselves at the Chat Noir, the Petite Hutte, l'Accrochage, and whom you rub shoulders with in such easy familiarity! What's the point of taking so much trouble to be nothing if a person has to be something just to pick up a few of those hours you throw away?

Call, don't refuse us that crumb. Call, a person feels so much better having done good by a couple of wretches, clods, hangers-on. Call, snug-gled in the warmth of your goodness you won't need Tranquilline, Equanil, Valium, to get to sleep.

There was only one hour – midnight – and it's gone. It's impossible to keep our eyes fixed on *The Wolf of Malveneur*, or even to keep them fast in their sockets; they're no sooner in place than they roll to the bottom of our cell, our closet, our trash can.

"Laãnou … D'you think Laãnou's back from Quebec City? … "

We phone Laãnou's. No answer. We can always boost our morale by imagining what she would said to us to boost our morale. It's not hard, she always says the same thing to boost our morale: "You're too sensitive."

Translated by David Homel

418

TWO OF US TOGETHER, EACH OF US ALONE

Claire Weissman Wilks

FIVE POEMS FOR DOLLS

Margaret Atwood

i)
Behind glass in Mexico
this clay doll draws
its lips back in a snarl;
despite its beautiful dusty shawl,
it wishes to be dangerous.

ii)
See how the dolls resent us,
with their bulging foreheads
and minimal chins, their flat bodies
never allowed to bulb and swell,
their faces of little thugs.

This is not a smile,
this glossy mouth, two stunted teeth;
the dolls gaze at us
with the filmed eyes of killers.

iii)
There have always been dolls
as long as there have been people
In the trash heaps and abandoned temples,
the dolls pile up;
the sea is filling with them.

What causes them?
Or are they gods, causeless,
something to talk to
when you have to talk,
something to throw against the wall?

A doll is a witness
who cannot die,
with a doll you are never alone.

On the long journey under the earth,
in the boat with two prows,
there were always dolls.

iv)
Or did we make them
because we needed to love someone
and could not love each other?

It was love, after all,
that rubbed the skins from their grey cheeks,
crippled their fingers,
snarled their hair, brown or dull gold.
Hate would merely have smashed them.

You change, but the doll
I made of you lives on,
a white body leaning
in a sunlit window, the features
wearing away with time,
frozen in the gaunt pose
of a single day,
holding in its plaster hand
your doll of me.

v)
Or: all dolls come
from the land of the unborn,
the almost-born; each
doll is a future
dead at the roots,
a voice heard only
on breathless nights,
a desolate white memento.

Or: these are the lost children,
those who have died or thickened
to full growth and gone away.

The dolls are their souls or cast skins,
which line the shelves of our bedrooms
and museums, disguised as outmoded toys,
images of our sorrow,
shedding around themselves
five inches of limbo.

THE LOVER

Joyce Carol Oates

No longer young? … Must remind himself of his age: thirty-seven. That was not exactly young. But when he had time to study his face in the mirror he was always shocked, subtly, by how relatively youthful he did appear, in spite of … Of course, the men in his family hardly seemed to age: his father had been energetic up until the very last week of his life. Tony had his father's gentle good looks, his dark, heavy eyebrows, his pained, distracted courtesy. *Yes …? Of course I'm listening.*

A woman whose face was a soft, lined, infinitely-lined glove: like a glove that has been crushed and let to fall. Aged. Elderly. Out of that pale, softly-wrinkled face her eyes peered at him with an intensity that was painful. Doctor, please. Doctor …? Tugging at his sleeve. Trying to pull him down to her where she lay; trying to pull herself up, up from the pillows. Her clawing fingers. His wrist. *You are too young to know … You don't understand.* It was necessary that he extricate her fingers one by one. Gently. With courtesy. The woman's voice was nearly gone now; he heard only a whisper. In fact he did not always hear the words, but he supposed he knew what they were: he had heard them so often from her. The woman's body was nearly gone now: 150 pounds some months ago, now 65 pounds. Yet she had that timid, desperate strength. Pulling at him, begging him. *Doctor, let me die. Tony …?*

The Huron Nursing Home: the daily and weekly and monthly records, the monthly insurance payments, the nurses, the Director who had been a friend of Tony's father. All were real, all were public. He was a public man. Thursdays at the Home, the other days at the hospital and in his office, in white, a public man. You are too young to know, the woman had accused him, but it was a lie. He knew everything. And he was not young.

Ah, lovely! At first, from the air, London had looked like any other city. And the crowds at the airport were like crowds at any airport. And the long ride in, the heavy traffic, the unmistakably gritty taste of the air, the dizzying, swarming sea of people at the very centre of the city: Leicester Square, Piccadilly. But nearing their hotel Tony began to realize how quiet it was. The traffic noises faded to a nervous, energetic hum, a constant hum, well within the range of what one could tolerate. The air seemed to lighten: a long stretch of park, the damp fresh chill of Spring. Suddenly he was happy to be here, it was lovely here, he would be happy here.

Mina had been saying for months: *You're so different now, so distracted all the time. You don't listen to me …* His mother criticized him, affectionately, pulling at his wrist as only she had a right to pull: *Must take a vacation this Spring, Tony, don't wait until August, you must take two weeks off and escape …* She had always been jealous of Tony's father, hadn't she, and jealous of his

427

patients and his success. But that was natural, wasn't it, and Tony tried not to mind her siding with Mina; his father had minded this sort of thing, had too often lost his temper. "Oh, isn't it lovely! ... Hyde Park," Mina was saying. "Aren't you happy to be here? It's so lovely here, look at all the daffodils and jonquils and tulips." Mina was leaning against the window as if she were slightly drunk.

"Happy," Tony murmured, unpacking. He took his things out with care; Mina had folded them and packed them with care. "Happy. Very happy, yes. Happy."

Such tall windows: floor to ceiling. Yet they were impractically narrow, hardly more than a foot across. Strips of glass, green-tinted. Tony counted nine windows in the room and wondered what was the point of it. Must be very expensive. And the room was oddly-shaped, one wall shorter than the others, so that he had the illusion of being inside a distorted cube, an art work that was a playful trick on the senses. The hotel was a tube, an elegant cylinder. The room was sound proof. Mina stood at the window pointing fourteen storeys below to the bright red double-decker buses and the stately black taxis that moved in countless lanes, streaming to the right, streaming to the left, a continual motion that was fascinating. And silent, unlike the traffic of Wisconsin Avenue.

"I don't want you to think of it while we're here," Mina said.

Her back was to him but he smiled in her direction. "Yes, that's right," he said.

No need for him to stoop as he knotted his tie, since the bureau mirror was immense. Tony was over six-feet-three; his dark-brown hair stuck out from his head stiffly, so thick it looked as if he could not comb it, only brush it out; his shoulders were wide. Yet his size was easily accommodated by the mirror and the long, highly-polished mahogany dresser. The bed caught his eye: almost as wide as it was long. Accommodations for Americans, for giants.

"Why are we staying here?" he asked. "Why aren't we staying at a ..." But he had let her do all the arranging. She and the very helpful man at the travel agency in Bethesda. The tickets, the reservations, the countless details worked out by Jessamyn Carlson, the cheques signed by Jessamyn in her neat, graceful handwriting. She was dressing in a corner of the room, out of his vision. Fortunately, she had not heard his question; he must have spoken too softly. So he said: "It seems to be very quiet here. The room is very attractive, it's like an American hotel."

When he glanced toward Mina he was surprised to see his own reflection: one of the mirrored closet doors was open, shielding her as she changed her clothes. His blue-gray suit looked good. Possibly he was tired, his complexion a little yellowish; he hated to travel. But the suit was attractive. Bought for this trip, especially for this trip, his first suit in two years ... *you'll need something light and yet warm, no matter that it's supposed to be Spring there, that crocuses started to bloom back in early March, England is always cold, always cold* ... Mina leaned around to smile at him. What had he said? She stood in a lacy white slip, her hands busy with her hair, pinning it up. Fast-moving little hands, the fingernails polished a very light pink, so subtly lacquered Tony could not always tell they were

428

lacquered. She was a very pretty woman, with her silvery-blond hair and pale-blue eyes and her smile. Barefoot, she was much shorter than he. Like a young girl, a child. But why did she wear white? – it reminded him of the paper smocks, those throw-away paper smocks patients wore for examinations. The smocks were a single size, large, with enormous armholes and a string to tie around the waist ...

Death is a privilege! he had wanted to shout at the old woman.

But Mina was not begging him for death, not even for one more quarter of a gram of morphine; she was not tempting him to commit murder for her sake. Instead, she was listing the events of their stay here in London. But one thing was disappointing: the travel agent back home hadn't gotten them very good seats for a certain play.

"We can get to the theatre early," Tony heard himself saying. "And if someone has turned in his tickets, then ...then... We can do that."

What good was it, to have money if you never spend your money? Money, too, was a privilege. Spending it, being happy with it, was a privilege. Two years since he'd bought a new suit; and his shoes were runover at the heels. Mina nagged him, laughed at him, argued with him. This vacation could be a second honeymoon, she said. Tony agreed. He sat with her on the second level of one of the buses, listening to her excited chatter as she read from a guidebook ... reading names of parks and streets and buildings and statues ... famous names, immortal names. Here, immortality was everywhere.

"So many people," Tony murmured.

Crowds along Oxford Street. A plunging stream of shoppers, tourists. Incredible, so many people. Yet an occasional square, glimpsed from the main road, looked almost deserted.

"Aren't you sorry you haven't travelled more? – you're thirty-seven years old!" Mina said, squeezing his hand. She was only a few years younger than he, but it had always been a tradition between them that she was much younger: girlish, sweet, sometimes audacious. He loved her very much and hoped he might learn from her.

It was difficult to carry on a conversation now that they were studying the menus.

Enormous ivory placards. The names of the dishes in French, in flowery script. *The White Elephant:* an exclusive private club on Curzon Street. Only a two-minute walk from the hotel, no need for a taxi. Their hosts were explaining things to them. Mina was listening attentively, but Tony's mind wandered. He had waited for Mina to shower, had been standing at one of the windows gazing down at the traffic, had found himself thinking that the value of travel might be a secret no one voiced: the realization that so many people existed, thousands upon thousands of people existed, quite unrelated to one another, unaware of one another, lives that scurried among lives without touching them ... and so it was liberating, wasn't it, to see how little one's own life mattered? ... How little one's own life-obsession mattered? And it was true, as Mina so often said, that people who had money might as well spend it. Money, too, was a privilege.

He was happy enough to be here, in this handsome dining room, studying this complicated menu. Their hosts were friends of friends. A connection through Mina's brother-in-law who worked in Washington with someone else's brother-in-law, something to do with the London-based subsidiary of a pharmaceutical company: not necessary for Tony to remember the exact relationships, but he should try to remember generally who was who, who was American and who was English. Odd, the New York accent of the man beside Mina, a handsome forty-year-old in a stylish suit, sideburns halfway down his cheeks. Tony listened to what was being said. Explanations of English holidays, bank holidays, indifference of workers to work and income and the old enticements of the materialist culture ... the terror that cynics had never considered, the possibility that God had retreated into Material for most people, into cars and television sets and semi-detached houses in the suburbs, and now the scornful intellectuals had done their work: now Material itself was losing its divinity. And could total chaos be far behind? Laughing over their cocktails and caviar and paté. Tony leaned forward. He wanted to ask whether that was really true? ... whether it had been offered as a serious remark, or only as part of the conversation? ... but already the subject was changed, already they had not so much backed away from it as leapt over it.

One of them asked Mina about their plans: which required her listing the plays and tours and museums and galleries once again. Flushed with joy, she was, hardly more than a girl after all. Blond and American and eager to live, eager for life to be made tempting to her. She was from Charleston, South Carolina, and in the company of strangers her soft gracious utterly charming accent re-asserted itself, without her knowledge. Tony felt a little jealous, that she should be so happy with other people and so unhappy with him, and not even know it.

During dinner Tony's mind wandered and he could not call it back. One of the men in their party reminded him of a patient of his who had died not long ago. Fifty years old, a wealthy broker, a sportsman with hundreds of acres in the Smokies, articulate about his own dying: witnessing with a kind of irritated awe the blemishes that covered his body and would not fade, the scales and itchy patches that gradually merged, scraggy, scabby patches of reddened flesh gone mad, wild, turned against the person who inhabited it. Was that death, was it that simple? Of course. Tony had been embarrassed for so long, he'd stumbled and reddened, as embarrassed as his father, but what good did it do to always resist? ... so many of them die anyway. Died. And not all of them seemed to mind. The dying man had smoked cigars and lay propped up in his expensive bed and spoke to Tony of the phenomenon of dying. Evidently he had begun to die, he explained, the day he lost all interest in the disease; like most educated people, he had taken an obsessional interest in "his" disease, had become rather a specialist in it (a rare kind of bone cancer). But that interest left him, one day. He saw that "his" disease did not matter, it wasn't disease that mattered, only the balance of power between life and death ... the shift of power and allegiance to the other side, to death, that was the beginning of dying. *I felt it with relief.*

One of the women asked Tony a question. He answered. He must have done well because she smiled, laughed, was obviously pleased with him. She was the wife of the man with sideburns. Behind her the panelled wall gleamed; her perfect honey-blond hair was reflected in it; and behind her image, beyond it, the amiable blur that must have been Tony's face. All was well. Tony found himself in the conversation without having anything to say, but that did not matter, not in the slightest. What had anyone to say? These healthy trivial people, strangers who turned out to be friends: what did they have to say? They praised the dishes, or complained about them. They commented on the wine. And was that James Mason seated at a nearby table? … or someone who resembled him? … and how long would the Carlsons be in London, or had they already asked that question? Tony heard himself laughing. He must have been happy to be with them, though not so happy as his wife was, it was like being with their friends in Bethesda or Georgetown or Chevy Chase, people turned out to be familiar, brothers and sisters, alluding to the same subjects and eating the same food, so long as their allegiance was to this visible, handsome, costly world. But how could they eat so much? Tony was amazed. Amazed at himself as well. It must have been because they were celebrating something important. They had to snatch at the food, had to snatch at whatever they were celebrating, not wanting it to end. Cocktails and hors d'oeuvres and appetizers and the courses that followed one another in an important sequence and then the after-dinner drinks and the after-dinner conversation … Jesus, so much food. So much of it wasted. Tony wanted to jump up and leave and get back to the hospital. He could shower there. Could change his clothes there. And …

The food must have been ornamental; he was missing the point of it. He was too literal. Not enough imagination. Without appetite he ate, as they ate without appetite, like geese force-fed for that expensive paté that people spread on crackers absent-mindedly and nibbled and forgot about and certainly did not notice. Tony's problem, Mina said, was that he never enjoyed anything; why couldn't he enjoy life as others did? He made an effort, he brought his spirit back to the table and listened to what was being said, trying to hide his discomfort. They must not miss Speaker's Corner at Hyde Park – did they know about that? – was it in the guidebook? There they could hear the most extraordinary speeches sincere people and obvious madmen, and fascinating people in the crowds, really fascinating. If you're interested in eccentrics. In abnormal psychology. *Will I, won't I, will I, won't I,* Tony heard himself thinking, while he agreed that he was interested in such things; he was interested in everything, that was why he and Mina had come, wasn't it? A small drunken voice, taunting him. *I think I will, I think I won't. I think I will.* And the old woman's face appeared in his mind's eye, begging him to leave these people, to fight his way past them, to release her from her agony. Tony half shut his eyes. He was smiling. His lips were smiling. *Will I, won't I. Will I.*

One of the women was telling an anecdote about an attempt made on the life of the Queen, some months before, and Tony's eyes filled with tears and he thought in a panic *Jesus Christ, what if I start to cry, what if I ruin this evening like all the others?* But there was no danger of that, the anecdote was really a joke, it resolved itself in laughter and all was well.

"You want to go home, don't you?"

"Of course not."

"You're not happy here, you want to go home ... You hate me. You're not happy with me."

"I'm very happy. I don't want to go home."

"You're always thinking of ..."

"No."

They went to famous immortal sites and yet time did not pass. The present could not be dislodged. The Tower of London: Americans tramping happily in the drizzle, taking pictures, crowding one another on the narrow, poorly-lit stone staircases, calling to the ravens ... *Look at the crows! Look at the crows!* a young father cried. His children were delighted. They went to the British Museum, where, grateful for Mina's awed silence, Tony gave himself up to *Will I, won't I, will I, won't I.* He had explained to that woman that he was not preventing her death. He did not stand in the way of her death. Not he. How was it his fault that, once she was hospitalized in that place, he could not cross any boundary established by the law? ... could not cross any boundary? ... he was sick with shame and terror, not knowing what to do. And yet: had her life evaporated to the point at which it was no more than a bubbling phosphorescence he could not have abandoned it, could not have given it up ... He was frightened, excited. He walked Mina through the enormous drafty rooms and kissed her where they were hidden, for a moment, by a marble wall.

Yet time did not move: only three calendar-days had passed.

In the Kensington Gardens Mina slipped her arm through his and accused him of being in love with another woman. Did she know the woman? ... was it the wife of one of his friends? Was it a patient of his? Tony laughed, she was so endearing, so absurd. He kissed her on the gravel path.

"Have you ever seen parks so very green?" they asked each other.

Mina was happy. Tony was happy, but he began to sweat through his clothes though the restaurants and theatres and museums were ill-heated, possibly not heated at all. At odd, unaccountable times he thought of his office, thought of the lights out and the shade drawn, *Dr. Carlson, M.D.* in gold leaf on the door, the waiting room empty and the *Réalités* and *Today's Health* and *Scientific American* and *Newsweek* and *Medic-World News* in their proper places in the magazine rack, everything in its place, silent, undisturbed, dustless. He thought of the hospital. He thought of the Huron Nursing Home ... Mina spoke wistfully of going to visit a cousin of her mother's, a spinster who lived in Highgate, but Tony did not reply, did not argue. In the end she went alone: he saw her off at the Underground near their hotel and they said goodbye bravely, as if they might never meet again.

Of course they met again, and though it was much later it seemed to Tony that time had not passed at all. He had wandered beneath the pavement, studying the crowds in the subway, his hands in the pockets of his raincoat ... a man with nothing to do, absolutely nothing to do. An observer, a stroller. A witness. A tourist. As soon as Mina was gone he began to notice, uneasily, how dirty it was down here. The corridors were depressing, especially one very long, poorly-lit one he wandered into by mistake, having misread a sign. He had intended to walk up to the Marble Arch, but had turned at the wrong place and found himself in a parking garage: huge, hideous place, smelling of exhaust. A man was sprawled at Tony's feet, humming to himself. Drunk. Sick. The corridor was puddled: some of it water, some of it urine. At the intersection with the main corridor an aged woman derelict sat beside her bundle of clothing or food, her hands folded, eyes shut, her expression peaceful. People streamed past her. Not far away were three guitar-playing beggars, all Americans, singing happily to the crowds that ignored them; a girl in blue jeans and a bright-yellow blouse rattled a tambourine that was also a kind of tin cup. It was quite cold down here. People hurried by, up toward Marble Arch or back in the other direction, not wanting to linger. Tony gave the girl in the yellow blouse a pound-note, but she did not seem to notice. She smiled vacuously toward him, nodding in time with the lively, thumping music. He wondered what the hell she was doing here and what the point of it was … but it was something to tell Mina about, at least. She could not accuse him of having nothing to say to her.

"What were you reading there, in that old book? … you missed what the guide was saying about …"

"About Indian customs," Tony said. "A Jesuit's journal … seventeenth century … North America."

She waited and he did not continue.

"What was so interesting about the book?" she asked.

He was light-headed from all the walking that day, from the miles of pavement and the crowds. Vague, blundering. He began to tell her, as they sat in this charming French restaurant in Mayfair, holding hands, began to tell his wife about a way of Indian torture … Indians torturing Indians … the pulverizing of the body's organs one by one and the necessity, the sacred necessity, of preserving the life of that body until the very …

She drew her hand away.

"You sicken me," she whispered. "You disgust me."

He pretended not to have heard and she did not repeat what she had said.

Rather small, cramped seats. Tony yawned. Familiar faces all around him: other tourists. The commotion five minutes before the ballet began was exciting, even Tony felt some interest, yawning after his heavy dinner. Mina seemed to be reading the program, studying it. She wore her glasses. In the theatre were women with bright, smiling, expectant faces, all wonderfully dressed, their hair wonderfully prepared. That was what they did with their splendid good health. The men were smiling too. But some were sleepy after their heavy dinners. A few of them red-faced, sluggish, uncomfortable. Hypertension, heart attack, Tony glanced at them and past them, not wanting anyone to catch his eye. Why are we here, what are we

433

doing here? But this was absurd: everyone wanted to be here. Obviously, everyone wanted to be here.

The music was delicate, enticing. The girl was shy ... the boy bold. The perfection of their movements charmed Tony: bodies, arms and legs, faces that were intelligent, feet that seemed to possess their own thought. Tony was fascinated by the stylized motions of power there on the stage: the male dancer now lifting the girl above him, as if redeeming her with his strength. She was very pretty. He was very handsome. And those muscular shoulders, those powerfully muscular legs ... to think of the power locked in them! Then another dancer entered, another woman. Tony's heart lurched. He realized this was only a dance, only an illusion. Images chasing one another in a pretense of being alive, bodies that mocked ordinary bodies with a supreme godly irrelevant strength, while the audience stared and smiled. The second girl had the face of a girl he had examined a few months ago, and when she entered the dance he seemed to lose the illusion before him in an instant. His mind shifted from the stage because it was not real. He wanted to cry out, wanted to protest, nothing could interest him except what was real, nothing could excite his passion ...

The dancer was tall; her black hair whipped about; lovely muscular legs, absolutely certain of each movement, each note ... absolutely certain of the dance. It turned out that this second girl was the important one, not the first. The man's interest shifted. The dance shifted. Tony was watching the girl and thinking of the other girl, of his patient, and he sank into an erotic daze, making no effort to concentrate on the dance or to avoid his memory of that day at the hospital, which he had very nearly forgotten. Of course he had forgotten it. He forgot, forgot everything; he had to. But the music and the black-haired dancer brought it back and he felt his yearning spread out everywhere in him, not concentrated in any part of his body. It was everywhere. In the brain. At the back of the throat, that dryness that could turn into a stabbing ache. In his lips, in his eyes. In the upper part of his body, in his chest, where the lungs yearned to take in air as fully and fiercely as possible, the violence of muscles never fully exercised, taking their pleasure. Jesus, how he wanted ... how badly he wanted ... But he didn't know what it was: he could not get it into an image, not into a single image. *Beautiful young schizo*, they had said. Brought in by police, found wandering in a railroad yard, clothing ripped, bare-legged though it was about twenty degrees that day, mumbling something about being raped, by a black man who said he would return to twist her head off if she told police ... *beautiful schizophrenic* they had said *though pretty battered at the moment.*

Intermission. Tony woke to applause. His desire mocked him: his spirit had swollen to the point of anguish, and now everyone was applauding, the dancers were taking their bows, he was sweating inside his clothes and Mina was saying things he must reply to, must respect. In the seat before him was a young German woman. Harsh-voiced, hair that was too blond, handclapping that sounded violent, hollow, out of proportion to whatever had happened on stage. His yearning was being mocked, his tender excited memories were being clapped out of existence ... He joined in the

434

clapping. He agreed with what Mina had said. With part of this mind he had actually been watching the ballet; he had been watching it. He had been listening to the music. With part of his brain he had concentrated on the dance, and it was not a lie, his applause, his willingness to join in the tumult of clapping. It was certainly pleasant to be here, it was a privilege to be here, and in a way he was grateful to be so suddenly awakened.

… Drinks in the lobby? … Ice cream? … Cigarettes?

Tony thought it touching, that adults would eat ice cream out of little cardboard containers, with wooden spoons. Like children, they were, eating with those wooden spoons. And so soon after their enormous dinners. Boxes of candy. Hard candies, mints. Would you like some, Mina? No. Thank you, no. Ice cream? cigarettes? a drink in the lobby? She countered by asking if he was enjoying the dance and when he said he was enjoying it, yes, very much, she turned away, offended by the sound of his voice. That he should not try harder to convince her! … that he should lie so unconvincingly!

They had not made love for so long now, the worry of it had become abstract, philosophical.

Sometimes she took on the burden of being at fault, not out of kindness but out of malice: she detested him. Sometimes he took on the burden, when he was genuinely tired or when he had had to leave the dining room, during dinner, because something that had happened that day returned to upset him. He loved her, he did not blame her for the rage she insisted she did not feel, and of course she loved him too: otherwise what was the point of it? The last several times they had made love Tony had had to convince himself that it was necessary, it was a scared necessity, and so far as he knew she believed him … she seemed to believe him. He was not to blame, that images rushed into his head. Was he? Nor was Mina to blame, that her warm eager body and her loving words seemed to fade, to become abstract and unconvincing. How am I to blame, she once sobbed, tell me how am I to blame … is it someone else, do you love someone else, what has happened and how am I to blame…?

They looked through the program together. They read the notes, commented on the dancers, studied the glossy advertisements, decided upon a restaurant in this very block where after-the-show suppers were a specialty.

"I'm enjoying this very much," Tony said.

And indeed he was eager for the dance to begin. The intermission was far too long. He got up to stretch his legs, made his way nervously through the crowds, returned to his seat and still there was a wait. A woman beside Mina turned out to be from South Carolina and the two of them were talking in warm, enthusiastic voices. So interesting here! … so unusual in so many ways!

The second ballet was by a contemporary composer named Fuhr and it was harsh, jarring, deliberately unrhythmic. Tony looked from one dancer to another, not knowing what would happen. The dancers seemed to pace and lunge … the black-haired girl appeared, her face grotesquely white, the features pencilled in, the mouth too red. The male dancer circled her. His movements showed passion, but passion restrained by the structure of

435

the music … And his face was heavily made up, like the girl's. Was it a parody? Was it serious, a serious monstrosity? Tony judged from the restlessness of the audience that they simply did not know: they hadn't the right cues, they didn't know how to react. A sickening sense of chaos, of unbalance … The music swerved this way, the dancers that way. *Will I or won't I. Will any of us.* Then there was a complicated turn and a spontaneous burst of applause from a few perceptive people in the audience, followed by a larger wave of applause. Tony seemed to catch the ballerina's joy as she felt the applause; she must have glanced out, a half-second, her exaggerated dark gaze acknowledging the audience … and Tony smiled, relieved and disappointed as the illusion broke for him, once again, and he was conscious of himself sitting in a cramped seat, perspiring, watching a contorted and very clever modern dance which he did not understand.

Beautiful? No. Why did they always exaggerate? So few people were beautiful, what was the point of demanding beauty? In fact, beauty now bored him. He was thirty-seven years old and hungry for other things, not beauty; the illusion of beauty could not hold his attention for long. The male dancer was like one of the guitar-playing boys in the underground tunnel, though more attractive. A very comely handsome face, carefully made up, stylized, unreal. And his strength was not real; it was a convention. It was art. He guided the girl not by the power of his own spirit, but by the power of the music and the power the audience gave him. He was the male dancer; he must be strong. His power was theatrical, stylized, coolly beautiful in its precision, and yet it was simply play … that quickening of the music, that outburst of percussion, suggested how the entire ballet was a cruel playfulness, a kind of abstract code. Gradually the audience caught on, gradually it began to respond to this code. The dance was one of asexual, graceful bodies that hinted at the dilemma of life in the flesh, without evoking it. Those thighs were muscular beneath the dead-white tights and, surely, the bodies were sweating inside the strenuous caprice of the music, but it was not visible to the audience; therefore it did not exist. Tony crossed his legs. He uncrossed them, with difficulty. So uncomfortable in here … On stage the dancers labored in an art that subdued the instincts by deadening them, by denying their existence. It was only a performance, Tony thought irritably. For him it was parenthetical interlude, but for the people around him, for Mina, it seemed to be much more: the intensification of their lives.

How he pitied them! … sad, ordinary people. Their passion had to be danced out for them, on stage. Otherwise they lost it.

Twenty years old, she was. But not beautiful. Why did they always exaggerate? Naked beneath the paper smock, her bare feet stuck in straw sandals, hugging herself, shivering. Not beautiful. Her skin was blemished, her forehead too broad, and rather bumpy, as if the bone were uneven; her teeth were discolored. But the eyes were attractive. Except for the shifting, the ceaseless evasion of her gaze, swinging to the ceiling and into the corners of the room and down to her long pale skinny feet. Dark red hair, would have been attractive, no doubt, if it had been washed. But it was greasy and hung about her face in snarled strands. Twenty years old. Dragged off the street and raped, she said. Could identify her attacker, she said. She spoke to Tony in a peculiar detached drawl. She would not look at him, but looked everywhere else. He wondered if she were really sane, and only pretending to be insane. She was obedient enough when he took her blood pressure, not resisting. She stared at the far corner of the room. For some reason he didn't feel afraid of her; he believed she was no crazier than anyone else. *Beautiful young schizophrenic!* ... And her legs hairy, unshaven. Her armpits unshaven. Fingernails broken, filthy.

Then he asked her to step into the lavatory; he handed her a container, for a urine specimen.

No.

She turned away, hugging herself. She was evidently embarrassed.

He offered her the container and she pushed it away with her elbow.

He explained what the procedure was. She must be examined – didn't she want to be helped? And he must make several tests, several more tests ... must try to determine what had happened to her ... see if there were live spermatozoa ... it was emergency room procedure.

She seemed to be listening, though she wouldn't look at him. He thought again that she wasn't crazy, only aping the mannerisms of crazy people; muttering to herself, turned away from him. Stop this! Stop! Go into the lavatory and get the sample for me and lie down on the table so I can examine you and all will be completed ... Then he had an idea. He told her he'd wait in the corridor. When she was finished in the lavatory she could come back into the examining room and lie down and prepare for the rest of the examination. How was that? More privacy for her.

So he went into the corridor. There were two orderlies by the drinking fountain, yawning and stretching. She's crazy, isn't she? She wasn't raped, was she? Like hell she was raped! ... she must be lying. It didn't look like rape, her legs and belly weren't bruised, she must be lying. Tony waited until he supposed she was ready for him. He went back into the examining room and there she stood, in the paper smock, her hands clenched before her. She was staring at the floor. He happened to notice the container with the urine specimen, partly hidden behind a filing cabinet. She had hidden it there out of modesty.

Tony thanked her.

And now for the examination: he saw at once that she wasn't bruised. But that might not mean anything. He asked her to put her feet in the stirrups and slide down to this end of the table, but she couldn't seem to do it. She whimpered. She lay still and obedient, and then tensed up at once, as soon as he touched her. He asked her to please relax, to co-operate. He had to complete the examination, had to get a smear. But she couldn't lie still. Tony tried to explain the procedure to her, but she didn't seem to be listening. So he called the attendants in and asked them to hold her down. A third attendant came along. Tony worked as quickly as possible. He felt light-headed, almost faint, that this girl should resist the examination and force him to hurt her; but this often happened, it couldn't be helped. He had to make four tests, it was for her own good, she had claimed to be raped ... the police would want as much evidence as they

437

could get ... She squirmed and whimpered, but he got the smear. Jamming his fingers up inside her: testing quickly for lumps for any disorder. Quickly, deftly, and it was over and she had not even screamed.

That didn't hurt, did it?

She was relaxed now. She seemed to go dead.

That didn't hurt, did it? Tony asked conversationally.

They let her go. She lay for a moment without moving, then rose to a sitting position at the end of the table. How she panted! ... like an animal. He could smell the stench of panic about her. But he had won, without really hurting her. He had completed the examination and would send the specimens to the laboratory and ...

He was taking off the rubber gloves when she attacked. She must have thrown herself off the table sideways – must have lifted herself by the sheer strength of her arms – jumping sideways at him, halfway onto his back, her hands around his throat. She was screaming now. Her screams came from every direction. She had grabbed Dr. Carlson by the throat and was somehow crawling up his back, literally climbing up his back. He fell heavily against the metal shelves. She was screaming and pounding his head against the floor ...

Mina was sobbing.

"There must be someone else. Another woman."

" ... no."

"Someone else. Someone else. Someone you love ..."

"For Christ's sake, no."

" ... and you don't love me."

"No. Can't you sleep?"

"Sleep. Can't I sleep," Mina laughed. They lay side by side in the enormous bed. The room was soundproof, nearly: from time to time they could hear a siren passing on Park Lane, but even that wailing noise was indistinct. Or maybe there were no sirens. Maybe the noises, faint and teasing, were from inside the hotel itself. Or maybe they were imagining it all. Tony sometimes heard his wife sobbing at a distance. But when he confronted her she was bitter and dry-eyed and waiting ironically to be loved. " ... So we'll leave a week early; we'll leave tomorrow afternoon, to please you. To get you back home."

"I don't want to leave early," Tony said weakly.

She required so little! ... only to be held in his arms, to be comforted. And so he comforted her. She wanted to be loved: it was what she deserved, as his wife. So he must love her. He must make love to her. Sobbing, her breath scanty as a child's, she lay in his arms and pressed her damp face against his ... his wife of eleven years ... so sweet, so anguished, so helpless and aggressive ... Of course she was innocent; she was not to blame. She was one of those who danced in the background, who could not rush forward and demand the audience's attention. She was his wife and required rituals appropriate to that role. *You don't love me. You love someone else. Please don't lie* ... She begged him to lie. His mind gave him images, flashes of the past: not bodies so much as entire scenes, experiences in which he and the other person were wedded, impersonally, irrevocably. *Tony ...? Do you love me?* The dying old woman: except she was not old, really, the disease had aged her. Sixty-four and she looked twenty years older, clutching at his hand, at his wrist, begging ... He was not guilty of her life or of her dying, but he would weep anyway, afterward, alone where no one could discover him: of course he was guilty, he was always guilty. And the others ... the others ... wed to him, and he to them, irrevocably. No other marriage could compete with those marriages. No other passion. ... And the black-haired girl who smelled of sickness, of panic, squirming on the examination table while he perspired over her, guilty, excited, nearly faint with the enormity of what she was forcing him to do and to be. Except she hadn't black hair, had she? ... dark red hair, dirty, sullen, lustreless ... and her eyes lustreless except at the moment he ...

The yearning was everywhere in him now. An ache, a wistful bewildered maniacal ache: that he might inhale so deeply, so wildly, that everything yet unknown to him, every secret, every terror, every adventure of the finite world, could be realized in one ecstasy. *Do you love me? ... Me?"*

Ah yes: he loved.

439

THE CAGE

John Montague

My father, the least happy
man I have known. His face
retained the pallor
of those who work underground:
the lost years in Brooklyn
listening to a subway
shudder the earth,

But a traditional Irishman
who (released from his grille
in the Clark Street I.R.T.)
drank neat whiskey until
he reached the only element
he felt at home in
any longer: brute oblivion.

And yet picked himself
up, most mornings,
to march down the street
extending his smile
to all sides of the good
(non negro) neighbourhood
belled by St. Teresa's church.

When he came back
we walked together
across fields of Garvaghey
to see hawthorn on the summer
hedges, as though
he had never left;
a bend of the road

which still sheltered
primroses. But we
did not smile in
the shared complicity
of a dream, for when
weary Odysseus returns
Telemachus must leave.

Often as I descend
into subway or underground
I see his bald head behind
the bars of the small booth;
the mark of an old car
accident beating on his
ghostly forehead.

LES RITES

Seán Virgo

1

The apple-wood peg hammered into the bank above their mudslide had reeked of beaver-cast seductively on the wind. The big dog-otter had nosed it, breaking water at the head of his family. He galloped up the bank towards the scent, undulating his sleek length over the moss while five cubs trod water, watching. At the last moment his mate whistled from the opposite bank and he swerved, distracted, to romp down the slide. So the trap, instead of breaking his back, closed on the hind legs and the great rudder, flinging a spray of wet fur a yard away. The otter rolled, thrashing and yickering, down to the water, uprooting the peg; and the cubs dived to join the game.

A coneybeare trap is no great weight, but the otter could only hold its own for so long, straining with his front paws. After twenty minutes the mate and her cubs let off nosing the tethered shape which swung with the current in the sombre gut of the pool. The last red bubble of breath had gone winking off down Kumdis Creek.

With the next freshet, body and trap had washed free of the pool, bumping and tumbling downstream with the sticks and moss-rafts through the coffee-dark water. It travelled a mile in the next three days, passing below the Tlell roadbridge and on into the darker forest. Two pools down, the trap lodged in the roots of a fallen hemlock and the stiff ottershape stretched with the flow in the deeper water. A week later the body rotted free and the head itself snagged on a sunken branch, wrenched off and drifted to the floor of the pool. Leeches seethed in its brain, the fur scummed off and followed the lost limbs downstream, and in the next rains the skull tumbled against a gravel bar and was left there, facing upstream, when the water subsided.

Kumdis Bottom is the most ruinous tangle of forest on the islands. Dark and saturated, it is a senseless grid of fallen trees smothered with mosses; and the ground a succession of trapped black pools, seeping into each other beneath a blotched and treacherous mask of liverworts. Most of the dead trees are young; stretched unnaturally in their search for light and finally starved out; leaning against each other and rotting swiftly in the humid air. There are entire husks of trees, in lichen and bark, thirty feet tall and crumbling into nothing about your face if you should lean on them.

Only the most ancient cedars and hemlocks, whose skins themselves are fire-scarred and marsh-textured, have stability; and as the ground lifts sharply to the South the original unfettered forest permits walking through the giant sleep silence. But down by the creek they stand half drowned or on islands of their roots' own making, blocking out all the light. When they fall they choke the water, which flows in places for many yards, invisible under the overlapping and half-sunken trunks. There is never any wind here, except when a raven, floating down through the cedar crests, breaks the air with its creaking pinions. That sound is like bats in a cave, and when the ravens call their belling cries hang echoing for minutes in the heavy silence. The texture is almost submarine.

Yet there is life. Underwater it is all one and the dwarf cutthroat trout arrow across the pools at any stir; while autumn brings a few lost dog salmon blundering up the shallows to spawn in the rare clean gravels. The beavers are young to the islands but they work half-heartedly along the creek; and the deer (who are immigrants too) find pathways somehow – their slots are printed everywhere among the liverworts and on the mud-banks, and bright piles of their droppings lie like berries among the sodden litter of hemlock cones.

Moss takes the animals as it does the trees. You will find the shoulder-blades of deer, bleached white with the first green lacing of the forest across their palms. Or the skull, in furry green, of a young buck with lattices on its eyes and bristling plumes on its antler hefts. Bone seems a finality, a certain resolution with the elements, but the mosscloak devours swiftly. Everything leaches back into Kumdis Creek through the filter of moss and rain.

But the otter's skull on the gravel escapes the moss, takes on the color and feel of its stoney bed, and stares back up the covered stream while a deer slips past on the bank with lowered head; and a little later, stumbling over the windfalls, a young man follows with a clamoring heart and a gun.

This pedigree of otter and riverbank must stand, because only an earth-quake, trundling the Queen Charlotte Islands back onto the dark sea bed, will prevent Kumdis Creek, which flows into and out of my story, from pursuing its slow and rack-choked way to the slough when our race, and perhaps the otter's, is quite forgotten.

2

The hotel coffee-shop in New Masset faces the volunteer fire hall and the R.C.M.P. station. On the wall, above the vinyl seats and formica table tops, is a picture of the Creation. It is in felt applique, white and black and red, a quaint and clumsy rendering twelve feet long of the Raven, hatching first man and first woman from the clamshell out on North Beach. The picture is by two ladies from Old Masset and their scene is bracketed by the two great clan figures of their people – Raven and Eagle, stiff and uneasy above the heads of the tourists, the loggers, the servicemen, the hippies, the natives.

The hotel bears the name of a great hereditary chief, and in the beer parlour that makes up the other half of the ground floor, there is a list a hundred strong of native people who are banned from the premises.

Behind the hotel is the sprawling reserve of the naval station. The crescents and circles of the married quarters, inturned and inspired as a turkey farm; the three-sided plaza of swimming pool, instruction rooms, and administrative offices; and all dependent on a little blockhouse five miles away on the same North Beach where Raven uttered his fiat. That building is ringed by a towering woodhenge of cedar poles and contributes doubtless to the vigilant security of the great white Lie.

The servicemen do not get involved in fights with loggers or indians: they are mostly overweight improbable warriors, lounging in the coffee-shop or driving through the town. Their wives seem to huddle in their Ottawa-plan homes – eating, dreaming, shopping through the catalogues or at the Capex built tactlessly on the high street. At weekends they may drive with their husbands and children out along North Beach in their dune buggies. It is their only contact with the environment, and in their suburban hearts they whine at the isolation, the rain, the mud, the monotony, the schools, the natives.

Often in the coffee-shop you will see a table filled with young men in green clothing, passing the time over coffee and soft drinks, communicating in their closed circle with a foreign tongue. They are so young, so clean cut and gauche, that their potential as fighting men seems if anything more unlikely than their chubby superiors'. They pass the time, they pass the time, they do not get into fights, they do not explore the wilderness, and they are french.

It is a pedigree of younger sons from families in St. Urbain, or Chicoutimi or the townships of Belchasse. Economic blankness, claustrophobia, perhaps an echo of *vingt-douze* legends, bring them into the forces. They group, they school, they take courses perhaps in radio technology; they are posted to the Pacific, to the furthest west point of Canada where, if they ever hiked up the beach to Rose Spit, they could see Alaska on a clear day. They pass the time.

One of them is Raoul Forrestier. He has been sitting here for an hour and a half, discussing cars, Guy Lafleur, the prime minister's wife; watching the other customers coming and going over his companions' shoulders. He drifts away from the group, his mind rewaking a dream from the night before as he hears two truck-loggers talk:

"I tell you – the rack on him. Seven points, no kidding. Biggest I ever seen!"

"Branch Seven is the place..."

"No I'm telling you, this feller Stays put. Got to be the one I seen there last spring. Even in velvets he was built like an elk. Next fall for sure I'll get him."

"Get him in the morning..."

"Fuckin' rights: camp out all night on the bridge. I'll get him."

And Raoul Fonestier has been dreaming of the deer too. Of endless dun herds, hooves clicking, passing before him over the muskeg. He has lingered in the Capex at the gun-rack, lovingly taken to himself a 30.30, seen himself tugging down the martini lever to reload, firing into the wave-like herd. It is the old glamour of childhood crazes at work. He is a boy still.

And he withdraws further, pale and certain in his vision, while his eyes take in abstractedly a table full of young natives. Normally he would watch them only in glances, covertly. The full mouth and body of one young girl, with her laughing black eyes, her carelessness of the destiny which leads her – they all know – down her mother's path. And the

444

beautiful young men, with naked gums, ten years away from beer-bellies and broken complexions.

But his mind is with the gun, with the two days, duty-free, ahead of him. The young indians sit, laughing, in their separate boredom, and he sees that he has money for the gun and the time to use it. He will rent a car – a pickup – he will go out and hunt deer on the muskeg. Most importantly, though he does not realize it, he will do this alone for his dream. He will brag to no one of his plans and he will go alone.

3

The dark blade settled between the rearsight's shoulders and travelled a little to the right. It dipped across the pale brow and steadied on the dark left eye. He eased it away slightly, aiming exactly between the staring eyes. One part of him remembered in time that the rifle was shooting four inches wide; another part noted how everything but the gun and the motionless face across the stream had lost focus, even the running water sound. In that instant the strain broke in – he realized he'd been holding his breath the whole time – the rifle began to leap slightly with each heartbeat. He lowered it and breathed deeply. The sound of the water rushed in. And a raven called, circling above the high forest roof.

The face before him merged back into its place on the bright gravel. He stepped out gingerly over the dark water on a rafting cedar bough, and along the crumbling bank. The shot would have been wasted anyway. Would have warned the deer.

He squats on the gravel spit, laying the rifle with care, and picks up the skull. Small enough to hold on the flat of his hand, it is still built massively in its own scale. It is the color of its gravel perch – dry from within though wet to touch from the lapping flicks of the stream. A flat head, snakey, the lower jaw hinged firmly into the skull, clacking in a dead bite when he releases it. The great overbite of the canines is a cold emblem of savagery – like a saurian fossil or a shark's jaw trophy – and he frowns at its mystery, his eyes going slightly out of focus as if he might clothe it again that way with flesh and fur and learn its name. The word comes suddenly – *loutre; l'outre* – as a blaze of dark, fearless eyes. Otter. It is a good omen not to have smashed it with an idle bullet. He cases it into his side pocket and picks up the rifle.

It has not felt right in these woods. His feet have betrayed him at every turn. Not just that he is a stranger under the trees, but that he has failed to condense himself into one simple being. He is out of balance. He had dreamed and foreseen how it would be, but now the clutter of his realities is a trammelling maze where he would walk straight.

And he had felt so straight, so clear this morning as he drove beside the calm inlet, with the truck and the gun, and the sun strobing along the spruce-ridge to his left. Till he had stopped by Blue Jackets Creek to give a ride to the young couple squatting by their rucksacks. They settled into the cab and within a minute their cool glances, their pachouli odour, their ease with themselves, upturned his patronage. He lost his grip on the helm, jarring the clutch clumsily as he climbed away from the inlet.

He lost himself, and his thoughts oscillated wildly between contempt, affection, communion, envy, confusion. He despised them as he would have on the base: then he was a generous, tolerant worldly wise man; then they held the answer to everything; secretly he was their brother; they were free spirits; he was a novice.

The 30.30 rested against the hippy's knee. "Going hunting?"

Raoul nodded, defensively. He did not like someone else to touch his gun. Or his dream.

"Bad time for it," the hippy said, easily. "Not much meat on them and you might get a doe."

"Sure, I'll be careful," he said, "just look around."

"We got all ours canned back in November" the girl said: "It's really good with rowanberries."

The hippy's hand rested on the gun barrel. Raoul winced. The hand was twice as big as his. The young man was huge and calm and knowledgeable. It seemed wrong and unfair.

He was rolling a cigarette now with a careful precision that belied the heavy fingers. "Remember the buck holds his head high" – he ran his tongue delicately along the paper – "though even then you can't be sure."

Raoul said "Sure, I know." He didn't know; he absorbed the lore. The girl looked out the window, laughing at the great parliament of ravens out on the gravel pits by the garbage dump.

"New gun?" the hippy gestured.

"Yes, I bought him this morning."

The girl moved to laugh at the 'him' but smiled and turned instead: "You're from Quebec?"

Raoul nodded.

"Quebec City?"

"Not too far. Across the river you know. Then Montreal for a while."

"Quebec is beautiful" she nodded gravely. "Really beautiful. Next to here."

Her friend murmured agreement, smiling as he inhaled from his smoke, ducking his chin. The rank Drum tobacco filled the cab. It seemed as exotic and dangerous as dope.

"You sighted the Winchester in yet?"

"No" Alain was in doubt.

"Should do, man – they get really shagged up in the crates sometimes. You want to stop along here someplace and I'll mark for you?"

He could not be unfriendly. He wanted these people to accept him. But his day was spoiled. He pulled over just past Watun Bridge, feeling as though he were following orders.

The other man picked two beer cans out of the ditch and walked up the road about fifty yards. Across the ditch was a big log pile, a mouldering mass of wasted timber from when the road went through. He set the cans up in front of a log's butt end and stepped back onto the highway. "O.K." he waved.

Raoul was shooting diagonally across the road. He was nervous of the girl beside him at the truck window, and of the hippy down the road not quite safely out of the way. He eased six shells into the gun, trying not to fumble, and yanked at the martini lever. That felt better. He was, after all, good with an FN on the ranges. What would the hippy make of that? Control was coming back.

He aimed the light gun, breathing carefully, sighting low on the cans because of the short range. He fired and missed. The sound of the shot came crackling back from some echo point on the muskeg. He aimed higher this time and missed again. He flushed and lowered the rifle to inspect the sights. The girl grinned vaguely, unconcerned. He flicked the lever again but when he aimed, the trigger wouldn't pull. He couldn't close the lever, pulled it down again, and the shell in the breech jerked upright, clamped in by its flange. He could not release it, shame overcoming his tenuous poise. "The son of a bitch jammed hup" he muttered to the girl.

The hippy sloped easily, bored, back down the pavement, buttoning his collar. He took the gun. "Yeh, they do that" he nodded, "You've really gotta slam the lever up." He took a Russell knife from his belt. Raoul fell at once in love with its leaf-shaped blade. This young man was so easy with his world, knowing the mysteries. The knife point twisted and the shell fell out onto the road. The hippy slammed the lever home twice and replaced his knife. "You're shooting wide," He said. "I saw your second bullet hit the wood."

He turned casually and aimed back across the road. His left hand did not even close on the stock. He fired and the lower can leaped, spouting ditch-water. Again, and the other flew out onto the verge. He handed the rifle back. "About four inches to the right" he said, his calm grey eyes resting for the first time straight on Raoul's. "Aim to the left, and you can fix it when you get home. See – the fore sight slides in that groove if you take the guard off." He smiled down at the soldier: "I'll set you up some more cans."

But it was not Raoul's weapon anymore. He ejected the last shell. "No, it's O.K." he said "I'll do it later." And rushed on: "Where you guys heading?"

"Down to Port" said the girl. "Are you going that far?"

"Oh sure" he shrugged "I'll take you. I've got nothing to do."

He dropped them outside Port Clements and drove on South towards Tlell. He'd go for ten minutes and when they were out of the way he'd come back. He didn't know what to do with his day.

And down the hill, by Kumdis Bridge, a deer crossed the road. It was big and unhurried; did not look up. It must be a buck.

The hunting spell reawoke: he pulled the truck in by the bridge, loaded the gun in the cab, and slithered fast down the bank into the trees. Inside there was frost on the moss still and a smothering silence. There was no sign of the deer.

He carried the gun at port across his body like a movie soldier; knelt to touch a bright pile of droppings like a movie indian. The hard black pellets were cold. He followed what might have been a trail once and floundered, breathing heavily, over logs and oozing pools, along the river bank and so to the resting place of the skull.

Now, he must take control of his day. He looks around. There is a trail, or clear ground anyway, across the stream again where a solitary crab-apple tree lies beaver-felled on the moss. He jumps from the gravel with a bootful of water and looks down at the litter of adzeshavings the beavers have left. The tree's stump points nakedly upwards, chipped round symmetrically as if by axe strokes. He would like to see a wild beaver.

He follows the untidy line of the river bank. There is more sky ahead, more light. For the swamp is not interminable. Someone, sixty years ago, cleared half an acre of the bottom, cut dykes and put stone drains down, and then left his forlorn dream of a homestead and family to die in a different ditch on Paeschendale. And Raoul is approaching a clearing of sorts – a space of mated couchgrass, hedged in by the grey embrangling of the wild apple trees –. The ditches are vestigial now – the roots of the coarse grass lie in water – but the clearing is firm. Frost has eaten into the mud and the grass mat will preserve it till nearly midsummer. The crabapples braid into one another – they are cruel, thorny trees and Raoul's toque is snatched by one branch, his left eye gouged by and streaming from its neighbor.

He crouches almost to his knees to win the clearing. When he rises the deer is watching him, thirty feet away across the grass patch. A phenomenal, alert stillness awaits him in the grey head and huge black eyes. The animal is poised for panic, but its nature wills stillness upon it. Raoul's mind is a bloody, racing confusion, but his nature, which he reaches for within, teaches him not to extend that to the deer. His heart knocks, but he fixes his eyes steadily on the animal's and keeps them from the gun which now – unprepared – he must load. He eases down the lever, imperceptibly, then with a prayer slams the breech closed. He winces at the sound, the movement, but his eyes hold steady. A muscle jumps on the deer's shoulder. The hind legs almost gather, but not quite.

He brings the gun round; touches the butt to his shoulder while the muzzle still points away across his body. His left arm swings slowly upwards. The deer holds still, staring. Raoul's left eye streams from its twig-lashing. He brings the sights to rest above the deep alert eyes. Then his finger jerks. Echoes rifle the clearing. The deer's ear is fanned by the bullet. Incredibly, the animal does not move.

Raoul has reworked the lever without thinking, straight after firing. The gun is still up and he is allowed another chance. *Four inches wide* he curses himself. The sights settle by the deer's right eye. He fires. The deer's whole neck and head flail backwards as though to a great hammerblow, and the body crumples down. The rifle breech is open, oozing cordite, and he has killed his deer. He steps towards the body.

But then, horribly, the deer is up again, or its hind quarters are up. Panic seeds the little grass plot. The animal forces its broken head, its paralyzed front limbs forward with a frenzied rabbit-like working of its back legs. It ploughs itself forwards, colliding with a young spruce tree, through the crabapples and into another open space beyond. It rams itself into a choked ditch and on again.

Raoul is dancing behind it in an agony of remorse and fear and the deer panic charging in his own blood. He would like to run away. He rushes upon the creature, the pathetic upturned tail, and does not know what he should do. But the seconds pass – from a mere foot away he fires the heavy bullet into the back of the deer's skull. The head is nailed to the grass, the body leaps once, electrically, and is still. It is over.

He lays the rifle in the grass and walks round and round the body, beside himself. He is waiting for his heart to still, for the possibility of balance to return. He knows that his crime is not to have done the thing but to have done it wrong. And when the next part comes, the cleaning of the carcass, he must be at peace with himself and calm among the witness trees.

He has not done this before but he knows how to. He kneels with his sheath knife and slices at the side of the deer's throat. The eyes are glazed into an impossible deep blue of their own – there is none in the sky. He watches his own face and hands, foreshortened in the blue mirror as in a teapot's side. Not very much blood rolls from the jugular: so much has been wasted already through the shattered skull and the pumping, running legs.

The stomach next. He tugs the deer onto its side and the legs swing against him, following gravity as if they were scarcely joined to the body. He wills himself into calm, rightness. He cuts from the breastbone, down through the long hammock of the belly. Already he knows that it is a doe (that had glared back at him as he chased the poor cripple down the clearing) but he notes the mild genital now, seeing human anatomy as he has all along.

He plunges his hands around the slick heat of the bowels. The smell comes up at him of rabbit guts, his only reference. Do people smell so? The bundle of intestines comes out heavy, but easily. There is no blood in the body. Only when he pulls the vivid liver free of its roots. He wipes his hands, front and back along the grass. A pink, flecked membrane covers the breast-cave, taut. He pierces it with his knife, and with a long sigh the warm, moss-scented breath comes back at him. The human heart is there, and after the lungs, with two more knife strokes the body is clean. He has done this right. He is redeeming himself.

But a shape has fallen free with the last knife stroke. Shrouded in its caul, the still eye and the smiling, lipless rabbit mouth of the foetus discovers him. He stabs the knife again and again into the frosty grass roots – to clean it, to clean himself. He is almost numb. Under one of the appletrees he slices out turf with his knife and chilled fingers and re-buries the fawn in limbo. He would pray for its rest and his atonement if there were words.

Carrying the carcass out is clumsy too, but the woods do not entrap him. He guesses at a drier route, circling round on the higher ground through the big trees; and soon he hears a truck thundering over the road bridge ahead and knows that he has chosen well. His load lightens. And as if in token of that, another deer trots through the shadows at his right, slips round an old cedar, and stops to stare back at him. He is seduced, outside himself, considering the feat of the hunter who, with one deer yoked across his shoulders, brings down another.

The deer is facing him directly and something in the forest air decrees that it shall not move. Raoul lets the body slip off his shoulders – it falls fast, top-heavy, and heaps against his leg. He has the hammer on half-cock this time. He pulls it back as he raises the gun, aims wide, and fires. The deer falls and then, like a shadow, is gone.

He comes back to himself – that the stricken animal may escape to die in pain is like a knife stroke. He lurches down the slope, jolting over tree-roots, his breath coming in gasps in a dowse of his victim's state. There is fur scattered everywhere – down the fibrous cedar bark and over the moss – and then, a few feet off, the first great scarlet star of blood upon the ground. And despite himself his brain begins to reason that the creature cannot get far, thus hurt; despite himself the thrill of tracking by a blood-spoon whispers to him out of his childhood reading. His breath comes easily. He is detached and keen.

The track is easy to follow. The blood is brilliant against the moss, the dead wood, the huckleberry stems. But when, across a log, he sees the deer, it is no longer a voyageur's quarry. It is so small and mute, furled gently on the ground, like a faun breathing. He kills it. A doe again, and very small, scarcely a yearling. He cleans it efficiently, his hands working across a cold distance, and drags it back up the hillside. Overhead and back the way he comes, two ravens invoke the forest's echoes. He is observed.

He leaves the smaller carcass and carries the first deer the last two hundred yards to the road. He lays it on the grass verge and tugs down the tailgate. A car is cresting Kumdis hill and his impulse is to leap like a thief to cover, but there isn't time. The driver sounds his horn three times, cheerily, as he swoops past; a passenger waves. Raoul slides the corpse along the truck bed.

Back in the forest he loses his way. It seems an hour of casting around on the slopes, looking for a landmark. As the afternoon wanes the shadows seem to spill out and eddy across the roots and brushwood. His eyes remember nothing. He is almost ready to work down to the river and retrace his whole journey when, a marker leaps at him. Draped on a low stump is a long, gritty shred of lung-flesh. And a few feet further on the gun and the deer at last.

Yet both piles of guts were far from this place. Something (the ravens?) had dropped this in his path. There is no sound from them now. The offal gleams obscenely against the moss as he trudges back to the road.

4

He'll drive up past Port Clements with his window rolled down, steering with one hand. He'll stop at the other bridge over Kumdis on the Masset road to wash the stink off his hands. And some Haida kids will be waiting across the bridge for a ride and he'll wave them over. There'll be three in the cab with him and one behind with the deer.

For a while they won't talk much, the two girls embarrassed, murmuring and giggling to each other, the boy remote, staring out with his cheek against the window glass. Raoul will be intensely aware of the girl next to him, her thigh pressed to his, her mocking eyes (however shy) when he glances her way. And the two of them off again in uncontrolled giggling.

450

Then there'll be a hand slamming on the roof of the cab and, jittery, he'll tread hard on the brakes and throw them all forward. Behind him the rear window will be running wet and red, and through that film the boy in the back grinning sardonically with teeth gaping, and brandishing a jug of Kelowna Red.

The boy in the cab will roll down the window and reach out and back for the wine. As they speed up he'll offer it across the girls. Raoul will hesitate and then take it, tilting it awkwardly squeezed between the girl Mary and the steering wheel. The wine will go back and forth, and the boy behind will hammer for his share, and they'll all begin to talk and laugh, while Raoul's speech slurs and the dusk grows happy.

The furthest girl Teresa will say "Hey come on down to the village, blue eyes." And he'll say "Sure, I always meant to go there." And all four of them in the cab will be laughing wildly while the girls chant "Beautiful blue, beautiful blue!"

"Hey, good-looking" Teresa will say "You gonna come to a party?" The boy will laugh nakedly in the darkening cab and say "Yeah, we'll stop at the bakery first" and they'll be laughing again because the bakery's next door to the liquor store.

It'll be dark almost at the top of Garbage Dump Hill, and a deer's eyes will glow out on the road. Raoul will swerve madly and the truck's wheels will wrench and skid on the gravel shoulder and almost lose control. But they'll laugh, laugh helplessly with the jug almost empty and the boy in the back beating on the cab roof and yelling "Goin down fast, goin down faast" as they plunge down towards the inlet where New Masset is fairy lights on the dark running tide.

Mary will lay her head on his shoulder and the boy Adam will put his arm round her sister and the postillion Henry will scream "Yea-aiii" as they tear along the inlet. "He's my cousin" Mary will say "He's reel crazy." Laughter will take them into the town to Collison Avenue: "Collision Corner, Collision Corner" the girls will chant, and Adam will roll the window down and fire the dead bottle onto the church lawn.

At the liquor store the postillion will jump down and Raoul will fumble a $10 bill from his pocket – "Put that in the kitty" – and hold it out. And Adam will smirk "Yeah, put it in your pussy" and Teresa will slap him hard on his brow and he'll laugh.

Then they'll run the dark and alien miles down to the village and on a ways, up the hill over the church, till the girls shout "Stop". The truck will come to a jolting halt and Raoul will know he's had too much already and his dream of Mary beside him will start to fade even as she grabs his arm by the house door.

They'll troop into the neat warm room where an old woman looks up from the stove. And she'll mutter *Tchi-ay* in disapproval at their state, yet grin in welcome too. She'll nod and nod her head at Raoul and ask his name and when he says it Mary will cry "No, he's Beautiful Blue Eyes" and Teresa will say "A reel French lover" and the old lady will cluck and chuckle and tell him to sit down, they've got no manners, they're *lumga* drunk.

451

In that small room, with its mirrors and gleaming stove and a photograph on the mantle of an old Haida man with a Hawk frontlet, the old one will take him over and say he must call her *Nonnie* Grandmother like the girls; and she will chuckle a lot but disapprove of the bottles going round. And Henry, the postillion, will stand apart by the door sneering.

To Raoul the words will come harder as the girls chatter on and the wine keeps ending up in his hand. But he'll cling to the immense affection that wells out of him to the old lady. To be able to sense the mother in this stranger from a hostile race, to feel what home and belonging mean after this year of prison life on the bases; after the rivalries, the bravado, the pin-ups on the walls.

He'll make of her the respectable Gaspe matriarch she resembles, and blush for her protectively when the youngsters make lewd jests and say they've brought down "a french stud for Nonnie." But she will laugh and laugh at that with them and poke his arm and pinch his chin and say he's "too skinny for me – I need something I can get a goood hold on." Raoul will love her the more for breaking his illusion of age and restraint.

He'll know he's letting go of something. That tomorrow he'll be starting in an empty square. Or he'll believe this anyway, and a wave of vertigo will wash around the walls upon him, as though he were poised to jump from a cliff and take his chances with the tides.

Another grandson Jimmy, maybe 13 years old, will bang into the house and grow shy instantly at the company. He'll ask about the deer in the truck and Raoul will say "Do you want them? Can you use them? Sure – they're yours. They'd only waste I mean." Nonnie will say she'd really like some fresh meat. "Henry never hunts for me no more." She'll glare at the door: "Lazy dog!"

The two boys will go out with Jimmy and carry the carcasses round to the back porch, kicking the dogs away. Raoul will offer to help and half-rise only to sink back to the couch as they laugh at him.

He will feel so fond of these people, yet struggle to keep his eyes from rolling upwards out of weariness and liquor.

Then Henry of the glittering eyes and impatient frame will be back at the door. "Hey, Row, I got to get down to Delkatla and pick up some shakes. Can I take the truck? I won't be half an hour."

He'll see he could never like Henry, but he's included. "Oh sure" he'll wave and fumble anxiously for the keys, but they're still in the dash.

Teresa will say "No, don't you let him take it – he'll smash it up for sure. He's always pulling mad stunts like that – he's crazy."

"No, it's O.K." he'll say.

And Mary: "Henry, you know you got no license now. You stay here." But Henry will have gone.

Raoul will slip down to the floor, his back against the chesterfield, and try to catch all their eyes. Maybe a minute later, it seems, he'll half-clamber up again, jolting out of sleep and realize he has been talking steadily but won't be able to remember what or for how long. He'll see some echoes in the others' eyes of the lanes and fields of his uncle's farm. And he'll realize that he has not been pretending to anyone and that they accept this and that it has all slipped by. He drifts again.

452

Then the girls will be by the door suddenly saying "See you Nonnie" and "Goodnight." Mary of the full mouth and limbs will catch his gaze for a moment and his eyes will reach up feverishly to salvage from the drunken shuttle a moment's touch for the darkness of her eyes.

There'll be no one in the room but himself and Nonnie and he'll mumble that he must leave her.

"You ain't going to do your nonnie no harm" she'll say. "You stay now. You're not going *any*where." And she'll squeeze his shoulder, laughing softly, as she limps by.

He'll hear her moving in the other room and he'll struggle out of his jacket from the stove's heat before he lapses into sleep. Maybe tomorrow, on the street, they won't even know him. Maybe they don't trust the things he has been learning. Never mind the truck and the gun – bad thoughts – never mind tomorrow.

His pocket will knock hollowly against the chesterfield's arm and he'll fish out the forgotten skull of the otter. The glow from the stove's grill will play over its deep eyes as he struggles to focus on them and bring back into his grasp the day's contrarities.

And Nonnie will be back at her door saying "What *is* that you got. Geee you're a funny feller, eh?" And he'll relinquish the otter's mask to the trembling hearthrug and slip away from everything while the old woman's voice is still speaking.

The tenses dissolve on that tableau in the hushed living room. Thirty miles down the inlet, over the muskeg, a raven shifts on its roost, dreaming under the cedar canopy high above Kumdis Creek. The water below checks and swirls blindly around the sunken branches. The stars of Orion hang, angled in the sharp January sky. The islands linger on the Pacific.

CONTRIBUTORS

Seamus Heaney of Ireland has published, among many books, *Death of A Naturalist, Door Into The Dark, Wintering Out, North, Field Work, Station Island, Sweeney Astray, The Haw Lantern* and *Seeing Things*. The sequence *Turas* appeared in *Exile* in 1973 and is not collected elsewhere.

Mercè Rodoreda of Spain is the finest of the contemporary Catalan novelists. Her best known book, *La Plaça del Diamant*, has been translated into more than a half-dozen languages, and it appeared in English as *The Pigeon Girl*. David H. Rosenthal, himself a poet, translated a collection of her work: *My Christina And Other Stories*. He is also the author of *Hard Bop: Jazz and Black Music 1955–1965*.

Leonard Cohen of Canada is a novelist, poet and songwriter who has published *Let Us Compare Mythologies, The Spice Box Of The Earth, The Energy of Slaves, Book of Mercy*, and *Death Of A Lady's Man*. A very substantial section of *Death Of A Lady's Man* first appeared in *Exile*.

Mavis Gallant of Canada, who has lived in Paris since the early 1950s, has written, among others: *My Heart Is Broken, The Pegnitz Junction, From The Fifteenth District, Home Truths, Overhead in a Balloon: Stories of Paris, Paris Notebooks: Essays and Reviews*, and *In Transit. Mau To Lew: The Maurice Ravel – Lewis Carroll Friendship* appeared in *Exile* in 1980 and is not collected elsewhere.

Ludwig Zeller of Canada has published more than a dozen books: *Mirages, Dream Woman, Alphacollage, In The Country Of The Antipodes, 50 Collages, The Marble Head and Other Poems, The Ghost's Tattoos*, and *To Saw The Beloved to Pieces Only When Necessary*, published by Exile Editions.

Victor-Lévy Beaulieu of Canada, one of the most prolific prose writers in Québec, is the author of several novels published by Exile Editions: *Jos Connaissant, A Québécois Dream, Satan Belhumeur*, and *Steven Le Hérault*.

Diane Keating of Canada has published three books of poetry, *In Dark Places, No Birds Or Flowers*, and *The Optic Heart*, and a novel, *The Crying Out*.

Italo Calvino of Italy was the author of many prose works: *The Watcher, Invisible Cities, t zero, The Castle of Crossed Destinies, If On A Winter's Night A Traveler, The Path To The Nest Of Spiders*.

Michel Deguy of France, central to that country's contemporary poetry, has published some twenty books, among them: *Fragment du cadastre, Biefs, Ouï dire, Actes, Poèmes 1960–1970, Reliefs* and *Jumelages suivi de Made in USA*. He is also the editor of the journal, *Po&sie*.

Robert Markle of Canada was a distinguished painter, sculptor, and maker of idiosyncratic whirley-gigs. He was also a man of letters and journalist. He died in 1990.

Timothy Findley of Canada, one of the country's finest novelists, has published with *Exile* from the beginning. His novels include: *The Last Of The Crazy People, The Wars, Famous Last Words, Dinner Along The Amazon, Not Wanted On The Voyage,* and *Stones*. His most recent book is *Inside Memory*.

John Montague of Ireland, one of two contributing editors to *Exile*, has published much of his verse in the quarterly. Books by John Montague that have been published by Exile Editions are: *The Dead Kingdom, Selected Poems, Mount Eagle,* and *The Love Poems: John Montague*.

Marie-Claire Blais of Canada has appeared often in *Exile*, starting with Volume 1 Number 1. Her novels include: *Mad Shadows, A Season In The Life Of Emmanuel, The Manuscripts of Pauline Archange, St Lawrence Blues, Deaf to the City, Anna* and *Nights In The Underground*.

Barry Callaghan of Canada, poet, prose writer, translator, is the author of: *The Hogg Poems And Drawings, The Black Queen Stories, As Close As We Came, Stone Blind Love,* and *The Way The Angel Spreads Her Wings*.

Yannis Ritsos of Greece was the most prolific of modern Greek poets. He wrote over twenty-five books of poetry. He was translated widely on the Continent and Louis Aragon called him the greatest European poet of his time. Our translators were Nikos Tsingos and Gwendolyn MacEwen of Canada. Mr Tsingos, born in Greece, is a musician and singer. His then wife, the poet Gwendolyn MacEwen, worked with him on two of Ritsos' major long poems, *Helen* and *Orestes*, published in *Trojan Women* by Exile Editions.

David Annesley of Canada, was born in Ireland and came to Toronto in 1963. He began drawing for the Book Pages of the now defunct *Toronto Telegram* in 1968. His work then appeared in *The New York Times, The National Review* and *The Atlantic Monthly*. He died young by drowning in 1977. Exile Editions published *The Annesley Drawings* in 1980.

Pierre Jean Jouve of France, who died in 1976, was the *doyen* of French poetry. His *Collected Poems* appeared in four volumes from Mercure de France. He was the author of a famous novel, *Paulina 1880*, and he was awarded the *Grand Prix des Lettres*.

Michel Lambeth of Canada, among the country's fine photographers, exhibited throughout the world until he died in 1978. *Nuescapes* was published during his lifetime as a limited edition.

Robert Zend of Canada was among the most singular and experimental writers in the country. His works include *Zero to One, My Friend Jerónimo, Arbormundi*, and *Beyond Labels. OAB*, in two volumes, published by Exile Editions, appeared in 1985, the year he died.

Jean Benoît of Canada has been a resident of Paris since 1947. His works have seldom been shown publicly, but *The Necrophiliac* appeared at the International Surrealist Exhibition in 1965, and so too *The Bulldog* in 1968. The *Object To Contain A Mummified Head* was exhibited in France in the summer of 1992.

Derek Mahon of Ireland has published several works of poetry, including *Night-Crossing, Beyond Howth Head, Lives, Poems 1962–1978, The Snow Party, Courtyards In Delft, The Hunt By Night, Antarctica, The Bacchae*, and *Selected Poems*.

Margaret Atwood of Canada has published poetry regularly in *Exile*, starting with Volume 1, Number 1. As a poet, she is well known for: *The Circle Game, The Animals In That Country, Procedures for Underground, The Journals of Susanna Moodie, Power Politics, You Are Happy, Two-Headed Poems, True Stories* and *Interlunar*, and *Selected Poems*.

Jacques Ferron of Canada was a story-teller who provided the most inclusive, complete account of his uncertain country, Québec. It was an account, rendered in dozens of tales, that was mischievous and mythic, appropriate to the man who was both a medical doctor and founder of the Rhinoceros political party. His novels published by Exile Editions are: *The Cart, Papa Boss* and *Quince Jam*, and his masterpiece, *The Penniless Redeemer*.

Tibor Déry of Hungary, who died in 1977, was one of Hungary's greatest writers. After surrealist and dadaist beginnings, he wrote post-war novels of such searing reality that he was imprisoned from 1957 to 1960. His novels include: *The Answer, Mr. G.A. in X, The Excommunicator, Imaginary Report about an American Rock Festival*, and *Cher Beau Père*.

René Lagorre of France, a painter, has exhibited in Paris and Washington.

John Meredith of Canada is a painter whose work is in many private collections and in such museums as the Art Gallery of Ontario, the Norman Mackenzie Art Gallery in Regina, The Vancouver Art Gallery, the Philadelphia Museum of Art, the Museum of Modern Art in New York, and the National Gallery of Canada.

S.W. Hayter of England settled in Paris in 1926 and opened a studio at rue Campagne-Premiere 17 a year later. After 1933, his studio was known as

Atelier 17, where he developed revolutionary graphic techniques. In 1940 he went to the United States and opened Atelier 17 in New York, but in 1950 he returned to Paris. His students came from all over the world to Atelier 17, presently on rue Didot. He was featured in *Exile* Vol. 8, Number 3/4, and he was always an advocate for *Exile* in Europe. He died in 1988.

Guillevic of France was born at Carnac, the place of sacred stones, in 1907. His christian name is Eugène but he signs his poems Guillevic. He is one of the most highly regarded of living French poets. Among his books are: *Terraqué, Exécutoire, Gagner, Sonnets, Sphère, Carnac,* and a fine bilingual edition translated by Denise Levertov, *Selected Poems.*

Ruth Andrishak of Canada published her first, and as far as we know, only story in *Exile* in 1979. *The Night The Rabbit Chewed My Hair Off* also was given the CBC fiction award in that year.

Louis de Niverville of Canada, whose paintings are in major collections in the United States and Canada, has had a distinguished career as a painter. *Family Album* is a work of some sixty objects.

Roch Carrier of Canada is one of the most prolific and popular writers from Québec. Among his many novels are *La Guerre–Yes Sir! Floralie–Where Are You?, Is It The Sun Philbert, The Garden of Delights, Heartbreaks Along The Road, Progress Of A Very Wise Child,* and *Canada Je t'aime.*

Breyten Breytenbach of South Africa published his first volume of poetry in 1964. Through six subsequent volumes of verse, as well as a collection of short stories and a short experimental novel, he won wide acclaim as the most important living poet of the Afrikaans language. The polarities of his work (Africa and Europe, White and Black, tenderness and violence...) were enhanced by living in exile in Paris after 1960. This condition was forced on him through his marriage to a Vietnamese woman who was branded as "Colored" and hence not socially acceptable in terms of South Africa's rigid racialistic legislation. His unrelenting crusade for human dignity and against apartheid won him wide international recognition but inevitably increased his private agonies. And in 1975, determined to express his convictions in other than aesthetic terms (he is also highly regarded as a painter) he returned to South Africa in disguise where he was arrested and tried on several counts under the so-called 'Terrorism Act'. In November 1975 he was sentenced to 9 years' imprisonment and all efforts to appeal against the sentence (whose harshness shocked even his Prosecutor) were quashed by the courts. After serving much of his sentence he was released and now lives in Paris again. Our translator is André Brink, man of letters, and one of that country's most important novelists.

Athol Fugard of South Africa is a dramatist whose works include: *Hello And Goodbye, Boesman And Lena, People Are Living There,* and *The Bloodknot. A Lesson from Aloes* had its world premier outside South Africa in Montréal, performed by the Centaur Theatre Company in 1980, directed by

457

Athol Fugard. Recently, he received The Obie Award for drama in New York.

David Goldblatt of South Africa is that country's most important photographer. Among collections of his work are: *Some Afrikanners Photographed*, and *On The Mines*. His photographs have been published all around the world and are in many collections, including the Museum of Modern Art, New York. In 1976, introducing these photographs, he wrote:

> "I have little faith in the strength of these photographs to stand unaided in Winnipeg, Ottawa or Saskatoon, or for that matter in London, Wollongong or Berlin. Not that I think them to be without merit. But because, I wonder, how can anyone not steeped in the life, ways, obsessions, graces, laws and particulars of this place and people, discern what is embedded of us even in these pale rubbings?
>
> It would be beyond me to convey in any number of words, yet I wish that I could so concentrate these few that you would have the same intimate grasp of these images as any child or adult from Naledi or Dube, Yeoville or Pageview.
> Most of the photographs were made in 1972 and 1973 in two parts of Johannesburg:
>
> 1. Soweto, the dormitory townships of the Africans who work in Johannesburg.
>
> 2. Hillbrow and other Northern Suburbs of white Johannesburg."

Jerzy Kosinski of the United States was born in Poland but resided in the U.S. from 1957 until he died by suicide in 1991. Among his novels are *The Painted Bird, Steps, Being There, The Devil Tree, Cockpit*, and *Pinball*. One of the strongest supporters of Exile in its beginnings, his essay, *The Art of The Self*, appeared complete in Volume 1, Number 1, in 1972.

R. Murray Schafer of Canada is a prolific contemporary composer, perhaps the most accomplished experimental composer in the country. He is also an author. His books include *The Book Of Noise, The Music of the Environment, The Tuning of the World*, and *Ariadne*, published by *Exile* in 1977.

Morley Callaghan of Canada wrote over twenty books: *Strange Fugitive, It's Never Over, A Broken Journey, Such Is My Beloved, More Joy In Heaven, The Loved And The Lost, The Many Colored Coat, A Passion in Rome, A Time For Judas, A Fine And Private Place*, and *A Wild Old Man On The Road*, and others. He died in 1990.

Ascher/Straus of the United States have published several works of fiction, including: *The Other Planet, The Menaced Assassin, Letter To An Unkown Woman*, and *Red Moon Red Lake*.

Robert Marteau of France is a unique voice among French poets. His books translated and published by Exile Editions are: *Atlante, Treatise On White And Tincture, Interlude, Pentecost, Pig Skinning, Mount Royal, River without End*, and *Venice At Her Mirror*.

Gwendolyn MacEwen of Canada died in the fall of 1987. Her works included: *Selah, The Drunken Clock, The Rising Fire, A Breakfast for Barbarians, The Shadow-Maker, The Armies of the Moon, Magic Animals, The Fire-Eaters, The T.E. Lawrence Poems, Earthlight, Noman's Land* and *Afterworlds*, which won the Governor-General's Award for poetry in 1987. Exile Editions published her play and translations, *Trojan Women*.

Yehuda Amichai of Israel has been a contributing editor to *Exile* since 1972, wherein he has since published several sequences of poems and a play. His books include: *Poems, Songs Of Jerusalem And Myself, Amen, Time, Love Poems, Great Tranquillity: Questions and Answers*, and *Selected Poetry*. *Travels* was published by Exile Editions.

Michel Beaulieu of Canada was the most productive and the most genuinely experimental of Québec's younger poets until his sudden death in 1985. Exile Editions has published *Spells Of Fury, Kaleidoscope* and *Countenances*.

Judith Thompson of Canada is in the forefront of the country's dramatists. Her works include *White Biting Dog, Tornado, Pink, The Crack Walker*, and *I am Yours*, published complete in *Exile*. Her collection, *The Other Side Of The Dark*, was given the Governor General's award, as was *White Biting Dog*.

Dennis Burton of Canada has paintings and drawings in many important collections including those of The National Gallery, Ottawa, The Art Gallery of Ontario and The Metropolitan Museum of Art, New York. Over the last fifteen years, there have been several retrospective showings of his work. Currently, he lives on the west coast.

André Frénaud of France, one of the dominant voices in that country, has published *Poèmes de Brandebourg, Il n'y a pas de paradis, L'Etape dans la clairière, Depuis toujours dêja, La sorcière de Rome*, and others. John Montague has translated a selection of his verse, *Novembre*.

Joy Kogawa of Canada is a poet who has published *The Splintered Moon, A Choice of Dreams, Jericho Road*, and novelist. Her prose works are: *Obasan* and *Itsuka*.

Yehia Hakki of Egypt was, after the Fifties, among the most important writers in the Arab world. He published his first story in 1925, the same year that he graduated in law. After that he played a prominent role in cultural affairs in Cairo, publishing several collections of his stories and editing an important literary/political journal.

Claude Gauvreau of Canada for twenty-five years, until his death in 1971 by suicide, wrote poems, plays, short stories, essays, prefaces, public letters and manifestos. But he published very little: only two small books of poems, so that when he died he was almost entirely unknown. His friends and admirers were those painters who banded together around the now famous Bourduas and Riopelle in the late Forties and throughout the Fifties. They were called the Automatistes. Their roots were in André Breton and Surréalism, and indirectly, they were related to the Abstract Expressionists of New York. Borduas, Riopelle, Gauvreau, and the others, were all powerful personalities, but he was the lone writer, and his was a key role. Their collective effort was not only aesthetic, but socio-philosophical, and he was the needed Porte-Parole out on the firing line. He collaborated in 1947 in the writing of the first Québec revolutionary manifesto, *Refus Global*, and he appeared at the subsequent political events of consequence, taking on all comers, denouncing the reactionary church, the political and poetic hacks, defending always that freedom of speech and print so rare in Québec until very recently. It is fair to say that all his life he had little regard for his own social or financial position. He died as he lived; poor and alone except for a few friends and admirers. His complete works have since been published in Québec. Recently, Exile Editions published his collected plays, *Entrails*.

Gérald Godin of Canada is the author of several books of poetry, including Poèmes et Cantos. He was a cabinet minister in the Parti Québecois, a party whose political aim is to separate from Canada in some form or other.

Tomi Ungerer, born in Strassburg, is now resident in Ireland. His books, satirical, and for children, have been published in numerous countries. He has won countless awards and prizes, including The Society of Illustrators gold medal, and The Art Director's Club Award for best children's book, and he has had major exhibitions and retrospectives of his paintings, constructions, and drawings on the Continent over the past two decades.

Margaret Avison of Canada, twice winner of the Governor General's award, is central to any consideration of Canadian poetry. Her books spanning four decades of sustained work, are: *Winter Sun, The Dumbfounding, sunblue, No Time,* and *Selected Poems*.

Harry Somers of Canada is one of the country's outstanding composers. He is versatile, having written orchestral and chamber music, pieces for chorus and solo voice, four ballets (including *The House of Atreus*), three operas (including *Louis Riel*), and much incidental music. His commissions have come from such diverse institutions as the Koussevitzky Foundation, Pan-American Union, the National Ballet of Canada, The American Wind

Symphony, and the Swingle Singers. His most recent work is *Mario The Magician*, an opera. *Kyrie*, first performed in Rome, was published in its entirety in *Exile* in 1973.

Irving Layton of Canada has over forty published books. He is one of the most passionate, grave, and technically accomplished poets of his time. *Selected Poems 1945–89: A Wild Peculiar Joy* contains all his most important poems.

Paul Celan of Germany, one of the most important poets to write in German, was born into a Jewish family in 1920. His parents were killed in the Holocaust. His sense of loss and suffering could not be healed. He died, a suicide, by drowning in 1970. The sequence of poems published in *Exile* became part of a splendid bilingual edition, *Paul Celan: Poems*, translated by Michael Hamburger.

Hugh Graham of Canada has published fiction and is a dramatist, essayist and broadcaster. *Where The Sun Don't Shine*, appearing complete in *Exile* in 1981, was his first published play.

Joe Rosenblatt of Canada, a singular and adventurous poet, has published, among many collections of poems and drawings, the *Bumblebee Dithyramb* and *Topsoil*, and with Exile Editions, he has published *The Sleeping Lady*, *Escape From The Glue Factory*, and *The Kissing Goldfish of Siam*.

Mary Meigs of Canada, born in the United States, has lived in Québec for nearly two decades. She is a distinguished painter, and has published *Illustrations For Two Books by Marie-Claire Blais*, with Exile Editions. She has also published two important books of memoirs: *Lily Briscoe: A Self Portrait* and *The Medusa Head*.

Thomas Kinsella of Ireland is among that country's most important poets. His books incude: *Another September, Downstream, Nightwalker and Other Poems, Notes From The Land Of The Dead, Poems: 1956–1973* and *Peppercanister Poems: 1972–1978*. He has also translated *The Tain*.

Alexandre Amprimoz of Canada is a poet, translator, linguist and story teller, and the author of over twenty books. His collection of stories, *Too Many Popes*, appeared in 1990 with Exile Editions.

Hannah Maynard of Canada was an extraordinary photographer who lived in Victoria at the turn of the century. Her work was edited by Claire Weissman Wilks and published by Exile Editions in *The Magic Box: The Eccentric Genius of Hannah Maynard*.

Miodrag Pavlović of Serbia is a poet, translator, essayist, and short story writer. Among his works are: *87 Persaura, Oktave*, and *Svetli i Tamni Praznici*. *Singing at the Whirlpool* was published in 1983, and *A Voice Locked in Stone* followed in 1987.

Mario Mascarelli of Serbia is an artist who is well-known in the republics that once were Yugoslavia.

Jennifer Rankin of Australia was a poet, and the author of one play. Introducing *From the Mud Hut* in *Exile* in 1979, Margaret Atwood wrote:

> "I first met Jennifer Rankin in England, as she was on her way to Australia and I to Venice. Later I stayed with her in Sydney after my visit to the Adelaide Poetry Festival in February 1978. At this time she was feeling very high. Her first major book of poetry had been accepted for publication in England by Secker & Warburg, and she was looking forward to this as an extension beyond Australia, where she was already well-known both as a poet and as a playwright, author of the controversial play, *Bees*. Three weeks after I left for Canada, she discovered that she had cancer. She underwent chemotherapy, with no positive results. Finally she turned to meditation, and began to improve almost immediately. She is currently practising meditation under the supervision of a medical doctor who speculates that meditation improves the body's natural immunity system and allows it to combat cancer.
>
> This would be unnecessary information if the poems in *From the Mud Hut* had been composed under ordinary circumstances. In fact, they were all written in the three weeks between the time I left Australia and the time Jennifer Rankin made the discovery that she had cancer. A number of them accurately predict the process she was later to go through, including her terrifying episodes in the hospital and her subsequent recovery. *From the Mud Hut* is thus one of the most startling examples I've yet come across of what Graves refers to as 'the proleptic imagination'."

From The Mud Hut was published complete in *Exile*. Not long after, Jennifer Rankin died.

Réjean Ducharme of Canada, the invisible man of letters of Québec – he is seldom seen, never photographed – is the author of several works: *The Swallower Swallowed, Le Nez qui voque, L'Océantume, L'Hiver de force, Enfantômes*, and a play, *Ha-Ha!*, which won the Governor General's award and was published by Exile Editions.

Claire Weissman Wilks of Canada has had exhibitions of her work in Rome, Venice, Zagreb, Jerusalem, and Stockholm. Her books include *In the White Hotel, I know Not Why The Roses Bloom, Hillmother, Tremors*, and *Two Of Us Together: Each Of Us Alone*.

Joyce Carol Oates of the United States is prolific. Among her many works are *On Boxing, You Must Remember This, The Assignation, Because It is Better* *and Because It Is My Heart, I Lock My Door Upon Myself,* and *Oates In Exile.* Her work appeared in 1973 in Volume I, and since then she has published eighteen stories and a play in *Exile.*

Seán Virgo of Canada is a poet, novelist, and story teller. *Les Rites,* which won the CBC prize for fiction in 1979, was among his earliest stories. Exile Editions has since published *Selected Poems,* his novel *Selakhi, White Lies And Other Fictions plus Two, Wormwood,* and *Waking in Eden.*

Susan Musgrave of Canada is a novelist and poet, and among her books of verse are: *Songs of The Sea-Witch, Grave-Dirt and Selected Strawberries, The Impstone, A Man to Marry A Man to Bury, Tarts and Muggers, Cocktails at the Mausoleum,* and with Exile Editions, her most recent selected, *The Embalmer's Art.*

John Montague

*Together we will undertake the extravagance of living under a
sharpened conscience, in open honesty, and we will see what happens.
The worst can only be catastrophe, which is better by far
than a false success.*

PAUL-EMILE BORDUAS

---

*The only true exile is the writer who lives
in his own country.*

JULIO CORTAZAR

466